Five Faces of Exile

ASIAN AMERICA
A series edited by Gordon H. Chang

The increasing size and diversity of the Asian American population, its growing significance in American society and culture, and the expanded appreciation, both popular and scholarly, of the importance of Asian Americans in the country's present and past—all these developments have converged to stimulate wide interest in scholarly work on topics related to the Asian American experience. The general recognition of the pivotal role that race and ethnicity have played in American life, and in relations between the United States and other countries, has also fostered this heightened attention.

Although Asian Americans were a subject of serious inquiry in the late nineteenth and early twentieth centuries, they were subsequently ignored by the mainstream scholarly community for several decades. In recent years, however, this neglect has ended, with an increasing number of writers examining a good many aspects of Asian American life and culture. Moreover, many students of American society are recognizing that the study of issues related to Asian America speaks to, and may be essential for, many current discussions on the part of the informed public and various scholarly communities.

The Stanford series on Asian America seeks to address these interests. The series will include works from the humanities and social sciences, including history, anthropology, political science, American studies, law, literary criticism, sociology, and interdisciplinary and policy studies.

Five Faces of Exile

THE NATION AND FILIPINO

AMERICAN INTELLECTUALS

Augusto Fauni Espiritu

STANFORD UNIVERSITY PRESS

STANFORD, CALIFORNIA

2005

Stanford University Press
Stanford, California
© 2005 by the Board of Trustees of the
Leland Stanford Junior University

Library of Congress Cataloging-in-Publication Data

Espiritu, Augusto Fauni.
　Five faces of exile : the nation and Filipino American
intellectuals / Augusto Fauni Espiritu.
　　　p.　cm. —　(Asian America)
　Includes bibliographical references and index.
　ISBN 0-8047-5120-x (alk. paper) —
　ISBN 0-8047-5121-8 (pbk. : alk. paper)
　　1.　Filipino Americans—Intellectual life.　2.　Exiles—
Philippines.　3.　Exiles—United States.　I.　Title.　II.　Series.
E184.F4E86　2005
973.91′092′39921—dc22

　　　　　　　　　　　　　　　　　　　　　2004022526

Printed in the United States of America
Original Printing 2005
Last figure below indicates year of this printing:
14　13　12　11　10　09　08　07　06　05

Typeset at Stanford University Press in 11/14 Garamond

Para sa minamahal kong Anna

Contents

Preface

When I first started the research upon which this book is based, I had no idea that I would soon be living the traveling life I was seeking to know in greater depth. For my dissertation, I went to the Philippines and lived there, for the first time in nearly two decades, from 1995 to 1996. I came to the United States in 1976 as an immigrant, and I had lived a comfortable life in Los Angeles. A few years later, I found myself at the University of Illinois at Urbana-Champaign, where I have been privileged to work among brilliant and supportive colleagues and friends. But my wife remains two thousand miles away in California, as do both of our families. Like many of my colleagues, I am torn between two loves and two homes, and I have become a traveler between two worlds.

Hence I have grown fond of the expatriate Filipino American intellectuals whom I chose as the subjects of this book, *Five Faces of Exile: The Nation and Filipino American Intellectuals.* My title echoes Matei Calinescu's *Five Faces of Modernity: Modernism, Avant-Garde, Decadence, Kitsch, Postmodernism* (1987), and the book looks at a different experience of the movements Calinescu describes, especially from the standpoint of those repressed "others" of modernity, colonialism, and nationalism.[1] The five intellectuals studied are Carlos P. Romulo (1899–1985), Philippine emissary to the United States from 1942 to 1985, and author of over fifteen books on U.S.-Philippine relations; Carlos Bulosan (1911–1956) and Bienvenido N. Santos

(1911–1996), two authors whose stories of Filipino workers and exiles scattered throughout the United States in the 1930s and 1940s have become required reading in Asian American Studies courses; and José García Villa (1908–1997) and N. V. M. Gonzalez (1915–1999), two Philippine National Artists whose poetry, fiction, and literary theory—although still unknown to many in academia—have decisively influenced Filipino, Filipino American, Asian American, and other literary communities over the past two decades.[2] At first, I was interested in Filipino American expatriate intellectuals as pioneers and precursors of the Filipino American intellectual communities of the post–1965 Immigration Act era, especially those exiles and U.S.-born Filipinos who resisted the Marcos dictatorship. Now my intellectual subjects have become valuable to me not only from a genealogical standpoint but also from an existential one, because their struggles mirror my own migrant life and provide visions of what the future might hold.

It turns out that more and more people today are traveling between the United States and Asia (despite economic crises and flu epidemics), which makes these early twentieth-century Filipino American experiences all the more relevant. In the first decade of the twenty-first century, we find ourselves in a world increasingly in flux. People are in motion on a larger scale than before, whether in search of economic opportunities and political freedoms or displaced by forces beyond their control. Filipino American intellectual expatriate lives combine both this search for mobility and freedom and the sense of loss that thousands, if not millions, of overseas contract laborers, refugees, domestic workers, and long-distance commuters are feeling.[3]

The subject of this book is how Filipino American intellectuals imagined the Philippines, Asia, and the rest of the world from their exile in America. Their story begins in the 1920s, when the United States ruled the Philippines as a colony, continues through the Japanese occupation, and concludes in the postcolonial era, when Filipinos and other subject peoples around the world were decolonizing under the banner of nationalism. Indeed, Filipino American expatriate intellectuals too, more than once in their lives, were caught between two loves and two homes, between an America that offered material wealth, intellectual challenge, and spiritual solace and a Philippines that commanded their allegiance and called out to them with memories of a cherished past. They too had to navigate between these two poles, and in the process, they became transnational travelers.

Out of the deracination and sojourning of Filipino American expatriate intellectuals, several common themes emerge. First, one finds the persistence of nationalism and other discourses of the nation in their self-representation, which overlapped or competed with discourses of American colonialism, ethnicity, race, and class.[4] Second, Filipino American expatriate intellectuals acted as a "bridge of understanding," to use the apt phrase of the Japanese American historian Yuji Ichioka.[5] Their thoughts and actions exhibited concern for cultural translation and diplomacy that brought "East" and "West" together and melded cosmopolitanism with the Philippines' "archipelagic" cultures.[6] Third, their constant shifting between two languages and world-views led to what Thorstein Veblen called "divided allegiance," or to the kind of double consciousness that Edward Said likened to contrapuntal reading and the counterposing of diverse cultural experiences.[7] Fourth, Filipino American expatriate intellectuals can also be grouped by a common tendency to favor a political approach that emphasized negotiation and evasion over confrontation, although there were exceptions. Such a view was consistent with their understanding of the importance of patronage and sponsorship in the Philippine-American context, upon which their survival as artists depended. Finally, performativity, especially as "practical consciousness" and as a process of "rearticulation" or "resignification," played a crucial role in the making and the expression of Filipino American expatriate intellectual identities.[8] Moreover, Philippine oral and theatrical traditions influenced their articulation of aesthetic and political ideas and sharpened their sensitivity to shifting audiences and sites of enunciation.[9] As I argue in the Introduction, these common attributes of Filipino American exilic intellectuals can only be understood in the context of the Philippines' history of colonialism, patron-client relations, nationalist assertion, and cultural dynamism, and of twentieth-century American wars, political developments, and artistic movements.

But while these common patterns connect Filipino American expatriate intellectuals, their diverse responses to the nation and their expatriation illustrate a rich variety of responses that signal the complexities of transnationalism. In Chapter 1, "Expatriate Affirmation," I adopt Carlos P. Romulo's designation of exile as "expatriate affirmation." A student at Columbia University from 1918 to 1921, Romulo came to regard displacement from home and overseas travel as constituent parts of Filipino nationalism. For him, exile, especially during World War II, when the Japanese occupied his homeland and prevented his return, conferred a sense of the differences between national cultures. It also made intellectual expatriates like Romulo, as well as Bulosan, Villa, Santos, and Gonzalez, who were similarly exiled, better appreciate their country's uniqueness, and it encouraged them to express their nationality in ways they had never thought possible. Exile, particularly in the colonial American motherland, also provided space for the performance of masculinity and the making of national heroes whose actions abroad and return home strengthened political careers in the Philippine colony. Romulo's political education between the University of the Philippines and Columbia and his travels among Asian nationalists, Western academics, and American politicians cemented these views of exile and nationality. Finally, his relations of indebtedness and reciprocity with Philippine Commonwealth President Manuel Quezon and (Philippine) Field Marshal Douglas MacArthur shaped not only his future political role but also his political discourse. Romulo understood Philippine-American relations in terms of *utang na loob,* or debt of gratitude, a pre-Hispanic Filipino value that helps explain his durability, despite charges that he was insincere and condemnation of his pro-American stances.

Carlos Bulosan and José García Villa arrived in the United States a decade after Romulo, and Chapters 2 and 3 describe their personalities, identifications, and responses to expatriation. In Chapter 2, "Suffering and Passion," I show how Bulosan interpreted the history of his Filipino countrymen on the West Coast, and his own social role, through the idiom of the *pasyon,* the Philippine folk Christian version of the suffering, death, and rebirth of Jesus Christ.[10] Excluded from the company of Filipino intellectual elites by distinctions of class, by a plagiarism charge, and by a virulent anti-Communist movement, Bulosan came to see himself as a Christlike martyr figure, whose sufferings helped to heal the social divisions and racial exploitation faced by his fellow countrymen in exile. Bulosan fused oral culture and traditional religious elements with the civil rights activism, labor radicalism, and proletarian literary values for which he has been posthumously acknowledged.

In Chapter 3, "Artistic Vanguard," I explore Villa's expatriate life against the backdrop of his rebellion against family, elite social class, and national culture. Villa left the Philippines for New York, where he lived a solitary life as an artist, disdainful of politics and propaganda, and symbolized the values of modernism for young Filipino writers. Yet Villa's rebellion against tradition, like all reversals, reinscribed what he opposed. While he rejected the tyranny of his father, who sought to control his career aspirations and to limit his inheritance, he became at times just as tyrannical toward his students and budding Filipino writers, who suffered from his cruel mind games and personal criticism. And while he sought to squash all traces of nationality, his love for the theatrical in everyday life hearkened back to earlier Filipino nationalist intellectual performative traditions. Likewise, his attack on American food and his defense of Filipino traditional cuisine suggests that alongside his self-perception as a member of the artistic vanguard, there was a latent nativism in him.

N. V. M. Gonzalez and Bienvenido Santos, the next two Filipino American expatriate intellectuals discussed, arrived in the United States over a decade after Bulosan and Villa and a generation after Romulo. In Chapter 4, "Nativism and Negation," I argue that Gonzalez's abiding literary and ethnic impulses were self-consciously nativist. Gonzalez drew upon the rich and diverse Philippine oral and literary traditions and languages—which he regarded as superior to the hybrid, middle-class, urban, or expatriate Filipino cultures that had alienated his generation—to describe the folk dwellers of his Mindoro frontier home. He was the oldest among Filipino American expatriate intellectuals at the time of his first American visit (he was thirty-three), and he was deeply influenced by the New Criticism and myth criticism practiced by his teachers, and, perhaps just as important, by their regionalist sensibilities. While Gonzalez lived in the United States for several decades, he denied being influenced in any profound way by his sojourn. He maintained his sense of Filipino nationalism, his Filipino citizenship, and his self-identification as Philippine writer. The realities of his life lived in two worlds, however, especially during the period of the Marcos dictatorship, when both he and Santos were intimidated from traveling to their homeland, placed great strains upon these attempts to fashion a mythology of geographic fixity and cultural authenticity.

In Chapter 5, "Fidelity and Shame," I explore the life of Bienvenido Santos, who shared Gonzalez's valorization of Philippine traditional cultures. Unlike Gonzalez, however, Santos genuinely enjoyed America, even as he professed his love for the Philippines. He obtained American citizenship in 1976, although this was in part to safeguard his well-being in the martial law era. Moreover, he embraced the rising American ethnic movements of the 1960s and was not averse to aligning himself with them. Nonetheless, his enjoyment of American comforts and his elevated class position in America filled him with shame (*hiya* in Tagalog; *supog* in Santos's Bicolano). Santos's Filipino nationalism continually brought to the surface questions of loyalty to the nation and memories of the past. All of these found literary expression in gendered themes of fidelity and betrayal, which infused his portrayals of friendship, class relations, and colonial encounters. Various images of traditional Filipino womanhood, particularly of the Virgin Mary, provided a recurring symbolic equivalent for the articulation of his nationalist ideals.

Finally, in the Conclusion, "Toward a Transnational Asian American Intellectual History," I argue for the importance of a Filipino American and an Asian American intellectual history that is simultaneously national and transnational. U.S. intellectual history remains sadly afflicted by American nationalism, a defensive stance toward transnational theories, and positive valorizations of "empire," ignoring the voices and perspectives of colonial and postcolonial subjects and intellectuals. American intellectual historians have also marginalized Asian Americans in the field of intellectual history. The challenge, I argue, is to construct a sound intellectual history that both brings together a concern for the nation and transpacific relations and connects Asian experiences on the American continent and in the Pacific world with critical histories of colonization, race, class, gender, ethnicity, and empire.

One will find in this book an approach that combines social history (especially as a reading of relations of patronage and reciprocity) with close, noncanonical readings of autobiographical and fictional texts. I have tried to analyze the important social and political relationships of my chosen Filipino American expatriate intellectuals, especially to the extent that such relationships impinged on their writings. I have paid particular attention to the elucidation of their texts for several reasons. First, there remains a need for synoptic readings that introduce the full range of Filipino American intellectual perspectives. Second, I strongly believe in the importance of highlighting Filipino American self-representations, not only because of their literary and aesthetic value, but also because postcolonial history and criticism cannot be taken seriously without the crucial perspectives of colonized intellectuals and a competent critical inventory of their ideas. And, third, I believe that intellectual historians must risk more readings of texts that respect their literary, aesthetic, and figurative properties but at the same time question unfounded claims to literature's autonomy from society and politics, which only isolate literature from history and vice versa.

This book would not have been possible without the active interest and participation of people from two continents and from the universities that provided me with positive intellectual environments. A postdoctoral fellowship from the University of California, Berkeley, Chancellor's Program in Academic Diversity, where I was resident from 2001 to 2002, was invaluable. I thank Waldo Martin, Paula Fass, Jon Gjerde, and Tyler Stovall of the Department of History and Ling-chi Wang of the Ethnic Studies Department for their encouragement and support.

I thank my colleagues in the History Department at the University of Illinois at Urbana-Champaign for providing such a conducive atmosphere for intellectual life and historical research, and particularly for their abiding interests in nationalism, transnationalism, colonial studies and postcolonial criticism, and the discourses of race, gender, and class, all of which have helped to enrich my own theoretical perspectives. I especially thank Jim Barrett, Antoinette Burton, Dave Roediger, Fred Hoxie, Poshek Fu, Clare Crowston, Chip Burkhardt, Peter Fritzsche, Mark Leff, Nils Jacobsen, Kristin Hoganson, Cynthia Radding, Ken Cuno, Caroline Hibbard, and Fanon Wilkins. In Asian American Studies, I would like to thank Martin Manalansan, whose work has inspired my own, Kent Ono, and Sharon Lee.

I would also like to thank Valerie Matsumoto, King-Kok Cheung, and Michael Salman at UCLA for their patience, wise counsel, and guidance over the years. I owe a great debt of gratitude to Michael Salman for his intellectual brilliance, his labors, and his boundless generosity. A special thanks also to Vicente Rafael, Carol, and Jack.

At the University of California, Irvine, I thank Yong Chen, Ketu Katrak, Linda Vo, and Glen Mimura; Douglas Haynes, David Theo Goldberg, Philomena Essed, and Ngugi wa Thiong'o for their support and friendship.

Various academic intellectuals in the Philippines provided invaluable help and welcomed me into their classrooms and offices. At the Ateneo de Manila, I thank the late Doreen Fernandez, Maria Luisa Torres Reyes, Cynthia Lumbera, Susan Evangelista, and Soledad S. Reyes. At the University of the Philippines, Diliman, I thank Gémino Abad, Franz Arcellana, Corazon D. Villareal, Priscelina Patajo-Legasto, Elmer A. Ordoñez, and Cristina Pantoja-Hidalgo. I also thank the staff of the Philippine-American Educational Foundation, especially Alex Calata.

I sincerely thank members of the Romulo family, including Beth Day Romulo, Roberto Romulo, and Ricardo Romulo, who took time out from their busy schedules for interviews and also provided helpful leads for further research. I likewise thank Gigi, Amparo, and I. P. Santos for their hospitality, guidance, and enthusiasm for this project and introductions to the Romulo family.

My thanks go to the family and friends of the late Bienvenido N. Santos in Camarines Sur and Albay provinces who warmly received me and gave so generously of their time and energy: Arme Santos Tan, Lina Santos Cortes and Jean Oreta Cortes, Lourdes Santos and family, and Dr. Aster Mancera-Reganit. I thank Tomas Santos for his encouragement and insights, as well as Michele Santos for sharing her recollections of her grandfather.

I thank Eustaquia Bulosan, who showed me around the home of his older brother Carlos Bulosan in Binalonan, Pangasinan Province. The late P. C. Morantte deserves special thanks for sharing his profound insights about his friend Carlos Bulosan, as well as for sharing articles and other writings. Morantte intimately knew all the intellectual expatriates I have chosen to write about.

Finally, special thanks to the late N. V. M. Gonzalez, who was a formidable, loving, stimulating, and thoughtful friend; Narita Gonzalez, with whom I was fortunate to spend many a wonderful occasion in California, Manila, and Mindoro; Chitty-Chitty and Bang-Bang in Diliman, Quezon City, and other members of the Gonzalez family in Mindoro. I especially thank Michael Gonzalez at Stanford, who has been of invaluable support.

Special thanks go to the staffs of various Philippine libraries: the American Historical Collection, in particular Lewis Gleeck; the José Rizal Library Filipiniana Collection, Ateneo de Manila; the University of the Philippines Library Archives; the National Library, especially Director Adoracion M.

Bolos; Aquinas University (formerly Legazpi College) Library; and the University of Nueva Cáceres Library. Special thanks also go to Cherry Puruganan, curatorial assistant at the Ayala Museum, for her invaluable help with the Carlos P. Romulo Papers.

In the United States, I thank Karyl Winn, University of Washington, Manuscript Archives, for his patience and support for research on the Carlos Bulosan Papers, and the staff of the Wichita State University Manuscript Archives Collection for their meticulous care and research assistance with the Bienvenido N. Santos papers. Thanks also go to Fred Cordova and Dorothy Cordova of Seattle's National Pinoy Archives, and to Barbara Posadas.

I wish to thank the late José García Villa, with whom I corresponded, with the help of Luis Cabalquinto and Carlos Angeles. I thank Luis Francia for an early draft of his excellent essay on Villa. I send a special thank you to Hilario S. Francia in Manila for sharing his insights on Villa and his collection of articles. I also thank Robert King and Arthur Vanderborg, former Villa students and poets, for their candid recollections. My special thanks go to John Cowen, Villa's student, friend, and literary executor, for his invaluable insights into the "master," and his sharing of books and articles. I also thank Leonard Casper, Linda Casper, and Jessica Hagedorn for sharing their ideas and/or agreeing to be interviewed.

Members of my family helped to sustain me throughout this period of writing. I thank my mother and father, Michael and Concepcion Espiritu, for their patience, their support, their invaluable recollections of language, family, and history, and their research assistance. I also thank the rest of my extended family—the Espiritus, the Rosanos, and the Lorescos—for their belief and support. I thank Gil Gonzalez for his love and support, as well as Concepcion Bernardo, and the Gonzalez, Sison, and Robledo families.

Lastly, there would be no book without Anna K. Gonzalez whose love and companionship, and commitment to these five special Filipino men made all of this possible. Over the years, I have been fortunate to share in her passion for ideas, her commitment to social change, and her sense of humor. It is to her that this book is dedicated.

Five Faces of Exile

Introduction

A historical background in Philippine history, especially of the late nineteenth and early twentieth centuries, is crucial to understanding the activities of Filipino American expatriate intellectuals in the United States. Three themes are especially significant. These include the emergence of the *ilustrados,* or "Enlightened" intellectuals, in the development of Filipino nationalism; the surge of popular nationalism among lower-class Filipinos and its foundation in folk religious beliefs; and the making of the colonial patronage relations that helped shape intellectual life during the American period.[1]

Filipino intellectual migrants to the United States lived lives similar to those of the ilustrados, who were the first Filipinos to be exposed to European modernity. They came from entrepreneurial families and included Creoles (called Españoles-Filipinos), Spanish mestizos, Chinese mestizos, and *indios.*[2] In the 1870s, they challenged racial discrimination, especially among the clergy, and were suppressed by the colonial authorities. Many fled to Europe, where they attended European schools and imbibed liberal, anticlerical ideas.[3] The ilustrados expressed themselves through patriotic writing and oratory and achieved notoriety for their outrageous behavior.[4] Moreover, they believed in Spanish conceptions of honor and manly displays, such as fencing and dueling, which earned them the respect of Spanish contemporaries.[5] Despite their attempts at assimilation, Spanish colonial rulers continued to regard the ilustrados as inferiors and blocked their efforts at political, educational, and penal reform in the Philippines.[6] Facing the reality of second-class citizenship at home and abroad, these expatriates began to develop a sense of nationalism, appropriating "Filipino" as a general term for all Philippine natives.[7] Perhaps the most important figure among the ilustrados was the Chinese mestizo José Rizal (1861–1896), whose incisive, satirical, and philosophical writings, especially the novels, *Noli Me Tangere* ("Touch Me Not") and *El Filibusterismo* ("Subversion"),[8] and unjustified execution would inspire the Filipino revolution against Spain in 1896, led by the secret society known as the Katipunan, founded by the plebeian Andres Bonifacio.[9]

Besides ilustrado nationalism, popular nationalist beliefs proved important in the constitution of Filipino American intellectual life. In large part, this occurred through the transmission of folk Christianity, a syncretism of Spanish Catholicism and animist beliefs. In his seminal work *Pasyon and Revolution*, Reynaldo Ileto argues that mystical beliefs in amulets and rituals that sought to concentrate "power" in individuals came to dominate Philippine folk Catholicism.[10] In particular, he contends that the spread of the *pasyon* (native versions of the passion of Christ, read during Holy Week) into the general culture eventually provided the idiom of protest in terms of which the lower classes interpreted their separation from Spain.[11] The values of folk rebels thus constituted a radically different worldview from the Enlightenment ideals that inspired the creation of the Philippine Republic.[12] Several aspects of the pasyon became important to Filipino American expatriate intellectuals. The first was the image of José Rizal as a Christlike figure that embodied traditional values of suffering, sacrifice, and fearlessness before death. The second was the interweaving of the myth of Bernardo Carpio with that of Rizal. Thus, the idea of separation, exile, and return became an integral part of Filipino thinking about expatriates. The third and last aspect was the pasyon's rearticulation of patronage and the concept of reciprocity, especially the values of *hiya* and *utang na loob*, or debt of gratitude, to justify separation from Spain.[13] Although positivistic social scientists before Ileto had utilized these values as essential traits that explained Filipino economic backwardness and the persistence of political factionalism and corruption, Ileto argued that such values had a historicity that challenged such fixed, static, and essentialist notions. Writing about the earlier period of Spanish conquest and Catholic conversion of the Philippines, Vicente

Rafael reinforced and expanded Ileto's initial insights with an analysis of the concepts of *hiya, loob,* and *utang na loob* that further highlighted their relational and dynamic aspects in the construction of community and in deflecting the power of Spanish conceptions of indebtedness.[14] During the American colonial period and afterwards, one finds in the client-based relationships between colonial white patrons and Filipino American expatriate intellectuals the uncanny survival of selective listening strategies, the persistence of the oral tradition, and tactics of displacing colonial discursive power that Rafael identifies only too well among native intellectuals of the sixteenth and seventeenth centuries.[15]

Indeed, political patronage became a decisive determinant of Filipino and Filipino American intellectual life, shaping among other things intellectuals' access to the means of livelihood, social rewards, and funds for travel. Modern patronage in the Philippines originated in the late nineteenth century with Spain's attempts to open up political opportunities for mestizos.[16] Patronage helped to launch the careers of future nationalist leaders like the scholar Trinidad H. Pardo de Tavera and the political leaders Apolinario Mabini and Sergio Osmeña.[17] During the U.S. colonial period, governors like William Howard Taft deftly utilized patronage to manage Filipino nationalism.[18] As part of America's mission of training Filipino "wards" in self-government, Taft established several institutions, including the Resident Commissioner's Office, as well as the *pensionado* system, which established the pattern of sending Filipino students (labeled *pensionados*) to the United States.[19] More important, he cultivated Americanized elite politicians, such as Sergio Osmeña of Cebu and Manuel Quezon of Tayabas, who soon dominated national politics. Quezon, in particular, towered over Philippine politics from the 1920s until his death in 1944.[20] He was instrumental in dispensing patronage to many young intellectuals, including Romulo and Villa, and indirectly to Bulosan, Santos, and Gonzalez.[21]

Patronage of Filipino American intellectuals was not, however, limited to the Philippine context. When they traveled to the United States, American institutions such as the Rockefeller and Guggenheim Foundations helped finance them.[22] Perhaps more important was the work of individual white American sponsors who recognized their talents and provided them with financial support, friendship, letters of reference, and introductions to networks that helped advance their careers. While the latter kind of patronage differed from the more binding Philippine version, certain studies, such as Nathan Irvin Huggins's exploration of patronage among Harlem Renaissance artists, show that racial difference, paternalism, and politics inevitably played important roles in shaping the outcomes of these associations.[23] Filipino intellectuals were just as likely to interpret their relationship to these individuals in terms of lifelong debts of gratitude.

Moreover, since they traveled back and forth between the two countries, Filipino intellectual migrants were affected by historical developments in both the United States and the Philippines. A few arrived in America during the Great Depression, which scarred them with its economic hardships and laws that discriminated against Filipinos.[24] At the same time, they were exposed to Popular Front culture and artistic modernism, which also had their counterparts in the Philippines.[25] World War II was especially important for Filipino intellectuals. No matter where they were, the Japanese invasion of the Philippines made them all exiles. Most of them worked in the headquarters of the exiled Philippine Commonwealth Government in Washington, D.C. The support of the U.S. government buoyed the social status of Filipinos (as it did that of others whose home countries became America's allies), and Filipino intellectual migrants benefited from new opportunities for speaking and writing.[26] However, the postwar anticommunist climate in both the United States and the Philippines either destroyed their careers or forced them into political quiescence or accommodation.[27] Finally, in the 1960s and 1970s, Filipino intellectuals encountered the ethnic studies movement and the transnational campaign to oust the Marcos dictatorship.[28]

The general issues raised in this book fit into the growing literature on the "postcolonial," especially with respect to questions of colonial discourse, performativity, and nationalism. Edward Said's *Orientalism* identifies the contours of Western colonial discourse about the East ("Orientalism"), which often pictured this socially constructed region and its peoples in contradictory racially stereotyped ways as either passively feminine or threateningly masculine, and the terrain with which Filipino intellectuals had to contend.[29] Said's *Culture and Imperialism* encouraged scholars to delve into anticolonial nationalist literature as a form of resistance. Nonetheless, Said often seems to express colonial culture either in terms of hegemonic Western literary discourses *or* Third World literatures of resistance.[30] In doing my research, I have observed that nationalist discourses tend toward both hegemony *and* resistance. How then could I conceptualize this double effect? Homi Bhabha's *Nation and Narration* showed one possibility by introducing the notion of the "ambivalence" that haunts nationalist discourse.[31] Paul Gilroy's exploration of "double consciousness" showed another through its exploration of the intersection between Enlightenment discourse and black culture among African diasporic intellectuals.[32] Finally, James Clifford's "Traveling Cultures" emphasizes the idea of travel as a cultural form and, more important, highlights the intellectuals' roles as cultural translators, something germane to intellectuals' self-presentation as a bridge of understanding between East and West.[33]

This book also engages the literature on colonial performativity, which has largely explored spectacles such as world's fairs, zoos, and museums, that has helped to define the reality of colonial rule.[34] While the idea of "anticolonial performativity" has not been fully articulated, works by Ed Cohen, Mary Louise Pratt, and Vicente Rafael have applied various understandings of spectacle in the development of nationalist intellectuals. Meanwhile, the cultural historian Doreen Fernandez has written extensively of the development of oral performances and the colonial Philippine theater, including its anticolonial aspects.[35] With respect to nationalism, landmark social scientific works such as Benedict Anderson's *Imagined Communities* helped to highlight the importance of the experiences of expatriate intellectuals in the rise of nationalism.[36] Through Victor Turner, Anderson himself used the insights of an earlier thinker, Arnold van Gennep, whose breakdown of the ritual process influenced both Turner's and Joseph Campbell's conceptualization of the hero.[37] This is important in my exploration of the importance of migration, exile, and return in the lives and works of Filipino intellectuals.

This book, moreover, fits into efforts to set Asian American Studies in a global or international framework. For some time, Asian American Studies was focused on the study of race, gender, and class within the *American* context.[38] Beginning in the late 1980s, however, a growing theoretical literature has called for a breakdown of the old paradigms of Asian American culture and of the disciplinary boundaries between Asian and Asian American studies.[39] In this regard, Sau-ling Wong's "Denationalization Reconsidered" is a landmark theoretical essay. While cautious about diaspora's long-term political impact, Wong provides the most succinct formulation of what she calls "denationalization," the diasporic cultural developments created by Asia's rise to economic prominence and the influx of recent migrants and refugees. She claims that the back-and-forth migration of Asian and Asian American intellectuals across the Pacific has contributed to the creation of new modes of imagining Asian American identity that are putting increasing strain on the disciplinary boundaries between Asian and Asian American Studies.[40] Yet while theoretical and literary explorations abound in this field, there have been relatively few historical explorations of transnational developments.

Likewise, this book's concerns dovetail with recent works reflecting upon the centennial celebrations of the Spanish-American War, and specifically, the U.S.-Philippine War, which overlap with Asian American Studies. These investigations, many of them responding to the marginalization of American imperialism in studies of the postcolonial, have focused on the origins of U.S. colonialism, its entry onto the world stage in the Spanish-American War, and its cultural legacies.[41] It is noteworthy that within this literature, there have been relatively few scholarly studies that have focused on post-colonization developments in the Philippines.[42]

Finally, *Five Faces of Exile* inevitably dovetails with the extensive literature on race, ethnicity, class, and gender. It provides instances of the colonial race discourse of "benevolent assimilation" that socialized Filipino intellectuals in the American colony into a desire for whiteness. It shows how "everyday racism," whether acknowledged, denied, or displaced, influenced the development of Filipino American nationalism and contributed to an understanding of Filipino American ethnic identity.[43] The book further demonstrates the complex dynamics of ethnicity, showing how differences of geography, language, and class bisected ethnic and national solidarity, while at the same time dramatizing the paradoxes of political and cultural citizenship.[44] The book also offers numerous insights into gender and sexual relations, from the masculinism of hero worship, self-mythologization, and male bonding to the figuration of national conflicts in terms of the imagery of motherhood, sex, and gender.[45]

This study of largely unrecognized Filipino intellectual migrants to the United States provokes reflection upon a number of significant themes in the "human sciences." These include the transformations of national or ethnic identity brought about by travel, the cultural legacies of colonialism, the question of hegemony and resistance, the overlap between tradition and modernity, and the impact of relations of patronage on literature and intellectual history. Filipino American intellectual experiences involve complex negotiations of identity, politics, and culture that subvert the very categories that have hitherto been used to study them. There is a serious need to reconceptualize various disciplines to allow for the exploration, rather than the marginalization, of these complex lives.

ONE

"Expatriate Affirmation": Carlos P. Romulo

World War I had just ended and the "Jazz Age" was just beginning when a young pensionado named Carlos P. Romulo arrived in the United States. From 1918 to 1921, he would study foreign trade service and comparative literature at Columbia University.[1] As an expatriate far from the comforts of an elite upbringing at home, Romulo would become acutely aware of the salience of race in this country. Soon after the start of classes, he found white and black college students divided by the "race problem," and each side questioned his association with members of the other race. While confronted by both groups to choose his friends, he found a third way, which would become characteristic of his approach to race and international relations. He refused to relinquish his friendships with both groups and continued to talk to "both sides."[2] Romulo also realized that while the American flag flew on Philippine soil, and Filipinos indulged in a feeling of self-importance as American colonials, they were unknown in America, and he himself was often mistaken for Chinese or Japanese. Romulo tried to remedy this invisibility and the larger society's inability to distinguish between Asians in America through education, by organizing, along with his fellow Filipino students, a José Rizal Day celebration, which was attended by Columbia University's president.[3] Indeed, racial experiences such as these would provide the young colonial scholar with a far wider education than he had expected.

Although rarely remembered in the United States today, Carlos P. Romulo was one of the most famous transnational Filipino political leaders of the twentieth century. He served at the highest levels of government, played a significant role in Philippine foreign affairs, and participated in the founding of the United Nations, where he argued for his liberal nationalist views. For many years, including those he spent at Columbia, Romulo resided in the United States. His diplomatic shuttle between Asia and America gave rise to a cosmopolitan, bicultural "Asian-American" outlook, which negotiated modernity and tradition. On the one hand, U.S. colonial rule of the Philippines was instrumental in shaping his political education, especially in patron-client relationships. On the other hand, living as an expatriate in America and encountering its urban industrial and racial landscapes shaped his ideas of modernity and national identity and helped fashion his diplomatic approach to the problems of nationalism and race relations. Moreover, Romulo drew on Filipino cultural conceptions to explain his political views. For instance, *utang na loob* ("debt of the inside") was important to his interpretive framework, suggesting cultural links with the age-old folk idiom of the pasyon.

Carlos Peña Romulo was born on January 14, 1899, the son of Gregorio Romulo and Maria Peña of the town of Camiling, Tarlac.[4] Carlos studied at Manila High School, the University of the Philippines, and Columbia University. He married a "beauty queen," Virginia Llamas, and together they had four sons—Carlos Llamas, Gregorio Vicente, Ricardo José, and Roberto Rey.[5] In the 1920s and 1930s, he worked as a professor of English at the University of the Philippines, as the secretary of Senate President Manuel Quezon, and as publisher of a multilingual chain of newspapers. During World War II, he was drafted into the U.S. Army as General Douglas MacArthur's press officer. He was decorated with the Silver Star, two Oak Leaf Clusters, and a Purple Heart.[6] When the Philippine Commonwealth Government was forced into exile to the United States by the Japanese, Colonel Romulo also fled, leaving his family in the Philippines.[7] Altogether, Romulo wrote four books about his wartime exile.[8] After the war, he brought his family to New York, where he served as Philippine ambassador to the United States and as the Philippines' chief diplomat to the United Nations. In 1949, he was elected president of the UN General Assembly.[9] In the 1960s, he served as president of the University of the Philippines. And from 1968 until 1984, he served as the foreign minister of President Ferdinand Marcos.

Despite the fascinating cultural intersections of his life, Romulo remains invisible in American ethnic history, especially in Asian American studies.[10] In the field of U.S.-Philippine relations, Romulo has often been portrayed as a pro-American diplomat whose stances border on the traitorous. In his 1969 biography of the nationalist Senator Claro M. Recto,[11] the historian Renato Constantino, a strident critic of Romulo's, expressed the characteristic nationalist view, speaking of Recto's "very low regard for Romulo" and his dislike of Romulo's "fawning attitude towards Americans."[12] On foreign policy matters, Constantino labeled Romulo the "Architect of Subservience."[13] Subsequent critics have charged Romulo with justifying authoritarianism. Romulo is portrayed as an apologist for the Marcos dictatorship in Raymond Bonner's critical account of America's foreign policy toward the Philippines, *Waltzing with a Dictator* (1987), and Pio Andrade's *The Fooling of America* (1985) accuses Romulo of covering up for Marcos.[14] Many of these criticisms are often on target. Yet without minimizing the force of these objections, one can go beyond the binaries of nationalism and collaboration, authenticity and duplicity, and profitably study Romulo's life in more complex and suggestive ways.

As one of the few transpacific Filipino intellectuals of the U.S. colonial period, Romulo provides a focal point for crucial discussions of colonial culture, patronage, national identity, gender, and race. Using his largely unexplored autobiographical texts and personal papers, I argue in this chapter that his identity was nurtured in a diverse cultural milieu involving a residual Hispanic influence, a dominant American colonial modernity, and an emergent Filipino nationalism.[15] Romulo's life thus teems with complex and ambivalent cultural and national identifications, embodying the conflicts of Filipino traditions and nationalism *and* Western modernity and Enlightenment principles. It is also replete with performances of national identity and masculinity that exemplify his uncanny ability to negotiate the multiple pressures of varying sponsors and audiences. At the same time, I explore the paradoxes of Romulo's career, which on one hand led him to pursue his personal ambition and on the other inspired him to articulate trenchant postwar analyses of transnational relations. Finally, I highlight Romulo's searching reflections on "the color line" in America and in colonial and postcolonial Asia. As simultaneously an "outsider" and a participant in America's racial dilemmas, with one foot outside and one foot inside America, Romulo provides a unique perspective on race and ethnicity, which not only reflects the prevailing postwar liberalism but also anticipates post–civil rights movement Asian American identity and Third World nationalism.

This matrix of transnationalism, performance, patronage, and race can be condensed in a phrase coined by Romulo toward the end of his American sojourn—"expatriate affirmation." For Romulo, expatriate affirmation reflects the positive valorization (rather than denial or negation) of the extraterritorial experiences that contribute to the social construction of national or ethnic identity. It is also an assertion of the performative dimensions of colonized intellectual life, given the pressures of personal ambition, colonialism, and national patronage. And, finally, it acknowledges the power of colonial racism and American race relations, while at the same time rejecting their dichotomies.[16]

Romulo as Ilustrado and as Quezon's Protégé

The intellectual influences upon Romulo grew out of a long historical tradition. They were the legacy of the creators of Filipino nationalism in the nineteenth century, the ilustrados. To a great extent, he inherited their sense of ambivalence, their social dependence upon patronage relationships, and their construction of national identity through performance.[17] Romulo had an intuitive understanding of ilustrado nationalism—he himself came from a similar class of respectable, multilingual citizens and rising entrepreneurs.[18] In his youth, Romulo's participation in spectacles, under the watchful eyes of American colonizers, was an important constituent of his identity. At the Manila High School, he participated in poetic declamations and debating clubs such as the "Cryptia" and the "Rizal," which extolled American moral values and acceptable Filipino leaders.[19] Through such performances, American teachers seduced Romulo and his generation to love English, American literature, and American heroes.[20] While still in high school, the young Romulo began his hero worship of Senate President Manuel Quezon. As a reporter for the *Manila Times*, Romulo covered Quezon's dramatic speeches and earned an invitation to his office.[21]

Reflecting several decades later on his first meeting with Quezon, Romulo explained in more traditional terms why he had idolized the Filipino politician and served under him for so long. He found Quezon attractive in a primitive, animistic way. He felt "the emanation of power" from Quezon, like an indescribable "psychic wave" or compelling "magnetic charm." These confirmed Romulo's belief in his heroic stature and his destiny as the future national leader of the Philippines.[22] Quezon "might have ordered me as he willed," Romulo confessed. "I was his creature." And he added: "Quezon could win any person he chose with the warm, personal charm that was his greatest asset as politician and man."[23]

Quezon's attraction for Romulo derived in large part from the politician's penchant for grand displays, a trait that Romulo would emulate. In particular, he recalled Quezon's dramatic entrance through the walls of Intramuros in 1916 after winning passage of the Jones Law through the U.S. Congress. A section of the historic walled city was demolished to make way for the parade that was to honor him, in a sense symbolic of the will to power of the new Filipino elites, like Quezon, trained in Philippine-American political culture. Moreover, Romulo claimed that Quezon was "the idol of Philippine youth." He was sartorially exquisite and "debonair."[24] Romulo's fascination with Quezon's charm, his diplomatic success and performance before crowds, and the energy that seemed to emanate from his body—all reflect the influence of traditional beliefs about leadership in Southeast Asia upon Romulo. Here, the power of the leaders derives from their dynamic ability to mobilize followers through personal relationships, and from their recurrent displays of strength, rather than static factors of heredity, blood, or birth.[25]

Like the ilustrados, Romulo first gained a sense of duality through his encounter with racial exclusion and inequality in his own country, particularly in social clubs dominated by white Americans, who determined the criteria for membership.[26] His sense of racial identity was further sharpened outside of his country. From 1918 to 1921, when Romulo attended Columbia University on a government scholarship, he encountered instances of white racism directed toward blacks and Filipinos. In Washington, D.C., he saw slums worse than in Manila. He responded to these challenges by rededicating himself to eliminating racial barriers and, in nationalist fashion, by organizing a rally to memorialize José Rizal, to which he invited the university's president, Nicholas Murray Butler.[27]

Romulo returned to the Philippines in 1922. His essay "The Tragedy of Our Anglo-Saxon Education" (1923) epitomizes his evolving synthesis of nationalism and American liberalism. He expresses his robust "faith in the spirit of America and its institutions."[28] Using the stages of his education as an example, he traces the growth of the Filipino's love for America.[29] He then severely criticizes the colonial governor-general Leonard Wood for reversing the pro-independence policies of the Wilson administration, thus nullifying the benefits of American tutelage of the Filipino in democratic government. Romulo ends in dramatic fashion: "We stand at the crossroads, uncertain but unafraid, the future imaged forth in our one supreme aspiration to freedom, the present a recessional that our faith in America shall not die."[30] The essay prefigures Romulo's brand of colonial discourse: he would begin with a glowing apostrophe to America, then follow this with frank criticism of its present-day policies,[31] and conclude with a reaffirmation of America's benevolence. Moreover, to Romulo, "America" transcended its immediate historical mistakes. It represented the synthesis of Christian ideals and American power, godlike and omnipotent.

Also in the early 1920s, Romulo was becoming more entrenched in Quezon's political machine. Quezon established the *Philippines Herald* in 1920 as his journalistic voice and hired Romulo as his assistant editor. In addition, Romulo worked as Quezon's private secretary and as publicity agent for the Philippine "Parliamentary Mission" of 1924.[32] During the apogee of the Filipinos' love affair with America in the 1920s and 1930s, the youth emulated Romulo. To them, he became the essence of the "Filipino as Yankee" and the "Little Brown Brother Who Made Good."[33]

Romulo's presence in the public arena was complemented by his love for the stage, which showed his complex national identity. As U.P. professor of American literature in the 1920s, Romulo wrote plays for the university. In his *The Real Leader* (1924), Romulo created the character of José Santos, a poor schoolteacher and ex-pensionado, who symbolizes the values of the new, modern American dispensation. José is faced with a dilemma. The rich, proud parents of his lover, Carmen, a U.P. coed, refuse to sanction their daughter's wish to marry him. One might have expected José and Carmen to flout the strictures of conventional morality. Instead, however, the two accept the decision of their elders. José honors Carmen's feeling of indebtedness to her parents and decides to bide his time.[34] Thus, he is portrayed not as a disrupter but as an integrator of Filipino family and gender traditions and American ways, something akin to Romulo's developing role as a bridge of understanding between East and West.

From the middle to the late 1920s, the friendship between Quezon and his protégé suffered as Romulo began to assert his independence and maneuver for a better position in their relationship. In 1925, the *Herald* suffered a string of financial setbacks. The affluent Roces family took over the paper and declared it politically independent. Romulo was asked to stay on as editor. Quezon responded by buying back the *Herald* with the help of his powerful friends. He then asked Romulo to be the editor of the reorganized paper. But having already committed to Roces and disdaining Quezon's attempts to muzzle the press, Romulo refused Quezon's invitation and went with Roces to establish the *Tribune* on April 1, 1925. The staff of the *Tribune* was made up of former *Herald* men who followed Romulo.[35]

Quezon attacked the *Tribune* for its critical posture toward him, and Romulo retaliated by berating Quezon for his escapades in the nightclubs and cabarets of Manila.[36] In further articles, Romulo questioned Quezon's "[exorbitances] of temper," which he believed were damaging the campaign for independence, and contrasted Quezon's leadership with Sergio Osmeña's "conservative conciliation devoid of theatricalism."[37] For over six years, Romulo presided over the *Tribune's* growth into the country's largest daily. Despite his difficulties with Romulo, Quezon, however, never gave up on his protégé. In 1933, in the heat of the campaign for Philippine independence legislation, he successfully enticed Romulo back into the fold with an offer that could not be refused: editorship and part ownership of the *Herald.* This time, Quezon used his group of wealthy backers to expand the *Herald* into a chain of newspapers, the *Mabuhay, Herald,* and *Monday Mail,* designed to compete with the Roces family's string of periodicals.[38]

As Quezon's political fortunes rose with the passage of the Tydings-McDuffie Act of 1934, which set a timetable for Philippine independence, Romulo's fortunes soared alongside those of his hero. In 1935, Quezon was elected the first president of the Philippine Commonwealth. Romulo stood closely behind the policies of the chief executive. In his essay "The Promise of a New Day" (1934), he echoed Quezon's concerns about the Philippines' declining economic leverage vis-à-vis the United States, calling for American consideration on trade issues on the basis of the Philippines' "special relations to America." As in his earlier essay, Romulo couched his request for trade preferences by playing up to American prestige in the colonial administration and tutelage of the Filipino people.[39]

Romulo's editorials on Philippine independence in the early 1930s earned him his first accolade in 1935, an honorary doctorate of laws from Notre Dame University.[40] His acceptance speech, "The Mind of a New Commonwealth," brings together Romulo's first articulation of liberal principles, juxtaposed with his traditional conception of reciprocity. Romulo expressed his adherence to the principles of free enterprise, equality of opportunity, and freedom of expression. He saw nothing "inherently vicious" in capitalism and rejected the Marxian notion of class because of its exclusion of "Oriental" hierarchies based upon "educational discrimination," "social heredity," and "religious modalities."[41] He employed symbols familiar to most Americans—"Bunker Hill," "Valley Forge," and "Saratoga."[42] He also touted American colonial rule in the Philippines as a model for peaceful decolonization efforts throughout the world. Finally, he couched the relationship between America and the Philippines in the language of debt. To Romulo, America was "a generous benefactor, a loyal and true friend." "If we can honor the debt in no other way," he said, "we can pay with our lives."[43]

In the late 1930s and 1940s, Romulo's career stagnated. On several occasions, Quezon baited the ever-loyal Romulo with promises to support his candidacy for political office, only to disappoint him each time.[44] Suspicious of his patron's motives, Romulo cultivated his ties with General Douglas MacArthur and his wife, Jean, and eventually became one of the MacArthurs' social favorites.[45] In the meantime, Quezon continued to exert greater control of domestic politics. He recognized the importance of patronizing the country's intellectuals for his own popularity. In 1940, he appointed Romulo chair of the English language segment of the Commonwealth Literary Awards, which gave prizes for the best poetry, short story, and biography entries in English, Tagalog, and Spanish. The awards were the brainchild of the Philippine Writers' League. Headed by the noted essayists Federico Mangahas, Salvador P. Lopez (a former Romulo student at the University of the Philippines), and José A. Lansang, the group promoted ideals of "social responsibility" and opposition to fascism. Their stances would influence expatriate writers like Carlos Bulosan and helped set the course of postwar Philippine literature.[46]

Romulo as Propagandist and Hero

In 1941, Romulo made his own assessment of the impact of fascism in Asia, in a series that won him the Pulitzer Prize for correspondence.[47] He sought to answer a basic question: would the colonized subjects fight on the side of their colonial masters, the Allies, should war break out with Japan?[48] His responses demonstrate his anticolonialism and suggest the expansion of his nationalist perspective toward an increasing pan-Asian and Third World perspective. Romulo especially singled out China's great importance to the future of democracy in Asia. In his first dispatch from the British colony of Hong Kong, on September 15, he criticized Britain's cavalier attitude toward China's determined nationalist resistance against Japan. He urged America to use her powers wisely, toward the enlightenment of the "benighted" millions. He believed that the United States was "the one power that [could] put its shoulder resolutely behind the wheel of progress . . . regardless of the opposing forces of colonial greed." To Romulo, the future of Asia depended upon the stirring for freedom that the Chinese had so far demonstrated. Having had a taste of democracy, the Chinese would no longer return to the "ancient ways." He urged Asians to fight alongside the "democracies," claiming that they stood to lose all of their freedoms under Japan. In other articles, Romulo presented the devastation wrought by the Japanese bombing of Chungking, Britain's acts of appeasement, and the resilience of the Chinese people in delaying the fascist advance.[49]

Romulo began to draw parallels between Chinese and Filipino nationalist leaders. He was impressed by the "unobtrusive personality" of Generalissimo Chiang Kai-shek. "He carrie[d] himself," Romulo observed, "in a manner that reminded me of General Emilio Aguinaldo . . . his 'Oriental reserve' and dignified mien instantly command[ed] respect." The Generalissimo reminded Romulo not only of Filipino heroes but also of American ones: "I could not help remembering the austere simplicity of that other man of the people, Abraham Lincoln, who broke the shackles of slavery

[like] this leader of China." In the meantime, Romulo found that Madame Chiang Kai-Shek "radiate[d] warmth and friendship" and her "bright intelligent eyes" held the "secret of her influence."[50] He went on to visit Burma, Thailand, Singapore, French Indochina, and the Dutch West Indies, meeting with nationalist leaders, often in secret.[51] He recognized in the development of these nationalist struggles much of the Philippines' and his own ilustrado history.[52]

Romulo's increasing identification with Asia and the Third World developed out of his own heartfelt reactions, which he expressed with a sense of tragic irony. Traveling on the Burma Road, with its fleeing refugees and bombed-out landscapes, Romulo spotted a serene park in Chungking, the only place in the city unscathed by Japanese bombs. It seemed strange to find such a symbol of peace and beauty. As he stood in front of "blood-red dahlias" and the "crystal clear water," Romulo caught "a fleeting impression of something incongruous and yet symbolic of the spirit of man—like a huge Amorsolo painting cast upon the ruins of a Tondo fire."[53] In Saigon, Romulo's anti-Japanese sentiments grew when he witnessed their intimidating displays in the former French colonial capital. Anxious "to show the natives who [is] master in Indo-China,"[54] Japanese soldiers chose "public parks and children's playgrounds . . . for their daily military exercises, especially bayonet practice. This latter they carr[ied] out realistically, accompanying their thrusts and parries with wild whoops and yells, while the natives watch[ed] amazed by the dexterity, strength and ferocity of the Japanese soldiers." The image of the Japanese sword was so ubiquitous in the city of Saigon that Romulo dreamt that he was suffocating under "a mountain of sabres."[55]

Upon his return to the Philippines, Romulo publicly thanked his immediate patron at the *Herald*, Don Vicente Madrigal.[56] Romulo credited him with having had the foresight to suggest the trip. "I am profoundly grateful to him," Romulo said, "and if my articles have in any way served to help our readers . . . I am sure that he who made the trip possible is entitled to their gratitude in equal measure." In his last article, Romulo recognized his great fortune in being under American and not European colonial rule: "As a Filipino I must acknowledge my indebtedness to the benign rule of America for the privilege of believing in democracy and enjoying its manifold blessings."[57] Applying this belief in democracy and freedom to Asia, he exulted in having given expression "to the just and natural aspirations of all peoples regardless of race or creed."[58]

World War II made an exile out of Romulo and again brought him into extended contact with American life. From December 1941 to May 1942, the Japanese laid siege to the province of Bataan and the small island of Corregidor guarding the city of Manila, where Filipino and American troops had retreated. Faced with a war on the Asian and European fronts, U.S. President Roosevelt, as planned, chose to concentrate American forces first in the war against Hitler, despite the pleas of Quezon and MacArthur for reinforcements.[59] Romulo found a new, powerful patron in MacArthur, who conscripted him to serve as publicist and gave him the rank of major. He rewarded Romulo's hard work on radio as the "Voice of Freedom" by promoting him to colonel and making him his aide-de-camp. When MacArthur was forced to withdraw to Australia, Romulo was included on a list of those to be evacuated from Corregidor. He soon followed MacArthur to Australia. From Australia, MacArthur sent him to the United States to publicize the Pacific War. Romulo obliged and went on a lecture tour of the country.[60]

For Romulo, Filipino identity during the war meant tireless travel and countless speeches on behalf of his occupied homeland to urban and rural Americans, and to white, black, yellow, and brown audiences. In the fall of 1942 alone, a biographical account claims that his schedule took him to 289 different cities, a total of 60,000 miles. He lived mostly in hotels and on trains. He helped raise war bonds in numerous rallies. As an eyewitness to the suffering in Bataan, Romulo called attention to the smug complacency of Americans, whom he addressed as "brother[s]" and "fellow Americans," and the need to ward off the Japanese threat in the Pacific.[61] His four autobiographical works make up a heroic nationalist narrative, with Romulo as the protagonist.

I Saw the Fall of the Philippines (1942), Romulo's first book, describes his separation and exile from the country and his identification with Filipino troops fighting the Japanese. Romulo says he is writing not as a soldier but as a journalist seeking to document the lives of the "heroes" with whom he has shared the experience of war, the more than 80,000 Filipino and American troops in Bataan. He recalls his peaceful life as publisher of the D-M-H-M Newspapers in prewar Manila, happy with his wife and four sons and numerous friends (2).[62] The Japanese invasion, however, cut him off from his family. He then faced two months of "hell" in Corregidor and witnessed the devastation of the Filipino and American forces in Bataan before he was rescued in early April 1942.

Romulo took advantage of *I Saw the Fall* to reinvent himself as hero and to advance his credentials as a cultural interpreter between Asia and America. He had a knack for what was newsworthy. Indeed, he shows his flair for the dramatic by claiming that "I was the last man out of Bataan" (1).[63] He likewise fashions himself as a cultural translator, claiming to be "the connecting link between the outer world and the decimated front lines of Bataan." He is "the Voice of Freedom." (320) Moreover, Romulo advances perspectives on U.S.-Philippine relations that he had stated before the war. For instance, he casts the relationship between America and the Philippines in spiritual terms and in the language of mutual sacrifice. Philippine freedom, he says, has now been "sanctified in American and Filipino blood" and an unshakable faith had been forged from the hearts of men and women waiting entrapped in the tunnel of Corregidor (322, 323). Finally, Romulo asserts that the binational sacrifice at Bataan has reaffirmed universal humanist principles: "I have learned that all men are fundamentally the same and that there is a kinship that race or creed or national ideologies cannot efface."

Romulo came to America with the blessings of *the* hero of World War II in the Pacific, General Douglas MacArthur. On the back of Romulo's book was a picture of the uniformed commander in chief of the U.S. Forces in the Southwest Pacific, standing sporting his Philippine field marshal's cap and smoking his signature pipe. Responding to an inquiry from American newspapers, MacArthur glowingly wrote of Romulo's heroic efforts on his staff, especially as the premier radio broadcaster of "The Voice of Freedom," which sustained Filipino morale in moments of desperation. Romulo, MacArthur said, stood "as a living symbol" of the Filipinos who died fighting under the American flag.[64]

As MacArthur rose in prestige because of his ill-fated defense of Bataan and Corregidor, Romulo became bolder in acknowledging MacArthur's patronage, rather than that of Quezon, who had become the nominal president-in-exile of the occupied nation. According to Francis Burton Harrison, Romulo claimed upon his arrival in San Francisco in 1942 that he was "on a mission for General MacArthur," not for President Quezon.[65] Romulo lionized MacArthur as the brave warrior who had defied the Japanese at Corregidor by leaving the safety of the Malinta Tunnel without even the benefit of a helmet to watch the Japanese planes bomb the island. MacArthur was a confident general, possessing boundless energy and enthusiasm, inspiring his men, and carrying out brilliant military maneuvers.[66] MacArthur's soldiers, however, did not share this heroic assessment. Short on rations and having very little contact with their commanding officer, they labeled him, perhaps unfairly, "dugout Doug."[67] Romulo was either unaware or indifferent to this version of history. He wanted to make MacArthur into a living symbol of America to the Orient.[68]

Romulo's actions enraged Quezon. He had been on the verge of firing Romulo because of his grandiose radio broadcasts in Corregidor and had asked MacArthur to put him under the censorship of a committee. Romulo protested—he thought the watchdog group was humiliating—but Quezon stood by his opinion.[69] Quezon's resident commissioner, Joaquin Elizalde, also outlined the president's objections to *I Saw the Fall of the Philippines*. Quezon objected to being upstaged by MacArthur. He also resented Romulo's publication of the details of his [Quezon's] personal entourage when he escaped from Corregidor, including mention of his personal servant, Ah Dong.[70]

Romulo's next two books, *Mother America* (1943) and *My Brother Americans* (1945), ponder the meaning of his exile and, the titles notwithstanding, show his ambivalence about the U.S. colonization of the Philippines. In the Author's Note in *Mother America*, Romulo uncharacteristically begins with a pro-Filipino rather than a pro-American statement. He claims that he has included in the book documents that show "[t]hat the Filipinos believed in democracy and thought along republican lines even before the advent of American rule in the Philippines." This bold statement seemed to undercut the legitimacy of American colonial rule. If it was true that Filipinos had already believed in democracy before the arrival of the Americans, then American instruction in democratic ideals and self-government (the professed aims of American colonialism) was pointless. Romulo recoiled from this conclusion, however, saying in his introduction that "under the most remarkable guidance in history, an Oriental nation [the Philippines] was converted to faith in democracy" and that America's work in the Philippines was "a masterpiece in human relationship" (xv, Prefatory Note).

Romulo's ambivalence about American colonialism continues throughout the book, as he discusses America's relationship with the Philippines, imperialism and race, and his idea for a Pacific alliance. In the introduction, Romulo points to the historic Atlantic Charter agreement between Roosevelt and Churchill that defined Allied war aims.[71] Romulo distinguishes between the promise of the Charter and its actuality, which he claims Roosevelt had already began to enact in the Philippines with the Tydings-McDuffie Act of 1934, which set a timetable for independence (xiii). Romulo then recalls the ceremony at Notre Dame when both he and Roosevelt had been honored with doctorate of laws degrees. In this dignified ceremony, the people and the symbols of the two countries melded in his memory, as both Filipino journalist and American president were honored by the same award and as the flags and the anthems of the two nations were successively unfurled and sung.[72] Romulo claimed his membership in the Filipino and the American world as he sang both songs "with equal emotional fervor." America must be an exceptional imperial power, he thought, because in no other colonial relation could "a representative of a subject race" share the same honors as "the head of a conquering country."[73]

Romulo, however, had his eyes on a deeper argument at the beginning of *Mother America*, a reinterpretation of U.S. colonialism in the traditional Filipino terms of *utang na loob*. The United States had been a "generous benefactor, a loyal and true friend" to the Philippines, and Americans always kept in mind the "dignity of the human soul" and regarded Filipinos as "fellow humans,"[74] in contrast to the cruel European treatment of other colonized Asians (xv, 31–36). Thus, while American colonialism had "interrupted" the Filipino fight for freedom against Spain, the Filipinos were "converted to faith in democracy" and became the beneficiaries of American rule (xiv, xv). These colonial gifts had created an imposing debt, which, he asserts, Filipinos could repay only "with our lives." Indeed, Romulo asserts, they had paid that debt when they "lined up to die beside their former conquerors" in Bataan and Corregidor and thus sealed their loyalty to American principles with "Filipino blood" (xv). Nonetheless, it seemed that despite this "blood brotherhood" there was a remainder that Filipinos still owed Americans: "I cannot see the Philippines in the position of refusing to America any [military] bases she might need to maintain her position in the Orient, for she owes everything she is and may become to America." Still, Romulo was quick to add (although with a timid qualification): "Nor can I imagine America refusing the Philippines anything they may ask for *within reasons*" (142, 136; emphasis added).

Romulo boasts of his qualifications as cultural translator and seeks to analyze the misunderstanding between East and West on the basis of race. "Let me," he says, "being neither of the Occident nor the Orient, but a Westernized Filipino . . . translate for the benefit of the Occident the 'inscrutable' Oriental mind" (47). Whites, he observed, were prone to call "Orientals" liars, little understanding that they in turn saw the white man as a "slippery character" who grabbed everything (46–47). Romulo's analysis of the Oriental, while interspersed with important observations, is itself permeated with Orientalisms that play upon the supposed division between a spiritual East and a materialistic West. The Oriental, he says, is "not mysterious," but acts on simple, age-old precepts of behavior. He cares more about the condition of his soul than anything else. The white man, however, has to have conveniences and luxuries to be content (47–48).

The Oriental is hypersensitive, "courteous to the point of appearing to fawn"—but the white man interprets this behavior as lying or sneakiness, rather than a fear of being hurt (49). On the other hand, the white man in the Orient often begins as a well-meaning, humble migrant from the metropolis, who often becomes corrupted. The chauffeurs, the availability of cheap labor, the household help spoil him and he becomes patronizing and greedy (55–56). He exploits the native and refuses to let him speak or disagree with him. Romulo uses the white man in the Philippines as an example. The white man may not even be conscious of it, but his "condescension" betrays him. He asks questions "without stopping to think of the hurt they [could] convey" (61). "Isn't there a white doctor here? . . . Where is the white man's hotel? . . . Isn't there a white manager here?" He may be speaking to highly educated, Western-trained Filipino doctors and hotel managers (60). He insults people by using "coolie talk" toward all those of Oriental blood, including servants who may be working their way through college and speak English as well as he does (61).

Because of such racist attitudes, Romulo says, many Asians had been persuaded by Japanese propaganda and fought on the side of Japan. But the Filipinos were different. Romulo identifies himself with a nation that holds no racial bitterness toward the white man. The Filipinos had benefited from

William Howard Taft's "Philippines for the Filipinos" policy and America's gradual training in self-government. The United States had never allowed the interests of imperialistic businessmen to become *official* policy. Given these reasons, Filipinos fight for their freedoms without personal animosity or "racial bitterness" toward Americans. Thus, America's Philippine experiment provides a model for other countries to follow (72–79).

"America's pattern" in the Philippines involved the opening of public schools, a period of training for ultimate sovereignty, transformation from local to national government, and, ultimately, independence. Democratic schooling, Romulo asserts, will eradicate the evils of militarism and the Japanese warrior mentality (126–28, 132). Romulo ends the book by calling for a Pacific Charter that will sum up the rights of Asians as the Atlantic Charter does for the Western world, a charter that will enshrine equality, protect national boundaries and resources, eliminate racism, and encourage constant vigilance for peace (145–46, 149).

Romulo's *My Brother Americans* (1945) departs from *Mother America's* analytical bent. While derided by critics at the time for its patchwork quality, it remains valuable today for its account of a Filipino's encounter with wartime America and for its perspectives on race. Upon his arrival in America, Romulo had become cynical and doubtful of America's pledge to grant independence to the Philippines.[75] However, his travels through dozens of American towns and cities reinvigorated his faith "like a religious experience" (41). With the eye of a social historian, he documents the gargantuan factories producing war matériel and training for war. On his travels, he made lasting personal friendships (38–43). New York City, where he had first studied in his Columbia University days, became his home away from home, and he grew increasingly fond of the city, to which he would return again and again (146–62). While America's preparations pleased him, he saw a serious threat to the war effort—the race problem.

White racism and racial difference proved crucial to Romulo's developing identity as a Filipino nationalist and pan-Asian, Third World advocate. Strangers made him feel like a "freak" in New York for wearing a U.S. army uniform, but with a Philippine Army fourragère. A drunk insulted his insignia (17). He was constantly being mistaken for Chinese, never for a Filipino. No one, it seemed, knew about Bataan or about Filipinos (18). But despite these incidents, Romulo still claims that he had never met any racial animosity in America (163, 164). He considered the race problem in the South, in the cities, and in California of greater consequence (165). As a "guest in the house," Romulo found it difficult to see why the race problem existed, for everyone seemed to agree that it was unjust and dangerous. But the problem lingered (166). Romulo believed that the fear of miscegenation was at the heart of the racial animosities, but judging from the Philippine experience, Romulo felt this fear was baseless, for wherever there was equality, the races practically did not intermarry (167–68).

Meanwhile, Romulo's sense of duality with regards to America was transferred to his relationship with fellow Filipinos in the United States. On a personal trip in 1944, he encountered Filipino laborers of the West Coast. He was eager to see his countrymen. He spoke to town leaders in "their homes, on farms, and in the factories and navy yards . . . in their native dialects." (169) He soon realized that unlike the nondiscriminatory policy of the United States in the Philippines, the California Filipinos were "discriminated against and often made to feel unwelcome" (169). He blamed the Japanese for the antagonism on the West Coast toward all Orientals, but he nonetheless saw the danger in xenophobia, especially during a time of war (170). Romulo again defines a unique place for Filipinos in the spectrum of race relations. He describes his countrymen as a group different from other Orientals in the United States, because, he says, they have never organized for the removal of the barriers to their naturalization. They are a "shy and unorganized group" who have "never looked beyond achieving the independence of their native land" (170).

Romulo says that he spoke to the white leaders of various towns and pleaded with them on behalf of Filipinos. He speaks in varying registers. At times, he seems paternalistic ("I have a plea. . . . They [the Filipinos] are humble, meek, timid, even . . ."). At other times, he criticizes anti-Filipino racism. (Filipinos, he says, have only done "backbreaking jobs which you cannot or will not do.") Then he resorts to the discourse of sacrifice and brotherhood: "See in their faces the image of the 21,000 Filipino soldiers who died for you in Bataan" (170–71). By the end of his trip, he says, he had persuaded a hotel owner to take down a sign on his desk that said: "No Filipinos Allowed" (171). In his desire to represent Filipinos, Romulo represents them as victims, and he fails to mention the countless fraternities, unions, activist groups, and newspapers that had lobbied for the right to obtain U.S.

citizenship, better working conditions, and an end to anti-miscegenation laws.[76] Romulo also fails to name or to give voice to a single Filipino he met in his travels to the West Coast, thus adding to their victimization.

In *I See the Philippines Rise* (1946), the heroic exile, who had now been appointed Philippine resident commissioner in the United States by President Sergio Osmeña, returns in triumph to the Philippines alongside the liberator, MacArthur.[77] In the famous picture of the Leyte Gulf landing, the diminutive Romulo strides immediately behind the gigantic figure of his hero MacArthur and the less impressive Osmeña. He reassumed his position as the "Voice of Freedom" and managed to accompany MacArthur in the "liberation" of Manila, before returning to Washington, D.C., to plead for rehabilitation funds from the U.S. Congress.

Before his departure for the Philippines, Romulo had felt his loyalties divided between Quezon and MacArthur, perhaps reflecting his ambivalence about his two great loves, Asia and America (9). As in his previous works, Romulo seems anxious to show Filipino loyalty to America, especially in pleading to Congress for rehabilitation funds. Filipinos working behind enemy lines, he says, have saved numerous American lives because of the completeness of their intelligence reports (36–42). Once again, he reaffirms the pattern of American colonialism in the Philippines as the pattern for the United Nations and the postwar world (262).

Romulo as Patron and as Critic of Colonialism

After the war, Romulo returned to the United States as resident commissioner under President Sergio Osmeña, but he soon found that American political leaders were not in a giving mood, and rejected any arguments based upon sentimental relations or incurred debts of gratitude.[78] Most Philippine presidents, and Romulo himself, were only partially effective in obtaining badly needed legislation for various Philippine issues, including a veterans' bill for Filipino soldiers who had fought in the U.S. Army.[79]

After having followed Quezon and served under MacArthur, Romulo cultivated his own following. During the war, he had briefly, under Quezon's initiative, brought together writers who would become famous in the postwar era, such as Carlos Bulosan, José García Villa, Bienvenido N. Santos, and P. C. Morantte, but they were not interested in political careers.[80] He soon recruited competent and promising Filipino intellectuals into the foreign service, like José Imperial and Manuel Adeva, who assisted him as resident commissioner. Both men would eventually become Philippine ambassadors. Romulo also recruited the Pacific Coast correspondent for *Bataan* magazine, Juan C. Dionisio, who would soon become Philippine consul general in Honolulu.[81] In the Philippines, Romulo was reunited with Mauro Mendez, his friend and city editor at the *Herald* in the 1930s. Mendez, who had stayed behind during the war, became Osmeña's secretary of public information and was launched on a diplomatic career. In 1948, at Romulo's invitation, he joined the Philippine Mission to the United Nations, where he met Romulo's protégé Salvador Lopez.[82] In turn, at Romulo's instigation, Lopez succeeded in persuading the newspaperman Narciso Reyes, an outstanding Tagalog writer, to work as his assistant in New York. Finally, Romulo also recruited two promising lawyers, José Ingles and Victorio Carpio, to serve on his staff at the United Nations.[83] Romulo claimed he had no method of selecting these talented young men, except on the basis of the quality of loyalty, which Romulo himself possessed.[84]

Despite Romulo's following, however, his failure to capture the Philippine presidency in 1953 shows his tenuous grasp of the intricacies of domestic patronage politics. However, he was to prove himself adaptable and managed to extract political advantage from apparent defeat. Early in the year, President Quirino had recalled him from Washington, D.C., to attend the Liberal Party Convention of April 1953 and to lend his stature as former president of the UN General Assembly to the deliberations. A "Romulo for President" campaign soon gained momentum and probably convinced Romulo of the viability of his candidacy. But before declaring his candidacy, he resigned from his post as Quirino's ambassador to the United States, citing the widely held view of the sad state of the Philippine economy, widespread government corruption, and the grave threat posed by the Huk peasant rebellion, which Quirino had failed to stem. In parting, he discouraged Quirino from seeking the party nomination.[85] On the campaign trail, he especially attacked Quirino's secretary of foreign affairs, Joaquin Elizalde, who was appointed after Romulo's resignation, for incompetence and lack of name recognition in America.[86]

During the Liberal Party Convention, Romulo and other Liberals, fear-ing intimidation from Quirino, called for a secret ballot. Quirino rejected this and leveraged enough delegates to scuttle the proposal and to preserve the voice vote. Under these conditions, Quirino, who wielded considerable power over provincial officials through his control of discretionary funds, won the nomination. Romulo, along with political leaders like former Vice President Fernando Lopez, who represented the powerful sugar growers of the Western Visayas, bolted out of the convention and set up a new party, the Democratic Party. Together, they developed a platform that selected Romulo as its candidate for president against Quirino and Magsaysay.[87]

Senator Tomas Cabili, a Romulo supporter, assessed his strengths and weaknesses as a candidate. His analysis showed the complex impact of Romulo's long years of expatriation to America upon his political fortunes. According to Cabili, Romulo's strengths included his leadership ability during war and peace, his international experience, and his reputation in America. Cabili noted that Romulo was smarter and more intimate with Americans than Magsaysay, more respecting of Americans than the anti-American Nacionalistas, and more honest than the corrupt, nepotistic Quirino.[88] Romulo's weaknesses included a lack of name recognition in the Philippines, the opposition of a segment of the press that labeled him hopelessly "pro-American," a late Third Party candidacy, and insufficient campaign organization. Moreover, he was short of funds. To shore up his sagging resources, he went on a two-week tour of the United States, but he failed to garner support there for his candidacy. He realized that many Americans were backing Magsaysay.[89]

The powerful sugar growers supporting Romulo soon lost confidence in his chances of being elected and, behind his back, sought a deal with the Nacionalistas.[90] The stalwarts of both parties worked out an arrangement, soon leaked to the press, that unified the two groups around Magsaysay's presidential candidacy. The sugar politicians obtained the promise of a Senate presidency for Fernando Lopez and three out of the eight senators on the Nacionalista ticket. The negotiators also agreed to return Romulo to Washington as Philippine ambassador to the United States.[91] Wounded by the machinations around him, Romulo disavowed any knowledge of the secret deal. He gracefully bowed out of the race, declared his support for Magsaysay, and became his campaign manager.[92] Referring to the promised ambassadorship, Romulo told his supporters: "I seek nothing, I expect nothing, I shall accept nothing."[93] Key political analysts, like Teodoro Locsin of the *Free Press*, marveled at Romulo's ability to gain political capital out of a sure defeat. Nacionalista Party stalwarts like Sergio Osmeña asked him to head the senatorial lineup, but, true to his word, Romulo refused to accept any political benefits from joining Magsaysay, at least in public.[94]

The presidential campaign revealed cleavages in Romulo's imagining of the nation—in particular, his class snobbery and his exclusion of cultural minorities from the Philippine nation. For instance, Romulo's attack on the front-runner, Magsaysay, played on his lower-class origins, highlighting the latter's poverty and lack of serious formal education. In response, Magsaysay's press secretary was only too happy to reveal that Romulo, despite all his learning, had plagiarized Adlai Stevenson's speech to the U.S. Democratic Party to use in his own acceptance speech to the Philippine Democratic Party.[95] And for this, Romulo had no defense, except to blame the error on one of his speechwriters.[96] Moreover, Magsaysay's men made an issue out of his wartime assertion in *Mother America* that the Igorots were not part of the Filipino nation.[97] A section of *Mother America* managed to find its way into the hands of students from the Mountain Province, home of the Igorots, and in a demonstration called against Romulo, Igorot leaders burned copies of his book.[98]

Correspondence between Romulo and an Igorot critic of his book shows the complex currents of nationalism and nativism to which Romulo's association with America gave rise. One Gabriel S. Castro responded to the passage in Romulo's book in a letter to the *Philippines Free Press*.[99] Castro felt that the passage was prejudicial toward the Igorots and misrepresented them to Americans. He marveled at Romulo's ignorance in calling the Igorots Philippine aborigines, when it was common knowledge that these were the Aetas, or Negritos. He rejected Romulo's attempts to distance Igorots racially from lowlanders. Castro claimed that the Igorot physique was no different from Romulo's own, and that if the lowland Filipinos from whom he sprang were more advanced or more civilized than the Igorots were, it was only because of environment, and not a matter of heredity. He discouraged Igorots from voting for Romulo. Castro then went on to call Romulo "The White Man in the Orient" and questioned whether he was truly a Filipino citizen.

In response, Romulo attacked the nativist tone of the letter and reasserted the authenticity of his nationalism. He took offense at Castro's insinuation about his identity, claiming that his Filipino citizenship was "the one proud possession and heritage which I shall bequeath to my children pure and undefiled." He quoted extensively from his editorial "I Am a Filipino."[100] He argued that his reference to the Igorots had been written ten years ago to combat a common misrepresentation in America (before the Philippines became independent) that the average Filipino wore a "G-string."[101] Beyond this, he sought to sidestep debating direct passages from the book by focusing on the upcoming elections and on the political issues of the campaign.

The attacks on Romulo abated as a result of the Nacionalista–Democratic Party deal and because Magsaysay had great respect for Romulo's diplomatic skills. Several years later, Romulo would capitalize on the mystique surrounding Magsaysay by writing two books, *Crusade in Asia* (1955) and *The Magsaysay Story* (1956).[102]

In *The Magsaysay Story*, Romulo heroizes his subject, using biography to expound moral values, mostly to the American audience at whom the book was aimed. He sets the details of Ramon Magsaysay's life in mythical terms and describes him as a kind of Filipino Abraham Lincoln. Ramon's *nipa* hut in Zambales becomes the equivalent of Lincoln's log cabin in Illinois (1).[103] His father, a high school teacher, who refused to change a student's grade in order to please a rich parent, was an exemplary model of honesty for Ramon (3). Romulo describes Magsaysay's backbreaking work as a metal worker as "slave labor" and compares his long walks to the University of the Philippines to Lincoln's long journeys to the library just "for the pleasure of reading a book" (5, 21). Moreover, Congressman Magsaysay had a passion for "the exact sum" and demanded complete honesty from his subordinates (75). Secretary of Defense Magsaysay had vigorously pursued the evil Huks and the Communist Party Politburo (105). He showed compassion toward peasants and became notorious for his "shampooing," or berating, of negligent officers of the Philippine Army. In defeating the Communist insurgency, Magsaysay, like Lincoln, saved the Republic at a crucial time in its history (117).[104]

Romulo's political writings of the decade, especially on international issues, show his critical response to American and European attempts to quell Asian nationalism and reestablish colonial rule. In an eloquent "private and confidential" letter to Secretary of State Dean Acheson in 1950, Romulo spoke for many Southeast Asian leaders when he expressed his pain and displeasure at U.S. support for the puppet Bao Dai government in Vietnam. Romulo began with familiar protestations of friendship for America and his claim to know "Oriental psychology" (99, 100).[105] However, he soon criticized America's decision to recognize Bao Dai, whom "the whole world knows . . . is helpless without the French" (100). As a result, the United States had buttressed French colonialism, given the Communists a propaganda victory as the sole anti-imperialists in the region, and undercut the positions of America's nationalist and noncommunist allies (like Romulo) who called for the establishment of a Southeast Asian alliance with the Americans (101–3). He sought greater understanding for Ho Chi Minh's intentions and expressed his opinion, based on personal experience, that Ho worked independently from Moscow (103).[106]

Romulo was to pursue these nationalist and anticolonialist positions in later writings, but in the context of articulating his liberal, internationalist outlook. *Crusade in Asia* (1955) showcases the Philippine counterinsurgency effort as an example to the world of a successful anticommunist strategy. This he rhetorically presents as a morality play. Evil Communism fed on the "morally diseased" environment of postwar Philippine society (Foreword). Drawing upon his wartime tour of Asia, Romulo connected the two evils of Japanese imperialism and postwar Communism, both of which attempted to seduce Asians by promising an "Asia for the Asians" approach (see 271).[107] The corruption surrounding weak leaders like President Elpidio Quirino aided Communism, as it had Japanese militarism (chapters 5 and 6). However, luckily, there were good, honest men in the Philippines, like Ramon Magsaysay, who remained uncorrupted and fought to end Communist infiltration (chapters 8 and 9).

In the latter sections of the book, Romulo is predictably more critical of the West's anticommunist strategy. He criticizes the French for their failure to convert "embittered" Vietnam into an ally and the United States for upholding French colonialism (247, 257). He counsels against including Japan, with no tradition of democracy, in a Pacific alliance and calls upon the United States to rely more on prodemocratic allies—the Filipinos, Thais, and Pakistanis (248–49). Moreover, he criticizes the United States, Great Britain, France, New Zealand, and Australia for excluding Southeast Asian countries from the so-called "5-Power Talks" on Southeast Asia. To Romulo, this was evidence of blatant racism and colonialism (263). In what would become a familiar refrain in his other books, he advises Americans to give assistance to poorer countries, not as a special favor with strings attached or as a disguised vestige of colonial imperialism, but on the basis of self-help and mutual respect (261). Finally, Romulo calls for more economic rather than military aid in Asia. He claims that the decision in Brown vs. Board of Education in 1954 did more to combat Communism in the area than any military assistance (293). In light of this, he repeats his wartime idea of a Pacific Charter that will outline the aims and principles of a regional, noncommunist alliance (274–75).

Romulo continued alternating anticommunist discourse with critique of the West in *The Meaning of Bandung*, written a year after the Asian and African Conference in Bandung, Indonesia, in April 1955, the first worldwide meeting of decolonizing countries. President Ramon Magsaysay named Romulo cabinet minister without rank for the duration of the conference. The first half of the book, "The Spiritual Offensive," describes the supposed machinations of the Chinese and Indian political leaders (Prime Ministers Chou En-lai and Jawaharlal Nehru) in cajoling delegates into making procommunist policy statements (3–4, 12–16).[108] Romulo claims that the noncommunist states thwarted these moves. In his official speech on behalf of the Philippine delegation, he restates their common agenda of political freedoms, racial equality, and peaceful economic growth (13–16; 23–27). In the second half of the book, however, "Asian Criticisms of America," Romulo relays a series of complaints against the West that he supposedly overheard from other Asian delegates (42–48). Many of them are familiar.[109] Others show expansion of previous themes. For instance, Romulo points to America's discriminatory practice of investing billions of dollars in postwar Europe and little in Asia. Romulo proceeds to dissect Americans' erroneous and chauvinistic assumptions about Asians and criticizes America's "sad lack of understanding" of the parallel between its own "revolutionary past" and "the libertarian aspirations of the peoples of Asia and Africa" (45ff., 48). He urges America, "[as] a child of revolution" to "seize the revolutionary initiative in Asia and Africa" (52–53).

Perhaps Romulo's most eloquent tract during this period was *Friend to Friend* (1958), written with Pearl S. Buck, when Romulo was propagating President Carlos P. Garcia's "Filipino First" policy.[110] After protesting his love for America, Romulo sets the Asian nationalists' case before the American public by formulating complex questions on American hegemony. Concerned with the problems of world power and disarmament, America has fallen behind the Soviet Union in its relationship with the non-Western world. Does the United States "represent the most hopeful wave of the future," he wonders, or is "it a declining power, gorged and weakened by its glutted wealth"? (16).[111] America is faced with two key postcolonial problems: eradicating the colonized's "slave mentality" ("counter-brutality, revenge, and racism in reverse") and the more important problem of "the psychological adjustment of the Western white man" to the termination of white rule (20). America seems ill equipped to deal with the world's complexities and, worse, it has failed to earn the respect of other peoples, despite its generosity in the shape of numerous aid programs. Romulo seeks to explain why.

Romulo finds that Americans entertain six "myths" about America's power. Americans believe that freedom will triumph no matter what the enemies of freedom do, that "progress is not possible without freedom," and that as the United States and the Soviet Union compete with each other, they are becoming more and more alike (34, 36, 40). One myth, that there is only the American way to freedom, is chauvinistic, while another—that it is better to tolerate an unfree Communist world than to be dead in a democratic one—is defeatist (37, 39–40). Romulo feels that America can repair its reputation by admitting its ignorance of "the ways of life and the institutions of other peoples" and disabusing themselves of the idea that they have a "mission" to require others to conform to American ideals (43). Moreover, Americans need to realize that their own social system is "no longer free enterprise in its purest form, but capitalism diluted with Socialist elements." Other social systems had, in fact, achieved progress in economy, science, technology and the arts (45). Finally, Americans have to recognize the media's occasional insensitivity and "careless misreporting of other people's customs" (46).

Once again, Romulo highlights the contradiction between America's rhetoric of freedom and its practice of race relations. Various issues rankle Third World leaders: racism in the United States, the dismissal of Latin American criticism of the West as communistic, America's refusal to come to terms with the Philippines on the future of the U.S. military bases (as it had done in Iceland and Japan), and America's lack of initiative in putting forward peace proposals (47–50; 51). As in his speech at Notre Dame and in *Mother America* in 1943, Romulo admonishes Americans that U.S. colonial rule in the Philippines can guide America's relations with Third World countries. While American colonialism had been a "strange combination of crude self-interest and high-minded purpose," it was nonetheless "eternally bothered with a conscience" (57, 58). That conscience, or "spirit of generosity," underlay the diverse motives, styles, and moods of American rule under various administrations and, aided by anti-imperialists, ultimately triumphed over "selfishness or cupidity" (59). Most important, the United States had granted the Philippines its independence (62).

Romulo makes no mention, however, of the inequality between American and Philippine trade relations after the war and the persistence of U.S. military bases. Instead, he takes pride in the fact that the Philippines has never asked for a handout, and that the American record rang "the death knell of colonialism" (63). Finally, Romulo says that Americans have to accept that the exercise of their imperial power makes abuses inevitable. He upholds the American practice of negotiating and coming to a mutual consensus with its allies, as opposed to the USSR's reliance upon coercion. The rest of the world, Romulo concludes, is better off with America with its mistakes than with the Russians. America, he affirms, can never lose sight of its final objective, human freedom (64–66).[112]

The Contemporary Nationalist

In 1961, Romulo decided to end his expatriate life and return home. He had lived in a "foreign" country for twenty years.[113] When President Macapagal offered him the position of president of the University of the Philippines in 1962, he immediately accepted. However, controversy would immediately stalk his new office. Macapagal had failed to follow the proper channels for selection of the president of the university, which went through the regents. Romulo, himself a former regent, seems to have been unconcerned by the irregularity of the process, but faculty and student leaders objected. Macapagal himself apologized to the university alumni, however, which cooled the controversy, and the regents soon elected Romulo.[114]

Romulo's nationalism found expression at the university in a climate of free speech and a host of spectacles designed to instill Filipino values. Some expressed the hope that Romulo, an avowed anticommunist, would rid the university of leftist influences, but he reaffirmed his liberal principles by opposing any witch-hunt, saying that McCarthyism had no place in a university.[115] On several occasions, Romulo outlined his nationalist educational goals: he sought to modernize faculty and research, to develop a university responsive to the needs of the nation, and to make the University of the Philippines "the center of Philippine nationalism."[116] For Romulo, spectacles, or what critics derided as cosmetic changes, would be crucial to the development of nationalism.[117] He filled hallways with portraits of heroes and martyrs, installed the first Philippine flag ever to be flown on top of the administration building, and required an ROTC cadet contingent to wear native Filipino garb. Moreover, on August 19, 1962, he renamed the administration building Quezon Hall after his idol Manuel Quezon. The date was designated "Quezon Day," and the occasion was celebrated with a scholarly symposium on Quezon.[118]

It seems fitting that Romulo's formal inauguration as president on April 7, 1963, reflected the penchant for performance he had once admired in Quezon. During the week of the event, the university held a plethora of programs: an open house of colleges, a "tea-musicale," a dinner sponsored by the regents, a gala concert by the U.P. Symphony Orchestra (with original compositions), a luncheon, and the presentation of the presidential collier, or ceremonial necklace. Onlookers were awed by the "spectacular fashion" in which academic colors mingled during the commencement procession, which involved universities from all over the world, but Silvino Epistola, a U.P. English professor, said he had overheard people say that "it was just too much pomp to grace a single occasion."[119] Nonetheless, President Romulo seemed to evoke a sense of ceremony and grandeur wherever he traveled.[120]

Romulo's political philosophy during this period seems to have wavered back and forth between nationalism, a critique of liberalism, and at the same time, reassertion of its fundamental principles. For instance, Romulo sought to develop practical links between the University of the Philippines and other Asian nations, especially with the Malay states. He sought to "redress the imbalance" in Filipino education, which had ignored the East and aped the West (2).[121] He saw the Filipino's role in Asia as that of a "catalyst" unifying the region's diverse cultures, which had to be based upon Asia's own needs, not the West's dictation (51, 52). Romulo's attempt to resituate the Philippines in the Asian mainstream stemmed from a growing suspicion that Western "humanism" had failed to match "the deep moral and spiritual crisis" ushered in by Western science and technology (116). Romulo was thus beginning to question his stated beliefs in liberal nationalism and progress. This doubt provided the basis for his discourses on contemporary nationalism in the Azad Memorial Lectures. There, Romulo praised India's "ethical imagination," recalling Gandhi's and Nehru's nonviolent resistance to the British. He argued that this "conscience" should be placed beside "the modern consciousness which [responds] to the idea of progress with a kind of mechanistic exuberance."[122] Romulo criticized the West for travestying civilized codes of conduct in war by dropping the atomic bomb on Japan and for subverting independent Asian and African nations (43).

Romulo seemed to be assuming a new role. He no longer played the anticommunist crusader or "friend" who advised Americans on the proper exercise of their influence in Asia, as he had done in the 1950s. Instead, he was charting a path for the emerging Asian nations. In this scheme, both East and West had to be carefully watched. The "dogmatism" of Communist countries and the "loyalty checks" of the Western alliance were "totalitarian on both extremes," while the alternatives of being "anti-West" or "procommunist" presented no real choice for Third World nations (28, 56). Rather, contemporary nationalism transcended the "orthodox dichotomies of East vs. West, or of Democracy vs. Communism" (31). Still, Romulo eschewed an exclusively Asian nationalist ideology. He was unable or unwilling to discard his liberal, progressive principles—in fact, he called for their reassertion. He believed the West had simply misinterpreted the impact of contemporary nationalism. Indeed, Third World countries merely sought to reassert the principles of freedom and the "equality of nations" trampled upon by both neocolonialism and Communism. Such a movement was based upon liberal, Enlightenment principles—it presupposed a higher law than that of men and provided the basis for an agreement on a common international order.

Nationalism thus appeared paradoxical—beginning from specific locations yet possessing international ramifications. "The emergence of [decolonizing] nations," Romulo said, had "done much to universalize history"

(21–23). Nationalism also shifted attention away from Cold War ideologies and toward universal human needs—freedom from hunger, freedom from thought control, human welfare—that were crying out for satisfaction (32). Ever the libertarian, Romulo challenged governments to eliminate censorship and obstacles to the free flow of information. He again condemned McCarthyism, opposed the death penalty, and challenged world leaders to follow a democratic path by allowing "contrary viewpoints" and "opposing political parties and programs" (55).

Even when Romulo sought to define Filipino nationalism for the youth, as in *Identity and Change* (1965), he continued to speak in broad, international terms. He elided the chauvinistic clichés that his performances at the University of the Philippines seemed to suggest. His view of Philippine nationalism, for instance, reasserted the necessary exile from motherland that led to the awakening of national self-consciousness. He writes:

> Nationalism, in the Philippines, for better or for worse, is an expatriate affirmation. It was so in the nineteenth century, with Rizal, del Pilar, Lopez Jaena, and the rest of the Reformist group. Then, in the twentieth century it was the central politics of those Filipinos within the country . . . who somehow felt that its culture and government were not our own. I had quite similar feelings during the American regime, but the physical fact of expatriation came to me as a member of the exile government in Washington during the war years. It was there that I began to be more analytical about our situation, to have the psychological experience of longing for identity even as I knew that I manifested it everywhere.[123]

This passage, so crucial to Romulo's thinking about nationalism and exile, deserves some discussion. For Romulo, Filipino nationalism was an "expatriate affirmation" with its roots among the ilustrados, the "Reformist group" that included Rizal, in nineteenth-century Spain. In the twentieth century, under the American colonial regime, a prevailing sense of expatriation dominated the politics of Filipino leaders even in the Philippines. Romulo shared this sense of exile, but it was not, however, until he was physically displaced from the Philippines by the Japanese invasion and spent the war years in Washington, D.C., that he truly understood these sentiments. For Romulo, expatriation was deeply tied up with a profound sense of paradox, a sense of division, between the desire for collective solidarity and the work of representing the nation in his own body.

Romulo's nationalism led not to certainty about one's roots but to critical self-questioning that stemmed from a psychological doubling of consciousness. He was reluctant to pin down Filipino identity, because he saw its roots as complex and heterogeneous (3–4).[124] For Romulo, national freedom need not involve "provincialism"—Rizal, del Pilar, and Lopez Jaena had not only dreamed of their native land, they had also craved freedom (5). Nor did nationalism require giving up the pursuit of "excellence" in the sciences and the arts. Romulo argued that Filipino artists had to accept an "international judgment." If Filipino artists were to be famous in America and in Europe, they had to be judged "within the circumstances of civilization itself" (5). In line with this nationalist outlook, Romulo traveled extensively throughout the Philippines, the United States, and Canada to seek grants for his programs. He succeeded in obtaining grants from the Philippine sugar industry, the Agency for International Development, and the Rockefeller, Guggenheim, and Ford Foundations.[125]

In the late 1960s, the rising tide of nationalism at the University of the Philippines led to protests against the sending of Philippine troops to Vietnam and the use of university facilities for testing chemical weapons to be used in Vietnam's jungles.[126] These militant and clearly anti-American protests put Romulo on the defensive. In the case of chemical testing, he was forced to end an agreement with the Dow Chemical Company.[127] The nationalist senator Lorenzo M. Tañada damaged Romulo's credibility with a letter published in the *Philippine Collegian* protesting the "Americanization" of the university.[128] Tañada charged that the university discriminated against Filipino faculty members (who received fewer benefits than their American counterparts), curbed nationalist speech, and tied up U.P. funds to implement American "aid" projects.[129] Romulo's response to these charges took twenty-three pages, but despite his thorough arguments, it failed to counteract the damage done to his administration.[130]

Nationalism, Dictatorship, and the Value of Loyalty

Romulo's term as U.P. president expired in 1968, and the regents elected his former protégé Salvador P. Lopez to replace him in December that year.[131] The transition from Romulo to Lopez was a vintage Romulo performance.

According to Lopez, who was then the Philippines' permanent representative at the United Nations and Philippine ambassador to the United States, Romulo had attempted twice to persuade him to take over the university presidency. "Romulo," said Lopez, "was no longer able to enter his office. The rebellious students barred his way." When Lopez refused, Romulo persuaded President Marcos to order Lopez home from Washington, D.C., to take over their "alma mater."[132] But Romulo had an ulterior motive for sidetracking Lopez from the diplomatic corps. Romulo was eyeing the position of minister of foreign affairs, Narciso Ramos, who was retiring after serving a single term. Since Lopez would have been the natural replacement for Ramos, Lopez's appointment to the University of the Philippines left the foreign affairs position open for Romulo. This, as Lopez put it, was "a perfectly Romulo operation."[133]

Foreign Minister Romulo found himself at home in President Marcos's cabinet. Marcos, who took a great interest in international affairs, sought to pursue an independent foreign policy, "from colonial status to special relations, to complete . . . self-reliance."[134] His foreign policy objectives of transforming the United Nations through a review of the UN Charter, strengthening the regional group, ASEAN (the Association of Southeast Asian Nations), and identifying with the Third World harmonized with Romulo's beliefs.[135] Moreover, the end of the Vietnam War and the vacuum left by U.S. disengagement from the area offered exciting challenges to Philippine foreign policy. Romulo took part in the novel opening of diplomatic relations with the Soviet Union and China and the establishment of more active ties with the Arab states to deal with the oil crunch and the Muslim secessionist movement in the southern Philippines.[136]

For a time, it did seem to many Filipinos that Marcos's martial law government might work. According to the historian Ruby Paredes, Marcos skillfully manipulated "the political system behind a rhetoric of social reform, [and formed] a broad base of support for his 'New Society.'"[137] Many Filipinos were not enthusiastic about Marcos's methods, but they agreed with his criticisms of reactionary oligarchs, a sensationalist and irresponsible press, and fraudulent elections determined by provincial warlords.[138] In the postwar Philippines, powerful families jockeyed against one another for control of the state, seeking concessions for their businesses and landholdings. Corruption was not unusual—it was an integral part of the political game.[139]

In the first few years of martial law, as Romulo thought, there was little difference between Marcos and the previous presidential administrations with regard to corruption.[140] Meanwhile, the seeming improvement of the economy and the redistribution of wealth, which resulted from the increase in USAID funds for rural electrification, rice production, and land reform seemed to many to justify giving up civil liberties. Romulo was among those who shared this fateful analysis. For him, the Philippines before martial law, where the possession of firearms had become ubiquitous, had become "a wild west country," a state of affairs resembling the aftermath of the Japanese occupation. He supported martial law because Marcos had obtained the surrender of hundreds of thousands of guns, which became the regime's "best achievement."[141] Moreover, Romulo argued, martial law instilled "national discipline." Even "when it was finally abolished, parents clamored for its restoration."[142] However, martial law would promote corruption and human rights abuses in the later years to a greater extent than under any previous administration, spurring widespread international efforts against the Marcos regime.[143]

Romulo defended President Marcos as he had defended all the other presidents he had served. He helped to create the appearance of a joint U.S.-Philippine agreement to establish martial law.[144] He was not above snobbery and distortion of the facts. In the early 1970s, he fêted foreign journalists and officials who visited the Philippines.[145] In the late 1970s, however, with the Marcos regime increasingly embattled with criticism, Romulo showed a streak of meanness by impugning and snubbing U.S. Assistant Secretary of State Patt Derian, President Jimmy Carter's chief diplomat on human rights.[146] Moreover, Romulo's participation in the National Assembly (Interim Batasang Pambansa, or IBP) elections showed a Romulo out of touch with reality. After six years of martial law, Marcos held the elections as a putative transition to a parliamentary system. While some ministers had to run for election, including Romulo, Marcos himself did not and remained as president.[147] From the start, the elections were fraudulent, and Marcos directed the results of the voting. Not surprisingly, Imelda Marcos garnered the greatest number of votes, while Romulo placed second.[148] The results caused widespread dissatisfaction and led to numerous protests. Yet one week after the voting, Romulo made the stunning announcement in the government-owned *Bulletin Today* newspaper that the "IBP polls were freest and cleanest yet."[149]

On a philosophical level, Romulo was retreating from liberal principles he had long espoused. For instance, although he had long advocated American-style democratic media for the rest of Asia, he now argued for the relaxation of a "universal" standard for press freedom, claiming that only a successful economy such as America could "afford to be self-critical."[150] This was a far cry from his lifelong opposition to censorship and his advocacy of unobstructed exchange of information. In various encounters with the Western media, Romulo skillfully adapted the discourses of liberalism, internationalism, anti-imperialism, revolution, and nativism to the defense of authoritarianism.[151] Even Romulo's speech at his granddaughter's graduation betrayed a subtle attempt to channel feminist aspirations toward the dictatorship.[152]

Romulo's friends began questioning his relationship with Marcos. William Safire's commentary in the *New York Times* expressed the sentiments of many Western journalists. Safire lamented Romulo's transformation from an "amiable ally of [press] freedom" to a mere media watchdog for Marcos. Romulo's behavior, Safire said, reflected the growing tide of resentment among dictators in Third World countries that the mass media would expose their denial of human rights. "The pity," Safire wrote, "was that in that tide, respected friends, like Carlos Romulo, without realizing it, are drowning."[153] But perhaps the most telling criticism of Romulo came from his former protégé Salvador P. Lopez, who bemoaned Romulo's political transformation. In the mid 1970s, the two had regarded each other with mutual admiration.[154] By the summer of 1980, however, Lopez was distancing himself from Romulo, whose life he characterized as a "tragedy." Lopez wished that Romulo had retired after his stint as U.P. president rather than becoming "one of the principal apologists of the regime." Romulo had become the opponent of all he had stood for, including "human rights," "democracy," and "press freedom."[155]

In a November 1981 interview, Lopez saved his most poignant commentary for Romulo's "terminal years" and his claim to have served *all* the Philippine presidents, of different political parties and persuasions, from Quezon to Marcos.[156] "Is that supposed to be cause for pride?" Lopez asked. It did not reflect, he thought, a positive "commitment" to "basic political principles." The great Romulo had been reduced to inventing slogans for Marcos, including that of his ruling party, the KBL (the Kilusang Bagong Lipunan, or New Society Movement), "There is no substitute for victory."

These, Lopez felt, were private thoughts that it now seemed indecent for Romulo to have uttered publicly (177–78). Romulo might have shot back that Lopez had served practically all the presidents Romulo had served. Still, Lopez's comments remain powerful criticism of Marcos's chief diplomat.

The August 1983 assassination of Marcos's principal opponent, Benigno Aquino, proved to be the turning point that led to Marcos's downfall, and in retrospect, to the eclipse of Romulo's reputation as world leader. Despite the brutality of this act and the international outrage against Marcos, U.S. President Ronald Reagan remained steadfast in supporting his friend. U.S. policy only began to change when Marcos began to lose control of the country and failed to contain the growing Communist insurgency.[157] The Aquino assassination aroused various sectors of the Philippine population and increased the tempo of the anti-Marcos movement. Even Romulo's son Ricardo, who had become an attorney, joined protesters in calling for the elimination of unjust laws that stifled "legitimate dissent."[158]

Romulo expressed to friends "how heartsick and humiliated" he was with the "recent turn of events" in Manila.[159] His letters to friends showed a marked ambivalence. On the one hand, he sought to distance himself from the government and to minimize his responsibilities by claiming that he was "apolitical" and that he had dealt with "foreign affairs" and not "domestic affairs." He said again that he had served all the Philippine presidents "irrespective of their political persuasions." Moreover, he claimed that he had tendered his resignation in January 1983 and had only remained upon Marcos's request that he reorganize the ministry.[160]

On the other hand, he expressed a different view in a confidential letter to Minister of Labor Blas F. Ople. In this, Romulo admitted that the Philippine government had suffered grave damage as a result of the Aquino assassination—"the American public's mind is poisoned against us." Philippine government attempts to correct dispatches from Manila were "wastebasketed," and even UN delegates were antagonistic. Romulo felt that his work of "40 years trying to build up our prestige internationally has been unfortunately destroyed." Nonetheless, he expressed to Ople his steadfast loyalty to Marcos. Indeed, to Romulo, loyalty to the president seemed to have become indistinguishable from patriotism. Given Reagan's backing, Romulo felt that Marcos could still make a comeback if there were reforms and an unassailable investigation of the Aquino assassination, and he tried to salvage the regime's credibility in the area of world peace and security, "to lay the groundwork for such a comeback," and to vindicate "the tarnished name of our people."[161]

Despite his failing health, the 85-year-old Romulo reaffirmed his loyalty to Marcos. He explained his refusal to sever his ties with the regime by saying that although doing so might make him a "hero" in the Philippines and in the United States, he felt in his "conscience" that it would make him a "cad" or "a rat jumping from a sinking ship" merely to save himself. He affirmed his steadfast loyalty to the president and his intention not to retire from service to him until obliged to do so because of age or "failing health."[162]

⌒

Carlos Romulo died in December 1985 with many of the tensions that had animated his life unresolved. The final chapter will no doubt remain controversial, but it was only the last installment in a long political and intellectual life characterized by complex positions. His own identity was itself a mixture of Filipino and American influences. Comfortable in two worlds, Romulo played the role of cultural translator and bricoleur. Performances were crucial to the development of his Filipino identity, whether these involved public displays or literary strategies of heroization, irony, paradox, self-invention, and juxtaposition. The contradictions of migrancy changed Romulo. During periods of prolonged expatriation—especially during World War II and as a diplomat in New York—he felt the pull of acculturation to America. Several decades of journalism and political networking in the United States had given him an extensive community of friends and admirers. And while he raised his children to be proud Filipinos, they grew up speaking English and playing with American children. Indeed, upon their return to the Philippines, they had difficulty adjusting to Filipino customs.[163]

Yet, like many Filipinos in the United States, Romulo experienced a racialization that differentiated his experience from that of white Americans and connected him to the ethnic American experience. That he has not been considered "Filipino American" says much about the cleavages within the Filipino American community and the cultural biases in Asian American historiography toward the second generation and the farm laborer experience.[164] Romulo's expatriate, exilic, diplomatic, and transpacific commuting experiences subvert the traditional binaries of American-born and immigrant, permanent resident and sojourner. Meanwhile, his access to the higher echelons of American government and elite status diverge from the experiences of marginalization faced by early Filipino migrants to America and often make him invisible to certain researchers.

Like the question of national and ethnic identities, Romulo's political positions would seem to admit of no simple answers. On one hand, Romulo helped construct the discourse of "special relations" between the Philippines and the United States, asserted Filipinos' debts of gratitude to American colonialism, and revered America's world "mission." At the same time, in seeking to develop a unique Filipino nationalist position that was both liberal and anticommunist, Romulo in his own way criticized or warded off America's overweening ambitions. Romulo did this through his sharp, although not loud, questioning of America's procolonial and anti–Third World policies and his exhortations that Americans accept the reality and the *responsibilities* of their country's status as a superpower. Romulo's nationalism, as we have seen, sought to make Filipino presidents national heroes comparable to prominent American and Asian leaders. At the same time, Romulo eschewed the fixity of official nationalism, affirming expatriate experiences and calling upon Filipino intellectuals to submit to "universal" standards of justice, art, and science.

Romulo's enduring support for Marcos attests to his adherence to the concept of *utang na loob,* or debt of the inside. From their first encounters, Marcos presented himself to Romulo, the elder statesman, as a genuine leader deserving of respect. Like Quezon and MacArthur, Marcos exuded charisma and confidence that won over the old diplomat. Romulo saw him as a studious and committed statesman, and as a member of Marcos's "team," he eschewed public criticism of the regime, as he had done many times in the past. Romulo had no problems expressing his disagreements with Marcos in private.[165]

Romulo developed a deep personal affection for Marcos, who reciprocated his admiration. Acts of generosity on both sides cemented the patron-client bond. Romulo no doubt remained appreciative of Marcos's provision for his material well-being—for example, in seating him on the boards of prestigious corporations—even after the regime had lost credibility in the eyes of many. In 1982, when the Marcos government conferred upon Romulo the National Artist Award for Literature, which he had long coveted, two earlier recipients of the award, José García Villa and Nick Joaquin, were so disgusted by the politically motivated decision that they sought to return their awards.[166]

Again and again in the following chapters, we shall see these difficult negotiations—between Filipino identity and American acculturation, between the power of American and Filipino patrons and the resourcefulness of their clients—repeated, with variations, in the experiences of Bulosan, Villa, Santos, and Gonzalez. These expatriates would choose career paths different from Romulo's and pursue their vocations as writers and artists. From time to time, they would rely upon Romulo's patronage, although, wary of political entanglements that might hinder their artistic work, they would always keep their distance from him. This did not mean, however, that Romulo's influence upon them was unimportant. As part of the first generation of intellectuals to study in the United States and to receive international recognition, and as a modern-day ilustrado, Romulo influenced the ideas of subsequent Filipino intellectuals about America. As an urbane cultural translator, committed to the importance of the word, and comfortable in both countries, he was also a model for the successful Filipino American intellectual.

In the Introduction, I argued that Filipino American intellectual history has its roots in the ilustrados' experience in Spain. Exile and the encounter with European modernity combined with tradition to produce the "Filipino intellectual." Romulo inherited this blend of Hispanic and Filipino influences and intellectual cultures from his father and grandmother, but he forged his own path under American colonial rule. He expressed a liberal, cosmopolitan, and bicultural ethos in his diverse capacities as pensionado, university professor, journalist, author, administrator, and, above all, as a diplomat adapting to and taking advantage of the rapidly changing winds of U.S.-Philippine relations. He was a true "Filipino-American," and his national identity shifted between the two poles of the hyphen.

TWO

Suffering and Passion: Carlos Bu

Like Carlos Romulo, the younger Carlos Bulosan inherited the legacy of the *ilustrados,* attended colonial public schools that taught in English, and sought to fulfill the American dream. He too became an expatriate and exile in the United States. Unlike the elite Romulo, however, Bulosan came from humble rural origins in the Philippines and remained poor in America. He showed no interest in a career in politics. Although he sought the patronage of Philippine political leaders, he limited their influence upon him. Bulosan focused his energies upon advancing working-class political goals and representing lower-class Filipinos. He rediscovered Philippine traditions in America and saw himself as returning to the Philippines through his fiction, but his early death in 1956 prevented a true homecoming.

Bulosan's peasant and working-class background implicates him in a cultural mind-set described in the introduction to Reynaldo Ileto's landmark study *Pasyon and Revolution.* For Ileto, one quality, in particular, distinguishes Tagalog folk Christian rebel leaders—their capacity to think beyond their often desperate predicaments under colonialist or nationalist regimes. As Ileto writes, they are able to project for their followers "a certain object, a certain future, that is to be actualized," suggesting their ability to interpret history in terms of myth and to mobilize the masses through visions of utopia. Thus, the illiterate Filipino poor, disparaged as "bandits, ignoramuses [and] in particular, failures," were not mere pawns of grand events but agents who generated their own meanings. Silencing *these* meanings, indeed refusing "to view them in the light of *their* world," Ileto says, has simply been a strategy of the "better classes" to subdue the lower classes.[1]

Ileto's insights into the Filipino lower classes in the Philippines, I argue, resound in the writings of Bulosan. Bulosan identified with the Filipino farm laborers and domestic workers who migrated to the United States during the first three decades of the twentieth century. From the vantage point of those "below" and through mythic images constructed by rural folk, Bulosan criticized the Philippine elite and articulated the deepest longings of the lower classes. Yet, in order to see how Bulosan captured this folk influence, it is not enough to use the familiar modernist lenses through which he has been seen. One must examine Bulosan through the prism of his successes and his "failures," in the light of *his* world.

↩

Bulosan was eighteen years old when he arrived in Seattle in 1930 aboard one of the President liners.[2] He was born in the northwestern Luzon province of Pangasinan, in a town called Binalonan, the son of semi-literate Ilokano peasants, who lost their land during the 1920s. The decade saw the expansion of commercialized agriculture, which disrupted traditional patron-client relations between tenants and landlords. Carlos had four elder brothers, two of whom left for the United States before he did. As a child, Carlos worked on his father's farm, and he later attended high school in the provincial capital, where he was exposed to American literature and began to write poetry for the school paper.

After he had completed only two years of high school, however, Carlos's family supported his migration to the United States. He arrived during the Great Depression, and for several years, he lived with his brothers Dionisio and Aurelio, washing dishes and picking fruit with migrant Filipino laborers. He also became involved in the labor movement, working as a publicist and essayist. Subsequently, he was hospitalized with tuberculosis for two years and read voraciously during this time. Aided by his brother Aurelio, who supported him financially, and by two white women authors from Los Angeles, Sanora and Dorothy Babb, who introduced him to the classics of Western literature, Bulosan blossomed as a poet. He had already published several books of poetry when he was given an assignment to write for the

Saturday Evening Post through the intercession of Louis Adamic, one of the many progressive white intellectuals who supported him.

Like many other Filipinos, Bulosan became popular during World War II as a result of the widespread American concern about the Pacific campaign, and because of the view that the few Filipinos then residing in the United States possessed a kind of "local knowledge" of their country, the Philippines.[3] Bulosan obliged Americans by writing poems and stories that expressed his faith in the United States and presented Philippine rural life in a humorous vein. In 1946, he wrote an autobiography more serious in tone, *America Is in the Heart*, which expressed his belief in American democracy. Understandably, this was read as an allegory of the triumph of American democratic ideals, which were then threatened by both external enemies and domestic turmoil.[4]

Toward the end of the war, an important turning point occurred in Bulosan's writing career. He was accused of plagiarism in a story he had published in the *New Yorker*, and while this was never fully explained, magazine publishers and critics in both the United States and the Philippines thereafter shunned his writings, and Bulosan never regained his wartime popularity. At the same time, many Filipino critics viewed his satires and revolutionary writings on Philippine society with suspicion, if not outright disdain. In fact, he lapsed into obscurity as a writer. From 1946, the year of the publication of *America Is in the Heart* (the last of Bulosan's books to appear during his lifetime) to 1973, when it was reprinted in the United States, Bulosan virtually disappeared from the American literary scene.

In Asian American studies and in a certain segment of Philippine literary criticism, Bulosan has nonetheless had a widespread and profound influence. His democratic vistas of America, and his view of art as a weapon in the struggle for socialism, won him support, and the critical literature has portrayed him as a writer committed to proletarian and Third World movements. Bulosan's authenticity as a revolutionary and his humanistic interracial vision have attracted activists for several generations.[5]

At the height of Bulosan's popularity in the United States, however, an American author sued him for plagiarism, an event that became of signal importance to Bulosan's relationship with Filipino elites in both the United States and the Philippines and marks a crucial shift in his perspectives of self and social class. Even more important, the issue captured much larger meanings. A close reading of Bulosan's story and the allegedly plagiarized story reveals not only Bulosan's literary strategy and ideology, indeed, his adaptation, storytelling, and writing practices, but also his connection to an oral cultural world that hearkens back to his early Philippine life. The plagiarism episode thus brings to light the "underside" of Bulosan's ideals of socialism and modernity: a folk spirituality and commitment to the *pasyon* idiom. In fact, Bulosan saw himself as a Christlike figure whose suffering held the key to the redemption of his fellow Filipinos. Although he was unaware or unwilling to recognize them, these folk religious conceptions fired him with a utopian vision that helped him to go beyond the limitations of his life and the impoverished lives of his ostracized and exiled Filipino compatriots in America.

Bulosan's Ambivalent Relationship to the Ilustrado Elite

Bulosan's connection to traditional cultures must be seen against the background of his relationship with fellow Filipinos on the West Coast and his aspirations to upward mobility—in particular, his quest to become accepted by the ilustrado elite as a Philippine writer and intellectual. Often, his desire for inclusion in high society cut across his desire to represent the cultural experiences of peasants and workers. He felt a simultaneous sense of difference from and camaraderie with Filipino migrant laborers in the United States. On the one hand, he possessed intellectual abilities that made him feel superior to them. On the other hand, as with José Rizal, his education fired him with a vision of educating his countrymen. In a 1937 letter to his friend Dorothy Babb, Bulosan complained that because of their "hard work" and "abnormal social life," most of his countrymen were uninterested in intellectual pursuits and "dead inside." To interest them, he talked about world events and about books, recited poetry, and sang with them, but much remained beyond their comprehension.[6]

P. C. Morantte underscores Bulosan's self-image as an ilustrado by pointing to his refusal to adopt the calqued term "Pinoy" (which was what lower-class Filipinos called themselves during this period) to describe himself. According to Morantte, Bulosan saw himself as having only a racial affinity with his fellow Filipino laborers. (As we shall see, however, Bulosan's cultural identification exceeded these attempts by Morantte to claim him for a certain nationalist perspective.) On one hand, although they observed and wrote about them, Bulosan and Morantte felt different from their "unlettered" countrymen. On the other hand, Morantte and Bulosan felt slighted by those Filipinos of higher social class who were sent to Los Angeles in the 1930s, the Philippine government-sponsored students, or *pensionados*.[7]

Moreover, Bulosan felt a kinship with the nationalist elites attempting to gain independence from the United States and to establish the basis for a postcolonial Philippines. He regarded them as his equals and at first saw himself as a member of their exclusive company. When Bulosan became famous as a writer during World War II, he succeeded in winning friends among the members of the Philippine Commonwealth government-in-exile, many of whom were writers. Only after his unpleasant social encounters with them and after they used the plagiarism charge against him as a pretext to discredit him did he realize the existence of limits to Philippine intellectualism. He became embittered and criticized their political stances, while at the same time clinging to the hope of a continued fraternity with Philippine intellectuals. But, in the atmosphere of the Cold War, many of them rejected Bulosan on the basis of his Marxist beliefs and sought to erase his memory.

However, the first public reactions to Bulosan that Filipinos would read about did not come from the Philippines. They came from the United States during World War II in response to his essay "Freedom from Want," published in the March 6, 1943, issue of the *Saturday Evening Post*. Bulosan was part of a select group chosen by the editors to write about Franklin D. Roosevelt's war aims, the "Four Freedoms."[8] In this manner, America discovered Bulosan. Hitherto unknown to most Americans, his name became a byword as a result of its placement alongside those of established American writers like Stephen Vincent Benét, Booth Tarkington, and Will Durant, and the illustrations of Norman Rockwell.[9] In 1944, Bulosan published *The Laughter of My Father*. The Office of War Information was so pleased by this collection of stories that it broadcast them by radio to American soldiers overseas, giving the go-ahead for critical acceptance of Bulosan.[10] Some critics, however, read these portrayals of Philippine rural life as reinforcing popular stereotypes of Filipinos as happy primitives.[11]

The Philippine Commonwealth government-in-exile in Washington, D.C., sought to harness Bulosan's reputation and literary skills for the war

effort, alongside Filipino expatriate intellectuals like P. C. Morantte, Bienvenido N. Santos, and José García Villa. One can see Bulosan's aspirations
for elite status in his relationships with leaders like Philippine Commonwealth President Manuel Quezon, Secretary of Public Information Carlos P.
Romulo, and President of the Philippine Republic Manuel Roxas. At first,
Bulosan catered to them. After all, Quezon had been the outstanding figure
in prewar Philippine politics and the principal architect of the Philippines'
transition from colony to U.S. commonwealth. Susan Evangelista and Dolores Feria accuse Bulosan of "snuggling up" to Quezon, as well as to the
American reading public concerned about the war.[12]

Bulosan was not wholly in favor of the government-in-exile's policies,
however, and he sought to maintain his independence on political issues.
For instance, although he revered Quezon, Bulosan was critical of the influence of fascism in the president's government. In a 1941 letter to A. V. H.
Hartendorp, editor of the *Philippine Magazine*, then under attack for its
anti-fascist stances, Bulosan expressed support for Hartendorp and the
Philippine Magazine's freedom to speak the "truth" against fascism. He,
nonetheless, found it "tragic" that "*important men in the government*" (emphasis added) were colluding with these groups.[13] Nonetheless, when Quezon died in 1944, Bulosan privately wrote about him with great admiration.

Bulosan had met the ailing Philippine president on November 18, 1943,
one year before Quezon died of tuberculosis. On the way to see him at the
Shoreham Hotel in Washington, D.C. (where Quezon presided over the exiled government), Bulosan made the acquaintance of Vice President Sergio
Osmeña, and Secretary of Public Information Carlos P. Romulo.[14] The sick
Quezon had a difficult time speaking, and Bulosan was quick to attribute
heroic traits to "the greatest man of my generation," seeing the roots of his
"humble origin" in the "heart-rending deprivations in his youth."[15] He described the "kinship" he felt for Quezon, "a feeling so great that it sustained
me on my perilous trip back to Los Angeles."[16] Bulosan's sense of affinity
was heightened by their shared illness. "For more than four decades," Bulosan wrote, "[Quezon] had fought against tuberculosis of the lungs, and
how well I know what effort and pain you have to go through with this disease."[17] Quezon asked Bulosan to write his official biography and a report
on the conditions of the Filipinos on the West Coast. But on the basis of his
brother's advice to stay out of politics and pursue his vocation as a serious

writer, Bulosan never wrote either of these. He did, however, consider his autobiography, *America Is in the Heart*, as a belated response to Quezon's requests.[18]

Nonetheless, in less confining circumstances of his own choosing, Bulosan was not averse to seeking patronage. For instance, he made effective use of war themes and symbols in publishing his collection of poems *Voice of Bataan*, with the wartime U.S. audience in mind. He dedicated the book to his brother, Aurelio, who was then serving in the 1st Infantry Battalion and who later saw action in MacArthur's invasion force at Leyte. Carlos also obtained the blessings of Colonel Carlos P. Romulo ("The Last Man Off Bataan") who wrote the foreword to the collection and compared Bulosan to the American poets Carl Sandburg and Amy Lowell. Bulosan also used a quotation from MacArthur—"Only those are fit to live who are not afraid to die"—as an epigraph.[19] A cablegram by Bulosan to Romulo on the occasion of Romulo's first extensive tour of Filipino communities on the West Coast shows Bulosan's attempt to utilize Romulo's patronage to heighten his own political prestige in the Los Angeles Filipino community:

> Enthusiasm of your coming to California is growing rapidly among our countrymen especially in Stockton-Sacramento Areas where American organizations and business groups are waiting for your presence. With *my* cooperation the American-Philippine Foundation is preparing a banquet of 2000 and an audience of 5000 people on April 8 or thereabouts as your introduction to the Filipinos in the coast. It seems to me that you should make a definite plan to appear here for the sake of our country because I personally believe that our people want you to be *Resident Commissioner* and Ambassador of the Philippines to the United States after the war. There is no doubt that they also would like you to be President. I am excited about all these things coming from our people who think *you are one of us* and I assure you *my* full cooperation through both American and Filipino presses and *my personal contact* and friendship with our people in the West Coast. Wire me back what possible date you could come in April which is also the first Bataan Day Memorial here. Mabuhay = Carlos Bulosan. (emphases added)[20]

After the war, Bulosan, who had become a celebrity in America, met a third Philippine nationalist leader, President Manuel Roxas. Bulosan's letter on this event was brief: "I met and interviewed the new President, Manuel

Roxas. Had lunch. We drove through the city [San Francisco] and traffic was stopped like hell. Never saw so many F.B.I.'s cops *[sic]*, and other barbarians."[21] Bulosan was at the peak of his career, sought after by the Philippines' most prominent political leaders, and by his cordial behavior, he showed his understanding of patronage and his willingness to utilize connections for personal gain.

For a time, it seemed that Bulosan would succeed in fulfilling the role of spokesperson. However, a series of events would lead to his increasing distance from the representatives of the Philippine government and the end of his active efforts to be recognized as an ilustrado intellectual.

First, his decision to refuse Quezon's patronage by excusing himself from writing the president's biography marked the beginning of a rupture between Bulosan and the elites. Quezon himself reacted by saying, "What, you have the nerve to refuse me?" And when Bulosan told Romulo that he had not accepted the offer, "Romulo was surprised as much as the president himself."[22] Such independence might have helped to fan the class prejudice against Bulosan, who, as a son of peasants and also a laborer, stood out among the Commonwealth staff. Indeed, as Morantte's account of a social encounter between Bulosan and the Commonwealth staff shows, his ilustrado aspirations came into conflict with the status-conscious governmental elites. Morantte writes that they viewed Bulosan and him with "condescension" because they lacked college degrees, although President Quezon himself had personally invited them to Washington. The staff regarded them as low-grade "Pinoys" from the West Coast and "freaky flukes."[23]

Second, in 1945, two years after Bulosan's trip to Philippine Commonwealth headquarters, and one year before the publication of *America Is in the Heart*, which marked the acme of his career, Bulosan was charged with plagiarism. At issue was his story "The End of the War,"[24] which Bulosan first submitted to *Philippines*, the official publication of the Philippine Commonwealth. Two of his colleagues, P. C. Morantte and Bienvenido Santos, the editor of the publication, consented to publish Bulosan's piece, but they were overruled by their immediate boss, Secretary of Information Carlos P. Romulo. After Romulo rejected the story, Bulosan submitted it to the *New Yorker*, which published it in 1944.[25] Several months later, Guido D'Agostino, a novelist and short story writer from New York, filed a suit against the *New Yorker*, claiming that Bulosan had plagiarized his own story

"The Dream of Angelo Zara," which had originally appeared in *Story* magazine in 1942 and had been reprinted in Martha Foley's edition of the *Best American Short Stories, 1943*.[26] In fact, it made Foley's "Honor Roll" and her list of "Distinctive Stories of 1942." Bulosan, an avid reader of literary magazines, could thus scarcely have failed to notice it. Rather than go to court, the *New Yorker* decided to settle with D'Agostino, and the matter was then dropped.[27]

That the plagiarism case was an issue of great importance in Bulosan's intellectual development and an obstacle to his efforts at social acceptance can be seen in his personal difficulties in its aftermath and in his attempts to evade any direct references to the case. Indeed, Bulosan suffered a writer's block in 1945 that was to last for two years and was to haunt him for many years thereafter. Bulosan wrote volumes of letters to family, friends, publishers, and others during the decade after the D'Agostino matter. Yet, in none of these did he make explicit mention of the plagiarism issue. His letters thus confront us with a strikingly "articulate silence."[28] Except for a few sporadic stories, Bulosan published little after 1946 and enjoyed none of the popularity he did during the middle part of the 1940s.[29] Several months before his death, Bulosan was to characterize the last ten years of his life as a "decade of silence and heartbreak and re-evaluation of my life and career."[30]

Both the snobbery of the elites and the plagiarism experience altered Bulosan's postwar view of the Philippine elite, and his writings reflect his growing bitterness. In December 1945, several months after the settlement with the *New Yorker*, Bulosan made extensive revisions to *America Is in the Heart* and probably used this time to polish what turned out to be a scathing indictment of the rich, especially in the first part of the book, where he writes of his life in the Philippines but at the same time seems to express the hurts he experienced in America during the war years.[31] Bulosan openly criticized the way governmental elites exploited the Philippine independence issue. While "agitation for national independence had been growing," he writes, "the government was actually in the hands of *powerful native leaders*"; the agitation had been exploited, to their own advantage, by "obscure men with ample education," which had plunged the country "into a great economic catastrophe."[32] Writing of the anger of peasants squeezed by "progress" in the Philippines, Bulosan makes it clear that the source of the discontent was racial. It stemmed from "*the few powerful Filipinos of foreign extraction*" (like those he had encountered among Quezon's Commonwealth staff members) "who were squeezing a fat livelihood out of it [the national economy]."[33] Finally, Bulosan records his contempt for the sons of the ilustrados, leaving little doubt that he recognized their abuse of patronage. He accuses the "sons of the professional classes" of "victimizing their own people and enriching themselves at the expense of the nation." He predicts that "once secure in their positions and connections," these young elites would also ruthlessly exploit the peasantry and the working class.[34]

In another segment of *America Is in the Heart*, Bulosan records the snobbery of Filipino elites toward the subject matter of *The Laughter of My Father*, his first book of prose fiction. He expresses his astonishment that because he had written about his fellow townspeople in the Philippines as "human beings," he had evoked "the philistinism of educated Filipinos and the petty bourgeoisie, and the arrogance of the Philippine government in Washington."[35] Dolores Feria confirms the similar reception of *The Laughter of My Father* among the pensionados in Los Angeles and notes the pride felt by Bulosan's poorer Ilokano compatriots. "None of the students and officials were interested," she writes, "for who *was* Bulosan?" Feria nonetheless notes Bulosan's own ambivalence about his class position, writing that if Bulosan could have afforded to do so, "he would end up at the bar of the Ambassador or the Builtmore [sic] Hotel, nothing less. For he had *very bourgeois tastes*, in spite of his fanatically proletarian sentiments."[36]

During the immediate postwar years, as his countrymen began to take note of his successes, Bulosan continued to bemoan the supercilious attitudes of his fellow Filipino writers. Frustrated, Bulosan wrote to Leopoldo Yabes of the University of the Philippines that it was gratuitous for Filipino writers to regard him as "ignorant" or feel themselves superior to him because he had no "formal education." Like them, he was simply a writer "trying to know more about his art" and struggling for "a more enlightened mankind."[37]

Apart from the reaction to his writings, Bulosan took note of other manifestations of elite snobbery toward him, as in the matter of governmental largesse and recognition that bypassed him as an "established" writer. He was "saddened by the fact that the Philippine government [was] sending several fellows to the U.S. to study how to write," while he remained "unrecognized" by his "own government and people."[38]

Bulosan's attitude to Romulo and Roxas also began to change. He privately criticized Romulo's writings for their elitism and their failure to accurately describe the "Filipino mind." "Genius is not the sole property of one race or one class of men," Bulosan declares. "Romulo's books and most all the other books written by Filipinos have failed as *Filipino* books; they fail to bring out the individuality of the Filipino mind, the shaping of that mind, its growth and possibilities."[39] He was also becoming dissatisfied with President Roxas upon whom he and other Filipinos had pinned such high hopes. By 1947, he was already upset that Roxas had supported the passage of treaties, like the Philippine Trade Act and the infamous Parity Amendment, that furthered U.S. neocolonial rule over the Philippines and made life more miserable for the country's laborers.[40] "The future is dark for the Philippines," he wrote, "but so is the rest of the world."[41]

Despite these discouraging signs from the Philippines, Bulosan continued to maintain his grand ambitions, especially of imitating, even bettering, José Rizal's literary accomplishments. He wrote often of a secret dream of writing a 1,500-page novel covering thirty-five years of Philippine history. "I will be long remembered for it," says Bulosan. One of the volumes would cover the period of the birth and death of José Rizal.[42] Reflecting on the dual impact of the Philippine national hero on his intellectual outlook, Bulosan identified with Rizal's sense of failure, his *sufferings* as an expatriate, *and* his ilustrado nationalism: "[H]ow I discovered that Rizal was not as handsome and glamorous as our ancestors would like us to believe; how, one night in Heidelburg *[sic]*, he wept over a glass of beer, thinking that he was a complete failure, so far away from home, so far away from the movement of freedom in the Philippines."[43] And he saw Rizal as a distinctly elite figure out of touch with Philippine tradition, a "leaf cut from the tree: perfect in itself, as a leaf, but separate from the mother tree."[44]

In the 1950s, Bulosan incurred the ire of the elites by openly backing the Huk rebellion and supporting the Communist intellectual Amado K. Hernandez.[45] The Huks were led by a charismatic figure of peasant origins named Luis Taruc, who became the object of elite fear and hatred. In the late 1940s, Bulosan participated in a campaign to have Taruc's autobiography (which was banned in the Philippines) published in the United States. Bulosan's association with Amado Hernandez, a Philippine labor leader and noted vernacular writer who was then a target of government repression, increased suspicions that Bulosan was a Communist and led to his final exclusion from the Philippine body politic. A newspaper clipping in the University of Washington archives notes that no less a person than Secretary of Defense Ramon Magsaysay, the future Philippine president, accused Bulosan of involvement in a Communist conspiracy. Magsaysay claimed that the arrest of a popular bookstore owner linked Bulosan to the "Communist parties in the Philippines and America" and indicated the existence of a "message center" for international "Communist activities." A captured note from Bulosan, however, reveals little more than expressions of appreciation for Luis Taruc, whose presence in America "cemented the progressive spirit" in both the Philippines and the United States and roused in Carlos the desire to write "a big book for the world."[46]

Anticommunists in the Philippines assailed Bulosan. He was blacklisted and government and publishing institutions sought to erase his memory. He paid the price for his stubborn adherence to his political beliefs and suffered alongside his comrades like Hernandez. Bulosan's death was ignored in the Philippines, with the notable exception of his home province of Pangasinan. Two weeks after his death, Binalonan, Bulosan's hometown, decided to rename the barrio of Mangusmana, in which he had grown up, Barrio Carlos Bulosan, "in memory of that well-known Filipino author who died recently."[47]

The Plagiarism Case

The plagiarism case, as we have seen, was a pivotal point in Bulosan's life. But what does it mean to say that Bulosan had "plagiarized" Guido D'Agostino's story? To answer this question requires a comparative reading of D'Agostino's and Bulosan's stories. Such an examination will help to explain both why the plagiarism case so devastated Bulosan and, at the same time, what he was trying to achieve artistically when he stumbled upon D'Agostino's story.

One of the great ironies of the plagiarism charge against Bulosan is that the story he was alleged to have plagiarized, D'Agostino's "The Dream of Angelo Zara," is itself a parable of plagiarism. Indeed, in recounting the essential events of the case, it seems as though life were imitating art. In

D'Agostino's story, an Italian immigrant and factory worker named Angelo Zara has a fantastic dream in which he has an audience with Benito Mussolini in Italy. The latter offers him a government job with a salary of 3,000 lire, equivalent to that of a general in the army. Suddenly, Mussolini dies. Zara has the dream on a Saturday night. The following morning, he rushes to tell the dream to his friend, Matteo Grossi, a bricklayer, whose "booming thunderous speech" and frequent cries of "Salamambitch!" intimidate Zara. In turn, Grossi takes Zara to see Ignazio Ferro, a shoemaker and dream expert. Grossi prevents Zara from telling Ferro the story, which prompts Zara to ask Grossi, "Was you have this dream or was me?" Grossi responds, "Is a dream like this no belong one man. Is pooblic property. We in America here. Everything for everybody" (52). Grossi begins to embellish the dream, "pointing it up here and there, giving it the little artistic touches," showing that it has indeed become his own. The 3,000 lire becomes 5,000 lire; from Mussolini giving him a general's salary, Mussolini now wants to make him a general. Ferro sees in the dream a "[v]ery big significanza . . . Is mean the finish for Mussolini . . . Il Fascismo, like I have been saying for ten years." As Grossi and Ferro walk through the rest of the neighborhood spreading the news of Zara's dream, Zara feels he has been cheated. "Fate had played a trick on him. It had given him a dream and he wasn't big enough to carry it. He walked along slowly, filled with a growing consciousness of his utter insignificance." However, as he walks along Washington Square, he sees the birds chirping and the kids playing. He begins to feel better and realizes that the dream has become the property of the community he shares (55).

Although the setting, the characters, and their racial and colonial milieu are different, Carlos Bulosan's "The End of the War" resembles the plot structure, the language, and the theme of "The Dream of Angelo Zara."[48] One finds here convincing proof of Bulosan's *adaptation* of D'Agostino's story, which at the very least, Bulosan should have recognized. In Bulosan's story, it is also Sunday morning. At Camp Beale, in Northern California, the protagonist, the harmonica-playing Private Fidel of the First Filipino Infantry, dreams that the "Japs" have met Filipino soldiers on a beach in Mindanao and surrendered to them. A few minutes later, he hears that the Germans have also surrendered (hence the story's title, "The End of the War"). He dashes out in his undershorts to look for his comrades, and tells his dream to his cousin, Sergeant Pitong Tongkol, whose promotion before him he resents, because before the war, Fidel had been a bookkeeper and Pitong a mere field-worker. Pitong decides to tell his brother, Mess Sergeant Ponso Tongkol. When Fidel tries to tell Ponso the story, Pitong plants himself in front of Ponso and pushes Fidel away, saying, "This dream is not for a small potato like you."[49]

The dream evokes Ponso's regret at the loss of his American dream. "Why the "salomabit come," Ponso exclaims, referring to the Japanese, who have destroyed his dream. Fidel's dream now replaces or substitutes for Ponso's, and the entire group goes on to tell Fidel's dream story to the rest of the camp. The text reads, "Private Fidel had dreamed the big dream, but it was too big for him to hold. It was a dream that belonged to no one now, yet it was a dream for every soldier. Hearing it told by another person, Private Fidel knew that it was not his dream anymore. . . . In utter defeat, Private Fidel backed out into the sunlight." Like Angelo Zara, he realizes the feeling of community that the dream has evoked among his comrades. Like Zara, he begins to feel better. He plays his harmonica "with great joy and inspiration."[50]

It does indeed seem that Bulosan borrowed D'Agostino plot structure, theme, and even language. Bulosan passed off as his own and presented as new and original another writer's idea. Unlike his forgiving character, however, Guido D'Agostino was not impressed by Bulosan's retelling of the story, with its "little artistic touches," and decided to sue him. Here, life diverged from art. However, Bulosan did both more and less than copy the story—he used the *language* provided by "Angelo Zara" to illustrate the Filipino migrant's life in the 1930s and 1940s. That language, in both stories, is the *dream* that crystallizes the latent frustrations and experiences of the workers and outcasts and prophesies an end they all desire.

Pitong Tongkol, Ponso Tongkol, and others transform the character Fidel's original dream story because of its usefulness in interpreting the complex circumstances of their lives. In effect, Bulosan, taking illegally from D'Agostino, was describing the making of folklore itself—the process of oral transmission, its aural aspects, its quality of being heard or overheard. The story's repetitious, aggregative manner links it to distinctive traits of oral cultures. Moreover, we can see the process of adaptation at work in the characters' attempts to embellish details of the original story as well as aspects of the story to suit their personal styles and tales.[51]

Bulosan *applied* D'Agostino's pattern to the West Coast Filipino American experience, perhaps creating a more meaningful story: his characters become the familiar farm laborers and cooks of Filipino American labor history who occupied the segregated jobs in the economic hierarchy. He includes their amusements—gambling (especially card games like monte), cockfighting, and cruising in fancy cars. The dream of the surrender of the Japanese emperor triggers a reflectiveness among the characters that brings out the tensions among Filipinos created by the war (the change in social rank occasioned by Pitong's promotion over Fidel) and the frustration of their ambitions (Ponso's love of money and cars). Just as Pitong and Ponso Tongkol use the language provided by Fidel's dream to articulate latent emotions, Bulosan himself uses the language provided by D'Agostino's "Angelo Zara" to create an altogether different story that captures something of the Filipino wartime experience.

During Bulosan's time, Philippine intellectuals eager to establish the basis for an authentic and original national culture (such as Manuel Arguilla, E. Arsenio Manuel, and Dean Fansler) also collected and adapted legends, myths, and romances, which they believed were endangered by "progress." Bulosan was aware of these folklorists and shared their vocation.[52] The principal difference between them and Bulosan was that most of their adaptations were obtained from interviews and personal recollections of folktales, whereas Bulosan, who had also drawn from similar experiences, lapsed into "adapting" a copyrighted work. His nationalist aspiration to unearth folklore and to adapt it perhaps accounts for his "silence" and feeling of great personal loss after the plagiarism case. Given his lofty aspirations to social mobility, his desire to put the Philippines on the map of world literature (especially through a recuperation of the folk tradition), and his own ambition to represent the concerns of his countrymen, the accusations of inauthenticity, lack of originality, and even lack of patriotism must have deeply hurt him. No doubt, he was aware of American colonizers' racist charge that the native Filipinos were incapable of original thought and only of mimicry, of which the plagiarism issue was but a subset.[53] Indeed, it seemed a lifetime before Bulosan would feel confident again in his vocation as a writer. But despite these personal setbacks, he was to continue, albeit more carefully, with his folktale adaptations.

Tradition, Supernaturalism and the Pasyon

Bulosan's adaptation of "The Dream of Angelo Zara" was not an isolated phenomenon but, in fact, an important and enduring feature of his writing: he also adapted other stories. Even at an early age, Bulosan (whose family was barely literate) was exposed to an oral culture in which storytelling, folktale, and myth suffused everyday conversation.[54] Even in the United States, Bulosan's fellow Ilokanos, the largest migrant population from the Philippines, exchanged folktales and oral performances, including some dealing with supernatural occurrences.[55] Like a bricoleur, Bulosan created by borrowing from a variety of sources, constructing, and improvising, leaving his personal stamp upon the work. What Walter Benjamin says of all storytellers is of special significance to the work of Bulosan. Benjamin writes of the storyteller's unique gift of being able "to reach back to a whole lifetime," combining his own experiences, those of others, and "hearsay." The storyteller, he adds, "could let the wick of his life be consumed completely by the gentle flame of his story"[56] A few examples from Bulosan's writings will demonstrate the salience of Benjamin's observations and the prevalence of this adaptive practice.

In *Voice of Bataan*, Bulosan's 1943 collection of poetry, the "Prologue," as Bulosan himself says in the footnote, is "a metrical paraphrase of the farewell radio message from Corregidor [before it fell to the Japanese] delivered by Lt. Norman Reyes."[57] The following year, Bulosan issued a collection of short stories, *The Laughter of My Father*.[58] In several pronouncements on this book, Bulosan reflected on the variety of influences from which he drew. In a preface written for a Philippine magazine, he explained that the "tragic humor" of the "common people" of the Philippines provided the material for his stories. These, he argued, were "satirical pieces" about the rich and the poor, written with the "great humorists" like Mark Twain and Cervantes in mind.[59] Even more telling is Bulosan's ambivalence in accounting for the sources of *The Laughter of My Father*. Apparently, when he was writing this collection, Bulosan was not aware of either the world's folktales or Philippine folktales and only became aware of them after the work was already published. He seems to argue for a kind of unconscious or practical memory of folklore. For Bulosan, *The Laughter of My Father* was a "book of modernized folktales . . . adapted to the Philippine scene and embellished with my kind of humor." He claims his total ignorance of Philippine or any other folktales and his surprise at reviews pointing to similarities with this literature. Bulosan felt he "had ventured innocently into a fertile ground of imagination and fancy."[60]

P. C. Morantte traces his fascination with folklore back to the village of Mangusmana where the young Bulosan "found himself a diligent listener to some fabulists or old story-tellers who, even when not drinking, liked to pass the time by telling stories to kids."[61] As Morantte further writes, "there was an *old man* [Bulosan] used to know . . . from him he drew the materials for many of his own tales which later appeared in American publications."[62] In "How My Stories Were Written," Bulosan discusses the influence of this old man, named Apo Lacay, who taught him all the stories of the village and of faraway places. Bulosan claims that his stories could just as well be attributed to the old man, whose voice he had assimilated as his own. It is noteworthy that Bulosan used the passive voice in his title "How My Stories Were Written," suggesting that he was as much a medium for the many voices in his stories as he was their creator.[63]

In his adaptations, Bulosan was fascinated by the sounds of language, not only as a form of communication but as remembrance of the living and the dead. "[Remember] the song of our birds in the morning [and] the sound of our language," Carlos's brother tells him as he is about to leave the Philippines. Bulosan continues: "Everywhere I roam I listen for it with a crying heart because it means my roots in this faraway soil; it means my only communication with the living and those who died without a gift of expression."[64] The flavor of his affection for the English language might be seen in *America Is in the Heart.* When he first began to compose letters to Dorothy Babb, he became fascinated with the musicality of words. He noticed especially how he "began to cultivate a taste for words, not so much their meanings as their sounds and shapes," such that he came "to depend only on the music of words to express [his] ideas."[65]

Traditional influences on Bulosan's adaptive practice were matched by both artistic vanguardism and humanism, suggesting the complexity of cultural influences: "I am not a good writer," he said, "but I will try my best to strive toward a certain form of *perfection*: that is, a perfection of thought and style" (emphasis added). Bulosan believed "that content and form are inseparable elements of good artistic creation: one generates the other, but both are generated by a noble theme of universal significance." He did not believe that *art* was "alien to life" but that it was "a crystallized reflection of life, deepened or heightened by our individual perceptions and sensibilities."[66] In another letter, he expressed awareness of the "dangerous path" created by his folktale adaptations in the context of his goals of artistic perfection and concern for social issues. Bulosan was probably referring to the possibility of plagiarism, which he had by then recognized. He nonetheless felt that the humanistic vision of contributing to "a better understanding of man and his world" made such a risk worthwhile.[67]

Finally, Bulosan's strategies of adaptation can be seen in his most popular work, *America Is in the Heart.* As we have seen, Bulosan retrospectively considered this book a response to Quezon's request for a report on West Coast Filipino life. The book, especially its second and third sections, is filled with accounts of Filipino encounters with racism that might be read as a kind of sociological "report." But the testament of other observers and the power of certain segments that stand out as tales or stories in themselves, suggest the possibility of more traditional influences at work in the book. Morantte's account of the writing of the book, for instance, shows the fragmented, storytelling style in which Bulosan originally wrote. In 1942, the year Bulosan started writing, the book was not originally titled *America Is in the Heart.* It was rather, Morantte says, a series of "loose" or "broken" narratives of "embellished" childhood experiences. Onto these were grafted Bulosan's stories about his life in America. It was not until 1944 that this amalgam of childhood fantasy and American life became a "personal account" hinged upon Bulosan as the narrator, part fictive, part real.[68]

The "loose" or "broken" narratives Morantte describes leave their traces in the book despite Bulosan's attempt to provide a coherent narrative over time. For instance, the very beginning of the work, in which Carlos sees his brother coming home from World War I, is reminiscent of a Philippine short story familiar to Bulosan, "How My Brother Leon Brought Home a Wife," written by Manuel Arguilla, a fellow Ilokano. Moreover, the genesis of one of Bulosan's most famous stories, "The Homecoming," a representation of Bulosan's fictive return home to his family, can be found in the extended dream sequence in the latter part of the book. There are even instructive fables, such as Bulosan's encounter with a rich white American woman from the Hollywood liberal establishment. The "white rug" of her luxurious house comes to symbolize Bulosan's attraction to the privileges of bourgeois white womanhood and the simultaneous repulsion he feels toward its racism and superficial leftist politics.[69]

Morantte claims that Bulosan was a good listener. Many of the stories he heard when he was living and working as a dishwasher in Lompoc in the 1930s found their way into *America Is in the Heart.* Bulosan's brother, Aurelio, confirms this fact. Carlos, he says, "used to mingle with the ordinary Filipinos, talk like them, and act like them. But they didn't know that Carlos was gathering materials from them." Carlos believed in being among the people, in putting emotion behind every word you wrote about them. But if Carlos would not tell others that he was gathering material from them, he did believe in being careful about the use of words, as much as the way one used people.[70] Morantte further adds that Bulosan was not interested in vicariously living as "victims" through his fellow Filipinos. Rather, "he deeply felt the realism of being himself the actual victim."[71]

In addition to the adaptive practice that Bulosan's "The End of the War" reveals, there is a second reason why his story should interest us, and that is in the element of the fantastic that pervades the story. The dream image probably attracted Bulosan to D'Agostino's story, for it speaks to the inclination to the supernatural that pervades Bulosan's writings. Dreams, visions, and visitations, as the anthropologist Stephen Griffiths shows, have been important parts of the cultural milieu of Ilokanos and Ilokano migrants to the United States. He notes especially the importance of "touching" in their interactions with persons possessing unusual healing powers and *anting-anting* (amulets). The folklore scholar Herminia Meñez also refers to "belief stories" that show the influence of the supernatural among Filipino migrants in California, which have "retained the status of legends." The Ilokano old-timers exchanged "[n]arratives about witches, ghosts, *kapre* (giants), and *ingkanto* (environmental spirits) . . . often during discussions involving the validity of supernatural beliefs."[72]

In a 1956 letter to the editor of Henry Holt & Company, Bulosan says, "It has always been my method to combine folktales, fantasy, autobiographical *[sic]* in my stories."[73] In *The Philippines Is in the Heart,* his posthumously published story collection, this combination of folktales, fantasy, and autobiography can be seen in his stories of ghosts, angels, and mermaids.[74] Many of the titles to these stories reflect their author's preoccupation: "Really, a

Ghost," "The Angel in Santo Domingo," "The Amorous Ghost Came to Town," and the "Return of the Amorous Ghost." In the last of these stories, the "amorous ghost," so named because he seeks to make love to every woman in the Philippine Islands, steals a young couple's baby. The town is aroused and decides to exorcise him, at the instigation of the character of Father. Father reveals his great powers of perception and courage in realizing that the world of the eternal dead ("night") and the world of the living ("day") are not "separate entities" but "interpenetrate" and sometimes even become one and the same thing, but with different names. [75] He decides to negotiate like a "gentleman" with the Amorous Ghost. He discovers that the Ghost had not intended to steal the child but only to play with it. The Ghost returns the child to its parents, and a dialogue ensues between Father and the Ghost. The latter's story is similar to that of an exiled, tragic figure reminiscent of the lonely Bulosan himself. The Ghost feels sad, misunderstood by humans, and plays with humans because this is the language they understand. Like the Father, he believes that ghosts and humans should live together, as they "used to do in the beginning of time, far away."[76]

The element of myth and the fantastical can also be seen in the more popular stories in *The Laughter of My Father*, especially "My Father Goes to Court" and "The Laughter of My Father." The latter story talks about an *anting-anting*, or amulet. At birth, Father "touched" his sons, conferring upon them sexual powers. In the story, Father and the young narrator attend a wedding feast. The youth's timidity in dancing with women makes the Father wonder whether he had *touched* this youngest of his sons at birth. However, toward the end of the story, Carlos is mistakenly accused of a sexual liaison with the bride. The Father erroneously sees this as evidence that he indeed touched his son, who has to exile himself to avoid a hasty marriage.

Finally, there are strong suggestions of the continuity of animist beliefs in supernatural power in *America Is in the Heart*. As a young boy in the Philippines, the narrator decided to work for a copra (coconut oil) company by climbing coconut trees and cutting the nuts. Attempting to speed up his productivity, Carlos falls and breaks a leg and an arm. His father takes him to an *albolario*, which Bulosan defines as a "chiropractor, little better than a witch doctor." He describes the albolario's work (in a somewhat condescending, sensational manner) of burning leaves, rubbing "ashes mixed with oil over my body, uttering unintelligible incantations and dancing mysteriously around me."[77] The young Carlos believed he would be healed and indeed he was.

In another instance, while surrounded by deaths in a Los Angeles hospital ward, Carlos and the surviving tubercular patients come to interpret a tree near his porch as a talisman. For him, it provided "soothing coolness" and began to mean "recovery" and "survival." But beyond this, he believed in its "potency," in its "mystical power." In his desire to live, he "worshiped" the tree "like a pagan" for its healing power over the patients who depended upon it. And Carlos stubbornly held onto his "faith," despite the "doctors" who "disputed" it. Against these agents of scientific rationality and modern medicine, he believed that the leaves of the tree "protected [him] from death."[78]

These scattered references to supernatural belief show Bulosan's familiarity with oral culture, storytelling, and the pre-Hispanic animist beliefs that survive among Filipinos in the modern period. They also implicate Bulosan in a larger folk Christian tradition. As the historian Reynaldo Ileto explains, these beliefs melded with Christianity during the Spanish colonial period in the Philippines and found expression in the pasyon, a native adaptation of the New Testament,[79] which became an integral part of popular culture. The pasyon narrated the betrayal of Christ and his trials and tribulations. But even more so, it was the centerpiece of Holy Week celebrations that were "annual occasion[s] for [their] own renewal, a time for ridding the loob ["the inner being"] of impurities (shed like the blood and sweat of flagellants), for dying to the old self and being reborn anew . . . for renewing or restoring ties between members of the community."[80] The point of these renderings of suffering—which included graphic descriptions of the shedding of blood—was to evoke emotions of pity (*awa*) and empathy (*damay*) that invited others to undertake their own journey or pilgrimage of redemptive suffering (*lakaran*), as Christ had done.[81]

Bulosan's works mirror the pasyon experience and also help to explain the pervasiveness of a religious idiom in his literary representation of politics and social life. For instance, the idea of suffering and sacrifice based upon faith in a redemptive future finds its expression in his poetry, where they are joined by motifs of blood and death. The Prologue to the long poem *Voice of Bataan*,[82] with the defeat of Filipino and American forces by Japanese troops as its setting, expresses Bulosan's belief in the power of faith and spirit (here tied to love of country). Although Bataan has fallen, the poetic narrator believes that what has sustained Filipinos through great hardship is "a force more than merely physical." Rather, it is "unconquerable faith," something "immortal" in the soul—"the thought of native land." In addition, the poem "Epilogue: Unknown Soldier" contemplates the possibility of renewal after death, of the soldier dying for his son and planting "new seeds" in "a new world" and "a brighter future."[83]

Even Bulosan's rendering of the case of Sacco and Vanzetti, two Italian immigrants falsely accused in Massachusetts of murder and executed, begins in characteristic Bulosan fashion, emphasizing how both had "suffered" because they were radicals and because they were Italians, with the emphasis being on their suffering.[84] It is easy to see Bulosan in this poem if one substitutes "Filipino" for "Italian."

The themes of the pasyon also permeate Bulosan's *America Is in the Heart*, a book whose connections to Philippine tradition are deeper than the modernistic readings of critics have yet to allow. The countless sufferings of the principal character of *America Is in the Heart* only make sense if they are seen as a social representation of the suffering of Filipinos on the West Coast. There is, first of all, Bulosan's choice of representing the plight of the Filipinos through a suffering, Christlike hero. Bulosan could have chosen many other heroic models, and his decision to choose this one was likely influenced by elements of the pasyon and by his deep understanding of the religious inclinations of Filipinos, for whom he felt great sympathy. Numerous tragedies afflict the narrator. For instance, part 1 involves the young Carlos in a string of mishaps—he falls twice from climbing coconut trees and suffers broken limbs, is knocked unconscious by an overflowing river, sees the death of his sister Irene, and witnesses the loss of his father's lands and the exile of his brothers near and far. In subsequent parts of the book, Carlos suffers the stings of racial violence and abuse in the United States—he is beaten several times by vigilantes, police, and armed guards and is hit on the head by a bottle, all because he is a Filipino. Meanwhile, he and his countrymen suffer the humiliation of arrests, illegal searches of their property, and violent opposition to their marriage or liaison with white women. The ending leaves us with sadness, as all pasyon narratives tend to do. The narrator succeeds in his quest to become a writer, but the bombing of Pearl Harbor and World War II itself destroy the unity of his family, the only people with whom he could share his success. Carlos reflects upon the irony that it took a war to provide outlets for the desires of Filipinos whose lives had been limited by race discrimination and economic exploitation.

The sadness of the book is not maudlin sentimentalism, however, but the narrator's attempt to empathize with the plight of his brothers and sisters, to evoke feelings of *damay* (empathy) or *awa* (pity) for the suffering, Christlike figure in readers, inviting a similar work of suffering. In this context, the final passages of the book assume a different meaning than critics have ascribed to it.[85] The emphasis on sacrifice, toil, and suffering symbolized by "America" seems far from the popular conception of a land of opportunity waiting for every profit-seeking immigrant or Horatio Alger. Rather, Bulosan's America hearkens to an idiom of protest in which compassion and empathy for the sufferings of others are paramount values, alongside an alacrity for self-sacrifice that is motivated by the attempt to give back to "others" (e.g., Christ, Rizal) for their sacrifices. Indeed, within this scheme, Bulosan's attempt to call the Filipino American community into being seems to be based upon a presumption of giving or reciprocal exchange (the supreme gift being one's own life) that appears limitless.

Other aspects of the pasyon permeate Bulosan's discourse, serving to reinforce the values of empathy and giving. The mood of sadness and tragedy, characteristic of the telling of the story of Christ's crucifixion, pervades almost every important poem of Bulosan's, even his love poems, infusing the political defiance in them with deep feeling. Meanwhile, in *America Is in the Heart*, the recurrence of certain images throughout the book creates an atmosphere of weeping, sadness, and nostalgia. For instance, in the first part of the book, a goat kid meekly allows itself to be slaughtered, and a *sibbed* (a bird) captured by his brother Luciano cries "because it has lost something" (21, 49–52).[86] Church bells resound, signaling sad moments, such as Carlos's tearful parting from his family as he heads for America (63, 73). The *kundiman,* a deep, plaintive love song, whether sung by a fellow countryman in the Philippines or in the United States, fills Carlos with memories of his childhood and makes him stop and listen to the "sound of home" (89, 97).

Apart from the feel for sound and the mood of sadness, the imagery of *liwanag* is of paramount importance in the pasyon and in Bulosan's discourse. Ileto defines *liwanag* as "light, illumination," a potent image used in the ritual ceremonies of popular organizations of the Philippine revolution against

Spain in the 1890s. Liwanag was a symbol of moral purification and religious redemption with political overtones, especially when contrasted to the darkness that had shrouded the colonized, abused, and fallen Philippines.[87] References to the redemptive power of light occur in Bulosan's poetry. For instance, the closing lines of the poem "Sacco and Vanzetti" assume its power with the repetition of Sacco's dream of a future that is unrealizable because of his death. That dream of "harmony of thought and action" is imaged in terms of "spheres of tragic light" and radiant "streams of vivid light."[88] The tragic, maternal character Marian, perhaps a symbol of the Virgin Mary herself, describes Carlos's positive qualities in terms of light, which reminds us of the "radiance" of those with power or *anting-anting:* "There is something in you that *radiates like an inner light, and it affects others.* Promise me to let it grow" (217; emphasis added).

In another passage, Carlos describes his dream of becoming a writer and of obtaining the poet Harriet Monroe's patronage. He describes her as a "famous editor" who sought to help him. She "had discovered most of America's leading poets and writers." Carlos wanted to follow in their footsteps, "arrive at a positive understanding of America," and thereafter return to the Philippines "with a *torch of enlightenment*" (emphasis added).[89] But in his personal correspondence with Monroe, Bulosan wrote with more overt religious symbolism of his dream. For years, he had been reaching for that "delight of humanity called Light" but had only encountered "darkness." He persevered because he had faith in myth, in the "mythology of Light," and he kept "marching into the morning" until he found Monroe, who led him to the "Light."[90]

The Spirit and Pasyon of Bulosan

Visions of the supernatural and the pasyon were not limited to Bulosan's poetry, fiction, and autobiographical writings, but spilled over into his life. Dorothy Babb, one of Bulosan's closest friends, testifies to the pervasiveness of the supernatural aura surrounding Bulosan, not only in his life but also after his death. Babb, a former member of the Communist Party in the 1930s, became a dedicated teacher, patron, and devoted friend of Bulosan's, as did her sister Sanora. It was no doubt with the deepest feelings that

Dorothy was moved to write about Carlos's continuing visits after his death: "It was for the best that Carlos died, but I don't think he is dead. His *spirit is living somewhere*. . . . I may have mentioned that I have twice received indirect communications from Carlos. . . . You may not believe in the after life, but I do" (emphasis added).[91]

Others testify to the element of liwanag that radiated from Bulosan's countenance. In 1937, P. C. Morantte had his first meeting with Bulosan in the Los Angeles County General Hospital. There, Morantte found Bulosan deathly sick with tuberculosis. Yet what stood out to Morantte was not Bulosan's physical frailty but something strangely reminiscent of a mystical, Christian life force. Morantte claimed to have seen "the incandescent *light* of hope glinting in his eyes, a latent *energy* coming to the surface from a *deep source of life*."[92] The writer John Fante, one of Bulosan's progressive American friends, also found it apt to use the imagery of light in describing the Filipino American author. He was moved by Bulosan's gentleness to make this comment: "If I were a good Christian, I think I might label him a *saint*, for he *radiated* kindness and gentleness."[93] Even his friends in the ILWU's Local 37 in Seattle felt this way about Bulosan's energy or presence. Matias Lagunilla, the union's secretary, commented in a letter explaining Bulosan's employment by the ILWU to Washington State's Department of Public Assistance that Bulosan had "many friends among us" and that "[w]e *need even just his presence among us*, that is how much we regard Mr. Bulosan's integrity and ability."[94]

Related to others' perception of Bulosan's radiance was their admiration for his sense of dignity in the face of physical suffering, an attribute Christ possessed, as did José Rizal, who was said to have walked calmly to the Spanish firing squad that ended his life. As Alfonso P. Santos, a Filipino poet and student at USC in the 1930s, wrote, "Bulosan was already suffering from poor health when I met him, but *he never complained about it*." And when Santos saw him walking with a cane into a Filipino restaurant in Los Angeles, he never showed "any expression that called for *pity*." Bulosan did not tell him about his sickness until much later and he only found out later "that one-half of his body was paralyzed and only one of his lungs was functioning."[95] What is interesting about this passage is how Bulosan's silence about his illness paradoxically magnifies his Christlike image for his fellow countryman. Indeed, among the poor Filipinos, the physically frail Bulosan was revered as a national or ethnic hero and a saint. "If he was broke," observes his friend, Dolores Feria, "he would limp patiently toward Temple Street and Montezuma in the heart of 'Little Manila' where the Pangasinan boys [from Bulosan's home province] always signed for the check." Feria writes that "they worshipped him as a kind of glorification of Rizal, Mabini, and Bonifacio all rolled into one."[96]

Bulosan himself took his sufferings with a modicum of self-pity and showed a remarkable resilience, despite the anticommunist attacks on him in the 1950s in both the United States and in the Philippines and his worsening health. A letter written toward the end of his life gathers his beliefs in Marxism (especially a teleological conception of History), religion, and the image of the suffering artist:

> Contemporary life is surely unfair to me; but history will vindicate it. I am not afraid of the present because I saw the future, and it is kind and good and rewarding. This is my own faith. And this is my conviction. . . . It is unlearned for me to say that I possess genius. . . . What I have is perseverance . . . and sacrifice, and also a basic philosophy of life which is untainted by the hypocrisies of contemporary civilization. I wish I can give this crystal-clear vision to you . . . it took me a whole lifetime of struggle to have it.[97]

↭

In the foreword he wrote to Luis Taruc's autobiography *Born of the People*, Paul Robeson describes the book in glowing terms, in the universalist language of Marxist dialectics, which had influenced Bulosan throughout his life in America. Robeson speaks of Taruc as a "new kind of human being," a "harbinger of the future," who was nonetheless rooted in the people, a person from "the working class" embodying the people's rich "humanist tradition," "wisdom," and "creative capacity," his life combining "theory and practice."[98]

According to Dolores Feria, Bulosan passed the book around for others to read and claimed to have ghostwritten it himself, which she thinks was a Bulosan fabrication.[99] Whether this was true or not, Bulosan was deeply moved by the Huk struggle, perhaps sensing in it an experience of sacrifice and faith in a redemptive future characteristic of the *pasyon*. Perhaps this experience of empathy and pity is what led him to write his own fictive version of the rebellion in *Power of the People*, also titled *The Cry and the Dedication*, a novel that was never published during his lifetime.[100] This was also meant to be a continuation of José Rizal's *Noli Me Tangere*, as this Bulosan letter shows: "I am writing a novel which will be the extension of Rizal's *The Social Cancer*. I say extension because he fought a foreign tyranny; I am fighting the coordination of foreign and native tyranny. There is no longer 'my nativeland', but 'my co-workers'; all national and geographical boundaries are scaled, and what are left are the class scaffoldings *[sic]* of society." The book betrays elements of Taruc's autobiography—Bulosan uses names like Old Bio, Mameng, and others that belonged to real-life characters. And like Taruc's, the book attempts to expose the relationship between anticolonial struggles in the developing world and the struggles of racial minorities in the United States.[101]

Perhaps more important, *The Cry and the Dedication* instances a tragic experience that recalls the pasyon. As the critic Gerald Burns states, the hero in Philippine literature is characterized neither by success nor by conquest, but by suffering, betrayal, tragedy, failure, and death.[102] In the novel, the "detached," educated proletarian Dante is perhaps the closest representation of Carlos Bulosan himself—he is a repatriate who has seen other lands and an intellectual who has returned to participate in the armed struggle. Dante returns to the Philippines with a dream of revolutionary transformation. He becomes involved with seven Huk guerrillas who attempt to rendezvous in Manila with another repatriate from the United States. However, the heroic aspect of the guerrilla struggle is marred by two failures—the other repatriate fails to appear, sabotaging the whole operation, and Dante's life ends in tragedy when he is betrayed by his own brother.[103] The narrator's positive assessment of these failures leads only to the conclusion that what Bulosan truly valued was neither success nor failure but the sense of sacrifice or laying down of one's life characteristic of the pasyon.

Scores of critical appraisals have for some time constructed a Bulosan consonant with the project of modernity, whether defined in terms of progress, ilustrado nationalism, socialism, exile, or mobility. But what I have tried to do in this chapter has been to question this modernist façade by unearthing submerged discourses in Bulosan that suggest his implication in a world that has often been dismissed as "pre-modern."

Bulosan's involvement in the world of oral culture, animism, and folk spirituality foregrounds the importance of religion and how it continues in vital ways to shape the perceptions, the worldviews, and the ideas of transnational Filipino intellectuals. It also suggests the vital links between expatriate or overseas Filipinos and their Philippine cultural world, despite the absence, or seeming absence, of visible manifestations of direct or continuing affiliation.

THREE

The Artistic Vanguard: José García Villa

Like Carlos Bulosan and Carlos P. Romulo, José García Villa belonged to the generation after the ilustrados and, like them, he dreamed of artistic success in America while he was still in the Philippines. He had even less to do with politics, however, and upon his arrival in America in 1930, economic survival and literary acceptance were more important concerns. Estranged from his family and his country, he avoided any hint of ethnic difference or national origin in his writings, although he personally clung stubbornly to Filipino cultural values. Villa would win poetic acclaim in the United States and return in triumph to his Philippine homeland several times in the course of his later life, shoring up the confidence of his people in their search for international respect as a nation.

Like many writers of the Philippine Commonwealth era (1935–41), Villa was intrigued by the question of the goals Philippine literature should adopt in the postcolonial, postindependence era. In line with his "materialist" conception of Filipino literature, based upon the history of the Philippine struggle for freedom from colonialism and class exploitation, Carlos Bulosan argued that Villa was an aberrant "phenomenon" and that his art was an example of a "declining" Hispano-Filipino culture and out of step with the emerging Filipino national culture.[1] Bulosan's view of art was, however, based upon social protest, ilustrado nationalism, and Philippine rural and folk traditions. For his part, Villa saw politics and history as irrelevant to art, and the artist's true vocation as a lifelong dedication to art itself. Consequently, he rarely included Bulosan in any of his poetry anthologies or took note of his accomplishments.[2]

Although there are difficulties in placing Villa's work in either the Philippine or the ethnic American literary tradition, excluding him would narrow the purview of both. The category of "ethnic" or "national" artists should include writers like Villa whose subjects and forms of writing have no recognizably "ethnic" content.[3] The definition of ethnic writers or poets, as Werner Sollors states, must be broadened to include the authors' origins, their audience, and their interactions with ethnic groups and not merely be limited to what is recognizable as "ethnic." The nineteenth-century ilustrado painter Juan Luna provides a Philippine example. Although most of Luna's works involve no recognizably Philippine themes, he was declared the country's "national" artist because of his social connections with Filipino propagandists in Spain and the anticolonial impact of his paintings. Indeed, Luna's career would seem an early prototype of Villa's.[4]

In this chapter, I explore a sphere of artistic modernism, patronage relations, and social behavior in Filipino and Filipino American intellectual culture that has hitherto been regarded as a separate phenomenon from Filipino nationalism and the construction of Filipino American ethnic identity. As poet, painter, short story writer, teacher, and editor and a founding figure of Filipino literature in the twentieth century, José García Villa exemplifies this overlapping relationship between nationalism, performance, and patronage. Indeed, this chapter identifies undercurrents of ethnicity and nationalism in Villa, especially in his pronouncements about art and social life and in his relationships with various patrons. I argue that such a thread can be found in Villa's theatricality and in his outrageous behavior as an expatriate. This performativity was foreshadowed by the social activities of the nineteenth-century ilustrados with whom he shared a similar social class background. Whereas Romulo utilized oratory and Bulosan storytelling, Villa employed shock, posing, and provocation to convey his artistic philosophy. He consciously utilized the power of the body and of sexuality. His *speech acts*—which included flattery, insults, and wit—ensnared his admirers and raked those he disliked. In other ways, Filipino nationalism and traditional culture expressed themselves through Villa. For instance, he had a lifelong ambition to be a patron of Philippine literature and to make it acceptable to an international audience. Many of his performances were designed to impress Filipino literary figures, whether in the Philippines or in New York. Lastly, Villa performed his identity in his attitude to ethnic food: he extolled the virtues of Filipino cuisine, which served him as an important marker not only of artistic taste but also of an essential Filipino American ethnicity.[5]

Poet and Fiction Writer

Born in 1908 in Manila, Villa became the poet par excellence of the Philippines. He died in 1997 in New York, but his stature remains undiminished in the Philippines. His reputation was based on a relatively small number of original works. From 1925 to 1997, he published one short story collection and five volumes of poetry, which included many previously published poems.[6] Some of the poems perhaps give evidence of Villa's "genius," but his reputation in the Philippines and among a handful of admirers in the United States probably rests on something other than his original work.

Villa's identity was shaped by his parents' attempts to fashion him in their own image and by his attempts to rebel against their wishes. Guia García, his mother, was a "rich heiress" who possessed prized real estate and a large income.[7] Simeon Villa, his father, was an insurgent against the United States. He was the personal physician of General Emilio Aguinaldo and notorious for his anticlerical beliefs. Something of this would rub off on his son José, who never became a churchgoer. Like many Filipino revolutionary leaders, Simeon was embittered by the American takeover of the Philippines, and he refused to speak English, although his son never learned Spanish.[8] From José's perspective, Simeon was an authoritarian father who pressured him into taking up medicine and was against painting, his first love. José's sister Anna believed that the basis of the quarrel between father and son was economic and social: "My father was very angry," she said, "because at the time poets did not earn [a decent living] and were considered *low class*" (emphasis added).[9] Later in life, when Villa was in dire straits in America, Simeon refused to give him any of the family property and incurred his son's hatred.[10] While still an undergraduate at the University of the Philippines, José Villa appeased his father by taking courses in medicine and later in law. At the same time, against his father's wishes, he pursued a career as a writer of fiction.

José Villa left the Philippines in 1930 and thereafter lived the life of an expatriate intellectual in the United States. He studied at the University of New Mexico and started a mimeographed publication called *Clay: A Literary Notebook*, which featured writers like Erskine Caldwell, as well as minor authors like Sanora Babb, and attracted the attention of Edward J. O'Brien, then considered the foremost critic of the short story.[11] O'Brien made the flattering gesture of dedicating *The Best Short Stories of 1932* to Villa and included twelve of his stories in his roll call of distinguished stories.[12] In 1933, Villa published his own collection of fiction, *Footnote to Youth: Tales of the Philippines and Others*, titled to take advantage of his exotic origin. O'Brien wrote an introduction to the book, in which he treats the self-exiled author with a mixture of admiration and Orientalist fascination, predicting a successful career for him as a novelist in the United States precisely because of his advantage in coming from "a totally unrelated civilization" (an obtuse notion, given that the Philippines was an American colony with an Americanized educational system, of which Villa himself was a product).[13]

Villa quickly, however, made a leap from the short story into a new literary vocation—poetry. In the mid 1930s, reading E. E. Cummings inspired him to abandon prose and to devote himself completely to poetry. Two years before the outbreak of World War II, Villa published *Many Voices*, his first collection of poems, in the Philippines, attracting the attention of, among others, Salvador P. Lopez, who in the same year founded the Philippine Writers' League, an organization that advocated a socially progressive literature and decried what it saw as the irresponsible "art for art's sake" credo of many Philippine writers, of whom Villa was, of course, one. (Ironically, the Writers' League would publish Villa's *Poems by Doveglion* in 1941.) In a review of Villa's poetry, Lopez wrote of visiting the poet in New York. Villa's theory of art did not impress him, but he recognized Villa's importance as a "pace-setter" for Philippine literature, suggestively calling him its "white hope."[14] The so-called "literature vs. society" debate raged on before the Japanese invasion of the Philippines, and Villa became an icon of those who believed in the preeminence of form and feeling over politics and content. The debate, as well as most Filipino writing, was interrupted by the war but resumed its hold upon Philippine intellectuals in the postwar period.[15]

For a brief period in 1941, Villa attended graduate studies in literature at Columbia.[16] After publishing a new collection of poems entitled *Have*

Come, Am Here (1942),[17] he won a spate of fellowships that helped stabilize his financial situation, enabling him to marry Rosemary Lamb, an Irish American, with whom he would have two sons, Randy and Lance. Lamb became the breadwinner of the family, while he took care of the children.[18]

Most of the critical literature on Villa has hitherto focused on his poetry. In large part, critics have neglected his life and failed to connect it to his overall literary posture.[19] But Villa was not only interested in remolding poetry but also in mobilizing the very life of the poet or the artist toward aesthetic ends. In a sense, Villa might be seen as an activist, not for politics, but for art. What links his art to his life is a performative thread, a love of play, exhibition, and acting, although not in the conventional sense of these terms, which presumes that theater must be divorced from life, fiction from fact, acting from serious behavior. Villa derided these categorical distinctions. He incorporated performativity into everyday life, such that every social setting (an art opening, a dinner table, or a classroom) became a stage providing an opportunity for performance and self-fashioning. Besides the cultural influence of the ilustrados described by Nick Joaquin, Villa was probably drawing here on a popularized notion of avant-garde movements, such as the Parnassians and Dadaism, that sought to explode all conventional aesthetic standards (as well as propaganda) and used unconventional literature and shock as instruments of revolt.[20]

The Artist as Rebel and Patron

Francisco Arcellana, one of Villa's younger contemporaries, highlights the key role played by performativity in Villa's construction of self. In one encounter with him, Arcellana was moved to ask, "Mr. Villa, why are you acting?" "I'm always acting," replied Villa. From this response, Arcellana had an epiphany. He realized that Villa's effort to discipline the social behaviors that most people take for granted was "deliberate" and "fantastic."[21] Strict in controlling the impression he made on others, Villa made this act of self-fashioning into a principle. Indeed, he seems to embody the kind of intellectual Edward Said has described, one who destabilizes social relations and sets off "seismic shocks," especially through "a series of discontinuous performances" in the ever-changing theater of everyday life.[22] In what follows,

I explore the stage of literature where Villa constructed a public persona through his pronouncements about the artist and literary taste. In the Philippines of the 1920s, Villa enacted the colonial Philippine version of the modernist's search for artistic freedom by defending himself against an obscenity charge. Indeed, in the history of Western modernism in the twentieth century, the motif of the artist persecuted by stringent Victorian or genteel morals was to be repeated many times over.[23]

As early as 1927, when he was nineteen, Villa and the "impetuous, iconoclastic" students who founded the University of the Philippines Writers' Club had already attracted the attention of the authorities. The group, among the first generation of writers reared in the U.S. colonial period, wrote that it was motivated by "a noble aim to elevate to the highest possible perfection the English language." Their credo was: "Art shall not be a means to an end but an end in itself." Villa was among the first editors of the club's publication, *The Literary Apprentice*, which was first published in 1928. Dr. George Pope Shannon, who was later to defend Villa, was the club's adviser.[24]

Villa's writings for the *Philippines Herald* had a greater influence on his generation, however. From 1927 to 1929, he submitted fiction and poetry to the *Herald*'s literary section, and in 1929 the authorities came to consider his work as subversive. In that year, he published two sexually suggestive pieces, both of which gave rise to obscenity charges. The first was a series of poems published in the *Herald* called "Man Songs." The second was "Apassionata," a short story published in the *Philippine Collegian*, the student newspaper of the University of the Philippines. Of the six objectionable poems in the "Man Songs" series, the one that drew the most commentary was "Song of Ripeness." The poem likens coconuts to nipples on a tree and makes the sensual leap to kissing one of the fallen coconuts because "it *is* the nipple of a woman"(emphasis added). "Apassionata" is the story of a seductress who entices young men by allowing them to see her naked body through a peephole.[25] Soon after the publication of these works, a Manila court charged Villa with printing obscene material. For the newspaper's sake, he admitted wrongdoing and paid a fine of 50 pesos. The question of disciplinary action was then assumed by a special committee of the university, headed by Jorge Bocobo, dean of the School of Law.[26]

The encounter between Bocobo and Villa exemplifies the cultural conflict between two generations of Filipinos socialized under different American educational influences, the former seeking to uphold the status quo, the latter to destabilize social conventions. Bocobo had been one of the first pensionados. His trip to America, which began in 1903, infused him with more than book learning. Upon his return to the Philippines several years later, he became a devout Methodist and a moral crusader. In 1922, a conference of American and Filipino Methodists identified five social evils in the Philippines: the saloon, the cockpit, the commercialized prize fight, the dance hall, and the uncensored "cine" [or movie]. True to his creed, Bocobo advocated prohibition in the Philippines and railed against cockfighting and prize fighting.[27] In 1928, while attending advanced studies in law at the University of Southern California, he campaigned for the closure of the taxi dance halls that he saw plaguing his countrymen in the United States. He visited these places himself and "exhorted" Filipinos never to come back to them. In one instance, taxi dance hall "girls" reportedly attacked him with "fingernails," "clubs," and "curses." This episode ended his crusading days in America.[28]

Villa was forced to defend himself before Bocobo's disciplinary committee, and the defiance and boldness with which he did so would inspire fellow writers to defy moral conventions. His statement provides a succinct formulation of his self-fashioning at this time and prefigures the themes that would preoccupy his life:

> The poems I wrote have been termed obscene, hence the action against me. My own conscientious belief is that they are not so; and if I have encroached on the sensuality of the public, that is literary license. *I am a writer and I am basically the artist self.* I am interested greatly in literature and in *the arts of painting and sculpturing*, which I am also studying . . . The artist sees *no connection between morality and art.* Art makes demand on everything and for it everything must the real artist suffer: *Art for Art's sake.* That he should paint and sculpture nudes, write about them—have [*sic*] nothing to do with his primary aim—which is *Beauty*; his efforts are aimed to attain beauty, nothing but beauty. And if in fulfilling this, he has to outline and make use of real natural fact he is not in the wrong. Artists find beauty even in physical ugliness, in grotesqueness, in what is dark—it is the beauty behind, the beauty *transcendental.* This the ordinary mind, the *untutored*, cannot see. (emphases added)[29]

Villa felt that Philippine audiences had misunderstood him. He suggested that the public was unprepared to understand "the more realistic side of art," for it still regarded writing about or sculpting nudes as "dirty," and it was so "narrow-minded" that it was intolerant of nudes even in "public fountains."[30] He called on his audience to reach for a higher morality and urged them not to be "prudes," but to accept the artist's vision and lift "the screen of conventional morality" that blinded them. Villa claimed that his motives were pure. "[E]ven if I am sad that I have been temporarily suspended from college, still I can feel proud that I had no such nasty motives. I am free. I am clean."[31]

In order to show that his use of sexual language was not extraordinary, Villa cited American literary figures. From Henry McBride, then editor of *Dial*, he cited a passage that makes the pseudo-scientific claim that "[a]rtists test morality by beauty, and recite the facts of Darwin's theory and the Laws of nature." Villa wondered how Walt Whitman's *Leaves of Grass*, a work with overt sexual references, could be circulated in the Philippines while "Man Songs" was deemed obscene. Finally, he provided a two-page list of references to sex in the poetry of Sherwood Anderson.[32]

Villa rejected the notion that the body was "dirty" and instead valorized it: "The human body is a beautiful body. And its feelings are beautiful feelings. These the artist endeavors to express. But aside from love and the sweetened emotions . . . the Filipino artist cannot express himself. If he does, he is restrained—he may even be imprisoned." In another passage, he argued that the body was a necessary path toward the "soul." "You see only the body, you touch it with Pharisai[c] fear, so you cannot reach the soul. But you must reach for the soul—always. However, our public does not even try to do this. At once it condemns." He equated artistic freedom with the freedom to explore the "body" and sexuality.[33] From Villa's liberal quotation of Sherwood Anderson, it seems clear that the latter's preoccupation with the body affected Villa.[34] In the end, he reaffirmed his literary license to write about "the body and its passions," citing the French naturalist writers Anatole France, Émile Zola, and Guy de Maupassant.

It did not take the committee long to decide against Villa and suspend him from the university for a year. As terms for his readmission, the committee demanded that Villa retract his writings, apologize to the law faculty, and refrain from publishing "any indecent or obscene article or composition."[35] Rather than submit to this, Villa decided to leave for America. In the same year, he won a short story competition, and he used the prize money to travel to the United States in 1930 in search of "adventure" and the opportunity to "pursue further studies in writing."[36] Dr. George Pope Shannon, his professor at the University of the Philippines, had moved to the University of New Mexico, which Villa attended for two years. He became the editor of a new magazine in Albuquerque and was something of a literary celebrity by the time he received his bachelor's degree.

Villa's performance before the university authorities, combined with his sudden fame in America, made him a hero in the Philippines and to a lesser degree among American literati.[37] The rumor spread that the University of the Philippines had "expelled" him, which added to his cachet. A biographical note in *Best Short Stories of 1932,* which may have been penned by Villa himself, describes his transformation. It speaks of his birth in the "Philippine Islands," which conjures up its exotic, insular, and colonial status. His father had demanded that he become a doctor, the note says, but instead he had chosen a literary career. He is said to have been "expelled," rather than suspended, and not for obscenity but for "immoral" writing, from the University of the Philippines, a victim of academic "old-maidishness." Finally, Villa is identified with New York, where he would live with few interruptions for the next sixty-two years.[38]

Villa's *Footnote to Youth* (1933) poignantly showed the Filipino expatriate's struggle with the memory of his Filipino ethnicity, symbolized by the narrator's soured relations with his father, the search for the lost hero in several stories, and the narrator's aspirations to an artistic vocation and upward mobility. The book, which helped to launch his writing career in America, contained twenty-one stories and sketches and was dedicated to his patron Edward J. O'Brien and to Villa's mother and father. In many ways, *Footnote* echoed the themes of his youth and his defense before the committee of the law school. Villa's confessional stories, such as the trilogy "Wings and Blue Flame," narrated the emotional counterpart of Villa's physical journey from Manila to New Mexico and his artistic self-discovery.[39] They also express hurt and sadness over his father's meanness and refusal to acknowledge his talent.[40] Another story, "Yet Do They Strife," might even be read as Villa's plea for tenderness from his father. Again, one can detect the influence of

Sherwood Anderson's *Winesburg, Ohio*, which portrays the warped lives of a small American town through the eyes of the artist George Willard, who in the end escapes to the metropolis. In several stories, Villa sketches the pathetic lives of his small town (i.e., the colonized Philippines), where numerous characters have become warped by religion and by their attempts to establish kinship ties with the national hero, José Rizal.[41] As in *Winesburg, Ohio*, Villa's artist seeks to leave provincial grotesqueness behind and risk everything in the big city.

In New York, Villa transformed himself from a short story writer into a poet, for whom language became a means for combating propaganda. Villa's literary experiments nonetheless increasingly led to the denationalization of his works. A reading of E. E. Cummings's *Collected Poems* in 1936 had led him to abandon prose and to pursue poetry full time. Villa first imitated the work of Cummings and other lyric poets, but he soon developed his own original style, over several years of painstaking study. Faithful to his credo, Villa suffered for his ideals. During the Great Depression of the 1930s, he experienced poverty, hunger, and racism at the same time that he won friends and supporters.[42] In the meantime, a Villa cult sprang up in the Philippines. The foremost followers of Villa, a group called the "Veronicans," included many budding Filipino writers: Francisco Arcellana, Narciso Reyes, Bienvenido Santos, Estrella Alfon, Manuel Viray, Delfin Fresnosa, and N. V. M. Gonzalez. They were inspired by Villa's rebellion against what they considered bourgeois morality and touted him as their artistic champion.[43] Toward the end of the decade, Villa enunciated his art for art's sake perspective, inoculating the Veronicans against the criticisms of the Philippine Writers' League. There was no reason, he argued, why other critics should demand of him literature of "social significance," which he termed "propaganda." The whole function of the "kind of art" to which he had given his "whole allegiance" was "to arouse pleasure in the beautiful."[44]

One of the things that continually attracted the attention of the Veronicans, and that reflected his continual self-creation during this period, was Villa's penchant for renaming himself. For instance, in the 1920s, he signed works "O. Sevilla." In the late 1930s, he renamed himself "Doveglion," a composite of "dove, eagle, and lion," meant to present the poet "gentle as a dove, free as an eagle, and fierce as a lion."[45] Each of Villa's pseudonyms roughly corresponded to his evolution. "O. Sevilla" recalled his ilustrado origins and his vocation as short story writer. "Doveglion" reflected his physical remove from the Philippines and his turn to poetry. As we have seen, he titled his second published work *Poems by Doveglion*.[46] The coinage appears archaic, recalling perhaps a medieval period of Christian ladies and gentlemen.[47]

During the 1940s, emulating E. E. Cummings' eccentric versification and wordplay, Villa earned a reputation in the United States as a poetic experimenter. He dedicated his collection of poetry *Have Come, Am Here* (1942) to Cummings and to his patron Mark Van Doren at Columbia University. Villa's technique of "reversed consonance" first appeared in this book, for which he also wrote a short commentary advertising his poetic experiments. In his "Author's Note Concerning Versification," Villa wrote that he was "pleased to announce" a rhyming method called "reversed consonance" that had "never been used . . . in any poetry." In this rhyme scheme, Villa explained, the "last sounded consonants of the last syllable, or the last principal consonants of a word, are reversed for [i.e., become the first letter of] the corresponding rhyme [word]." Hence, the word "near" would rhyme with words like "run," "rain," and "reign," and "light" would rhyme with "tell," "tall," "tale," and so forth.

Villa's device has never been adapted into American poetry, but what matters here is his attempt to claim a place for himself in the literary history of English and his pose as a technician or craftsman. This pose continued in Villa's "comma poems," in *Volume Two* (1949). Here, Villa wrote a longer commentary about his new technique of placing a comma after every word in a poem, perhaps suggesting his greater stake in its success.

Villa wrapped his claim to originality in the English poetic tradition and Western art around a punctuation mark. He claimed that the commas could be used as aesthetic devices, as a means for commenting about time and space, and as a way of making comparisons with the plastic arts. Whether the commas serve the functions that Villa claimed for them is debatable. After all, poets like Shakespeare, Blake, and even Villa's idol, E. E. Cummings, did without them, instead using the natural pauses in language. Moreover, they can be obstacles to the appreciation of the poem. Nonetheless, Villa once again showed his commitment to experimentation and the new, which provided its own justification as far as he was concerned. He offered a superficially plausible analogy between the comma poems and Seurat's "pointillism" and sought to intimidate his audience with remarks such as "Only the uninitiate would complain . . ." and appeals to "the more poetically and texturally sensitive reader."[48]

This survey of Villa's self-fashioning would not be complete without comment on his attempt to influence the development of literature in the Philippines and the United States as an anthologist and editor. From 1927 to 1941, Villa published an annual Roll of Honor of the best Philippine stories. This was a direct imitation of Edward J. O'Brien's own roll of honor. Villa used O'Brien's criteria, the "test of substance" and the "test of form," and a rating system of from one to three stars, with three stars for the stories he judged most enduring.[49] Villa sought to develop "a school of Filipino short story writers or authors, partly as filling a want in the local literary field and partly with a view to the possible development of some literary genius who might make a name for himself in the United States."[50]

Especially after Villa's expatriation to the United States and his success as editor of *Clay* and short story writer, Philippine writers eagerly awaited his annual selections. His stature as an American poet authorized his patronage of Philippine writing and set him on a par with the Philippine print media's chief editors: A. V. H. Hartendorp of the monthly *Philippine Magazine*, A. E. Litiatco of the weekly *Graphic*, and McCullough Dick of the *Philippines Free Press*. Villa's literary judgments attained the status of revealed truth and reinforced his reputation as a shaker of convention. When Francisco Arcellana published the avant-garde magazine *Expression* and was charged with immorality, Villa came to his defense. He culled several stories from the magazine, included them in his *Best Philippine Stories of 1934*, and helped introduce the new magazine. "This is the first radical 'little magazine' to appear in the Philippines," Villa said, "and I am glad to welcome it—it has a worthy spirit behind it and fosters experimentation and has no stupid bourgeois-moralistic taboos."[51]

Yet while almost every Filipino writer respected Villa's critical judgments, many of them came to resent his imperious attitude. For instance, the *Philippine Magazine* carried this exchange between Villa and the author Amador Daguio. Villa had fired the first shot by complaining in a previous issue: "I can not understand how Mr. Daguio, who has written some very fine poems, can produce prose of complete illiteracy." Incensed, Daguio replied: "I don't give a snap for what any Villa says about me." Daguio took a jab at Villa's literary tastes: "I know that if I wanted to write a story to sat-isfy Villa . . . I'd write of a woman who is lonely, who goes to her room and imagines things and . . . [deleted] . . . and Villa would swallow a lump in his throat and call it a 'find.' We cannot depend upon a man who lets the caprice of the moment prejudice his opinion."[52] The poet Angela Manalang Gloria, later considered one of the country's best poets, resented the young Villa's manner of passing judgment on the work of others, offering unso-licited opinions, and "pontificating" about poetry.[53] She was shocked by Villa's calling her a "third rater" as a poet and "a writer of merely pretty po-etry" and "pleasant amateur verses." He dubbed her "Miss Nostalgia," full of "melodiousness" but lacking "passion" and "drive."[54] The fiction writer and critic Edilberto K. Tiempo recalled with disdain that Villa was "the unques-tioned literary dictator in the Philippines in the 1930s." Speaking of Villa's attitude toward other writers, Tiempo wrote, "Villa was like Jove descend-ing from Mt. Olympus to dispense judgment upon subservient mortals."[55]

Villa's attitude of superiority was only matched by his self-effacing, if not flattering, attitude toward his white superiors. In the latter part of the 1940s, Villa edited the E. E. Cummings number of *Wake*, a Harvard journal; a spe-cial issue on Marianne Moore in the *Quarterly Review of Literature*; and *A Celebration for Edith Sitwell*.[56] Villa showed his skills as arranger and copy-editor in these publications, but his presence in these works was slight. For instance, in *A Celebration for Edith Sitwell*, the only time Villa's name ap-pears is on the title page. He presents the major poets and writers of the time and their commentaries on Sitwell, as well as works by Sitwell herself, but he himself wrote neither an introduction nor an encomium for Sitwell. Nor did Villa write a biographical note about himself. That the contributors, includ-ing Sitwell, failed to mention Villa, added to his invisibility. Villa disap-peared into the background of his own text.

This particular instance seems to contradict Villa's pattern of self-fash-ioning until one recalls his worship of Sherwood Anderson, E. E. Cum-mings, and Edith Sitwell. Sitwell was, like Villa, noted for her religious verse, her own distinctive styles of clothing, and eccentric social performances. She became a patron of sorts for budding American poets and took an interest in José García Villa, who had sent his poems to her during the war. She even-tually included his poetry in her anthology *The American Genius*.[57]

Sitwell wrote of Villa to other writers. These limited exchanges provide some idea of her attitude toward Villa, and vice versa. For instance, in 1948, Sitwell went on a much-publicized tour of the United States with her brothers Osbert and Sacheverell to read and perform their poetry. She saw Villa at a large party thrown on her behalf at the Gotham Book Mart in New York.[58] Sitwell enjoined her friend Stephen Spender to find a publisher for Villa, her "new protégé."[59] As her biographer, Victoria Glendinning, writes, Sitwell was motivated by an Orientalist curiosity about Villa. She was fascinated by him as a Filipino "magic iguana," writing "sharp flame-like poems." She hastens to add, however, that some of these poems were bad.[60]

Something of Villa's attitude toward Sitwell can be deduced from a passage in a letter of Sitwell's to the publisher John Lehmann, a fellow poet and critic, who had objected to Sitwell's decision to include a liberal selection of Villa's poems in *The American Genius*. Sitwell's reply to Lehmann shows a maternal concern for Villa and a glimpse, perhaps, of a Villa performance on behalf of his "experiments." Sitwell confessed that she thought Villa's comma poems "bosh." She nonetheless felt that to slight his explanations for them would have broken his heart, especially because he was a Filipino. Villa "began to weep . . . on the evening before I left," she said, and he went on crying "throughout the evening," claiming that he *had to* have his explanations for the comma poems.[61] Whether these were genuine tears of sadness at the failure of a friend and patron to understand him or a calculated performance is difficult to tell. But the story shows that Villa was not averse to showing vulnerability before those whom he admired or considered superior, which stands in marked contrast to his severe, condescending attitude toward those whom he regarded as his inferiors. This tendency in Villa became more pronounced after he shifted his attention to high society and to the unsuspecting students of his poetry courses.

The Postwriterly Career of the Genius

Villa stopped writing poetry in the 1950s, but this did not end his career as an artist: it only gave new life to his passion for performance before fellow Filipinos and before his students in American universities and private classes. In accounts of his public interactions with friends and admirers, Villa's self-fashioning assumed new theatrical forms. Outrageous behavior now supplemented the performance of his early years as an artist persecuted by an "old-maidish" University of the Philippines and as a purveyor of literary taste. Villa's performances were calculated to get the public to recognize his achievements and those in power to provide for his material welfare. Being averse to taking up any occupation he regarded as unworthy of his name, Villa suffered constant privation. Paraphrasing Nietzsche, he was "overtaken by awe of himself" and of his "exceptional rights." He resisted "criticism" and thus began to decline as his "pinions" fell "out of his plumage."[62] However, in another sense, the post-poetic Villa did not degenerate; rather, he was regenerated by the enjoyment of his newfound fame and social life.

To understand Villa's activities in the 1950s requires some knowledge of his previous performances for patrons. According to P. C. Morantte, Villa had been financially insecure even before the war and had depended on the generosity of an Irish American friend, a janitor from the Bronx. In 1941, Villa received a $250 award from the Philippine Commonwealth Government for his book of poems entered in the First Commonwealth Literary Awards.[63] In 1942, the same forces that had brought Romulo and Bulosan to Washington, D.C., to work in Quezon's Commonwealth government-in-exile brought Villa to the national capital. According to Morantte, Quezon had "tried to help Villa several times by giving him a job; but Villa, after tiring of the job, would walk out, without even going to the trouble of writing a letter of resignation."[64] For a time, the impoverished Villa was hired to clip news items about the Philippines, alongside Bienvenido Santos. He hated the mestizos and Spaniards he encountered in Quezon's government and blew up over his first assignment (to write an article about *abaca,* or Manila hemp).[65] The publication and success of Villa's *Have Come, Am Here* later in the same year persuaded Quezon to settle a pension on him of $100 a month, which Villa received for two years. On this and the funds he received from a Guggenheim fellowship, Villa mostly lived well during the war years.[66] After Quezon's death, however, Philippine political leaders were less inclined to patronize the poet. Both President Sergio Osmeña and Ambassador Carlos P. Romulo denied him a government post.[67]

Various Philippine writers criticized the government's neglect of Villa. The journalist Teodoro Locsin warned: "The government of this country may profitably . . . remember that a nation is known for the work of its exceptional men, and a job or a pension is a small price for the honor that such

Filipinos as Villa are bringing the Philippines."[68] Amador Daguio, who had tussled with Villa during the 1930s, now viewed Villa's plight as a symbol of public indifference to the country and its artistic geniuses. He feared that America would "claim Villa for her own" and the Philippines would "lose him forever." Daguio thought it would be a cause for great "shame" (and here, one hears the overtones of *hiya*, as embarrassment) for the entire country not to have developed the habit of patronizing its authors so that they would be able to "live on their royalties." He especially thought it shameful that the "wealthy of our country" gave little to support artists, thus denying them "freedom from want."[69]

In the late 1950s and 1960s, the celebrated fiction writer and dramatist Nick Joaquin reported on attempts to provide Villa with a government post and on Villa's trips to the Philippines. He compiled these into an essay titled "Viva Villa," which I draw upon for the following account. The essay provides a rich and fascinating account of the aging artist's social life. Few writers and critics had at that time appreciated Villa's theatricality. Joaquin's understanding of Villa shines through in these accounts, which draw upon numerous interviews with the poet. The result is a sympathetic portrait that brings to life Villa's numerous outrages.[70]

In the 1950s, Villa's economic problems continued. Through the work of his friends in the foreign service, he obtained a sinecure in the Philippine Mission to the United Nations in New York in 1954. He was put on the books as a chauffeur. Thus, living on a chauffeur's income, Villa continued his literary activities during the 1950s, a period of great experimentation in American poetry, which saw the rise of the Beat poets.[71]

In 1959, Far Eastern University (FEU) in Manila decided to honor Villa with an honorary doctorate. No one expected Villa to return for the ceremonies, but he surprised many by making the trip back to the Philippines. He returned to New York two months later. The following year, Villa returned to the Philippines for a vacation and a yearlong teaching assignment at FEU. He was reputed to be an excellent teacher of poetry. A distant cousin, Carmen Guerrero Nakpil, recalled meeting Villa at this time. She introduced him to members of her family; Villa later quibbled about being upstaged by them.[72] In 1961, Villa received the prestigious Rizal Pro Patria Award, and in 1962, the Republic Heritage Award for Literature.

When Villa returned to work in New York in 1962, he encountered a Foreign Service that had faced severe criticism for its patronage practices and now saw reform as its top priority. A standardized test on Philippine history and economics was instituted (197).[73] Vice President and Secretary of Foreign Affairs Emmanuel Pelaez considered maintaining Villa in his post, but his refusal to take the civil service examinations doomed his chances (198ff.). Villa saw the examinations as Pelaez's attempt to persecute him, not considering that the reform led to the discharge of forty other ineligible employees in the mission (207). Joaquin quotes Villa as saying: "I shall refuse to take the exam because the idea is absurd and an indignity to subject me to it . . . I have reached a position in Philippine life that they should *respect*" (199). Moreover, Pelaez found Villa's desk empty and was told that the poet only showed up on payday (208). Not surprisingly, in December 1962, Villa was fired from the Philippine UN Mission.

Filipino intellectuals interpreted the latest action against Villa as the work of a bureaucracy that had little appreciation for culture. Headed by Lydia Arguilla Salas, one of Villa's good friends, they launched a petition drive among fellow writers calling for President Macapagal to grant Villa a pension worthy of his national achievements, something akin to poet laureate status.[74] They managed to obtain over two hundred signatures, with about six refusing to sign on the basis of personal antipathy toward Villa and objections to his alleged freeloading. In his report, Joaquin tried to put a positive spin on the Villa affair, waxing eloquent to the effect that Villa had been "our oldest ambassador in point of service." "Even when he is dead," Joaquin said, "he will continue to be our most brilliant ambassador abroad, carrying into every nook where English and poetry are read the name of our country, the name of our people . . . his country certainly owes him a debt of gratitude" (212).

In 1965, Villa met then Senator Marcos and his wife Imelda at a party in New York and implored the senator to help him. He also sought the help of Carlos P. Romulo, then U.P. president. Villa claimed that Marcos had had the "gallantry" to respond to his request, while "[t]he great General Romulo just ignored me" (216). Soon after his encounter with Marcos, Villa was re-hired at the Philippine Mission as a "commercial attaché," sending out tourist folders to high school students doing book reports on the Philippines (216–17).

On another occasion, Imelda Marcos paid a visit to Villa in New York.

Villa described her as "a vision of delight" and likened her to the "Venus de Milo" (216). Imelda asked Villa a favor—to buy for her husband $2,000 worth of the best books on politics, history, and social science. Villa went to the New York Public Library and in two weeks had a list of books that he ordered from Scribner's. Mrs. Marcos brought the books back to her husband, who was impressed by them (217–18). Convinced of Villa's usefulness to the Marcos government, Imelda and Ferdinand invited him to return to the Philippines in 1968. They granted him the highest position he had ever attained in government—foreign affairs officer, with the rank of "vice-consul." For the occasion, Villa wore the national garb, a *barong tagalog,* and happily commented that he had not "worn a barong tagalog in ages." He bragged that "[w]hen I put on a barong tagalog I feel like an angel, because I look so handsome in it, I feel so beautiful. I guess it's the Filipino in me, it brings out the Filipino in me" (219).

On the social scene, Villa's return in 1968 created a sensation among Filipino intellectuals and helped to reinvigorate his reputation as a Filipino national artist, although an American resident. He socialized with entertainers, artists, politicians, and models, appearing (to Joaquin) as a knightly figure who brandished a peculiar sword: "Lip is what he cuts you up with, this Peer of the Realm who was born with a silver cheek in his tongue," Joaquin wrote. "When he wields it, the bodies lie strewn about." Moreover, Villa was "a Happening all by himself." He especially loved to pronounce on the things that struck him the most, the same preoccupations that had guided his fiction and poetry—beauty, sexuality, the body (his own and those of others), and, finally, his newfound philosophical sensibility.

An important part of Villa's performance of national and gendered identity was his love for sexual banter. He asked women if they were virgins and dismissed men who annoyed him by saying that they should be castrated (182). Villa often slept during the day and roamed the clubs at night. Joaquin recorded this particular evening: "[Villa] went to an art opening wearing a pendant of red glass balls that everybody touched curiously. But poetess Virginia Moreno cupped the pendant in her hands, whereupon Villa congratulated her. 'Virgie,' said he, 'you are the only one who has known how to handle my balls.'" In a restaurant, Joaquin wrote, "a woman painter confronted [Villa] with: 'Why didn't you come to my opening last night?' The poet cocked an eyebrow: 'Your opening?'" In another venue, he was asked when he had last been home. Villa replied, "I come only once in five years," and then broke down laughing over his own words (213–14).

Next to sexual raillery, Villa loved to call attention to himself, especially as an artist of high sophistication. At a nightclub, a crowd gathered around to see what he had suddenly scribbled in his notebook: "*I was born evolved. I did not have to rise higher than myself*" (214). Introduced to an actress, he revealed his essential self-staging: "Do you think you can act? *I* can act. I act all the time" (215). Villa often sought to upstage other stars—in a sense, he saw himself as a kind of male diva. This love for self-staging went hand in hand with a disdain for the "pseudo-culture" of ballet, opera, and the theater (196), a dislike that extended to fashion models: "I detest all models," said Villa, "except me. I want to be a male model. I'd make an intelligent model" (215).[75]

Joaquin describes a scene at a fashion show in which Villa made an appearance with Elvira Manahan, the beautiful mestiza wife of a prominent Philippine senator, and stole the limelight. Joaquin highlights Villa's story of his and Manahan's entrance. As Villa tells it, Manahan arrived in a "white classic evening dress," while he wore a "Nehru jacket overladen with necklaces." The crowd "gaped" at both of them, but chiefly at Villa (221–22).

Despite all Villa's clowning around, Joaquin found that the effect of his performances was independent of how he acted. Villa conveyed "an impression of . . . dignity, [without need of] title, position, or the right clothes, or the important manner to prop it up" (223, 224). Villa, who had stopped writing poetry in the 1950s now presented himself to Joaquin as a "thinker," a "philosophical mind" capable of making fine distinctions that immature creative artists could not (225). Villa claimed to be at work on philosophical essays on the relationship of language to life and literature—a major four-volume treatise for which he would be remembered, even more than his poetry (226).[76]

Five years later, in 1973, still in the good graces of the Marcoses, Villa returned to the Philippines to receive the National Artist Award, along with six legendary figures in the Philippine literary and plastic arts.[77] Through the initiative of U.P. President Salvador P. Lopez, the university also conferred upon him an honorary doctorate in humane letters, which he received in May of that year, thus ending his long banishment from his alma mater.[78] One month later, Villa received the National Artist Award in a formal ceremony on June 12, Philippine Independence Day.

Villa's National Artist Award was tied to the nationalist political project of the Marcos dictatorship. In their own words, the Marcoses sought "to elevate creative expression to its rightful status as the vanguard of the country's spiritual development." In fact, the Charter of the 1973 martial law constitution included a clause that stated that "Filipino culture should be preserved and developed for national identity. Arts and letters shall be under the patronage of the State."[79] According to a journalist covering the awards, Villa stood out among the crowd honored by the Marcoses because his work had so little that was Filipino in it, either in style or in content, unlike that of his fellow awardees, who utilized Filipino folk motifs, building materials, music, and images.[80] But his performance for the nation was implicitly acknowledged in the award's mention of the "international recognition" he had brought to the Philippines and of his having uncovered the Filipino soul through "new idioms."[81]

The expatriate Villa's homecoming, as in 1960, was marked by jovial celebrations and a spate of new aphorisms and outrageous remarks. Villa's sexual banter proliferated, some of it suggesting homoeroticism. For instance, as he told the journalist Lorna Montilla, "The trouble with you, Miss Montilla . . . is that like me, you like very young boys."[82] On another occasion, Villa encountered the movie sex symbol Fred Galang and proclaimed, "We love each other" as he looked at Galang, whom the reporter Letty Jimenez-Magsanoc described as "seductive," with "several buttons open down his shirt the better to show off an un-nerving physique."[83]

There was some mention in the press of minor criticism of Villa. Jimenez-Magsanoc reported that some believed that Villa was a "burnt-out case . . . a has-been . . . turning to exhibitionism to attract public attention." (To this criticism, Villa is said to have responded that still, "the least of me, is most.") Others believed that the only reason he was still in the limelight was because of the New Society's emphasis on reawakening pride in everything Filipino. (Villa could only agree with this and cautioned against too much patriotic zeal.)[84]

At a banquet during this same year, Villa and Imelda Marcos had an apparent falling out. A leading Filipino poet, Carlos Angeles, claimed that Villa resented the First Lady ("Madame") for a breach of decorum. According to Angeles, Villa felt aggrieved that at a party called in his honor, Imelda Marcos had called on the "Russian poet" to sit with her and deferred doing the same honor to Villa. He reacted by refusing to sit with the First Lady throughout the whole night, preferring to sit at "the far end of the hall" and subsequently leaving with Angeles for drinks somewhere else.[85]

Mindful of his financial dependence on the Marcos government, Villa never said anything incriminating in public against it. Upon his return to New York, he continued to live in relative isolation. One writer, however, claimed that Villa detested the Marcoses and mocked them with impersonations at the Philippine Center on Fifth Avenue.[86] Villa's only public comments against the Marcos dictatorship both involved Carlos P. Romulo. In 1981, Romulo pleased Marcos by winning a lucrative deal from the Americans on the U.S. bases.[87] Marcos decided to reward the aging Romulo with the National Artist Award for Literature, which he had long coveted. Incensed by Marcos's decision, Villa and Nick Joaquin made the gesture of returning their National Artist Awards to the Philippine government. They were told that they could not do so because the awards were "unreturnable." In a 1982 interview with the literary historians Doreen Fernández and Edilberto Alegre, Villa lamented Romulo's unexplainable attempt to derail his reappointment to the Philippine UN Mission. The basis of Villa's criticism of Romulo was personal and revealed his bitterness toward the general. As Villa explained, "President Marcos had already signed my extension, but (General) Romulo resubmitted it to (President) Marcos for reconsideration on the grounds of my age. He [Romulo] is at least 17 or 18 years older than I am, and he has an appointment for life. (President) Marcos gave him a life appointment. At his age!" Reminded of Salvador P. Lopez's relation to Romulo, Villa defiantly replied: "Romulo helped S. P. and S. P. owes Romulo a lot: I don't owe Romulo anything. You see, without his post, Romulo is nothing. . . . He claims that his post is important . . . So he wants power through his position. Sad, sad."[88]

Later Life: The Persistence of Tradition and Ethnicity

In the last few decades of his life, Villa's classrooms or small workshops provided the arena for his daily performances, and his activities showed the persistence of Philippine family and social class upon his art.[89] Villa developed paternal relationships with some of his students, especially those who admired him. When Villa was laid off from the Philippine UN Mission in 1962, he supported himself by teaching poetry at the New School for Social

Research, close to his own home in Greenwich Village.[90] Through the New School, he met several students who were to study under him for a long time, including John Cowen, Robert L. King, and Arthur Vanderborg.[91]

Villa's extreme pedagogical antics—his use of "cajolery, threats, and insults to bring out the best from his students"[92]—recall the extreme, controlling influence that his own father had exerted upon him. Villa's students recorded his terrifying or humiliating classroom environment. For instance, a student of Villa's at the New School, the African American poet Calvin Forbes, wrote that "José and the class had laughed at my first poem, yes, a crude poem I see now, though their laughter hurt me to the bone back then. But I learned my lesson, heeded José's advice, and came back two weeks later with a poem that everybody praised. I became one of his special students."[93] Villa, Cowen said, "was not at all reluctant about going for the jugular, and many students often dropped his course to avoid his ridicule and insulting barrage of verbal assaults about their lack of intelligence." Students broke down in tears when they failed to match Villa's "verbal diatribes."[94] Cirilo Bautista added that, "In front of his horrified class . . . he once threw into the trash can the newly-published book of poems by a leading American poet that one of his students was raving about because, according to Villa, that was where it belonged."[95] Robert King summed up the underlying message of Villa's first course: "If you think you know poetry, forget it—you don't know poetry!" The second course seemed to say to him, "I am going to teach you the few formal things that can be taught about writing poetry, but do not expect to be a poet when we get done, or ever." King deduced that Villa's intimidating manner and insults were a kind of "litmus test" to weed out the unserious students.[96]

Not all of Villa's admirers, however, accepted his harsh tactics. In 1972, the Philippine poet Leonidas V. Benesa provided a highly critical evaluation of Villa's pedagogy. Benesa had come to New York to visit the legendary Philippine exile, having written a hagiographic review of Villa's *Selected Poems and New* in 1962. However, he found Villa's teaching methods distasteful and spoke his mind.[97] He described a meeting of Villa's class at Euro's Bar, at the corner of Fourteenth Street and Sixth Avenue. Villa "came in, like a true guru," surrounded by his students, Benesa wrote. The group had just come from their poetry class and all were still "shaking," especially one named Marshall, who blurted to Villa, "I could have killed you!" Villa simply ignored him and said for Benesa's benefit, "I call them the New Barbarians . . . They come to me to be civilized." "To be chastised," retorted Benesa, "there's a distinction between the two, you know." Villa ignored him and began to discourse on poetics.

Benesa described his observations of Villa in words that suggest the transference of Villa's difficulties with his father onto his students. Villa, Benesa wrote, relished "playing the role of the Nasty Old Man . . . he was living and loving—and hating—with them [his students], a combination of the existential approach and the Socratic method." Benesa concluded that Villa was "definitely a sadistic person" who enjoyed "the discomfiture he inflicts on his subjects, believing . . . that the traumatic treatment is absolutely necessary to establish the rapport needed." While he saw one workshop with Villa as effective in developing students' ear for poetry, he found it "tragic" that many of them stayed on. He described the psychological bondage that developed in preternatural terms: "Villa casts his spells, like a witch, so that his students fall into some kind of thralldom forever. . . . The more successful they are, the less able they are to break loose, to unhex themselves of his bondage. The abuse that the guru heaps upon them seems to bind them more closely to him in a very subtle form of Machiavellianism."[98]

Villa continued to teach even after officially ending his duties at the New School, fashioning not only students' aesthetic sensibilities but also their moral identities. He assembled students who wanted to continue studying with him and developed an "Advanced Poetry Workshop III," which met at his apartment at 780 Greenwich Street. Villa continued to intrigue his students with his integration of poetry and ethics. His courses usually began at 8 or 9 P.M. and would go on until well past midnight. Villa offered his students martinis on the house. He began his sessions with "table talk," in which he would pass around news clippings, cartoons, occasional poems, and his own aphorisms, asking students to consider their relationship to literature or life in general. Robert King would later call the class "Life 101," while John Cowen remembered Villa saying that his was "a course in humanism" in which poets refined "not only their craft, but their own lives," and weeded out "uncultivated" poets as much as poetry. Villa likened the workshop to a "reform school," where students shaped their "spiritual" and not just their "aesthetic lives."[99]

After "table talk," students' poems were circulated, analyzed, refined, and criticized in a seemingly freewheeling manner. Students applied Villa's "adaptation technique," which he had first used in *Selected Poems and New* (1958). Villa described the sessions as "experiments in the conversion of prose through technical manipulation," drawing on "published letters, journals, [and] notebooks"; at times, they took the form of exercises in piecing various parts of a prose work into a new unity, or what he called "Collages."[100] In his classes, Villa gave more specific guidelines for the use of titles, removal or repetition of words, and the manipulation of grammar and syntax.[101] Luis Francia described these sessions of reworking poems as intense, "no-holds barred" affairs, even "critical jousts," where poets had to be on their toes, especially in articulating their opinions of a poem.[102] In these sessions, Villa highlighted his conceptions of poetry, which were linked to a fundamental notion of performativity.

Indeed, the sessions reinforced Villa's own dogma of the primacy or peremptory place of form over content, or narrative. "Meaning didn't matter much . . . that was the prose or narrative mentality," Francia continues. "Anathema to the poet's creed." Even more telling was Villa's chivalric injunction to poets "not to read fiction, to purify ourselves . . . and have that lyric spirit fly unfettered."[103] Villa's mantra was "Form, form, form . . . without it matter was immaterial. Never mind your poetic soul (a word he hated): You either had it or you didn't, so there was no point in worrying about it." The end result was that the poet "emerged leaner, meaner, a sainted warrior poet armed and dangerous."[104]

While made up of those who personally admired him and had devoted themselves to Villa's poetic theory, Villa's workshop provoked strong reactions. Luis Francia complained of an inability to sleep whenever Villa praised or castigated his poetry. Luis Cabalquinto, a close friend of Villa's, provided a sobering assessment of his friend and mentor. Villa had attempted to mold Cabalquinto, but the latter objected to his attempt to make "clones" out of his students.[105] He found Villa "very controlling," not only imposing his aesthetics but also his moral values upon students' lives, insisting on a "sophisticated" lifestyle, with "courtly manners," in a domineering way, "like his father." Even worse, Cabalquinto complained of Villa's intolerance for dissenting views: "[Y]ou had to toe the line . . . You don't get influenced by other writers. Only Villa, E. E. Cummings, and Marianne Moore were valid."[106]

Beyond teaching, the manner in which performativity and ethnicity meshed in Villa's life manifested themselves in his refusal to relinquish his Filipino citizenship and in his extraordinary championing of Filipino food. Villa once described himself as a "Filipino, but an American resident." His choice of eschewing American citizenship in favor of remaining a Filipino national might have been rooted in economic reasons, such as his continuing need for Philippine government patronage.[107] He nonetheless believed that there were times when he had suffered because of his choice of nationality. For instance, he claimed that he had been denied the Bollingen Prize in Poetry for *Volume Two* because he was not an American citizen, and that Oscar Williams had refused to anthologize his poetry for the same narrow-minded reason.[108] At the same time, there were prominent intellectuals in the Philippines who questioned the sincerity of his Filipino nationality. The prolific Philippine novelist F. Sionil José said of Villa: "He's not Filipino. There's nothing Filipino in his writings, in his thoughts. He's a third-rate poet and I don't know why they made him a National Artist. Although he has a Philippine passport, he hasn't lived here. He hasn't done anything for this country. He wants to be this universal artist. He's self-serving. He only comes here when they give him an award. He enjoys all these accolades. But he hasn't written anything since the 1950s."[109] Arnold Azurin, a notable anthropologist at the University of the Philippines, echoed José's sentiments: "Villa has retained his Filipino nationality, or so he constantly reminds his friends from the Philippines who pay homage to him at his flat in New York. . . . He has become . . . naturalized as a bohemian New Yorker. . . . Hence his nationality as a Filipino may be documented through his passport but hardly in his 'ethnic or national soul,' to put it in a nativistic manner."[110]

Villa's early conceptions of ethnicity were rooted in disdain for national particularities and a belief in the universality of human values. The poem "The Country That Is My Country," for instance, disavows patriotism ("flags") and "all separations" of nationality. Instead, the poetic narrator embraces "Fellowman," "The Human Being," or "The Man."[111]

Villa loved to play with his place, identity, and ethnicity. For instance, in his ,,A Composition,, *[sic]* of 1953 (the title of which is a play on punctuation), the poetic narrator claims to be either "José" or "Villa" [a blurring of names], to have been "born on the *island* of Manila, in the *city* of Luzon" [an inversion of actual geographies], and to be from the "*Country* of Doveg-lion," hence not from a nation-state but from a country of myth and romance, which transports the reader to another time and place (medieval Europe, perhaps), perhaps even eternity (for "Boundaries it has none . . .") (emphases added). The poet, nonetheless, decides later that he does belong to a territory after all. He claims a country, but one whose boundaries are determined not by politics but by Art. In this artistic land, the poetic voice says "subhumans" may not reside, only "Earth Angels," whom he calls "the true humans," because they are the only ones who "perceive" the "hazards" that he must endure as an artist. The sovereign power of that mythic land grants these people "citizenship," and at the same time, he humbles himself before them and claims their camaraderie.[112] Toward the end of his life, Villa would reaffirm his distance from ethnic or nationalist politics and the fact that he "was never and [could] never be an activist."[113]

Yet, while he frowned upon activism, he reveled in extravagant displays of ethnic nationalism and nostalgia whenever the topic of Filipino cuisine was involved. The critic Jonathan Chua wrote that Villa was "finicky about food" and that he could be "as supercilious about it as about Philippine literature." Consuming authentic Filipino food appears to have been Villa's token of returning home: "He misses authentic Philippine longanisa [Chinese Philippine pork sausages] and wants only fresh shrimps 'na may ulo' [with heads] and sotanghon 'na walang sabaw' [rice noodles without the broth, cooked traditionally]."[114] Perhaps no topic could make Villa immediately revert to code switching, between Tagalog and English, or Taglish, more quickly than food. What his poetry could not say about his ethnicity, his palate and his stomach did. Hilario Francia wrote that Villa thought American cooking tasteless. He loved Filipino cooking so much that he would travel to Francia's brother and sister-in-law's house in Haworth, New Jersey, just to partake of Filipino food and cooking. "Villa's stomach is so Pinoy, it was impossible to convert it to any other nationality," Francia said.[115]

Villa's obsession with food was in part rooted in the hunger he encountered as a struggling poet in the 1930s, but it was also based on a mixed sense of propriety and a celebration of the sensuality he found in Filipino culture. When he returned to the Philippines in 1959, at fifty-two, he said: "All my life I have been underweight and underfed. Now my ambition is to weigh a hundred and sixty pounds."[116] But the gourmand's scrupulousness about food equally stemmed from absolute standards of food's place in society (or society's manner of consumption). John Cowen recalled, for example, that

Villa had once been invited to read his poetry at the house of Rita Drag-onette, a New York poet. Villa refused to read his poems but asked Cowen to read them in his place. The poetry reading, said Cowen, "was followed by a buffet at which Villa began to insult his hostess's poor American style of cuisine. 'In the Philippines, one does not serve cereal and beans at a recep-tion; several fine meats and outstanding accompanying dishes glorify the table: this food is only fit for horses!'"[117] Finally, Villa's love for Filipino food was a celebration of pure sensuality. Villa's enjoyment of the sensual delights of food perhaps extended his attempts at valorizing sex, animality, and the body. When Luis Cabalquinto made his monthly visits to Villa in 1994, he brought three of Villa's favorite foods—*tuyo* [salted dried fish], *tinapa* [dried fish], and canned mangoes from the neighborhood Philippine grocery. Villa was elated: "I love Filipino food," he said. "I can't live without our tasty dishes—*adobo, kare-kare, pansit, crispy pata, lumpia.*"[118]

⌒

Villa lived long enough to receive the highest honors his country could give him. But even as late as 1978, he was again deprived of his job at the United Nations, only to be reinstated in October 1980 through the help of the writer Adrian Cristobal. Villa was shaken by his insecurity. Yet once he re-gained his composure, he challenged the Philippine government in 1985 to grant him an Honorary Lifetime Diplomatic Passport that would allow him to go in and out of the country.[119] Toward the end of his life, Philippine in-tellectuals showed genuine concern for his well-being; many wished to repa-triate him, because he remained their National Artist. A. Z. Jolicco Cuadra called upon the government to pay for Villa's New York apartment for three months to enable him to serve as resident poet of the University of the Philippines. Cuadra went so far as to say that Villa deserved the Nobel Prize.[120] When Villa's health worsened, Adrian Cristobal called upon the public to remember Villa's accomplishments and argued that "he is the near-est to a great poet that we have."[121] Upon learning of Villa's worsening con-dition, Philippine President Fidel V. Ramos himself ordered the Foreign Af-fairs Department to assist him. Upon his death in February 1997, the National Commission on Culture and the Arts (NCCA) paid for his burial plot in New York. President Ramos, whom Villa had respected, publicly eu-logized him.[122]

In various ways, Villa's life highlights the continuing influence of Philippine letters and Philippine culture upon his extreme modernism. While he drew his artistic principles from Western avant-garde movements, he was also influenced by the Filipino American colonial and postcolonial cultural milieu. Through his reliance upon Philippine state patronage (especially the diplomatic corps) and his attempts to patronize Filipino writers from his location in America, Villa remained institutionally connected to Philippine society. While he suffered the governmental neglect experienced by most Filipino English writers and expatriates, Villa was eventually recognized by a government that had once judged him unfit for foreign service and was rewarded by various political patrons. Moreover, his poetical pedagogy revealed the return of family and social class beliefs that Villa had repressed or had attempted to exclude from his poetic experiments. Finally, in daily life encounters with other artists, Villa performed his ethnicity by staunchly maintaining his Filipino citizenship and championing Filipino cuisine, which evoked his bilingual and bicultural heritage and his nostalgia for the Philippine past.

FOUR

Nativism and Negation: N. V. M. Gonzalez

In 1997, an American writer, James McEnteer, recounted his journey to Romblon with N. V. M. Gonzalez (1915–1999) and his wife Narita. Along the way, McEnteer writes, Gonzalez struck up a conversation with two *balikbayan* women also returning to the province.[1] One of them sighed, "Growing up here I didn't appreciate this place. . . . Now I just want to come back and leave the rest behind." The other woman asked Gonzalez when was the last time he had gone back. Gonzalez replied, "I never left home." McEnteer noted Gonzalez's "raised eyebrows and [his] wide, open mouthed smile, sharing in the surprise and delight of his own answer." He added, "[D]espite his long, often expatriate career, Gonzalez has kept his focus fixed firmly on the Philippines and the lives of Filipinos." Gonzalez, he said, described his "long absences from the Philippines" as "'merely physical, a concession to geography.'"[2]

This anecdote condenses the main themes of Gonzalez's life explored in this chapter. The elements of nationalism, performance, and reciprocity found in the repertoires of Filipino American expatriate intellectuals like Romulo, Bulosan, and Villa are suggested here by the motif of homecoming and Gonzalez's relationship to other Filipino migrants, particularly with women of a lower social class.[3] In this scene, Gonzalez seems to deny that he has ever been an expatriate ("I never left home") and conveys the message that his history as an immigrant in America ("merely physical, a concession to geography") is unimportant. What mattered for Gonzalez was the imagination, which remained "fixed firmly" on Philippine soil, despite several decades of absence. Denying his historical location and the passage of time away from the Philippines also suggests the desire for an unchanged and authentic identity. Moreover, the passage captures Gonzalez's humor and charm and his understatement for effect. These signs of everyday performance and consciousness of audience link Gonzalez to the ilustrados and pensionados, to Romulo's oratory, Bulosan's storytelling, and Villa's theatricality. At the same time, in his attempt to erase his migrant history, Gonzalez seems to depart from Romulo's "expatriate affirmation," Bulosan's diasporic consciousness, and Villa's cultural exile, which in various ways accept, if not celebrate, "foreign" experiences as constitutive of national identity. Gonzalez gestures toward a Filipino nativism that informs much of his postwar writing. Such an ideology attempted to reconstruct Filipino history and culture not only on the foundations of secular nationalism, folk culture, and oral tradition, and Philippine pre-Hispanic myths but also upon a mythicized personal history. In this way, literature and biography, text and context become inextricable in understanding Gonzalez's life and work. This combination had a complex evolution. Gonzalez was, after all, a fiction writer and literary theorist par excellence, and it is through his works of fiction and criticism and the reciprocal personal relationships that grew out of them that his ideas evolved. Indeed, any intellectual history of so complex a thinker requires that one be attentive to the paths that he took, as well as the disguises that might throw one off track.

Gonzalez was born in Romblon and grew up in Mindoro. He began sending his writings to the *Philippine Magazine* in the early 1930s when he also wrote for the weekly *Graphic*. The emerging fields of anthropology and folklore studies and the influence of literary realism during the 1930s and 1940s affected his anthropologically mediated literary theory (centering upon the trope of the "native"), especially after World War II. Throughout much of his career, this would provide the unique line of commentary about his works. Magazine editors found Gonzalez's stories "haunting." They praised his use of "local color" in describing the Mindoro *kaingin*,[4] the clearings of the impoverished slash-and-burn agriculturists, while others read them as charming "tales."[5] While some postwar critics focused on his literary craftsmanship,[6] others addressed what I regard as his fusion of nativism and formalism. They pointed to the influences of myth and literary artistry in his work and his humanization of the lower classes, particularly women and children.[7] They praised his attempt to rejuvenate Philippine postwar culture with mythic "life symbols" such as the bamboo and traced his themes of class conflict to older Philippine literary traditions.[8] During much of his stay in the United States, from 1968 to 1999, Asian American critics largely ignored his "Philippine" fiction and literary theorizing.[9] In the last years of his life, however, in the wake of the rethinking of theory in Asian American studies, interest focused on the element of "displacement" in Gonzalez's writings, his tropes of "wandering" and "nomadism," and his imaginative returns to the Philippine homeland.[10]

These considerations of formalist method, myth, tradition, and migration constitute important aspects of Gonzalez's complex, heterogeneous nationalism, but they need to be seen in the context of his life, especially its institutional contexts and networks of obligation. His life and work represent the tension between a desire for nationalist community and authenticity and the individual urgings of literary ambition. More important, Gonzalez normalized the complexities arising from this tension through what might be termed "expatriate negation," or a denial of the value of expatriation in Filipino intellectual life. Gonzalez at times concealed his life's rough edges, the irritations, and the hardships he had encountered, especially while away from his homeland, in an effort at self-mythologization. As with many "postcolonial" intellectuals, Gonzalez's striving for "roots" grew as he traced various "routes" across the Philippines, the Pacific, and throughout the world. Recurring obsessions with place, language, and home found expression in tropes of rootedness, authenticity, and indigenousness.[11]

There is nothing simple about Gonzalez. The dislocations of his life and the multiple layers of his fiction subvert and provide ironic counterpoints to his nationalist desire. His nativist discourse tends to hide his ambivalence to shifting geographic and cultural locations, which compelled him to reassess the meanings of Filipino-ness. My task in this chapter is to show the possibilities and limits of this approach. To do this, I shall explore Gonzalez's career and his intellectual genealogy. The first segment traces the origins of Gonzalez's poetics through the reassessment of the Filipino past that emerged out of World War II, his advocacy of vernacular writing, and his relations of patronage. In the second phase, from the late 1960s to the mid

1980s, Gonzalez experienced his longest period away from the Philippines as a result of martial law, and during this time he taught at California State University, Hayward. The segment explores his diagnosis of the postcolonial *problems* of Filipinos and Filipino Americans, his psychological prescriptions for their overcoming, and the limitations posed by his solutions. Finally, the third and final segment explores Gonzalez's career from the mid 1980s to the late 1990s as a post-Marcos transpacific commuter whose energies were equally divided between the Philippines and the United States. It explores his simultaneous reassertion of nativism and his reaching toward a pluralistic and eclectic poetics.

Gonzalez and the Colonial Basis of Filipino Nationalisms

The period beginning with the Japanese occupation of the Philippines in 1942 and ending in 1968, when Gonzalez's second sojourn to the United States began, was the most active phase of Gonzalez's life. During this time, besides writing most of his fiction, he mentored a new generation of writers through the courses and writers' workshops he taught at the University of the Philippines,[12] where he began teaching in 1950. He founded the critically acclaimed *Diliman Review,* served as editor for the young publisher Alberto Benipayo, and launched the Philippine Writers' Union. At the same time, he raised four children with Narita and traveled on fellowships to three continents.[13] As we have already seen, these two decades coincided with a turbulent period in Philippine history and Philippine-American relations. Gonzalez spent the first two years of the Japanese occupation in Manila. Late in 1942, he married Narita Manuel, a graduate of the University of the Philippines. The Japanese interrogated and tortured his father, and after hearing rumors of his arrest, Gonzalez and Narita fled to Mindoro. There, they spent a "forced vacation" for the duration of the war.[14] Echoing Narita, Gonzalez recalls that his "family's main concern was food," but they "sat it out there for the next two years with the guerrillas." Gonzalez also continued writing. He managed to obtain a typewriter and "used and re-used" its ribbon, occasionally "moistening it with coconut oil."[15]

Gonzalez's statement perhaps downplays the hardships of travel and survival during the war, which confronted him and other Filipino writers with drastic intellectual changes. He describes the shock of the American defeat. "The Japanese advance," according to Gonzalez, "was preceded by a lot of American propaganda calculated to make the Filipinos [feel] completely safe from attack." Most Filipinos believed that the Japanese were "no more than *apa* [ice cream cone] vendors," one of their popular occupations, and that the Americans were invincible. However, after the third day of the bombing of Manila, the city was "inundated by [Japanese] soldiers." Filipinos, with great difficulty, "had to learn how to bow." The "reality" of the [Bataan] Death March was "too much to accept."[16]

The Filipino historian Teodoro Agoncillo describes the predicament in which Manila intellectuals found themselves, which forced writers like Gonzalez to reexamine their pasts, laying the foundations of his postwar nativist worldview. For Agoncillo, the problem of Filipino writers during the war involved "identification and culture" in a time of isolation from "Western thought." Since the present was "dismal" and the future "nebulous," the writers "began to think of the past" and they soon "re-discovered [their] forebears." They realized, "although painfully and, perhaps, reluctantly," that their heritage had been "blurred by centuries of foreign domination."[17] Moreover, the word "foreign" here became equated with "Western," not Japanese, domination. Hence, self-examination kindled an anti-Western feeling that had been prevalent in Japan's own propaganda in Asia. In the interests of its plan for a "Co-Prosperity Sphere," the Japanese colonial government instituted a cultural policy that discouraged English and instead institutionalized Tagalog, or "Pilipino," above and beyond other vernaculars, as the official national language.[18] Moreover, the Japanese encouraged Tagalog literature and even published an anthology, *Ang 25 Pinakamabuting Maikling Katháng Pilipino ng 1943* (The Twenty-five Best Filipino Short Stories of 1943).[19]

Filipino English writers like Gonzalez were practically forced to write in Tagalog in order to survive, and to do so they had to relearn a language that had become like a foreign tongue as a result of what had been their total immersion in English. Gonzalez himself was not a native Tagalog speaker. Having grown up in Romblon and Mindoro, two remote provinces at the crossroads of major linguistic communities, he spoke Hiligaynon and some Tagalog, which he probably had more occasion to use as an adult in Manila working for the prewar *Graphic*. Gonzalez claims to have learned "Tagalog by listening to politicians deliver their promise-loaded speeches."[20] In Agoncillo's appraisal of Tagalog writers during the war, Gonzalez deserves both criticism and praise. Agoncillo argues, on one hand, that Gonzalez's short story entry in a Tagalog writing contest, "Lunsod, Nayon, at Dagat-Dagatan" ("City, Countryside, and Lake") suffers from anglicisms that make the narrative sound awkward, if not comical, in the vernacular. He claims that like many other anglophone Filipino writers, Gonzalez had originally written his story in English and then had it translated into Tagalog. On the other hand, Agoncillo praises Gonzalez for writing in Tagalog even after the war, when other writers had reverted back to English. This, to Agoncillo, was a sure mark of Gonzalez's genuine commitment to the language and by implication proved his authenticity as a Filipino, even though Tagalog was not even his mother tongue.[21]

Japanese language and cultural policy led to a breach in Gonzalez's and other Filipino intellectuals' self-understanding as exclusively Western, if not white, in identity and culture. Tagalog usage compelled not only linguistic but cultural reexamination. Agoncillo's account is useful here. According to him, the writers were painfully "confused," especially since conquest had caused them to forget the "*brown* man with a simple culture," which was part of their own "personality." After the war, Filipino writers were "told to be ourselves," but alas they "did not know how." Agoncillo cites a legal scholar and writer in Spanish, Manuel Briones, who called upon Filipinos to junk the "ridiculous mimicry" of the West, return to "the ancient virtues," and find nourishment in "the Oriental cultural foundation."[22] Agoncillo uses the popular tropes of identity crisis and a return to the past, which recall the ilustrados' nationalist narrative of a "golden age" of Philippine civilization and its decline under Western exploitation. But while the ilustrados were guilty of exaggerations in the interests of claiming social justice and cultural equality with the Spaniards, the intellectuals of the 1940s, under the sway of Japanese power and racialism were coming to a different solution to their confusions. What is telling in Agoncillo's account is the reduction of what is authentically Filipino culture to Philippine pre-Hispanic culture and the Orientalist alignment of the Filipino's psychology with the East, "whose way of life, philosophy, and culture were more adapted to his *personality.*" These claims in effect denied the hybridity and heterogeneousness of Filipino culture and psychology, disparaging its Western graftings as "ridiculous mimicry" while at the same time denying the mimicry of imitating Japan's anti-Westernism and Orientalism. These historical shifts in the character of Filipino nationalism, which find parallel in the experiences of other Third World nationalist intellectuals, would have a profound impact upon Gonzalez and other Filipinos.[23]

The Japanese occupation's cultural policy, which discouraged English and American culture, led intellectuals of Gonzalez's generation to two approaches, both aiming at the reconstruction of Filipino identity and the Philippine past and defining the essential elements of being Filipino. One group, led by the fiction writer Nick Joaquin, asserted Filipinos' Hispanic heritage. While Joaquin would become one of the Philippines' most successful writers in English after World War II, he inherited the convictions of Filipino writers in Spanish who had, like the Japanese, criticized American imperialism, among them Isabelo de los Reyes (a.k.a., "Don Belong"), a folklorist and founder of the Philippine Independent Church and the country's first labor union, and Teodoro M. Kalaw, the former editor of the Spanish-language newspaper *La Independencia*.[24] Joaquin advocated a rethinking of Filipinos' Hispanic history. Opposing attacks on the Spaniards and the attempt to root Filipino culture in the pre-Hispanic period, Joaquin argued that Spain, not the ancient Philippines, had created the "form" of Filipino national identity—"religion and national unity"—which he deemed more important than its content. For Joaquin, Spain had "give[n] birth" to the Philippines and Filipinos "as a nation, as an historical people" out of "numberless tongues, bloods, and cultures."[25]

The other alternative possibility for Gonzalez and Filipino nationalists was that embodied by Japanese cultural policy, which encouraged Filipinos to rely upon their native cultural resources by writing in Tagalog and expressing "who they were." Filipino writers, as Agoncillo says, saw through the propaganda aims of the Japanese colonial linguistic strategy.[26] But they did acknowledge the truths that Japanese cultural policy revealed, although they may have been forced upon them. "Suspect or not," Agoncillo continues, "the Japanese succeeded in projecting Tagalog to the consciousness of the Filipinos as a language to be desired and developed."[27] Inevitably, the imperative to write in the vernacular led to a new consciousness of the tradition of Tagalog writing in the Philippines, which had experienced a renaissance in the 1930s, during the era of American colonial rule. Many Filipino intellectuals "discovered," moreover, that this tradition had its roots in the precolonial and Spanish colonial eras. Tagalog vernacular writing was rich and heterogeneous, from the riddles and love songs of pre-Hispanic times to the literary modernists of the twentieth century who borrowed techniques derived from English writing, infused by themes from animism to socialism.[28] All of these vernacular genres embodied notions of time and space, and, perhaps most important, myths, metaphors, and symbols that differed from the anglophone world to which Filipino writers in English like Romulo, Villa, Bulosan, and Gonzalez, and others like them in the Philippines, had inevitably been drawn. This subsequently forced a rethinking of culture that validated not only the vernacular but also the Philippines' indigenous, pre-Western, and especially oral cultural legacies.

World War II and the postwar period would have a profound impact upon the evolution of Gonzalez's nativist poetics. Given his own class and regional backgrounds and a temperament that emphasized austerity and understatement in writing, Gonzalez eschewed Joaquin's version of nationalism. He did, however, follow the cultural nationalists in calling for a return to pre-Hispanic culture. Over time, his recuperation of Tagalog oral culture and literary tradition was to become intertwined with the moralism of the postwar nationalist discourse of authenticity. Gonzalez's arrangement of his prewar fiction, for instance, signaled these nativist literary influences. After the war, Gonzalez returned to Manila, where he accepted a position as editor of the *Evening News*. He simultaneously published a collection of his prewar short stories, *Seven Hills Away* (1947). According to Gonzalez, these stories of the Mindoro *kaingin* reflected near literal renditions of events he had heard of or experienced as a teenager after he had failed to gain admission to the University of the Philippines. "I had two years," he said, "of what you might call apprenticeship [in his father's meat business] in towns and villages, inadvertently living the life I was later to describe—talking to people, finding my way around, committing to memory . . . every turn of the road, every bush by the wayside."[29] This had brought him into contact with the *kaingineros*, including the indigenous tribal people of Mindoro Oriental's highlands, the Hanunoo-Mangyan, who regarded the lowlanders as *sandugo*, or "of one blood."[30] Gonzalez's *Seven Hills Away* and many other subsequent writings thus made up a kind of ethnographic record of lowland Mindoro during the 1920s and 1930s.[31]

The stories of *Seven Hills Away* are arranged so as to create a vivid portrait of life in the hinterlands of Mindoro. "The Pioneer," "Life and Death in a Mindoro Kaingin," and "The Planting" tell of the pioneering spirit of the kaingineros, the struggles of husbands and wives to work and to raise children, their animist belief in the spirits residing in nature, and their movement deeper into the forest to find new clearings. Through the experiences of sailors returning home, "Far Horizons" mirrors the restlessness of the kaingineros and shows the illusions of those they leave behind, who must cope with their prolonged absence. A series of stories deromanticizing the kaingin then follows. "Owl in the Moon" narrates the shame of a kaingineros's wife who spends an adulterous evening with the landowner. "Hunger in Barok" depicts the seasonal hunger in the kaingin and a landowner's exploitation of his tenants' initiative. "White Mare in the Corn" shows a boy's guilt for his uncle's spearing of a stray horse. And "Pare Lucio" and "The Old Priest" narrate the journey of an accused murderer and his police captor to town and the moral decline of a beloved priest. Finally, a series of stories focus upon children. "The Baby" is about a couple's journey to present their infant child to their parents and in-laws. In "Seven Hills Away," we glimpse the life of a pioneer landowning family (and their struggle to rebuild their homes after a fire destroys their property) through the eyes of a seven-year-old boy. And, finally, the teenage child of "The Happiest Boy in the World" journeys away from the drudgery of his father's farming life to fulfill his dream of an education.

Gonzalez's stories fulfilled the prewar thirst for realistic renditions of the Philippine scene ("local color").[32] As one critic wrote of the so-called Period of Emergence of Philippine Letters in English (1930–44), "The overall concern of writers and critics alike . . . was the creation of a *national literature.*" Reflecting the themes of *Seven Hills Away*, he writes of what critics thought a national literature should consist: "simple barrio life, the rugged virtues of simple folk, tropical nature and the great national heroes," which they believed could reveal "something of the *Malayan Spirit*" (emphasis added).[33] This simultaneous emphasis on regionalism and nationalism linked Gonzalez's nuanced stories and Philippine colonial literature in general to the rise of nationalism and ethno-racialist thinking—here I am thinking of Herder's *Volksgeist* and Anglo-Saxonism—that captured European and American imaginations in the nineteenth century. The irony of this nationalist impulse in Filipino literature, however, was that colonial white American intellectuals had encouraged and laid the foundation for it in the early twentieth century, given their interests in cultural anthropology, folklore, religion, and myth.[34]

Gonzalez's year of study in the United States during his Rockefeller fellowship in 1949 would expand the creative and critical basis for his prewar nativist ideas. His teachers exposed him to literary theories and literary critics that would be lifelong preoccupations. Gonzalez spent a semester at Stanford University's Writing Center under Wallace Stegner and summer at the Kenyon School of English in Ohio. He also attended lectures at Columbia University and the notable Bread Loaf Writers' Conference in Middlebury, Vermont. New Criticism, which owed its origins to T. S. Eliot, I. A. Richards, and William Empson in the 1920s, was becoming a mainstay of English departments throughout the United States during the Cold War as a result of the academic positions of its adherents and its conservative political bent.[35] Many of Gonzalez's teachers studied or supported New Criticism. These included Stegner, Katherine Anne Porter, and Yvor Winters at Stanford; the so-called "Southern Agrarians" (Allen Tate and his wife Caroline Gordon, John Crowe Ransom, and Robert Penn Warren), René Wellek, and Herbert Read at the Kenyon School of English; and Mark Schorer and Susanne K. Langer at Columbia University. Gonzalez was exposed by the New Critics to Henry James and the importance of technique in fiction writing. New Critics highlighted James's deft use of point of view, especially of limited narrators, not only as a technical innovation but also as a way of setting limitations to consciousness and truth. Gonzalez also learned the importance of "intrinsic" versus "extrinsic" criticism, of the value of the "text" and "close reading," and the irrelevance of the biographical, social, moral, or political context to an assessment of a work of art. As Gonzalez himself would later say, he learned how to read his texts with "objectivity," a hermeneutic practice related to the New Critics' attention to the formal aspects of texts—narrative structure, symbol, metaphor, and characterization. Finally, Gonzalez imbibed the value of irony, paradox, and ambiguity, which reinforced his already understated prose.[36]

Perhaps more important than their teachings was the example that the New Critics provided Gonzalez of the possibilities of synthesizing modernism and nativism. As much as they loved the sublimity and universal appeal of literature, Tate, Schorer, Gordon, and Porter wrote with passion about their home region, the American South.[37] As young adults, these Southerners had been separated from their home. Ransom, Tate, and Penn Warren studied abroad as Rhodes Scholars at Oxford. At various times, Tate and Gordon lived among expatriates in Paris. Like colonial intellectuals, they became more nativist (embracing Southern regionalism) at the same time as they were becoming more cosmopolitan and more modern in outlook. When they returned to the United States, however, many of them would find teaching opportunities not in the South but in the North, which only exacerbated their nostalgia for home. Perhaps it was their very "expatriation" that made the Southern Agrarians, for instance, cling onto their image of the South, providing an existential analogue to Gonzalez's expatriation to America in 1949.

Similarly, the very avant-garde modernism of the New Critics was at least in part the result of the sublimation of their feelings of displacement from home, which led them to look back at the traditions of the South, of family, geography, and history. In the case of Katherine Anne Porter, Gonzalez's professor at Stanford, it also intensified other traditions, such as white supremacy, a topic that Gonzalez almost never broached. During the postwar civil rights era, Porter's southern nativism would lead to advocacy of segregation. Porter disliked black writers like Richard Wright and Ralph Ellison and excluded them from her list of readings for writing courses. Gonzalez never mentions reading these writers. It is also telling that Gonzalez never met Carlos Bulosan while in the United States, but sought out Villa in New York.[38]

But myth criticism was also gaining vogue during the period of Gonzalez's first sojourn in the United States and would have an even more profound impact upon his nativism. Susanne K. Langer, Carl Jung, Joseph Campbell, and Northrop Frye—all of whom were profound influences upon Gonzalez—were united in their common view that myth is inherent in the thinking process and fulfills a basic human need.[39] Langer, one of Gonzalez's favorite writers, exposed him to Ernst Cassirer's *Philosophy of Symbolic Forms* (1925), which argues that myth is a form of thought, a "symbolic form" that is fundamental to the human response to the world. According to Cassirer, myth is even more basic than language in involving the primal, emotion-laden language of experience.[40] From these basic premises,

Langer would argue that emotional and aesthetic experiences were best rendered by structures of myth, ritual, and art, and not by discursive, "syntactical" language.[41] Carl Jung was, of course, central to the dissemination of myth theory among Western scholars of religion, literature, and art, especially by way of his concept of the "collective unconscious," a kind of "racial memory, consisting of 'primordial images' or archetypes."[42] These archetypes included the recurrence in widely divergent cultures around the world of figures such as "the Earth Mother, the divine child, the wise old man, [and] the sacrificial death of the god." Campbell extended Jung's uncovering of "timeless human patterns in myth and literature" with the idea of the "monomyth," the theory that "all heroes were one hero and all myths were one myth."[43] Campbell also reflected a universalism that for some time influenced Western liberal intellectuals and Gonzalez himself—he was hostile to cultural particularism and nationalism, believing that "accidents of geography, birth-date, and income" were not the essentials of human life.[44] Finally, the widely influential Northrop Frye argued for the hierarchical superiority of myth criticism above all other criticism in his masterwork, *The Anatomy of Criticism*, which was published in 1957, but whose ideas were already circulating in the literary and academic world at the time of Gonzalez's arrival at Kenyon in 1949. Frye believed that all literary forms, including realism, came from myth, especially from biblical and classical Greek sources, and that they over time increasingly returned to their basic mythical origins. He also argued for the "quest myth" as the source of all literature and its many ramifications, an argument that would be of profound significance for Gonzalez.[45]

Upon his return to the Philippines later that year, Gonzalez set about applying the lessons he had imbibed overseas to his own nativist conceptions of literary art. He began to stake out a position critical of urban and foreign influences on the Philippines and to assert the values of rural and indigenous lower-class Filipino life. One senses the immediate impact of Gonzalez's American education in essays, still unpublished in book form, and fictional works that present art and myth as twin answers to the problems of colonialism, the construction of a national literature, and the nuclear age. Gonzalez's prewar essays for the *Graphic* dealing with points of cultural interest, books, current events, and happenings in Manila seem mundane compared to some of the essays he subsequently wrote upon his return from

America.[46] Several of these, including an exploration of "time" in Joseph Conrad and a reading of one of his own stories, "On the Ferry," which shows his increased awareness of *technique* in fictional narration (e.g., "objective correlatives"), reflect the influence of New Criticism. His love for New Criticism shows in an essay on language, which reflects his quasi-religious belief in the power of art to heal worldly problems, and in his appropriation of a pre-Hispanic Philippine riddle as a precursor of New Criticism's reading strategies.[47] Meanwhile, the influence of myth criticism, in tandem with New Critical strategies, is apparent in his searching essays on the importance of tradition in Philippine letters, his exposition of myth and "life symbols" in *The Bamboo Dancers*, and his reading of José Rizal's novels as instances of the "monomyth."[48] Finally, we see Gonzalez expanding his readings of literature to Asian writers who were responding to colonialism and nationalism by using their native languages, folk forms, ethnic literary traditions, and popular myths.[49] In sum, these essays show the compatibility, if not the inextricability, of aesthetic and cultural nationalist concerns in Gonzalez's art, which found their quintessential expression in his fictional works.

In his 1957 novel, *A Season of Grace*, Gonzalez combines the narrative restraint, density of detail, and ironic sensibility of New Criticism and simultaneously conveys a strong sense of place, mythic time, and the importance of anthropological "life symbols," which he had learned from reading Campbell and other myth critics. The novel represents Gonzalez's vision of the Philippines, his passionate feeling for the land, and the rural folk who labor upon it. Gonzalez is a master of understatement, of showing not telling, and of rich descriptions that create a "semblance" of life. He describes the rich landscape and the everyday activities of an archetypal husband and wife, Doro and Sabel, swidden farmers from the island of Tara-Poro who migrate by boat to Sipolog and establish a new life working the land there. As the critic Richard Guzman has argued, Gonzalez is less concerned with chronological events than with embedding everyday events into the cyclical rhythm of mythic time. The protagonists suffer hardships caused by human and natural causes, including a usurious tenancy system, corrupt police officials, and the onslaught of rodents, but they are not perfect; they endure their sufferings with dignity, honesty, if not a sense of humor, only to undergo the same process all over again the next season. Moreover, the central life symbol of the novel, the coconuts that wash up on the shore of the island of Mindoro originating from other islands, come to symbolize the very values of the people and their commitment to rooting themselves in the land.[50] This commitment to the land—that is, the determination to plant seeds upon it or to be washed away—is, for Gonzalez, what distinguishes the authentic from the unauthentic, who can be regarded as a native and who will remain a "foreigner." For instance, the antithesis of Doro and Sabel are Epe Ruda, a firewood "concessionaire," and Tiaga Ruda, his wife. Like Doro and Sabel, they have come from somewhere else, but their inability to plant seeds and to grow crops on native soil stems from their baser qualities rather than from their external origins. Epe Ruda, as we shall see below, fails to live up to his end of reciprocal patron-client relations. Meanwhile, his wife Tiaga, who has brought white sugar from Batangas to remind her of the wealthy life she has left behind, is a harbinger of "progress."[51] Tiaga is described as slick with the rice measurements and quick to advise Epe Ruda on how to get more from his workers.[52] Tellingly, the couple are childless, which in Gonzalez's organicist view of the world is a sign of physical *and* cultural sterility.

Gonzalez's second novel, *The Bamboo Dancers* (1959), continues this dialectic between modernity and tradition, art and myth. The book is a novel within a novel, written in the voice of Ernie Rama, a 26-year-old Filipino sculptor. Like Gonzalez himself, Ernie has studied on a fellowship in the United States in 1956 and traveled to Japan and Taiwan, before returning to the Philippines. The novel, as Gonzalez writes, is a "confession,"[53] Ernie's recollection of his life as an expatriate in America and his journey across the Pacific with two other expatriates, Helen (his writer friend) and Pepe (his doctor brother). It is also about their encounters with Filipinos of their generation, other Asians, and Americans. Of passing importance among the last group is the writer Herb Lane, Helen's fiancé, who dreams of writing a book about the Philippine bamboo dance, or *tinikling*, before he is shot in Taipei for having run over a teenage girl.

The Bamboo Dancers is a quintessentially modernist novel in subject matter and form, the type most favored by the New Critics. It is complex and intellectually challenging, and it would be no understatement to say that Gonzalez had great ambitions in writing it. The novel reflects the influence in particular of Herbert Read, whose analysis of the shift in Western art from an ideal of imitation to one of symbolization and suggestion Ernie

Rama happens to read in a New York library.[54] In line with these reflections, Ernie says in the novel's epilogue that writing it led him to discover "an essential unity" and "the figure" that might have emerged "out of that mass of time and place, out of the speech and dress and fripperies of our day, from all of which, alas, New York and Sipolog have now sprung as one" (329–30). This passage reveals Gonzalez's great faith in art and his meticulous concern with "controlling metaphors," or the "image" that will capture his ideas (which we also see in his essays and in *A Season of Grace*), as well as with the power of the imagination to bridge geographic, temporal, and cultural differences, despite the superficiality and pretensions of the cosmopolitan urban middle classes and the threat of nuclear extinction.[55]

But if the epilogue captures these artistic aims, it also expresses an attitude about America that differs from that articulated in Romulo's *Mother America*, Bulosan's *America Is in the Heart*, or even Villa's *Have Come, Am Here*. Rather than a place of realized kinship, love for the land and its people, or an opportunity to "claim America," the America of *The Bamboo Dancers* is a place of alienation, ghostliness, and disembodied existence.[56] For Ernie, Helen, and Pepe, it is a place to recover *from* rather than to recover *in*. With reference to America, Ernie describes "a fragment of a sidewalk in some faraway city in Summer" as "our tomb," as something the three of them "had gone to America to learn" (330). The passage indicates that perhaps exile and expatriation itself symbolizes death, and that complete renewal can only come about through a sense of responsibility for one's native land. Indeed, the three characters experience alienation in America and only regain a sense of wholeness upon their return to the Philippines. Meanwhile, their experiences in Japan and Taiwan represent a transitional point, embodying both possibilities of estrangement and care and responsibility.

Ernie Rama in America embodies the suspicious, ambiguous, binational intellectual that nationalists like Claro Recto were warning Filipinos about.[57] He is a lonely expatriate in America, distanced from his cultural, national, and even proper sexual identity. The title of the first chapter, "A Lament for Tammuz," a poem recited by the American Mrs. Rice, signals the sterility of the Philippine-American cultural landscape.[58] Among fellow students and expatriates in New York, Rama is cynical about the Philippines' future. He dislikes most of his fellow Filipinos and puts down the *tinikling*, the national bamboo dance, performed by world famous touring Philippine dance troupes such as the Bayanihan, whom he encounters throughout his travels. The Americans he meets in his travels have come to equate the dance with Filipinos and Philippine culture as much as with Bataan, World War II, and the American soldiers who died there, but Rama hardly identifies with any of this. Everywhere he goes, old people he meets on the street and in parks inspire him with a phobia, and he runs away from them as though from death itself. Finally, he has sexual relations with Helen, whom he had dated in the Philippines, which is quite surprising given the suggestion of his homosexuality.[59] When Ernie leaves her, she pursues a romantic and unrealistic liaison with Herb Lane, a budding American writer and one of those who exoticize the Filipinos as bamboo dancers. Rama thinks his sexual liaison with Helen could never have happened in the Philippines, which reinforces the suggestion of the unnaturalness of the American moral landscape. Finally, before his departure to board a ship bound for the Philippines, Ernie visits his brother Pepe, whom he discovers has been having an extramarital affair, predictably with a beautiful blonde, betraying his wife, Gaya, and his daughter, Meding, who also happens to be Ernie's godchild. Instead of confronting him, Ernie rationalizes his silence in terms of the importance of being loyal to his older brother.

The resolution of the alienation experienced by Ernie, Helen, and Pepe, Gonzalez seems to suggest, involves a return to their home province of Sipolog and to wholesome Filipino values. Japan and Taipei are intermediate steps toward their reintegration into Filipino society. In Japan, Ernie meets Americans involved in the anti-nuclear movement, from whom he hears criticism of the United States by Americans for the first time. In performing an errand for them, he visits Hiroshima and has an extensive audience with survivors of the 1945 atomic bomb. While he seems indifferent to them, reflecting the extent of his own indifference to the world, he is in fact profoundly affected by their stories and by the threat of human extinction, which reveals itself upon his arrival in the Philippines as an almost imperceptible sense of social responsibility and "civic-mindedness." Meanwhile, things seem to change little for Helen and for Pepe. While Helen feels burdened by their unwholesome liaison in America and now finds herself pregnant, she cannot bear to tell Herb Lane (on a USIS trip to East Asia), who she surmises would immediately call off their engagement if she did. Finally, for Pepe, Japan is no more than a series of trips to the red-light district, or the Nichigeki, which he subsequently brags about to his friends in the Philippines over drinks.

In Taipei, Ernie comes down with a debilitating flu, even as he reads in the newspapers of a flu epidemic engulfing the Philippines, perhaps suggesting the contagion of cultural malaise that is spreading among Filipinos. As if to underscore the point, a few of the touring Filipino "terpsichoreans" he meets at his hotel snidely remark on how lucky they are to be putting some distance between themselves and the Philippines. While Ernie is sick, a domestic servant named Chan takes care of him, and from him he learns that Herb Lane has run over a 13-year-old Chinese girl and been shot by an anti-American protestor. Meanwhile, Helen, who was with Herb Lane when this happened, suffers a miscarriage. Ernie surprises himself with his new-found sense of responsibility for Helen, whose well-being and reputation he makes sure remain intact.

The Philippine segment of *The Bamboo Dancers* is full of suggestions of renewal and of Gonzalez's vision that return to one's native land is crucial to moral and cultural regeneration. On the plane bound for Manila, Ernie sits among Chinese women and feels shame (*hiya*) because they seemed more excited about being home in the Philippines than he is. This is a sure sign that being part of a community matters for Ernie. When he arrives at their house in Manila, Gaya and Pepe are quarreling. Gaya and his mother have found out about Pepe's illicit affair with the blonde and are giving him the silent treatment. Soon both women leave the two men behind and journey to Mindoro. Left alone by the women, Ernie sees a new maturity developing in Pepe, who becomes a pioneer of sorts, visiting patients in several neighborhoods beyond their housing project and caring little for his pay. Ernie too sees a new civic responsibility growing in him, and he criticizes the profit motives of the developers of the housing project and their failure to build parks and schools. Soon he too returns to Sipolog, enters the bamboo gate of their house, and is reunited with his father (who walks with a bamboo cane, because his legs were broken during the war by the Japanese), fear for whose welfare has caused his phobia of old people. Indeed, Ernie realizes he has been running away from an entire generation of Filipinos and now confronts his fear of the death of his father and the values of his generation.

While Gaya had feared it would not happen, Pepe soon returns too and is reunited with his family, suggesting his transformation from immaturity and selfishness to family responsibility. In the fashion of myth criticism, in which water and earth are pervasive symbols of rebirth and fertility, Ernie is reborn in the end when he nearly drowns between bamboo outriggers while on a fishing trip in Sipolog. The near drowning symbolizes baptism and hope for Ernie's eventual wholeness. As if to underscore the point, the narrative chronologically ends in the prologue with the theme of the power of life to regenerate. Helen has now fully recovered from the shock of Herb Lane's death and the miscarriage and is full of energy again. Ernie writes to the editor of a Manila newspaper about the resurgence of life even at Ground Zero of the atomic bomb in Hiroshima. He also discovers that, imitating the Japanese, he can grow plants outside his Manila residence, because the land is rich and fertile.

In the meantime, Gonzalez's notions of the shortcomings of the middle class are reflected in several of his prominent short stories. For instance, the progressive feminist of "Where's My Baby Now?" is engrossed in self-improvement and women's activism, but the price she must pay for this, the story suggests, is the peace and stability of her family.[60] Meanwhile, in "On the Ferry," Mr. Lopez, an engineer responsible for the construction of a collapsed dam, conceals his failure to pay for his son Nilo's college education from his fellow passengers on the ferry from Manila to Mindoro. Reflecting the disturbance growing inside his soul, the frightening sight of a boat shipwrecked on an island confronts Lopez with his own failure, for he is as unable to explain this to his son as he is to explain the lies he has made up "to conceal his having failed him."[61] Finally, in "The Popcorn Man," a Filipino professor at a military base, Mr. Leynes, rationalizes his great life as an "educational concessionaire" teaching English to the children of Americans (who cannot get used to the idea of Filipinos teaching them) on a foreign military base in his own country. The "popcorn," provided free of charge to the Filipino teachers, but monetarily worthless, symbolizes his self-delusion.

⌒

If Gonzalez's writings seem to preach the importance of Filipinos' remaining in their homeland, or returning there, his life exhibits a restless desire to go abroad that seems to subvert the nativist tendencies of his fiction. After his one-year visit in the United States, Gonzalez consistently applied for fellow-ships that allowed him to travel outside of the Philippines on a regular basis. In the 1950s, he visited Japan, Korea, British Malaya, Singapore (then part of Malaya), Indonesia, Taiwan, and India. In 1962, he traveled on a cultural exchange program to Taiwan for two weeks for dialogues between Filipino and Chinese writers. In the same year, he sought opportunities to teach at Iowa University's Creative Writing Program with Paul Engle. And in 1965, he spent a year in Europe on a Rockefeller fellowship with his family, including Narita and all of their four children. The family lived in Italy and while there Gonzalez spent some time at the Rockefeller Foundation's Bellagio Study and Conference Center on the shores of Lake Como. Gonzalez and his family were subsequently based in Spain, where he and his children took classical guitar lessons. From there, he toured West Germany and England upon the invitation of the West German government and the BBC.[62]

Gonzalez's travels throughout Asia and Europe did more than provide him with the ability to write about faraway lands, as exemplified in *The Bamboo Dancers* and *A Grammar of Dreams*; they also confirmed his cultural nationalism. Some writers he met throughout Asia, for instance, had realized their dream of writing in their native tongues, something Gonzalez had been concerned about since the war.[63] Other writers with similar concerns about colonialism and the process of decolonization, like Raja Rao and Wang Gungwu, had succeeded as literary or academic writers in English.[64] Wang recalls meeting Gonzalez in Manila in 1951–52 "at a young writers' gathering, where he was host together with Wallace Stegner, and then again a couple of times later." Wang was at the University of Malaya (located in Singapore at that time) and remembers the Filipino author's "cheerful face and generous praise for young budding writers."[65] In England, Gonzalez was for a time reunited with Herbert Read, subsequently Sir Herbert Read, his former professor at the Kenyon School of English sixteen years beforehand. Although Gonzalez makes no mention of it, Read had also become a staunch opponent of the Vietnam War.[66] In Rome, Gonzalez encountered what he felt was the snobbery of Italian writers at the time, consumed as they were by New Criticism, which Gonzalez already regarded as old. In Spain, he had a special kind of illumination, for he learned that the word "Filipino" had its origins among Spaniards who were born in the Philippines and had died there, recorded in a book that detailed their activities away from "home."[67] This insight, however, did not necessarily lead to a conceptual appreciation of expatriation, even though he had traveled to more places outside of the Philippines than most Filipino intellectuals of his time.

Gonzalez's relationship to patronage or reciprocity provides a second indication of how biography and social practice tended to subvert his nationalist discourse. In 1955, for instance, in his introduction to Bienvenido Santos's first work, he questioned the compatibility of literature and government service.[68] In an interview several decades later, Gonzalez regarded his rejection of political patronage as one of the crucial decisions that led him to a literary and artistic life. As a young man who had failed to gain entry into the University of the Philippines, he said, a family friend and former Quezon aide named Mang Tomas had brought him to the offices of the then Senate president in order to repay him and his father for previous acts of kindness. Quezon had promised him a job if he came back the following day. But instead of reporting for work the following day, Gonzalez said, he had decided to return to his home province of Mindoro. The interviewer, Doreen Fernández, asked, "You did not want to go and see his secretary?" Gonzalez replied, "No, I didn't. I didn't want to have anything to do with the arrangement."[69] He drew an analogy between his experience and that of Narita's father when the latter had been invited by the Japanese to serve as a dummy or token Filipino plantation manager. As he described it, this literal turning away from political patronage made his artistic career possible, conveying the message that art and political patronage are incompatible, and that genuine artists have to forego such favors if they want to preserve their authenticity and integrity.[70]

Did such a moral square with Gonzalez's experience? Did he consistently avoid patronage and thus preserve his authenticity and integrity as a Filipino writer in the terms that he had set for himself? The reality of Gonzalez's relationship to patronage is more complex than his tale of Mang Tomas suggests. Although by different means, Gonzalez was often the beneficiary of some kind of artistic or political patronage or sponsorship. Indeed, what his tale leaves out is the extent to which a Filipino intellectual (like any intellectual, for that matter) needed patronage during the American colonial period, and even afterwards, as we have noted in the cases of Romulo, Bulosan, and Villa. Few were likely to be discovered or to succeed without recognition and acceptance by a "superior," with the accompanying honors and remuneration. For instance, the praises of the editor A. V. H. Hartendorp and his publication of Gonzalez's works in the *Philippine Magazine* in the 1930s were crucial to Gonzalez's development and acceptance as a writer, as was José García Villa's crude but much anticipated Honor Roll, an annual collection of best Philippine stories that had received a maximum rating of three stars, or asterisks, from the renowned master.[71] In the 1940s, the Commonwealth Literary Awards, sponsored by the Quezon government, gave Gonzalez recognition as an artist, as did the colonial Japanese government's Tagalog writing contest and publication of his story. And during the postwar period, he obtained the special patronage of the Rockefeller humanities director, Charles Burton Fahs, who was responsible for Gonzalez's trip to the United States and probably for his two other subsequent Rockefeller-sponsored trips to Asia and Europe. Sponsorship and patronage had a snowball effect. His year as a Rockefeller fellow in 1949 and the publication of his *Seven Hills Away* by Alan Swallow, a publisher who assiduously sought to provide an outlet for beginning writers, helped Gonzalez secure the patronage of high-ranking members of the University of the Philippines, who promptly appointed him to a position as assistant professor of English, ahead of other qualified candidates, although he did not even have a bachelor's degree. It was his classmates at Stanford in 1949, Edward Loomis and Robert V. Williams, and possibly his former professor Wallace Stegner, who recognized his literary and academic capabilities. They helped him to land positions at the University of California and California State University, Hayward, which aided his immigration to the United States in 1968.[72] Indeed, while Gonzalez often railed against patronage as a corrupting influence on art in his public pronouncements, this list of his patrons shows that he himself was a beneficiary of that system. In more sober moments during the 1950s and 1960s, he would acknowledge the necessity and importance of patronage, as did many intellectuals and artists of his generation.[73] The defensiveness about patronage in his 1981 interview with Edilberto Alegre and Doreen Fernandez underscores Gonzalez's increasing shift toward cultural nationalism, and his increasing concern for authenticity, which seemed to demand a rigid moral purity.

Finally, Gonzalez's conflicting statements about language and art exposed the ambiguities of his linguistic nationalism. While Gonzalez later admitted that his entire literary output in Tagalog amounted to only four stories translated from English to Tagalog (including his classic "Bread of Salt"), one story rendered from Tagalog to English ("Tigang Langit," or "Dry Heaven"),[74] and perhaps a similar number of essays, the issue of whether to write in Tagalog or English became an obsession for him. It would be a topic explored in numerous essays, letters, and discussions with friends for five decades, from different perspectives, reflecting ambivalence and vacillation on the subject. At times, he believed that the language in which one wrote was irrelevant and that the more important issue was clarity of expression and form, especially in the postwar climate of nuclear war and postcolonial nation building. At other times, he would advocate a shift from English (which he described as a "borrowed tongue") to Tagalog, convinced of its indispensability and satisfied at the oneness of thought in the native language and the expression of those thoughts. At yet other times, he would retreat from his advocacy of Tagalog for fear of losing a favored reader and friend whose language was English or some other Philippine vernacular.[75] In the early 1950s, Gonzalez wrote several essays for the popular Tagalog weekly *Liwayway*. He claims that the editors judged his prose as *pampanitikan*, or for the highbrow, which in the Philippines was synonymous with the mestizo elite class. He felt that *Liwayway* was more interested in the *pambakya* (literally, wearers of "wooden clogs" [*bakya*], like those recently arrived from the provinces, who came to symbolize low-class tastes in the eyes of the urban middle class).[76] Writing, Gonzalez rationalized, "meant following the conventions of the trade as practiced by that *class* for which the industry provided profits. It did not mean pursuing the demands of an art form, and least of all the demands of an idea." The end result, Gonzalez claimed, was that he had been "forced to return to English."[77] In the language of opposition to the upper classes, he thus blamed the publishing industry for pandering to popular tastes and frustrating his Tagalog literary aspirations. But while this rationale might have been understandable in the 1960s and early 1970s, Gonzalez never published any books of fiction or nonfiction in Tagalog during the last four decades of his career. In contrast, he published six books in English. Contrary to the bleak picture he painted of the prospects for an audience for *pampanitikan*, a new generation of writers did find themselves at home in the vernacular and wrote poems or stories, some of which Gonzalez himself favorably reviewed, as well as novels, in the new creole, "Taglish."[78]

Gonzalez at Hayward

Gonzalez's cultural nationalism gained a new urgency in the context of his expatriation, indeed, exile, in the United States. He had come to the University of California, Santa Barbara, in 1968 as a visiting associate professor, been in residence at the University of Hong Kong in 1969 on a Leverhulme fellowship, and then moved to a tenured position in the English Department at California State College, Hayward, where he was to remain until his retirement in 1983. Like many Filipino and Asian immigrants to the United States, he had come as a classic "sojourner." He had planned to work in the United States for only a few years, earn enough to improve his family's material conditions, and then return to the Philippines. A respite from his hectic teaching load at the University of the Philippines, where, after eighteen years of teaching, he was receiving a recently tenured faculty member's salary was also an added incentive to leave.[79] Finally, as Gonzalez explained to his former professor Wallace Stegner, he intended to use the time away from the Philippines to write—"[F]or the sake of my writing, so long deferred, I'm prepared to be an exile for at least ten years."[80]

The declaration of martial law in 1972, however, disrupted Gonzalez's dreams, as it did those of numerous Filipino immigrant intellectuals and activists. While Gonzalez was under no immediate threat from the Marcos government insofar as his personal safety was concerned, he worried about the fate of his children, his friends (especially those in the literary community), and his relatives in the Philippines during this uncertain period. The barrage of news of the doings of the conjugal dictatorship and the comings and goings of immigrants lured to the Philippines by the dictatorship's ingenious *balikbayan* program, which provided travel discounts and special privileges to Filipino Americans "returning home" as tourists, kept the question of home in the minds of Gonzalez and other intellectuals.[81] The dictatorship was not limited in its powers to Philippine territory, however, as the participation of Foreign Affairs Minister Romulo in the infamous blacklist attests. Indeed, it was able to cow many of its critics in the Filipino American community by a successful propaganda campaign, disinformation about the Philippines, and frequent intimidation.

As we have seen, many Filipinos stood by the Marcos government, at home and abroad, although the international resistance against Marcos developed immediately. In this context, Gonzalez, who was not predisposed to criticize the government or participate in militant politics, chose to remain silent about martial law. Silence was his way of surviving, because it allowed him to avoid being detected by the Marcos regime, which was keenly aware of its national intellectuals and political leaders in the Filipino American community. Moreover, Gonzalez's allegiances were torn between his son, Michael, then a student at the University of the Philippines, who took a stand opposing Marcos, and former writing students, like Rony Diaz, and established writers visiting him in the United States who had decided to collaborate with Marcos.[82]

At the same time, one might regard Gonzalez's silence about the regime as noncooperation (which he intended), a sign of resistance to being assimilated by the dictatorship, serving it, or legitimizing its policies. Indeed, Gonzalez only grudgingly paid his taxes to the Philippine government.[83]

Instead of addressing political issues in his writings or in interviews, Gonzalez directed his attention and that of his readers and critics toward a subject that preoccupied him, the question of "culture," especially the influence of American colonial culture upon Filipino writers and intellectuals like himself. He eschewed the subject of what was *politically* wrong with the Philippines and instead displaced his energies into exploring the question of what was wrong with the Filipino. In this way, Gonzalez's gaze remained fixed upon the Philippines without touching upon or commenting upon its political realities. This kind of thinking informs his literary autobiography "Moving On: A Filipino in the World" (1973), written for a conference on Southeast Asia that seems to have been founded, ironically enough, upon essentialist assumptions of cultural differences between the "East" and the "West." In this essay, Gonzalez used the ideas of Franz Fanon to analyze the way race paralyzed the Filipino writer, whose bodily motions, including speaking English, seemed to suffer from the continuous surveillance of an invisible colonial gaze.[84]

He was just as fascinated with applying Jungian psychology to Philippine realities and had a penchant for labeling psychological problems "complexes" (e.g., the "Mother Complex," etc.). For instance, Gonzalez identified what he called the "Magellan Complex" and the "Jones Law Syndrome."[85] Named respectively after the European "discoverer" of the Philippines and the American congressman who gave his name to the Jones Law of 1916,[86] these theories provided historical rationales for what Gonzalez observed as the preoccupation with awards and the hunger for American approval among fellow Filipino intellectuals of the colonial and postcolonial eras. He described both as "two of the stresses upon our imagination as a creative people."[87] The Jones Law Syndrome he regarded as the "solicitation of foreign, and generally American, approval," which had become not only a "national habit but an expression, alas, of national character."[88] Moreover, he adds, this neurosis "caused us to will our efforts toward contributing to the welfare of the nation so that it could claim political freedom as a right. Generations of *pensionados* became conscripted as intermediaries toward a new era of dominance, at the expense of our creativity, particularly literary."[89] Meanwhile, the Magellan Complex was Gonzalez's statement on the "provincialism" of Filipino writers, "the claim that one was first at something or other."[90] Moreover, Gonzalez writes, "the Magellan Complex is something of a passionate need to be first in some endeavor, to literally claim, on behalf of the nation—in this case, Inang Bayan—new territory in the form of achievement and honors."[91] Both of these problems Gonzalez traced to the misguided desire to prove to Americans that Filipinos had the requisite qualities to become an independent nation.

Yet, while these explanations shed light on the mind-set of Filipino intellectuals, they clearly reflect their postcolonial, nationalist interpretation of colonial and postcolonial realities. By labeling the preoccupations of the colonial-era intellectuals as such, Gonzalez was appropriating that intellectual history for a nationalist politics that regarded elites as having betrayed the Philippines with their avowed love for America and things American, erasing the very agency of this social class, the intricate relationship of collaboration and resistance between the elites and the lower classes, and the larger transnational colonial political context that all Filipinos had to navigate. This was clearly a projection of present concerns back to the U.S. colonial period. On the one hand, it is doubtful that most Filipino intellectuals of that time were so misguided as to betray their country, as Gonzalez seems to imply. On the other hand, Gonzalez's reduction of colonial intellectual psychology to these neuroses could be read as an attempt to exculpate colonial intellectuals, including himself, from any responsibility for their actions. Neither position seems tenable. As historians like Alfred McCoy, Ruby Paredes, and others have shown, political leaders like Manuel Quezon were *con-*

scious about accepting American hegemony and, moreover, strategically navigated the patron-client system, often to their advantage. Quezon and the elite social class he represented saw Philippine-American rapprochement as sound *nationalist* strategy, especially in the matter of free trade that benefited their haciendas and cash crops. Moreover, as Michael Salman has argued, Quezon and other nationalist intellectuals rearticulated American slavery and antislavery ideology in the service of Philippine anticolonial nationalism, showing their creativity in using American colonial rhetoric against itself.[92] As I have also shown in earlier chapters, seemingly pro-American or apolitical authors like Romulo and Villa, completely educated in English and American "tutelage," could and did register political and social criticisms of the United States. Bulosan and other Filipino English writers abroad also criticized America's cruelty to immigrants and ambivalence toward them from progressive and folk Christian perspectives. Finally, there were the anti-imperialist thinkers and intellectuals of the period, like Maximo Kalaw of the University of the Philippines and Isabelo de los Reyes.[93] Gonzalez "forgets" these diverse political perspectives under American colonialism. Influenced by the postwar and postcolonial nationalism of Teodoro Agoncillo, Claro Recto, and Renato Constantino, and perhaps by the ethnic nationalist movements on American college campuses, which he kept at arm's length, Gonzalez's characterization of colonized intellectuals was elitist in implication, allowing him to claim a paramount *decolonized* status vis-à-vis those who still suffered from the "colonial complex" or "colonial mentality." In this, he was echoing the analyses and the biases of both Recto and Constantino.[94]

The great irony of Gonzalez's cultural nationalist perspective, highlighting Filipinos' colonized culture and precolonial cultures' promise of liberation, the notion of a "golden age," already advanced by ilustrados like Rizal and criticized by Isabelo de los Reyes, was its compatibility with the Marcoses' nationalist project.[95] Throughout their regime, Ferdinand and Imelda Marcos manipulated animist folklore, legend, and Philippine traditional cultures in their attempts to rewrite Filipino history in their own image. They also remade Filipino archaeology (museumizing), theater (dramas), and pageants (beauty pageants, parades, and spectacles) in the interests of preserving the dictatorship.[96] The conjugal dictatorship could easily assimilate psychological and cultural analyses of Filipino problems. However, fictive or nonfictional narratives that provided a mirror of life under the dictatorship and exposed the workings of authoritarianism did prove threatening, as we shall see in the case of Bienvenido Santos's novel *The Praying Man*. Perhaps more than Gonzalez cared to admit, his political and artistic freedoms, even in exile, had been curbed by a transnational regime that demanded political conformity and brooked no disagreement.

↭

Closely tied to the problem of consciousness among Filipinos was a second, related problem—what Gonzalez perceived as Filipinos' inability to read, to interpret, and to decode the signs of a deeper, more significant reality, the world of myth. Much of Gonzalez's concern with reading was probably motivated by the way his own works had been misread in the past, given his dialogue with Father Bernad and the animus of E. K. Tiempo. Filipino intellectuals, he argued, had been inculcated with the wrong values, expressed in catch phrases such as "the human condition" and "universal values," influenced by postwar existentialism and liberalism that disguised their Eurocentric assumptions and tended to mislead, not only the writing of fiction, but also its interpretation.[97] This problem of reading was in part rooted in the complexes suffered by the Filipinos and in part arose from their lack of exposure to reading protocols during the colonial era. Although he was teaching many non-Filipinos at Hayward during the 1970s and early 1980s, Gonzalez's main concern remained how *Filipinos* read.

Gonzalez's solution to the problem of reading, as much as the Filipino's colonial neurosis, emphasized the importance of competence in Filipino tradition and a return to the Filipino past. Gonzalez's hermeneutics did not, however, involve a simple retrieval of the past. As he said in an interview, the past had to be *interpreted*.[98] His admonitions about reading reflected his long-standing concern for formalism and myth criticism—on the one hand, he stressed the importance of understanding "technique," and on the other hand, he highlighted the importance of "myth." In his response to Miguel Bernad's reading of *The Bamboo Dancers*, Gonzalez had explained what he meant by technique. In the reading of fiction, he made a distinction between "subject" and "theme," which he had adapted from Mark Schorer. Gonzalez redefined these two concepts. "Subject," conventionally understood as the topic or subject matter of a story, was expanded to include the "moral idea," the structurally recurring mythos of the narrative, which linked it to the larger themes and philosophical currents of world literature. He subdivided these mythic structures, following Campbell's notion of the monomyth and Frye's centralizing of *the quest* motif, into "the journey," "the battle [or] conflict," the "establishment of a home," "the endurance of suffering," and "the search for perfection." Gonzalez believed that "if any of our stories are worked out with these things in mind, the world is ready to listen, anywhere, anytime."[99] In the case of Filipino literature, Gonzalez identified four recurring subjects—"The Barrio and the City," "The [Artist as the] Hope of the Fatherland," "The Lost Eden," and "Illusion and Reality." To these, one might also add two sources of Filipino writers' values—"feudalism" or "the hacienda society" and "a serious concern for social justice."[100] "Theme" not only meant a recurring preoccupation, idea, or motif, but, more specifically, a commentary upon the moral idea or subject, the attitude toward a particular quest or search, whether thwarted or attained, diverted or deferred. The theme is that aspect of the narrative that most closely reflects the author's viewpoint.[101] Not surprisingly, Gonzalez emphasized the importance of narratology, the study of narrative. Especially in *The Father and the Maid* (1990), he explored the role of narrators in Philippine, Third World, Russian, European, and American fictional works, examining the ways they determined points of view and consciousness and set limitations upon their craft.

In particular, Gonzalez displayed an evident fondness for the archetypal resonance of the Filipino short story "How My Brother Leon Brought Home a Wife," one of Philippine literature's classic pastoral love stories, written in the 1930s by Manuel Arguilla, one of the Philippines' first and best short story writers.[102] This depicts the journey of a recently married couple from Manila to the husband's home province to present his bride to his father, a veteran of the Philippine revolution. On the last leg of their journey, they ride on a carabao sled driven by Leon's younger brother, Baldo, who hears them singing "Sky Sown with Stars," an old love song in the vernacular, learned from their father. Gonzalez marvels at Arguilla's effective use of the child Baldo as a limited first-person narrator. However, this technical achievement points to an even greater accomplishment: the expression of archetypal native values. After his meeting with the newlyweds, symbolic of the urban and the modern, Father summons Baldo and asks him what they did on the carabao sled. Reassuringly, Baldo tells him that they sang "Sky

Sown with Stars." For Gonzalez, it is the element of song, this lyricism that ineffably resolves the story's essential conflicts—between city and country, modernity and tradition, fathers and sons, and the Spanish colonial era and the new American dispensation. The presence of the song in the story was, for Gonzalez, a reflection of the Filipino "collective unconscious," a part of that heritage of lyricism that goes back to the epics of the precolonial era and even to mythic times, *in illo tempore*. As Gonzalez writes in an earlier essay, "Whistling Up the Wind," songs have for many centuries bridged the conflicts that have divided Filipinos across generations and across time.[103] Arguilla's accomplishment was to have embodied both technique and archetype in his short story, creating a work of beauty.[104]

Finally, for Gonzalez, sensitivity to myth, history, and tradition led to the ability to decode or interpret contemporary events. He gave an example of what he meant by this in "Even as the Mountain Speaks," his lecture to the "Columbus Conference Paradox" of the UCLA Center for Medieval and Renaissance Studies.[105] For him, the volcanic explosion of Mt. Pinatubo in 1991, which buried Clark Air Force Base in a blanket of ash and ultimately displaced the American military from Philippine soil, helped to reconceptualize the American colonial presence. The volcano's eruptions were both temporal markers and a metaphor for colonialism. Volcanic eruptions had bracketed American colonial rule—the explosion of Taal Volcano in Batangas in 1898 had marked the start of the Spanish-American War, and the eruption of Mt. Pinatubo in 1991 led to the end of the American military presence, a feat that several decades of anti-bases politics had not been able to accomplish. Just as important, erupting volcanoes and *lahar*, a mudflow of volcanic fragments on the sides of a volcano, provided a metaphor for Filipino history. Gonzalez described colonialism in terms of powerful volcanic explosions that spewed out a "*lahar* of colonizations," reflecting the Philippines' multilayered, syncretic history.

Yet while Gonzalez saw the potential that myth or literary symbols had for clarifying historical events, he nonetheless sought to limit literature's potential social and political effects. He made this explicit in an interview with Roger Bresnahan. "A successful story, in the sense that it is artistically achieved, does not raise an argument or beg a question," Gonzalez said. "Nor does it move one to action *beyond* inviting contemplation. Its text is a tangible object, its narrative structure a perceptible shape of a specific feeling or emotion."[106] Moreover, he was evidently unshaken in his allegiance to the absolutist New Critical idea of one text, one reading. This can be seen, for instance, in his interpretation of Wolfgang Iser's "reader-response theory."[107] Gonzalez recounts the difference between the "implied reader" and "the actual reader" of literary texts and the gaps that form in the process between the intended and the actual reader. The text provides a "virtual world" *distinguished* from the "actual world" (44). For Gonzalez, as for Iser, "virtuality" comes from text and imagination working together in an endless process of anticipation and retrospection, creating a gestalt. Gonzalez tellingly argues, however, that the text "*cannot . . . exceed what has been provided.*" Hence, while "our perception of the world varies with each reading" (46), Gonzalez sets a limit on meaning that denies literary texts anything but "aesthetic fulfillment" (*Father and the Maid,* 51). How, then, are we to account for the novels of Rizal, for example, which do raise arguments and go beyond Gonzalez's dictum of inviting contemplation, indeed repeatedly inspiring revolutionary political activities in the Philippines and elsewhere? Moreover, Gonzalez often sets up history as a straw man against literature. His formalist theory privileges literature above history, fiction above society, and rhetoric above action. Gonzalez asks, for instance, "How well do we understand the *hermetically sealed* text that a novel, or fiction, for that matter, *must have* so that it does not get mistaken for history?" Such a view creates an impermeable barrier between literature and history, denying the complex interrelationships between the two. He refers to "the rigidity of history" without simultaneously addressing the ways literature could itself become rigidly isolated from society. And finally, he seems to reduce history to mere "fact" rather than address the complex rhetorical maneuvers, temporal emplotments, and problems of memory—topics that have concerned historians in the last three decades—that complicate the boundaries between history and literature.[108]

Gonzalez's tendency to a univocal reading of texts often manifested itself in the classroom in my own personal experience with his Philippine American Literature Class.[109] While he encouraged his students to read carefully, he tended to dampen the multiple interpretations that arose from the reading of a text by hewing too closely to his own interpretation, which tended to close off discussion and led to some frustration in the class. In retrospect, one source of interpretative friction especially relevant to his nativist approach was his tendency to reduce "Filipino American" texts to "Philippine" texts, which tended to negate the perspectives of Filipino Americans in the class, especially those of U.S.-born or U.S.-raised Filipinos. Indeed, Gonzalez was skeptical, if not at times hostile, to the construction of Filipino American literary criticism, seeing the current state of affairs (perhaps not without justification) as self-absorbed identity politics.[110]

Gonzalez's fixed focus on the Philippines has tended to obscure the realities of his life as a new immigrant professor at Hayward and the challenges that this new environment posed. As a professor of creative writing, he had a full teaching load that required a lot of direct contact with students, burdensome for one who had been teaching for nineteen years and was starting a new job at fifty-five, ten years from retirement. Teaching multicultural classes in the era of the counterculture and the youth rebellion was in any case a challenge. Gonzalez taught the standard courses and workshops on creative writing.[111] His colleagues at Hayward included his former Stanford classmate Robert V. Williams and Ben Johnson, an African American translator of Italian short stories.[112] Adjusting to American life was sometimes a strain too. He was upset, for example, about a Department of Labor finding that his holding a teaching job deprived a more deserving American of the same position. Perhaps as a consequence of all this, his health suffered.[113]

Gonzalez also never learned how to drive. He took buses, and relying upon bus schedules led to feelings of isolation and an unwanted dependence on friends or family to get around and perform everyday chores, such as carrying his groceries home. He found this life "difficult" but enjoyed the time he had to think, read, and write.[114]

Gonzalez arrived in the American university system during the late 1960s, a time of great turmoil and student activism. The University of California campus at Santa Barbara was a center of the racial unrest and the antiwar protests that were raging throughout the country. Gonzalez stayed aloof from these developments and attempted to concentrate on his writing and teaching. The problem was that there were few students to teach, because many were more interested in extracurricular activities than learning about fiction.[115] Gonzalez decided to leave Santa Barbara, if only to find a place where he could continue his work on Filipino literature. One year after starting at the University of California, the 54-year-old Gonzalez and his wife moved to the California State University at Hayward. Gonzalez rightly claims that his former Stanford classmate Robert V. Williams was responsible for his appointment there. Williams and his wife, Hatch, both of them avid readers of Gonzalez's early work, had occasionally provided shelter for Gonzalez during his year at Stanford. They now helped by housing him until such time as he could find a house and get settled in Hayward with Narita.[116] The English Department wanted him as much because of Williams's advocacy as for his ability to teach a variety of courses, including creative writing workshops. It was only later, after he had already been hired, that many faculty members came to appreciate his intelligence and sense of humor.[117]

Politics was the last thing that was on Gonzalez's mind, and he would remain aloof from activism at Hayward, as he had in Santa Barbara. If he did get involved in departmental politics, he stuck with his conservative friend Williams rather than aligning himself with the younger, more politically radical faculty and the student protesters.[118]

Gonzalez's avoidance of politics was ironic, however, for it was in part the student unrest that was responsible for Hayward's interest in him. A member of the search committee that hired him to teach in the creative writing program said that affirmative action recruitment had been an important consideration in doing so.[119] The Hayward campus had experienced militant protests, particularly from members of the Chicano and Latino minorities on campus, who questioned the absence of Latinos in the English Department. The hiring of Gonzalez solved not only the problem of staffing the creative writing program but also the department's ethnic and racial problem, helping to deflect criticism of its record on racial issues. Although not Latino, Gonzalez was, after all, a member of a racial minority and had a Spanish surname. According to this search committee member, Gonzalez was not unaware of these circumstances but took them in his stride, never allowing himself to be distracted from his gaze on the Philippines.

At different times, the realities of growing old in America fed Gonzalez's insecurities and led to ambivalence about whether to stay on in California or return home. In 1974, he felt that a government raid on a seminary in Metro Manila signaled the end of his *balikbayan* ambitions, but the following year, he concluded that he would rather brave life in the Philippines than suffer the uncertainties and "loss of identity" faced by Filipinos in the United States. Joking about entering "the desert called senior citizenship," however, he subsequently decided to postpone going home for five more years in order to obtain social security credits in the United States and be in a position to support his son Mike's graduate education in Australia.[120]

In the final analysis, Gonzalez remained steadfast in his adherence to Philippine citizenship, which not only expressed his love of being Filipino but also his staunch desire to remain unsullied by "hyphenated" identities. Gonzalez was proud of the fact that he had never become an American citizen. "Although we lived in California for more than twenty years, we have remained Filipino citizens," Narita Gonzalez writes. "On one occasion," she says, "we visited the Philippine Consulate in San Francisco to renew our passports. [The consul] observed that we deserved some kind of award for remaining Filipinos after all these years."[121] For N. V. M. Gonzalez, there was an inherent contradiction between altering one's citizenship and claiming Filipino identity. "I can't be an American citizen if I continue to be a Filipino writer," Narita quotes him as saying. "I am not a Fil-American writer either." And, as she speculates, Gonzalez's "insistence on not being a 'hyphenated' writer may have been the reason behind his not being represented in an anthology of Asian American fiction [perhaps *Aiiieeeee!!!*],"[122] hence the victim of an Asian American nativism. His former mentor Wallace Stegner once asked Gonzalez whether he had considered becoming a U.S. citizen. Gonzalez said he had not and had no wish to seek it.[123] The issue was to resurface in the mid 1970s in an odd way. The Philippine historian Carlos Quirino had inaccurately reported to a Philippine magazine that Gonzalez had a comfortable job at Hayward and had become a United States citizen.[124] This was, of course, the ultimate insult for a Filipino nationalist. To be grouped among those who were living comfortably while the motherland suffered was bad enough, but to be mistaken for an American was worse, for this was the ultimate sign of having abandoned one's nation. Privately, to his compadre Ben Santos, Gonzalez expressed consternation at Quirino's groundless claim.[125]

Gonzalez the Transpacific Commuter

As was the case with many political exiles and others who had been deterred from returning to the Philippines for one reason or another, Gonzalez's ordeal as an expatriate ended in 1986 with the collapse of the Marcos dictatorship and the emergence of Corazon Aquino's government.[126] For Gonzalez, the ability to return home was salutary, and it infused him with new energy. The new space for travel across the Pacific opened up by People Power and the subsequent end of the Cold War made Gonzalez a transpacific commuter, shuttling between the Philippines and the United States.

Gonzalez's life had grown considerably more complicated in the years since he had left the Philippines in 1968. Although he dreamed of returning to the Philippines, there was to be no final return for him. As one might have expected of someone who fiercely maintained his Philippine citizenship and claimed never to have left home, Gonzalez did not live the rest of his remaining years solely in the Philippines. Instead, his new, bifurcated life simply gave new form to the ambivalent multinational, multicultural reality that he had in fact inhabited for several decades.

His family was now spread out on two continents. He and Narita owned homes both in Northern California and on the grounds of the University of the Philippines, and they hosted travelers in either direction. In 1987, after being awarded an honorary doctorate in humane letters by the University of the Philippines, Gonzalez served as international writer-in-residence there. At the same time, he helped establish a center for Filipino and Filipino American studies at Hayward and continued to teach there on occasion, as well as at various other colleges in the western United States.[127] In the 1990s, he wrote for Philippine newspapers, launched his own column in the *Manila Times,* and became literary editor of *Katipunan,* a Filipino American newsmagazine that had played a crucial part in the fight against martial law.[128] He not only traveled extensively throughout the Philippines and the United States but hosted many scholars, artists, and filmmakers visiting the Philippines, where he gave friends, including myself, tours of his home provinces of Mindoro and Romblon to visit his family and see the sights he had described in such detail in his stories and novels. Meanwhile, Filipino friends, former students, and scholars who traveled to the United States continued to seek him out, as they had done for several decades.

The realities of his transnational world hardly seemed to transform Gonzalez's nativism. In various ways, he continued to express a Philippine-centered view. For instance, when asked about his friend and fellow writer Bienvenido Santos, who described his sojourn in the United States as "exile,"

Gonzalez was critical. He said that Santos made too much of the word "ex-ile," which did not apply to the life of Filipino intellectuals like him, claiming that the English word's equivalent could not be found in any of the vernacular languages of the Philippines. He implied that if it was not in the vernaculars, it must therefore not exist in Filipino psychology. This view dovetailed with the structuralist perspectives of Sikolohiyang Pilipino ("Filipino Psychology"), a movement led by the psychologist Virgilio Enriquez that criticized the colonial basis of ideas about psychology and sought to reestablish the discipline on the foundation of native psychological concepts derived from the Tagalog vernacular. Gonzalez was an occasional member of the *kapihan*, or coffee-table talks, in Northern California sponsored by the group.[129] While socially conscious and resistant to Western colonialism, Sikolohiyang Pilipino inclined toward a linguistic nationalism that recalled some of the problems of Agoncillo's approach and a methodological reductionism of Filipino culture that paralleled Gonzalez's own structuralist, mythic hermeneutics.

Nor did his transnational life detract from his need for literary recognition, the "Magellan Complex" notwithstanding. For instance, one critic commented on the incongruity of Gonzalez's claim that his collection *Bread of Salt* (1993) showed the evolution of a master storyteller, when most of the stories had been written in the 1950s and 1960s and Gonzalez could boast of only a few original stories in the past three decades.[130] Likewise, his longing for the National Artist Award, while never publicly expressed, was all too apparent to at least one former student. Caroline Hau, a critic of Philippine literature, writes of Gonzalez's silences: "I also felt that he wanted to be National Artist—and was embarrassed by what I took to be the nakedness of his yearning, even though he never alluded to it."[131] Privately, Gonzalez confided that he was unhappy with the recognition that other Filipino authors, notably F. Sionil José, had received in the United States, when he had been in the United States for several decades and had failed to attract that attention.[132] In 1997, then Philippine President Fidel V. Ramos named him the National Artist for Literature in a ceremony at the Malacañang Palace, which cemented his literary monumentalization in the Philippines. Among other things, it entitled him, as it did Romulo and Villa, to burial in the Libingan ng mga Bayani, or Cemetery of the National Heroes. In the following year, Gonzalez also received the University of California Regents Lecturer award in 1998, after being nominated by younger admirers and friends at the Asian American Studies Center at UCLA. Even in the matter of recognition, the diverse provenance of the awards he received tended to subvert the tendencies toward nativism in his works.

～

Although it is almost imperceptible, one can perhaps note an expansion of Gonzalez's outlook toward a plurality of perspectives. *The Bread of Salt* (1993) attests to the growing importance of life "beyond" the Philippines in Gonzalez's work. By 1993, Gonzalez's exploration of Filipino life in America amounted to only six stories, which was, however, a large output by his standards, since he emphasized quality over quantity. These stories explore the lives of expatriates and demonstrate an increasing concern for how they remember the Philippines, given their changing lives in the United States.[133] Gonzalez's depiction of his literary art and philosophy on the back jacket of *Bread of Salt* displays a bricolage that reflects a growing understanding of the multiplicity of his borrowings, from New Criticism to myth criticism, liberal humanism, reader-response theory, postcolonialism, Marxism, and social history. With *A Grammar of Dreams* (1997), Gonzalez was charting new directions in his fiction, influenced perhaps by the spate of interest in Philippine historical reconstructions and "globalization." The Filipino American setting had entirely disappeared, and Gonzalez now wrote (after thirty years) of his European journey in stories of the pretenses, tensions, and intercultural encounters of Filipino expatriates in Italy, France, and England. Gonzalez was likewise breaking an old stricture. For the first time, he was trying his hand at historical fiction, something that Gonzalez, the New Critic, had abhorred. There seemed to be a loosening of his demands for separation between history and fiction and the utter subordination of the former category to the latter.

Gonzalez was among the last of the colonial generation of Filipino English writers. He died in the Philippines on November 28, 1999, preceded by Romulo, Bulosan, Villa, and Santos, and soon followed by their friends and fellow Filipino writers of the colonial era Manuel Viray, P. C. Morantte, and Carlos Angeles, as well as by their younger interlocutor, the important literary historian Doreen Fernandez. If by legacy, one means one's place in a system of social relations and the immortality that comes from being remembered, then Gonzalez had little to worry about. One can hardly contest the provocative impact of his sophisticated nativist poetics, which have spurred his students and many with whom he came into contact in the Philippines and the United States to expand their literary and cultural horizons. His place as one of the Philippines' canonical literary writers seems secure. Likewise, for someone who hardly craved the uniform of an "Asian American" writer, Gonzalez has had a limited but significant impact in Asian American studies and among other ethnic American writers and academics. Gonzalez's impact on Filipino Americans in the western United States parallels José García Villa's in the Northeast, and Bienvenido Santos's in the Midwest, although one doubts whether any of the three can duplicate the continuing impact on American culture of Bulosan's life and his *America Is in the Heart*. Gonzalez's signal contributions, apart from his stories and novels, have been to heighten awareness of reading, to spur writing in English, Tagalog, and other vernaculars, and to serve as a father figure to many who have profited from his challenge to aspire to artistic achievement.[134] Ironically, it may be the complexity of Gonzalez's own transpacific life and his wide-ranging intellectual curiosity and commitment, embedded in his writings, that will prove to have a more lasting impact than Gonzalez the master artist and proponent of a nativist poetics.

FIVE

Fidelity and Shame: Bienvenido Santos

To-day, I heard a direct broadcast from Manila by Bert Silen, Ted Wallace, and Don Bell, describing the bombing of Clark's Field, 4 A.M. in Manila. They spoke of the moonlight guiding the bombing planes. It was 2 o'clock in the afternoon here in Illinois, and I was in my room, writing my term paper in the development of prose fiction in the 17th century. Don Bell's familiar voice was too much for me. I remembered how I used to listen to his 12:45 P.M. broadcast, right after lunch, as I lay in bed half-asleep with Aquing beside me, tired after the morning's work and also half-asleep. Even the children knew how to say, Don Bell and the News of the Day! And here I am, far away from that all, from my loved ones and home, in a strange country, writing a term paper while my country is being bombed! The tears roll down my cheeks and fall on my sweater, and I write on bravely, brushing away the tears. And I write something like: "for realism, as it is now understood, often borders on the gross, the misshapen. It is often the cry of the bitter; it is the sound of the wings of man's frailty beating the air in futile helplessness."[1]

By the time Bienvenido Santos wrote this entry into his wartime diary (much of which he destroyed),[2] he had been in the United States less than two months. He would spend the duration of World War II in the United States. Santos arrived in San Francisco on board the SS *Ruth Alexander* on Columbus Day, October 12, 1941, after a 26-day voyage from Manila. He would leave the United States on board the SS *Uruguay* on January 17, 1945, and arrive back in the Philippines in early February.[3] Like Carlos P. Romulo, who had arrived in the United States twenty-three years before him, Santos was a pensionado. He had already received his degree in education from the University of the Philippines, taught several years in the Bicol region in the southeastern part of Luzon, and published short stories and poems in magazines. He had left his wife, Beatriz Nidea, and his three daughters, Arme, Lina, and Lily, behind in the Philippines. Santos had come to take graduate courses in English at the University of Illinois at Urbana-Champaign, which he chose because it was a small school, where, he felt, he could learn more. It was one of the less popular destinations for pensionados, many of whom studied at Columbia, the University of Washington, or the University of Southern California.[4]

Hence, when the Pacific War broke out on December 7, 1941 (December 8 in the Philippines), with the simultaneous attack on Pearl Harbor and the invasion of the Philippines, Santos was enrolled in a mandatory survey course in English for the one-year MA program.[5] He feared he might not ever see his wife and children alive again. Reality had not only interrupted his study of realism; it was overwhelming it.

These moments of anxiety and nostalgia would lead to a transformation in Santos's sense of identity and national consciousness, wounding him and leaving lasting scars. Florentino Valeros, a critic who was intimately connected with Filipino English writers before the war, registered the surprise many Filipino intellectuals felt in reading Santos. The choleric and hopeful prewar writer seemed to mature before Valeros's eyes, introducing new literary and historical subjects into the national literature, shedding all affectation and absolutism, and mixing laughter with pain and silent wisdom. Valeros remarked especially on the transformation of Santos's "humor," from the carefree aspect of his prewar stories to the "knowing, suave, edged humor" of the postwar ones, as though of "a man hiding tears in his laughter." Santos remained "the optimist," but one who "had acquired deep and perhaps older wisdom."[6]

In previous chapters, we have seen how intellectual travel led to various modes of expatriate consciousness, from the affirmations of Romulo to Gonzalez's negation of the expatriate experience. In this chapter, I argue that Santos experienced expatriation neither as affirmation nor as negation but through intense feelings of guilt, or more properly, shame (*hiya, supog*),[7] brought about by his perceived inability to meet the demands of family, community, and nation for authentic subjectivity. What also emerges in Santos, however, is an imagining of masculinity that is Southeast Asian in texture—charismatic, patriarchal, sexually virile, eloquent, and religious, combining traditional animist religion and Catholicism.[8] Santos's representations of women valorize both the self-sacrificing maternal figure (*Inang Bayan,* or "Mother Country") and the demure, virginal rural maiden who has become a "cult figure" of Filipino womanhood, known as Maria Clara.[9] He reserved his ire for modern, urban, cosmopolitan women who were self-confident and assertive, although ironically, he remained dependent upon them throughout his life.

The Expatriate and the Nation

One good reason for an intellectual history of Santos is that the subject of so much of his creative work was his life. He loved and excelled in writing letters to family, friends, and patrons, many of which found their way into collections of his selected letters. During the last three years of his life, in direct contrast to the reticent Gonzalez, Santos published over 1,000 pages of autobiographical writing, including two memoirs and two volumes of letters.[10] As suggested by the title of his first book of memoirs, *Memory's Fictions,* he had a deep concern for how memory, especially as imagination, shaped and reshaped biography and history, often blurring the lines of distinction between reality and fiction. Like Gonzalez and many other writers and artists, Santos believed in the imagination's preeminence over history and truth. This logocentrism, as Jacques Derrida would call it, was a long-standing theme in Santos's autobiographical writing.[11] For instance, in a 1941 letter to Estela Detera, a former student, he writes of the power of dreams. "Reality is too drab," Santos writes. "[I]t must always be silver-lined with dreams. Refuse to dream as much as you will, but dreams shall ever wander about until they find you; and yielding, one day you will find yourself rubbing your eyes, awakening to a reality more beautiful than the dream."[12] The imagination was in a sense more reliable because memory, like time, was unreliable and, worse, a traitor. The narrator of "The Day the Dancers Came" writes, "Like time, memory was often a villain, a betrayer,"[13] and at a conference, Santos himself claimed that "history tends to be reduced to what is verifiable, while fiction provides emotional information: truth *felt*, not merely declaimed."[14] Finally, *Memory's Fictions* abounds in playful and eloquent interrogations of truth and historical memory that alert the reader several times over to the constructed nature of "personal history."[15]

Yet, if memory is unreliable, it was perhaps in part due not only to Santos's advanced age when he wrote his memoirs but also to the stresses and strains of a life of travel. Like Romulo and Gonzalez, Santos traveled back and forth between America and the Philippines several times over the last five decades of his life. He stayed in America for long periods, as mentioned, from 1941 to 1945, and then again from 1958 to 1961, 1965 to 1969, and from 1970 to 1981, after which he began spending half the year in America and half in the Philippines. Santos successively inhabited different modes of expatriation—pensionado, war exile, postwar literary student, political exile, and transpacific commuter. Against the American colonialist and Filipino nationalist mappings of the Philippines, Santos created his own countercolonial, transnational, and translocal mapping of America and the Philippines.[16] He also reimagined, humanized, and complicated the image of the Filipino poor in America and the Philippines. In doing so, he, like Romulo, Bulosan, Villa, and Gonzalez, defied colonial and racist stereotypes of Filipinos as invariable and primitive "tribes," "wild people," and "social problems" for American whites.[17]

Although Santos's works were published almost entirely in the Philippines, they had transnational subjects and heterogeneous origins and contexts of writing. Both the Philippines and America became his fictional subjects, especially the hybrid, the migrant, the exile, and the traveler, reflective of his own experiences. His first three novels—*Villa Magdalena, The Volcano*, and *The Praying Man*—have the colonial and postcolonial Philippines as their subject matter. His two later novels—*The Man Who (Thought He) Looked Like Robert Taylor* and *What the Hell for You Left Your Heart in San Francisco*—occur entirely in the United States. This does not address the overlap, however, for the action of most of the novels in part takes place in another country—whether in the United States, the Philippines, or Japan. It is noteworthy that all of Santos's novels were written in the United States, testifying to the importance of his American expatriation to his literary construction.[18] Meanwhile, of the seventy-three stories he wrote, gathered, and published in several story collections, about one-third have the United States as their setting.[19] As in the case of Gonzalez, however, temporal anomalies, and not only shifting geographies, complicate the reading of Santos's stories. For instance, when Santos collected most of his stories, much time had elapsed since they were written. A significant number of stories from *Brother My Brother* (1960), for instance, were written before World War II, and *Scent of Apples* (1979) gathers stories that go all the way back to the mid 1940s. Hence, these stories illustrate the arbitrariness of chronologies and a double life and a double temporality, changing their meaning with shifting historical and narrative contexts.

As I have been arguing throughout this book, Filipino intellectual travel and expatriation, including Santos's, did not occur in a vacuum but in the context of colonial and postcolonial relations of obligation and reciprocity. Santos's expatriation must be seen in the light of the expectations of the Philippine colonial state. The American colonial government continued to place a high priority on education in the colony, and an American, Luther Bewley, ran the Bureau of Education until World War II. Americans established a Philippine Normal School and other teachers' colleges and scrutinized the teacher training of their Filipino wards. There were also rewards for excellent teaching. For instance, Santos's exemplary teaching in the 1930s earned him a trip to Teachers' Camp at the Baguio Vacation Normal School.[20] Moreover, as the example of numerous returned pensionados shows, an American college education was a tremendous asset for any Filipino aspiring to middle-class status.[21]

Bewley himself interviewed Santos and other teachers who had done well in the examinations to determine which of them would go to America and which universities they would attend.[22] At the end of their terms abroad, Santos and other pensionados were expected to return to the Philippines and teach for the state, in which capacity, they would receive much lower salaries than teachers at the private colleges that were springing up throughout the country.[23] The state's expectations notwithstanding, the Philippine postwar era was a high point of both nationalism and antinationalism, and the task of nationhood included the problem of encouraging the return of Filipino university scholars on fellowships abroad.[24]

Intellectual travel and separation also placed stresses and strains upon

Santos's marriage and family relations, because he was separated for extended periods from his wife, Beatriz Nidea (1907–1981), or "Aquing."[25] Santos and Nidea were married on December 23, 1933, when Santos was twenty-two and Nidea was twenty-six. She was also more advanced in her teaching career than Santos.[26] Santos's frequent absences from the Philippines also led to the construction of a translocal, transnational family. After the war, Santos and Nidea raised their children—Arme, Lina, Lily, and Tomas—together in the Philippines for twelve years. They took the ten-year-old Tomas with them to the United States during Santos's Rockefeller and Guggenheim fellowship stints from 1958 to spring 1961, but they were separated from their daughters both during those years and for sixteen years, from 1965 to 1981, during the Marcos era (1965–86).[27]

Individual Ambition—the Pleasures of Performativity

Besides the pressures exerted by state and family obligations, Santos had personal ambitions that exerted pressures that were equally strong upon his psyche. Foremost among these was his desire to become a writer. This had its roots in a love for performance and audience approbation that he had acquired during his youth. One can see this in Santos's frequent references to the influence of his American English teachers, the enthusiasm he felt for declamation and oratorical contests, and his love of words.

One of the most frequent expressions of performativity in his autobiographical and fictive writings is of his colonial experiences with American women high school teachers who inspired him to write, although in drastically different ways. Mrs. O'Malley taught him to love the English language with her recitation of poems that expressed her nostalgia for the New England she had left behind. She exemplifies the sentimentality of colonialism, its quasi-religious, paternalistic (or maternal) belief in the benevolence of the colonial pedagogical mission of reforming natives.[28] Santos discusses the larger ramifications of this colonial encounter in an essay on Filipino writers that downplays the importance of meaning and instead emphasizes rhythm, bodily movement, and sentiment. Santos credited the Americans with fostering Philippine oral tradition through the public school system. In particular, Santos noted the emergence by the 1920s of "the *rhythms* of an Ameri-

can tradition of eloquence," which excited Filipino students. While they recited speeches or poems from memory, "accompanied by *gestures, body language, and corresponding mien*," they were unable to comprehend the meanings of these works, except through the "coaching" of their teachers. Santos
fell in love with the "sound" of English, and he later became an "orator of
the purest ham." Hence, his conclusion that "the language chose me" because he had at an early age been "predisposed to appreciate its *rhythms*."

There were other aspects of American instruction to which Santos was
predisposed, which brought out cultural, if not racial, incongruities. Santos
recounts his grammar school experience of listening to his American woman
schoolteacher recite a poem called "Snowbound." While he and his classmates were "enthralled" by her "obvious nostalgia" for her New England
home, their "brown faces" looked up with wonder, for they "had never seen
snow in their lives" and were in fact suffering from the tropical heat.[29] For
Santos, the irony of the reference to snow mattered little—indeed European
events had long provided the subject matter for the Philippine stage, even
during Spanish times, so this was no surprise. What mattered, however, during American as in Spanish times, was the sound of the language. American
teachers selected American authors "known for their musicality," and it mattered little to the Filipino schoolchildren "what they were saying."[30] Indeed,
the high value Santos would attach to sentiment in his moral and literary
values might have stemmed directly from the influence of this imperial and
gendered sentimentality.[31]

As opposed to Mrs. O'Malley, Mrs. Sage represents the other side of colonialist performativity—racist speech.[32] Santos describes her as a "red-head"
who appeared to "hate her work," and who severely chastised her students,
always seeming angry that they were "so dumb."[33] On a day especially traumatic for Santos, she charged him with plagiarism. Having "shuffled" the
corrected themes for the day, she interrogated him about the authorship of
his paper. He was terrified "by the sound of her voice," by her standing up
to wave the paper in front of her and exclaiming, "'No Filipino can write
this.'" She asked, "Where did you copy this?" After denying that he had
copied it, Santos broke down and cried.[34] Here, the "voice" Santos heard was
colonialism's terrifying voice, not its soothing, sentimental sound; the performance he saw (her standing up and waving the paper) was calculated to
humiliate an upstart native intellectual and to impress the audience with the

worthlessness of their fellow Filipino. Mrs. Sage's charge of plagiarism plays upon the archetypal racist assumption we have seen several times that natives were of a lower level of intelligence, that they were imitators and mimics incapable of original ideas, thus requiring "tutelage."[35] This charge psychologically devastated many, but Santos used it as a motivating factor to succeed as a writer, to prove his old high school teacher wrong.[36]

What colonial racism does, however, is to repress examination of the varied cultures of the colonized. As Santos hinted, he was already "predisposed" to accept the rhythms of English as a result of his exposure to performance. He traces his love of performing to his childhood experiences in a family that combined Tagalog and Pampango influences. Apart from his mother's chanting of the pasyon, of which I shall say more, and a Capampangan *zarzuelista* from Tondo named Kaka Martin, his brother used to set him up on a chair to perform Tagalog riddles before a crowd, with quite comical effects, which his Tondo neighbors would reward with loose change.[37] As a child, Santos also used to visit cousins in Pampanga, and while there, he would watch the theatrical performances of the *moro-moro*, a hybrid Spanish colonial theater form that featured distant wars between Christians and Moors (*Moros*), with their motifs of heroes rescuing maidens and their flashy swordfights.[38] Indeed, something of the melodrama and theatricality of the moro-moro probably suffuses Santos's fiction, with all its dramatic betrayals. The cultural traditions of performativity that Santos imbibed from the vernaculars, especially in his native Pampango, which he spoke with his parents and his only brother, and through which he imbibed the moro-moro, did much to shape his foundational, if not romanticized, encounter with the English language. It recalls the ways in which the Filipinos' encounter with Spanish, then the new colonial language, in the seventeenth century, as in the Ladino printer Tomas Pinpin, was shaped by indigenous, pre-Christian cultural traditions of poetry, song, and epic.[39]

Moreover, as a young man, Santos had aspired to be a lawyer, not for any lofty purpose but to be able to demonstrate his eloquence in the courtroom. Responding to a student's request for his advice on becoming a lawyer, Santos confessed, "I had dreams of success: of brilliant performances in a crowded courtroom; of spell-bound multitudes straining to hear every word I uttered; of laboring masses being swept off their feet through the sheer power of a lawyer's eloquence; of fame and laurels; even of wealth." His eventual choice of a teaching career was in a sense a displacement of this dream of performance in the courtroom to the classroom.[40]

During World War II, Santos found another arena for performance, expressing a kind of extravagance that made him feel guilty about his own well-being in comparison to the situation of his fellow countrymen at war. He was chosen by the U.S. government to go on a lecture tour of the United States to inform audiences about the Filipinos and the war. The involvement of the War Department, which obligated his hosts to pay for his accommodations and to provide his audiences, determined his reception, as it did for Santos's boss, Romulo. With such support, Santos excelled in his forte and relished his travels, which broke the monotony of his editorial work for the Philippine exile government in Washington. Reflecting several decades later on the experience, Santos was ashamed (*hiya*) that he had a nice time touring the United States, traveling to twenty-two universities as "Exhibit A" (what a Filipino looked like), and speaking passionately about his people and his country.[41]

Indeed, it was through his travels that Santos met Bulosan's Filipino old-timers, who had apparently been abandoned both by their own government and by their adopted country. Their plight touched Santos and became a recurring subject of his short stories. A visit to the real-life German prisoner-of-war camp in Fort Hays, Kansas, became the basis for "The Prisoner," while a stop in Kalamazoo, Michigan, led to an encounter with a real Celestino Fabia, whose name appears in "Scent of Apples."[42]

Finally, Santos's love for performativity found expression in his ironic, comical approach to life. For instance, he had a penchant for self-deprecation. In his memoirs, he satirized his inability to drive a car and his lack of a family connection to anyone important, of great concern to status-conscious Filipinos. He poked fun at his odd appearance—his weight, his baldness, and his dark skin. But his sense of irony could also take on a more serious tone. He drew attention to the paradoxes of World War II, the few rewards for writers and the availability of administrative positions he detested, and the ways he and his wife were prevented from returning to their Philippine homeland by the Marcos dictatorship during the martial law period.[43] Santos took his expatriation and exile with humor. To his closest friends and correspondents, that humor often combined sexual innuendoes with the playfulness inherent in code switching between the five different languages—Pampango, Tagalog, Bicolano, English, and Spanish—he spoke.[44]

Identification with the Outsider and Marginality

If performance provided one of the motivations for Santos's desire to be a writer and an important constituent of his national identity, he found an equally powerful motivation for writing in being an outsider, which stemmed from his life experiences. He had grown up in poverty. He felt insecure about his family origins.[45] Moreover, his early experiences with death, which made him an orphan by the time he was twelve, raised by a brother who was twenty-three years older, fueled his emotional insecurity. He loved rhetorical displays, but no member of his family showed up to attend his oratorical contests or graduation ceremonies at Manila North High School.[46] At the University of the Philippines, he felt like an outsider because of his poverty as he worked his way through college as a proofreader for the *Philippines Herald* and the *Woman's Outlook*.[47] To Santos's insecurities of family and class, one might add language and geography as well. Santos never learned Tagalog well enough to truly feel comfortable in it. While he could speak it and read well enough to read Balagtas, the national poet, Pampango remained his first love and the language in which he felt most at home.[48] During the 1930s, Santos's decision to move to his wife's home region in the Bicol provinces probably made him more comfortable in Bicolano than in Tagalog. His location in Legazpi or Naga from the 1940s to the 1960s made him geographically and culturally far from the center of Manila literary life. While he visited the capital on occasion, his Bicol residence led to his isolation from young writers.[49]

Santos felt like an outsider in his social roles, however privileged he might have been. After the war, Santos obtained higher-paying jobs as an administrator, first as vice president of Legazpi College, a private school founded and owned by Don Buenaventura de Erquiaga of Albay.[50] As a writer, he felt out of place in running a university, even though the "Founder" made him president in 1958. In that same year, Santos fled his job and returned to the United States on a Rockefeller fellowship that allowed him to take courses on novel writing at the University of Iowa's Creative Writing Program at the ripe age of forty-seven.[51] Upon his return to the Philippines three years later, Santos was to experience the same thing. He assumed the position of vice president of the University of Nueva Caceres, but his heart was not in it. He lasted there no more than five years before returning to Iowa again, this time as a Fulbright lecturer.

In the 1970s and 1980s, Santos frequently imagined himself an outsider in several ways. During the 1970s, he thought that there was a conspiracy to exclude him from the company of fellow Filipino writers because he had not been invited to the University of the Philippines for creative writing workshops, whereas his friend N. V. M. Gonzalez had been.[52] Santos was devastated by Beatriz Nidea's death in 1981, and felt even more alone thereafter. He resumed what he called the "tramping" life of his fictional characters, traveling to several schools to teach, including at Columbus, Ohio. He felt so isolated there that in his letters, he invented "Charlie," a character who, like Santos, misses his home, and who seeks to return to a place in China that no longer exists.[53] At times, Santos even felt isolated from his own family. He was haunted by the thought of being a burden to them, so he "shuttle[d] from place to place" so as not to overstay his welcome. Rather than being a financial burden to them, he helped out his needy children.[54]

The sense of being an outsider was not only important to Santos's identity but also became an important facet of his literary and pedagogical theory. Santos believed that constructing believable and compelling characters was the most important aspect of the short story, and for him, the compelling characters were not the successful, integrated figures but the outcasts of the society. One can see this in Santos's admonition to his students that there are two kinds of fictional characters—"winners" and "losers." "With winners," he said, "there is no story. But with losers . . . how they handle their loss, that is the story."[55]

Indeed, Santos had feared he might not succeed as a writer because the people he wrote about were the Filipinos who suffered the exclusions of race.[56] He often felt his life approximating fiction, ironically taking on the shape of his characters, always coming and going, "touching the strangest ports," and "always burdened" with "memories," "dreams," and emotions.[57] Santos later spent a great deal of time in the 1980s interviewing pioneering Filipino laborers in Manilatowns on the U.S. West Coast, who had aged along with him. This sparked memories of his first encounters with them and recognition of their plight. While he had first been apprehensive about being able to talk to them, they surprised him by carrying on the conversation in a lively way, speaking with longing about their native land, and even singing and dancing. He came to the conclusion that "[t]hese exiles never really left home." Indeed, they had become terrified by the idea of returning, which Santos found "tragic."[58] Moreover, as Santos says elsewhere, the old-timers felt like "outcasts" and "misfits" in a world that had "swept them beyond moorings." What remained of life became "an endless floating in a shoreless sea."[59] This led Santos to say that perhaps, "in a special sense, I too, am an old timer."[60]

That Santos wrote about the old-timers with great empathy should not, however, conceal the differences between his own social status and theirs, as often happens in literary criticism that ignores Santos's life. After his return from the United States, his wife Nidea invested their money in various business ventures and in property, and when she died in 1981, the couple owned two houses in Greeley, Colorado, had successfully raised a middle-class family, many of whom had master's or doctoral degrees, and had leisure time and ample funds for travel.[61] These were over and above the obvious disparities in education and social mobility that differentiated Santos's life from those of the old-timers, such as Santos's command of the English language, degree from the premier university in the Philippines, and graduate degree from an American university. By contrast, the old-timers of this period, now retired from decades of low-wage work, were struggling to live on meager incomes in the Manilatowns of various West Coast cities, fighting to hold on to low-cost housing in the midst of urban renewal or redevelopment projects, as the plight of the residents of the International Hotel in San Francisco dramatizes.[62]

Devotion and Betrayal: Kinship, Reciprocity, and the Nation

If colonial and national performance and a sense of being an outsider helped to shape Santos's motivations, family relationships, religious beliefs, friends and patrons, and nationalist ideology provided the stable foundation and support for his endeavors as a writer. To the extent that historic social and political circumstances provided a favorable climate for such relationships and perspectives, Santos thrived as poet and fiction writer. But the modernization of the Philippines during the Commonwealth period, his expatriation, the coming of war, and exile shook these foundations, testing not only his ability to fulfill his roles as husband, father, and citizen but even his loyalty to his mother, wife, and country.

The "Mother" of Childhood, Religion, and Marriage

The observation of Santos's critics that Filipinos idealized the nation through the image of the Filipino woman might be regarded as an understatement when seen in the light of Santos's life and work. Women and gender are not only important in Santos's fiction but were key to the relationships that mattered in his life. At the heart of his youth, his marriage and family life, and his religious belief was the foundational figure of the "Mother," or the maternal woman, a central, mythical figure we have seen before in the pasyon in terms of the mother-son relationship. In Santos's descriptions of his formative childhood years in his memoirs, letters, and stories, it is the image of the mother that predominates, and only much less so that of the father. He describes his mother in terms that recall the Virgin Mary. She had the most beautiful eyes and the gentlest gaze he had ever known. She was fair-skinned, elegant, and beautiful, although she could be provincial and earthy, fond of the Southeast Asian custom of chewing betel nut. Most important, Santos remembered the soothing power of her voice. Every year during Holy Week she would sing the *pasion* in Pampango. She sang sad, lilting songs to make him fall asleep. Her voice became ingrained in his memory.[63] Along with the voices of Pampango and Tagalog actors, his mother's voice became part of Santos's emotional, religious, and literary sensibilities.

The connection between Santos's real mother and his spiritual mother becomes explicit in his devotion to the dark-skinned Virgin of Antipolo.[64] A fundamental part of Santos's own identity was his miraculous birth aided by the Virgin. Like the biblical parents of John the Baptist, Santos's mother and father longed to have a child because they were lonely and their only son, Gregorio, had married at the age of twenty-three and left to start his own life. They did what remains popularly known as the *alay lakad*, literally "offering journey" or "offering walk" up the steps of the mountain leading up to the shrine of the Virgin of Antipolo in Antipolo, Rizal. They had faith, says Santos, and they believed in Fate. Santos's mother promised the Virgin that if she were granted a child, he or she would make the annual pilgrimage to the shrine. Soon after this, Santos himself was born, a miracle child, and thereafter began to make the yearly pilgrimage to Antipolo with his mother.[65] Santos's mother and the Virgin of Antipolo recur in his life stories, often indistinguishable from each other in their faith, beauty, and lyricism. For Santos, the image of the Virgin of Antipolo and his religious devotion to her worship, whether in actually visiting the shrine or in imaginatively re-membering it, became his stable foundations during times of hardship and exile.[66]

The poignancy of Santos's remembrance of his mother lies in the fact that she died when he was only ten. She survived in his life, however, through a strange incident that brought together his biological mother, his spiritual mother, and his wife. Some time after his removal to Albay and his marriage to Nidea, Santos forgot to fulfill his mother's vows to make the annual June pilgrimage to Antipolo. He contracted mysterious black spots on his body that baffled the provincial doctors. Nidea took him to doctors in Manila, but they too failed to identify the illness. While he was asleep, however, San-tos dreamed of the Virgin's gentle face looking down on him. He then woke up and realized his error. In his ruffled state, he awakened Beatriz and cried out to her, "*Inang*" ("Mother"). The following day, rather than going to the hospital, the couple (for the first time) made the pilgrimage to Antipolo, and soon afterwards, Santos's mysterious black spots disappeared. Although San-tos might not have intended it, the story suggests that his mother survived death through Beatriz. The disease was not only a sign of the son's way-wardness (his migration away from home), the dangers of potential betrayal (of a sacred vow), and the need to return to one's familial and religious re-sponsibilities (to remember mother, Virgin Mother, and the pilgrimage). It also became the means through which the maternal continued in new form in Santos's life, through his wife, consecrated by their joint sacrifice—their journey to the shrine at Antipolo, offering, and prayer.[67]

After this incident, Nidea became Santos's faithful companion for nearly fifty years and their relationship reflects their love for each other, and in par-ticular Nidea's loyalty to Santos and devotion as both wife and surrogate mother. From the very beginning, however, there was a great deal of anxiety in their relationship. The letters they exchanged before marriage, during their first prolonged separation between 1931 and 1933, when he remained in Manila to finish his studies at the University of the Philippines, display both his fear of betrayal and his own sexist masculinity. Santos demanded sexual "purity" from Nidea—virginity—despite the fact that he never questioned his own sexual purity. He dreamed that Nidea had married another man and abandoned him. His readings of fiction by Sinclair Lewis, Sigrid Undset, and Fyodor Dostoyevsky seemed to compound his worries. The novels that Santos read involved adulterous wives whom their husbands forgave and welcomed back. The women characters were thus portrayed as wayward children and the men as paragons of civilized masculinity and nobility. Yet while Santos demanded purity from Nidea, he wrote about his flirtations with various women and their attraction to him.[68] Being insecure and hungry for the approbation of others, Santos also proved susceptible to sexual flattery. Of a high school student who wrote love notes to him, Santos confessed: "I couldn't in all honesty ask her to stop writing me because secretly I wanted it to continue." And during their wartime separation, after being married for eight years and having three daughters, it was Santos, not Nidea, who was to experience a lapse in marital fidelity. Fully aware of what he was doing, he developed a relationship with a white American woman named Dorothy. It is noteworthy that even here, Santos chose someone who had shown maternal concern for him. Dorothy had taken care of him when he was sick and had looked out for his welfare. Undoubtedly, the pain caused by this affair and the guilt he felt affected the way he felt about such dilemmas.[69]

Over the course of their long marriage, Nidea must have faced considerable pressures as she took care of Santos and their transnational family and at the same time pursued an academic career that her husband at times wanted her to abandon.[70] Nidea, after all, was an intellectual in her own right. She had received her doctorate in education, co-wrote several widely used textbooks, and constructed various tests for the states of Iowa and Kansas.[71] When she died, Santos brought her body back to the Philippines and showed his loyalty to her by commemorating her death on All Saints Day every year.[72] Although he had liaisons and at times searched for permanent partners afterwards, Santos never remarried.

While Santos valorized the ideal woman in his life, he would express his displeasure at what he regarded as her antithesis—modern, liberated women who, in effect, betrayed the national ideal. At the heart of Santos's displeasure was women's departure from Maria Clara (the archetypal demure Filipina of Rizal's *Noli Me Tangere*), their apparently "shameless" display of self-confidence and sexuality. Influenced by the notion of *hiya*, Santos too frowned upon public displays of affection. At one time, he even sought to write a novel, suggestively titled "Maria Clara Revisited," contrasting the woman of propriety and *hiya* with the women of today.[73] On the one hand, Santos was cognizant of unscrupulous men victimizing innocent, defenseless, and pitiful women.[74] On the other hand, despite whatever social factors might frame the plight of women in the Philippines, women remained pitiful to Santos, if not ultimately responsible for what happened to them. He rarely ever held men accountable for their plight, even in the case of prostitution. As he said, "My heart cries out for the young and lovely Filipina who would sell her body and soul to any foreign guy willing and able to take her abroad. Yes, I understand that at the bottom of all this is economics, a deprivation that has worsened through the years. That's why my heart cries out in pity and helplessness."[75]

Patronage and Friendship

Beyond the maternal figures in his life, Santos cultivated relationships with important people who believed in his abilities and supported his literary career; his relationships of loyalty and betrayal with them provide an important avenue for exploring the ambivalent emotions produced by his transnational intellectual life. Much like Gonzalez's, Santos's most devoted literary patrons were white, male Americans and a few powerful Filipinos. The Americans included A. V. H. Hartendorp, editor of the *Philippine Magazine,* Charles Burton Fahs, Paul Engle, and Dean Paul Magelli, while among the Filipinos were Don Buenaventura de Erquiaga and the Hernandez family. Hartendorp was among the first to publish Santos's stories, which he admired, although he despaired at their "sad" themes.[76] Meanwhile, Fahs, humanities director of the Rockefeller Foundation, granted Santos not one but two consecutive Rockefeller fellowships.[77] The first Rockefeller allowed Santos to bring Beatriz and Tomas to the United States and escape from administrative work to study novel writing at the University of Iowa with the poet Paul Engle. In leaving his position at Legazpi College in the Philippines, Santos felt he had disappointed Don Buenaventura de Erquiaga, the Spanish founder and owner of the college, who had recently appointed him its president.[78] In Iowa, Santos continued work on a novel he had started in the Philippines, *Villa Magdalena*. The second Rockefeller granted by Fahs allowed Santos to complete the novel. He did more than that, however, for during the same year, he worked simultaneously on a second novel, *The Volcano*. With the recommendation of Engle, Leonard Casper, and Manuel Viray, Santos then applied for a Guggenheim and won the prestigious fellowship the following year, much to the delight of Engle, who got him an Iowa teaching fellowship and brought him to his speaking engagements to raise funds for the school.[79]

Santos's relationship with Engle seems to have been friendly, supportive, and profitable. When Santos arrived in Iowa, he stayed at Engle's house and reveled in his extensive library. In turn, he and Nidea often invited Paul and his first wife, Mary Engle, as well as other instructors in the Creative Writing Program, to their house. Engle, a former ministry student and Rhodes scholar, who was from Cedar Rapids, had founded the Creative Writing Program to teach his brand of writing to the world and directed it with missionary zeal.[80] He provided an atmosphere that allowed Santos to overcome his initial trepidation about writing a novel. He also took Santos to literary receptions that introduced him to the way "artistic and affluent Americans lived." There were disappointments, however, in their relationship, principally in Santos's unsuccessful attempts to have Engle house his fellow writers N. V. M. Gonzalez and F. Sionil José.[81]

Upon Santos's return to the Philippines in 1961, a new patron, Jaime Hernandez, appointed him as dean of the University of Nueva Caceres (UNC) in Naga, Camarines Sur. Hernandez, who founded the university, had been secretary of finance in Quezon's exiled Commonwealth government during World War II and at one time had been Santos's boss. At UNC, Hernandez provided Santos with an air-conditioned car and chauffeur for various meetings. Being a good friend of Hernandez's, Santos had even contemplated the possibility of writing his patron's official biography.[82] When Hernandez stepped down as president, Santos continued his relationship with the family through Dolores Hernandez Sison, Jaime Hernandez's daughter, who assumed the presidency of the university. In 1965, four years after Santos began work at the university, he again left for the United States, this time on a Fulbright lecturer fellowship at his old haunt in Iowa, where he was to remain for the next seven years, with a brief interruption between 1969 and 1970.

If Santos had a relationship of indebtedness with the Hernandez family, it seems to have been essentially between himself and Jaime Hernandez, not with his daughter. While Santos respected her, he complained of the "subtle form of slavery" she was practicing in leaving the country for extended periods and delegating the tasks of administration to her subordinates, especially Santos. He also mentioned how he tried to evade meeting with her when she traveled to the United States. Nonetheless, their letters speak fondly of working together on graduation ceremonies and other social occasions.[83] At times, Santos's flirtatious comments and sexual banter ("Send me your latest pictures, preferably in miniskirt") even hint that perhaps something beyond work was involved.[84] At one point, Sison had to challenge Santos and Nidea to articulate their terms for returning to the university, especially since Santos's *hiya* seems to have prevented him from doing so. The contents of her letter and Santos's own request suggest that Santos and Nidea were in a stronger position in this transnational negotiation because, although Iowa was not a high-paying institution by U.S. standards, they were earning far more in dollars there than what they had been making in the Philippines. When Santos returned to the Philippines in 1969, he succeeded in getting another extended leave of absence from Jaime Hernandez of no more than three years, and so he returned to Iowa once again in 1970, this time armed with an immigrant visa.[85] The declaration of martial law in the Philippines in 1972 subsequently overrode his agreement with Hernandez.

In the wake of martial law, Santos and Nidea found an accommodating patron once again in the Midwest, at Wichita State University, and in Dean Paul Magelli. Santos and Nidea had just spent a few months with their longtime friend P. C. Morantte in San Francisco, before resuming their positions at the University of Nueva Caceres. While they were there, however, President Marcos suspended the constitution of the Philippines and declared martial law on September 21, 1972.[86] Santos and Nidea now had to remain in the United States, uncertain of the situation in their home country and concerned about the well-being of their daughters in the Philippines. They applied unsuccessfully for teaching positions in California, but Santos eventually obtained a post as Distinguished Writer in Residence in the English Department at Wichita State University (WSU). He credits President Clark Ahlberg and Dean Paul Magelli for his appointment. Over the years, Magelli treated Santos and Nidea with the respect, as well as the pomp and circumstance that their accomplishments deserved, including a sumptuous celebration of the launching of *Scent of Apples*. Santos's position, which had been a temporary but renewable one, was made permanent in the late 1970s. In 1982, at age seventy-one, Santos donated his personal papers to the WSU Library and retired. Yet, even after his retirement, Magelli and Santos continued to have a close relationship. When Magelli became president of Parkland College in Champaign, Illinois, Santos followed him there and taught in the school. He repaid Ahlberg and Magelli for all they had done for him with his loyalty and friendship.[87]

Santos's long-lasting friendship with Leonard Casper was much more complex and at times turbulent. Casper was both friend and patron to Santos, although he was thirteen years younger, simply because of his more senior position as professor of English at Syracuse University and later at Boston College. Initially motivated by the desire to understand his Filipina wife,[88] Casper carved out a niche for himself as a critic of Philippine literature over a number of years of writing reviews of Philippine English writings, befriending Filipino writers, and participating in symposia on Philippine literature.[89] As Casper gained influence, Santos grew to depend upon his patronage to advance his career.[90] That his relationship with Casper in particular was growing can be seen in this brief acknowledgment: "Thank you for this and other past favors. I don't know of any other student of Philippine literature who can equal your critical ability, your understanding of what the Philippine writer is truly trying hard to say, not to mention your dedication and unselfishness." Casper's support included incisive criticisms of Santos's works. He also wrote letters of recommendation, as we had seen in Santos's Guggenheim application.[91] Moreover, with Casper as one of his recommenders, Santos obtained a grant as a Fulbright-Hays lecturer, which allowed him to return to the University of Iowa's Creative Writing Program in 1966.[92]

This friend-patron relationship with Casper, however, was not free of stress. A few years into their relationship, Casper once exploded over his perception that Santos was trying to gouge him when Santos's agent charged him for reprinting one of his stories, "The Common Theme," which Casper had sought to republish for a largely nonprofit venture.[93] On another occasion, Santos was hurt by Casper's rather low ranking of his works in a listing of the best works of Philippine literature in English in Alberto Florentino's

Midcentury ("I was way down the list, barely making it, thanks to you").[94] Nonetheless, Santos's diplomacy and genuine feeling of friendship for Casper apparently helped to restore the client-patron relation. With calculated hyperbole, Santos wrote to Casper that the "Philippines should give you a cultural heritage award for the service that you have been and are rendering Philippine letters."[95]

The hurts of this and perhaps other points of friction in the relationship would recur in the 1980s and 1990s. Motivated by *hiya* and never one to be considered *walang hiya* or *walang utang na loob* (shameless or incapable of honoring a debt of gratitude), Santos was deeply affected by Casper's charge that he had been ungrateful in failing to acknowledge his role in selecting and arranging Santos's second book of poems, *Distances: In Time*, and, as a consequence, by some of his sarcastic ad hominem attacks.[96] In his own way, however, despite all his protestations of gratitude for Casper and his acknowledgment of his skills as a critic of his works, Santos seems to have stood his ground whenever he perceived that Casper overstepped his boundaries as critic and patron (as for instance, when Casper putatively told him to give up on writing novels and go back to writing stories). On another occasion, pressed by Casper about his omission of him as an important literary influence on his writing during the interview for *Writers and Their Milieu*, Santos continued to exclude him, especially because he thought the interviewers were asking him about influences upon his writing, which included Sherwood Anderson, T. S. Eliot, Graham Greene, and others.[97] Santos's relationship with Casper embodies the classic and complicated relationship between Filipinos and colonial rulers ever since the sixteenth century, which Vicente Rafael has described,[98] and which I have explored through the lives of Romulo and Bulosan in particular. While acknowledging the power of colonial patrons and seeking their approval and friendship, native Filipinos have always found ways to deflect their criticism and in turn to register their criticism of colonial authority. As we shall see, this insight was not only important in Santos's relationships with patrons and friends but also an important part of his fictive representation of colonial and postcolonial relations, particularly in his novel *The Volcano*.

Colonial and Postcolonial Betrayals

Running parallel with his relationships to his mother, his wife, and his patrons, Santos also had a more abstract, ideal attachment to the Philippine nation. His inability to serve his country at various critical historical junctures led to feelings of shame and guilt. As we have seen, Santos felt guilty about living a life of relative comfort and safety during World War II, even as his family suffered danger and privation. At the conclusion of the war, he told Nidea, "If there be any suffering yet left, let me share some of it too." Santos also feared the "disfavor" of the government if he did not return to serve and the insinuation that he had become too proud or too accustomed to luxury to share in the hardships of life in the Philippines. "If anything scares me," he said, "it's the suspicion that I don't want to return to the Philippines anymore." He also felt this intensely when he returned to the Philippines after the war, started teaching, and witnessed the devastation and the hardships that people had to endure. While he had complained to the authorities about his unchanged salary since before the war, the sight of buildings under reconstruction, schools full of bullet holes, critical shortages of equipment, makeshift offices constructed of bamboo, and fellow teachers wearing donated United Nations Relief Association clothing tempered his attitude.[99]

Just as important for Santos's nationalism, and reminiscent of Romulo's views, was his perception that both America and the Philippines should fulfill their debt relationships to each other. Unlike Romulo, however, Santos was angered that America had provided such meager funds for Philippine rebuilding but nonetheless boasted of its contributions (on his travels through Albay province, for example, Santos found plaques on walls proclaiming that the buildings had been "reconstructed with financial aid from the United States of America").[100] America had failed to honor its debts to the Philippines and to even live up to its own claims, he felt. Santos criticized the ingratitude of Americans for the sacrifices Filipinos had made for them. This was the exact opposite of Romulo's argument that the Philippines continued to owe a debt to the United States, even after the sacrifices made by Filipinos at Bataan. Reflecting a more militant attitude, Santos pondered alternative messages for the plaques in Albay boasting of U.S. aid. One of them, he wrote, should have read that the wartime destruction was mainly "caused by trigger-happy American soldiers," while another should have advertised how woefully short American spending had been compared to "what Americans really owe[d] the Filipinos," especially in terms of "the broken lives of the survivors."[101]

Perhaps ironically in the circumstances, a few decades later, Santos

nonetheless made the painful decision to renounce his Philippine nationality and apply for U.S. citizenship, motivated by his fears of the martial law
government of President Marcos. The Philippine ruler had confiscated the
farmland that he and Nidea had been paying for over several years to provide them with a living when they retired. Marcos also muzzled freedom of
expression, including the publication of Santos's own novel *The Praying
Man*, which was banned by Philippine censors in 1973.[102] Despite all of this,
Santos and Nidea still hoped to return to the Philippines and to end their
life of exile. One of Santos's close friends at the time, F. Sionil José, regarded
this as "sentimentalism," and advised him to remain in the United States. In
this context of political uncertainty and their own nostalgia for the homeland to which they hoped to return, Santos and Nidea decided to become
American citizens.[103]

Santos's statement to a Filipino American newspaper in 1976 on his naturalization expressed his view that a "bamboo curtain" had been drawn over
the Philippines, which had once been described as "the show window of
democracy in the Far East."[104] It is noteworthy that Santos never blamed the
United States for its support of the Marcos dictatorship, although he had
criticized postwar U.S. policies. With an eye toward those who would see his
change of citizenship as a form of betrayal, Santos claimed that he would
continue to love his country, his people, his friends, and his kin and to feel
proud of being Filipino. He expressed this pride through the objectified gender representation of the Filipina beauty queen. "[W]hen I see a 'Miss
Philippines' crowned 'Miss Universe,' twice in recent years, I get all soft inside me." In a burst of romanticism, which disguised his own desire to return to the Philippines as well as his love of American comforts, he cried
out, "I would rather live in exile, missing the land of my birth, its glorious
sunsets, the scent of fruits in and out of season, familiar scents and sounds
of childhood, and yes, why not, its hurricanes and floods and blistering days
and humid nights." And finally, he sought to change the Marcos regime, not
through political action, but through prayer, using words that would be
prophetic: "I have been patient . . . wishing deep in my heart for a *miracle* of
change without violence, without anarchy."

Yet, deep inside, Santos felt he had betrayed his own country by acquir-
ing American citizenship, which dovetailed with his feelings of guilt about
having lived away from the Philippines and enjoyed the fruits of a better life

in the United States. Santos also felt guilty about the consequences of his decision to remain in the United States. He believed that his wife Nidea had died in 1981 without ever seeing her dream home in Albay because of his selfish desire to remain in a more intellectually stimulating environment in America, with its great libraries and tennis courts. Santos felt "embarrassed" by people pointing to the fact that he had "dollars," instead of pesos, and hence had much greater spending power than most Filipinos, a sign of high-class status that he could not accept. And finally, he felt guilty for having been away from his home country teaching American students creative writing, rather than teaching Filipino students. Thus, after his return, to make up for lost time, he took lower-paying teaching jobs in several Philippine universities.[105]

Loyalty and Betrayal: Fiction

The contrasting themes of loyalty and betrayal, responsibility and guilt, and genuine nationalist citizenship and inauthentic individualism find greater articulation in Santos's fiction, which approximates his life closely enough to allow for a similar investigation of themes, with the possible exception of his patronage relationships. The first set of fictional representations explores the interplay between familial and spiritual devotion and the mother-son relationship. The second section explores the fictive counterparts of Santos's representations of marriage, an even more ubiquitous trope of Santos's mature fiction, both in terms of devotion and of the various tensions that undermine the conjugal bond. And the third will explore the question of loyalty and betrayal writ large, in terms of the transnational, colonial and postcolonial, cultural relations between Americans and Filipinos, especially through the lens of Santos's quintessential postcolonial novel, *The Volcano*.

These distinctions, however, should not be taken as discrete segments, self-contained and unrelated to one another. Indeed, representations of loyalty and betrayal on one level will reveal relationships with another. One hallmark of Santos's writing is the way in which his literary themes wrap around each other like a helix. Familiar experiences and recognizable symbols transcend the individual and cross over to the realms of the family, the nation, and the transnational. Moreover, imagined conflicts often find expression through gendered representations and relationships that show Santos's heightened awareness of gender. Nonetheless, they often reflect his conservative views as well. Here, as in his autobiographical writings, not only do traditional conceptions of femininity emerge but also a construction of masculinity that is decidedly patriarchal. Finally, many of Santos's characters often reflect aspects of his own experiences, especially the different places in which he had lived or to which he had immigrated, his changing occupations, and his relationships with people. By citing these biographical parallels, however, I seek to suggest the connections between Santos's life and fiction and the common problems he grapples with in both, as opposed to indulging in the affective fallacy of reducing his stories to biography.

Familial and Spiritual Devotion

One poignant expression of family and spiritual devotion can be seen in Santos's prewar story "Child,"[106] which portrays the sentimentality of the archetypal mother-son relationship, showing how it provides a subtext to the ostensible world of work, social life, and organized religion inhabited by adults. Selmo, a sugarcane worker, town bully, and male chauvinist has committed sacrilege, tearing the attire of the town's patron saint on the eve of its feast day and extinguishing "the ever burning oil lamp on the altar" (11–12). The townspeople believe that the ensuing rains, which threaten the coming fiesta, are a result of this desecration. On the day of the fiesta, however, Selmo skips the festivities and heads away from the town, drawn by a mysterious "yearning." He walks past the symbols of town life—the music in the background, the voices, and even the roaring of trucks and cars on the provincial road. He heads to the "mountain," walking past the "house of the friars," with its big white cross on the roof, and then to a little house beside a tamarind tree. There, Selmo's mother, a nondescript old woman with bandaged head is sitting feeding two pigs. Selmo runs to her, crying out "Inang" ("Mother") (15). He weeps when he sees her, embraces her, and buries his head in her "withered breast," like a little child finding comfort and peace.

Two subsequent stories, "Far from the City" and "Early Harvest," build upon this literal and figurative return to the safety and stability of the traditional Earth Mother figure.[107] Compared to these two stories, "Child" appears secular in its approach to family devotion, for the two stories assume a decidedly supernatural quality. In "Far from the City," Santos continues his valorization of the traditional and rural, with its superstitious worldview, and affirms the ways in which simple folk religious beliefs lead to both miraculous healing and marital harmony. Like Santos himself, the male narrator and protagonist has recently migrated from a large city to the province of Bicol, where he joins his wife, Toria, and they share a house with a view of the beautiful Mayon Volcano, the scene of many of Santos's stories. In this traditional setting where everyone knows each other, where the houses recall the Spanish colonial era, and where the narrator can take pleasant walks and sing songs with his wife, the natives tell superstitious tales that disturb the narrator. They talk of a house that drove its menfolk to hang themselves on a tamarind tree. The narrator learns to pray to an image of Santa Rosa, especially when his wife becomes deathly sick. His prayers save her, and other local people come over to pray and to kiss the image. When she gets well, Toria becomes angry with him for talking to a "dark girl." To heal the rift between the two, his mother-in-law tells them folk stories about jealous birds that make them forget their quarrel. In the end, his wife's face reminds him of the image of Santa Rosa. The juxtaposition of the image of his wife with the woman saint recalls the persistence of the desire for the maternal and the spiritual in Santos's life and fiction, which we have seen in his misidentification of Nidea as his mother, in a crisis that could only be resolved by renewing his interrupted annual pilgrimage to the Virgin of Antipolo. And we shall see this same confusion of the marital with the maternal in yet another story, "Schoolhouse in the Foothills," discussed below.

In "Early Harvest," a beautiful story of resistance to the Japanese occupation of the Philippines, which Santos wrote in wartime Washington, D.C., he advances the view that human activity and reason alone are inadequate in solving the problems of human beings. Rather, divine, supernatural aid is necessary and forthcoming, especially when one strives to help oneself and maintain one's dignity. The story is seen through the eyes of a child, again named Selmo, and his observations of his people's struggles during the war. With the memory and indignity of the first Japanese confiscation of the fruits of their labor fresh in their minds, the people of the hills deceive the Japanese by telling them to come back for the harvest day celebration on a Wednesday. The folk, however, work night and day before then to harvest all the rice, with the aid of the guerrillas, with whom presumably they would have had to flee. However, their prayers to the blessed image of Santa Rosa, led by a saintly American priest, come to their rescue. Late that night, after they have completed the harvest, it miraculously rains, and the resulting flood saves them from Japanese retribution.

In Santos's postwar novels, the theme of maternal devotion and divine intervention in human affairs assumes a more pessimistic cast as Santos's characters grapple with the consequences of war, displacement, exile, family division, and corruption. In *Villa Magdalena*,[108] Santos's first novel, the quaint animist beliefs of the prewar stories are replaced by a deistic view. The connection between divinity and traditional superstition is weakened and what remains are superstitions in a postcolonial Philippine world that has become both amoral and immoral. Fred Medallada, the protagonist of the novel, is a poor but promising young man from Sulucan. He has been apprenticed to a distant relative named Don Magno, an unscrupulous businessman and the patriarch of Villa Magdalena, who has acquired his wealth by taking over and successfully running the family leather business of his rich but estranged wife, Doña Magdalena Conde. The novel traces Fred's decline from his simple roots and his warm, human qualities toward the corruption and ruthlessness of his patron. A strange figure in the story emerges in the life-like bust of Don Magno, which is pictured alongside a woman saint (52, 55–56, 60). After a confrontation with Doña Magdalena's strong-willed sister, Doña Asuncion, who accuses Don Magno of transferring the Condes' fortunes to himself, Don Magno confides his problems to the bust (61–69). The bust, however, acquires a significance apart from its confessional role for Don Magno and begins to symbolize the wayward journey that Fred is undertaking. Ordered to repair a crack that has appeared in the bust, Fred increasingly finds the Baal-like idol hateful but irresistible. It seems to sneer at him and assumes for him, as it does for Don Magno, a life of its own (71, 72–75).

In Santos's next novel, *The Praying Man*, representations of the mother-son relationship occur in the context of a weakened relationship between religion and folk spiritual beliefs and a postcolonial world of political intrigue and corruption.[109] As in *Villa Magdalena*, the protagonist, Cris Magat, hails from humble beginnings in Sulucan and has now become part of the corrupt ruling clique through his pharmaceuticals empire, his manipulation of high officials, and his participation in a free-wheeling, masculinist culture of booze, pornography, and womanizing. He senses a plot to get rid of him, and the novel is ostensibly about his attempts to remain one step ahead of the conspirators, including a trip to Chicago to hide out with a childhood friend from Sulucan, Kosca. But, as the title of the novel suggests, Magat is not only a *preying* man but also a praying man. The rough, mother-seeking creature of "Child" has here turned into a political animal that nonetheless still longs for maternal comfort and spiritual guidance. Magat's dual world is symbolized by the contents of his wallet. In one compartment, he keeps a medal of the Virgin Mary, while in another he keeps a package of prophylactics, both of which have served as talismans that have saved his life (44–45). Just like Santos himself, Magat also makes an annual secret pilgrimage to the Virgin of Antipolo, there confessing to his fallen state and vulnerability and seeking the Virgin's maternal and spiritual love. He prays, "Virgin Mother, take care of me, the worst of your sons . . . I'm a human animal, but I'm your son and I love you . . . I'm alone, Mother, alone without you" (45). He also has a special reason to pray this time because his son, Junior, has run off with a "hostess," a high-class prostitute named Janet. The Virgin Mother apparently grants his request, for he soon discovers his son's whereabouts and tells him to go home to his worried mother. Meanwhile, the preying man resurfaces. Magat takes Janet into his obscene apartment with its sexual gadgets and has sex with her. Cris Magat's devotion to the Virgin Mother comes to symbolize the doubleness of the Filipino as simultaneously religious and corrupt, steeped in prayer and preying upon his fellowman, but without the salvation of the earlier stories.

Solomon King in Santos's next novel, *The Man Who (Thought He) Looked Like Robert Taylor*, although a close fictional relative of Kosca's, shares the same sense of double consciousness as *The Praying Man*'s protagonist, Cris Magat, in the context of a motherless world in which God has stopped intervening.[110] King is a Filipino who has lived in the United States for a long time. He has no medallion of the Virgin to symbolize his longing for his dead parents and for spiritual fulfillment, as Magat does. Neither does he have a bust, like Fred Medallada, that becomes a touchstone for the changes in his own life. Rather, what anchors him is his superstitious, animist belief in Fate, which has two sides. First, King believes in the notion of the "double," the inevitability of "lives that are extensions of other lives . . . running parallel but close, so close they touched at certain points ever so lightly but palpably, like pure coincidence—and mystical because unnatural" (55). Second, Fate comforts King, because it is inexorable. It has preordained his death, whose sign is embodied in a dream. In this dream, a long-dead family member—his mother—will offer him something sweet to eat. This he must accept, and when he does, he too will die.

Santos's nationalist ideals become wrapped up in the superstitious notions of the novel. The death of King's idol, Robert Taylor, signals his own end to him, and he decides to embark upon one final journey across the United States to revisit his old haunts and to say farewell to his friends. Through the character of King, Santos seeks to convey that there is an unchanging national cultural essence underlying the experience of the Filipino. In an interview, he began with a familiar cultural nationalist trope, that the Filipino, in trying to be an American, had "lost his identity." For his generation, the popular movie actor Robert Taylor exemplified the ideals of masculinity and physical perfection. Santos grafted this idol-worshipping quality upon a Filipino character, King, who "felt that his and Robert Taylor's lives [were] one." Santos's aim was to demonstrate that despite all of the Filipino immigrant's efforts "to be an American . . . on the outside," he remained "a pagan of sorts, believing in magic, believing in superstition."[111]

For Santos, then, Robert Taylor is a symbol of American modernity and a measure of the extent of Filipino American men's self-delusion. Indeed, Taylor comes to stand for the same thing in Santos's world as the modern women he dislikes, whom he represents as symbols of modernity that erode Philippine tradition. What Santos does not say is that Taylor is not only an emblem of a desired modernity and cosmopolitanism but also a symbol of a desired *white* masculinity they can never attain. As with Santos's other novelistic male characters, this self-delusive quest for masculinity and whiteness goes hand in hand with King's patriarchal view of women. On the one hand, King displays fatherly concern for a homeless woman and her child, strangers whom he meets, shelters, and clothes. On the other hand, he can be misogynistic. For instance, King is obsessed by sex, and his girlfriend Morningstar leaves him because she becomes exasperated with his exploitation of her as a sex object. King has also left his wife, after a bitter argument and lived without contacting her for years, although in his final days, he attempts to reconcile with her.

Fidelity and Infidelity

These last two examples of the overlap between intimate relations and superstition suggest Santos's central metaphor for representing his own guilt
and the subject of fidelity and betrayal—marital relations. In this, he was
not unique. As we have seen, in the 1930s, Santos had soaked up the writings
of Sinclair Lewis, Sigrid Undset, Anatole France, and Fyodor Dostoyevsky,
with their recurring theme of the unfaithful wife and the devoted husband
who accepts her back,[112] hence the impression that the woman is immature,
fickle, and childlike, and the husband is responsible, noble, and mature.
Critical of Dostoyevsky's story "A Gentle Spirit," Santos observes that "he
entirely neglects all that is beautiful and everlastingly good in woman."[113]
Yet while Santos questions such one-sided representations of women in
these European and American fiction writers, his women characters hardly
represent the "beautiful and everlastingly good." Instead, both his male and
female characters often live lives of lies and unfaithfulness.

Santos was obsessed with the motif of marriage in his novels, and especially with marital infidelity and betrayal. We have already seen the womanizing Cris Magat of *The Praying Man* and Solomon King who deserts his
wife in *Robert Taylor*. To them, we might add Don Vicente in *The Volcano*,
whose symbolic importance is examined below, and the characters of *Villa
Magdalena*.[114] Yet as complicated as these liaisons are in his novels, Santos
best explores the subject of loyalty and disloyalty in his short stories, where
it sometimes figures as a kind of gendered allegory of the Filipino nation.
Santos's preoccupation with the subject, and the shifts in his views, can be
traced in these stories.

In two prewar stories, "The Portrait" and "Schoolhouse in the Foothills,"[115] Santos dramatizes loss and separation in marriage relationships on
the Philippine rural periphery. The pathos of "The Portrait" is in a woman's
love for her husband, her remembrance of him, and her devotion—religious
in its passion—to both Church and Cross, symbolized by the tolling of
church bells and the wooden cross on top of an ancient church near the
house of the story's protagonist. A religiously devout old woman named
Apung Sabi has lost her husband of many years. To deal with the pain and
to honor him, she and her children work hard to have an obscure picture of
her late husband enlarged and framed into a portrait, a big undertaking for
a poor farming family and something that only those with means could af-

ford. Over many months, the family manages to save enough money to send the picture to Manila and to find someone who speaks Tagalog to carry out the errand. Ironically, when they finally receive the enlarged picture, Apung Sabi has a hard time recognizing it. She has gone blind. Despite its ironic ending, it is precisely the presence and the self-sacrifice of the Virgin Mother–like figure of Apung Sabi that preserve a sense of wholeness for the prewar rural Filipino family in the crisis they face.

Meanwhile, in "Schoolhouse in the Foothills," a schoolteacher is separated from his wife in the Bicol region by an assignment to teach in one of the outlying areas in the province of Sorsogon. (Hence, the scene of the story is twice removed from the colonial capital and center, Manila.) The teacher feels homesick and misses his wife and daughters, and the sight of his young pupils playing in the yard reminds him of them. As he is about to return, a heavy storm crashes down on the region, and he endures the difficulties of finding transportation home and the cutoff of all contact with his wife. After a long wait and increasing fears for his family's safety, exacerbated by a rumor that Mayon Volcano has erupted, he returns by bus on Christmas Day, although he is unable to get home in time to spend the holiday with them. When he arrives, he sees his wife "standing at the door with our child in her arms." Recalling the biblical image of Mary and the child Jesus, he thinks, "I had a feeling I had seen that same picture before, of the mother and the child" (57). As in the case of Apung Sabi, loss, separation, and feelings of displacement are healed by the self-sacrificing wife and caring mother.

In comparison to these prewar stories, Santos's postwar marriage stories exhibit a divided allegiance that goes beyond the domestic core-periphery relations between city and the country and between regional center and hinterland to explore transnational dimensions. Displacement from the Philippine homeland resembles the separations of the prewar era for Santos's exiled characters, but gone now is the caring Filipino woman who mends the hurts, keeps the family stable, and restores the male to his home. World War II destroyed not only much of the landscape of Manila and various Philippine provinces but also a way of life, including the expatriates' idealized traditional Filipina. Prior to the war, there were already tensions in gender relations caused by the rise of the Commonwealth in the 1930s and the advance of modernity.[116] However, the war greatly accelerated this process.

Many Filipinas became prostitutes or were coerced into becoming "comfort women," or sex slaves, by the Japanese overlords.[117] Meanwhile, the few educated Filipinas in exile were exposed to changing gender norms that made them more assertive and self-confident.[118]

In Santos's postwar stories, the true Filipina—rural, demure, virginal, self-sacrificing—is either highly idealized or else relegated to the background. The expatriate, modern, urban, articulate, and assertive woman is *never* valorized as a true Filipina and indeed is often a symbol of an encroaching and despised modernity that leads to social and fraternal fragmentation. Simultaneously, we see the reemergence in Santos's narratives of the figure of the white American woman in the lives of Filipino males. Whereas the white women of his prewar narratives, like "Surprise Ending," had been truly maternal figures, the postwar white American woman now becomes wife or partner in interracial liaisons or marriages. Only this time, the white woman is a simulacrum—hence a lesser figure—a surrogate for the true Filipina, who is forever lost. Nonetheless, just as in his stories of Filipino women, the mother image or ideology persists in Santos's views of women in the ways in which the white wife becomes acceptable as she slides over into her maternal role.

In the classic story "Scent of Apples," devotion to an ideal Filipino-ness comes to be represented in the twin values of proximity to a "first-class Filipino" and faithfulness to the ideal of the Filipino woman.[119] On a speaking tour during the war, Ben, an educated Filipino exile, stops in Kalamazoo, Michigan, where Celestino Fabia, a Filipino old-timer, asks him a loaded question, full of nostalgia and a host of associations shared between them: Are the Filipino women of today still the same as they were twenty years ago? Ben knows that women like those of the past are no longer to be found, but he answers in a way that allows Fabia to preserve his ideal. Fabia then invites Ben (whom he calls a "first-class Filipino") to his house, thirty miles away, for dinner with his family. On the way there, Fabia tells Ben the story of his difficult life. When they arrive at the house, Ben smells the scent of apples, which becomes a symbol for him of the nostalgia of this meeting. He meets Fabia's white American wife, Ruth, described as a plain, portly woman. The couple have a son, Roger, described as a clean, handsome boy. Before dinner, Ben walks around the house and notices an old photograph of a Filipina in her traditional Philippine dress, perhaps the wife or lover, or

maybe even the mother, whom Fabia left in the Philippines. The face is beginning to fade, symbolizing the passage of time and the disintegration of
Fabia's ideal. Ben afterwards asks Fabia to show him where the scent of apples is coming from, and Fabia takes him to a room, where he speaks of
Ruth's loyalty in staying with him when he was struck down by appendici-
tis. Ruth's devotion is not the sexual or romantic attraction or beauty that
the idealized Filipina represents, but it suffices as a kind of surrogate. When
Fabia takes Ben home, we realize that Fabia is much more aware of the gulf
that separates him from home and from his ideals than suggested by the initial question about Filipinas he asked. Ben offers Fabia a chance to send a
message to his family in the village, but Fabia refuses, saying they will have
forgotten him.

A thematic reversal takes place in "Footnote to a Laundry List."[120] This
time, it is romanticized loyalty to the memory of an American woman that
provides the tenuous basis for a Filipino professor's action in a postwar
Philippine university. Dr. N. B. Carlos, a former Filipino expatriate, defends
a young coed at the University of the Philippines who is charged with having had illicit sexual relations with the husband of a faculty member. The
young woman appears before a faculty committee, which acts as though it
were the Inquisition. (Suggesting the sexist environment, the faculty member involved and her husband are not even interrogated, so the trial is
skewed from the outset.) Dr. Carlos is moved to defend the young student.
However, he does not do so out of love for social justice or women's rights,
but in memory of an idealized love affair with a white American woman in
the United States. It is noteworthy that his defense of the young Filipina is
just as sexist as the arguments against her.

If these two stories highlight the theme of loyalty, however tenuous or
equivocal, stories about domestic violence and adultery dramatize disloyalty
and the problems of attaining marital and family stability given the dislocations of modernity. "The House on the Hill" depicts a patriarchal reassertion
of authority and power over women's bodies in the postwar era of changing
gender roles and greater sexual freedom, although sexual license is reserved
for the male.[121] A rich proprietor named Salazar decides to build a mansion
on top of a hill for his wife, Mercedes. His goal is not to honor her, however,
but to exile her for her "indiscretions." He accuses her of having such a good
time dancing with his employees that she has neglected their daughter

Marichu's upbringing, even though he himself has meanwhile been pursuing his mistresses. When the house is finished, he throws a party, but by this time, Mercedes is crushed. She soon dies, and the mansion becomes a mockery of him. Only Salazar and Marichu remain there, and decay sets in. One day Salazar goes out hunting and brings back a strange, bloody, dying bird. A cry issues from the forest. The bird's cries continue into the night and frighten the servants, who have buried it. Salazar is perturbed, while Marichu dreams of her mother with stained red wings.

The second story, "Brother, My Brother," reveals the persistence of secret longings and desires brought about by an idealized expatriation, this time represented by the memory of a liaison with an American woman, whose image threatens the stability of a postwar Filipino family.[122] The narrator, now a professor at the University of the Philippines, has a very unhappy marriage. (He says little about his wife.) His desk cabinet, which is chockful of letters, memories, and secrets, is suggestively also full of termites, and the wood is already becoming hollow, metaphorically suggesting his corrupted soul and his dysfunctional marriage. The source of his marital problems is an adulterous affair he had in wartime Washington, D.C., while studying for his PhD, a time of which he often dreams. He had fallen in love with the white American wife of Mike, a fellow Filipino, who had gone to Leyte (in MacArthur's invasion) and entrusted the care of his pregnant wife to him. When Mike returns, he leaves his wife, without saying goodbye, and rejoins the Army, perhaps sensing her unfaithfulness. She is devastated. After going away on a trip, the narrator returns and searches for her but cannot find her anywhere. He frequents the Manila House, a popular Filipino restaurant and watering hole for the expatriates, and watches as Filipinos go across the street to a bar and a brothel. Identifying with these suffering "little" men, he apostrophizes them, perhaps not without condescension, as "Brother, my brother." He rationalizes his guilt and his continuing distance from his wife by saying that she should have married Nick, a rich suitor who had once taken them out. All along, he has been deceiving his wife and his daughter with his memories of America. Toward the end, he hears a dirge, an ambiguous ending that may signal either the death of their marriage or perhaps his realization that what transpired in America and his relationship with his "brothers" is over.

Colonial Reciprocity

Santos's thematic obsession with themes of loyalty and betrayal also found expression on the larger canvas of the novel, in particular, his classic postcolonial novel *The Volcano*.[123] Santos felt a particular fondness for this work. Compared to his first novel, *Villa Magdalena*, he thought it was much easier to write, "as if writing novels were like giving birth."[124] Moreover, as with the ethnographic character of much of Gonzalez's work on Mindoro, *The Volcano* captures a rich social history of the Bicol region.[125] Perhaps, more important, Santos's triangulation of postcolonial relationships provides a useful framework for exploring the swirling cross-currents of colonial and postcolonial racial, gender, and class relations that are dramatized by the text. As he writes, the cast of characters of both the novel and the colonial Philippines include "the Filipino, the Spaniard, [and] the American" grappling with and "surviving one crisis after another," from World War II to the volcano's eruptions, "each lost in his/her own private concerns."[126] Here, one sees the conflicts and the dilemmas of the American and the Spaniard in relation to each other and to the native Filipino majority during the difficult transition from the colonial era to the postcolonial period. An important point that Santos leaves out is how the theme of betrayal and exploitation occurs within the context of the *utang na loob*, or "debt of gratitude," and, even more important, *hiya*, or "shame," which we have already encountered in Romulo's *Mother America* and Bulosan's *America Is in the Heart*. The difference between Santos, on the one hand, and Romulo and Bulosan, on the other, is Santos's focus on the minds of the American colonial rulers and postcolonial Spaniards, rather than just on the Filipino psyche. Moreover, Santos's account emphasizes the importance of *hiya*, or shame, which suffuses the natives' perception of their relationship with their colonial rulers.

Perhaps the most compelling predicament in the novel is that of the Americans. Their arrogant relationship to the natives recalls Santos's two contrasting schoolteachers and reflects the doubled character of U.S. imperialism itself—as sentimental imperialism and as white racism. In *The Volcano*, sentimental imperialism, with its accompanying racial paternalism, is represented in the characters of Paul and Sara Hunter.[127] As both doctor and Protestant minister, Paul Hunter symbolically represents America's paternalistic goals of civilizing and Christianizing the natives. Hunter preaches "brotherly love" and seeks to convert the predominantly Catholic and superstitious natives to Protestantism. It is only much later in the novel that we realize that the Hunters, although caring, can also be blatantly racist. Like the Thomasites (so called because they arrived on a ship named the SS *Thomas*), who came to teach English after the 1898 Philippine Republic was conquered by the U.S. invaders, the Hunters have come to the Philippines, specifically to the region around Mayon Volcano, in 1928, believing that they know what is good for the Bicolano-speaking native population.[128]

When they arrive, the natives are suffering the effects of a volcanic eruption, and the Hunters unfortunately come to see them as victims, and not as complex, self-determined agents with whom one must "contract" relationships of indebtedness (as they see their colonizers). Rarely do the Hunters notice the people's sense of dignity and faith in the face of extreme adversity or sense their determination to remain free of entangling debt relations. The Hunters shower the natives with gifts—medicine, food, and clothing—available to them as a result of their membership in the Board of Foreign Missions. They fail to notice the natives' reluctance to accept their gifts, indeed their great shame (*hiya, supog*) in having to accept gifts they can never fully repay, in the same way that the peasants of the Spanish colonial land system (perpetuated by the Americans) remained in perpetual debt bondage.[129] To such an overabundance of signs of power, the natives respond by giving what they can—chickens and eggs, for instance, or by performing services for the Americans like cleaning the Mission barracks. They also attempt to displace their discomfort by joking about the gifts and their inability to repay. They resent Paul Hunter's probing into their lives, but instead of confronting him, they make a joke out of everything—"they had found a way of looking disaster in the face and smiling."[130] What Santos presents through the traditional Filipino discourses of reciprocity are cultural representations of what is today called "global restructuring." The Hunters' relationship to the natives presents the classic burden imposed by American "aid," both governmental and private, around the world after World War II on the basis of uplifting the peoples of the Third World from poverty. This aid, of course, always comes with strings attached—foreign debts, loss of control over domestic economies, devaluation of currency, and the destruction of national industrial capacities—all of which breed a hated dependency upon the West. A critical study of global philanthropy, for instance, expresses much the same sentiment that Santos expresses through his fiction. "Donors," it says, were often "shocked" and "sad" when they realized that "even their best intentions [were] often suspect," and perhaps worse, when "supplicants . . . resent[ed] the gift for which they [were] asking."[131] The Hunters can only see one dimension of the natives with whom they have coexisted for thirty years. Indeed, they find the natives' fatalism and their day-to-day lives incomprehensible, as well as resistant to their Christianizing efforts.[132]

But the sentimental imperialist is only one face of American colonialism. The other side is the classic racist, afraid of racial impurities, of contamination, of miscegenation. The hostility of the Filipino Exclusion movements of the 1920s in the United States, which produced antimiscegenation laws targeted specifically at Filipinos, finds its Philippine counterpart in Paul Hunter's dilemmas about his daughter Florence's interracial relationship and subsequent marriage to Badong, their dark-skinned, loyal resident helper at the Mission. Shared suffering does little to diminish these fears. When the Japanese invaders arrive, the natives and the Hunters alike are forced to flee to the mountains and to live a difficult life hiding in caves, often visited by guerrillas, who requisition their food. Badong risks his life for the Hunters several times. In the context of shared misery under the Japanese occupation, the Hunters come to feel that these people have accepted them. The outdoors even makes the Hunters look dark brown now. "How strange, they felt like one of them, not Americans or Filipinos but people struggling to survive in a land overrun by ruthless men."[133] But colonial racism dies hard, especially in the most intimate matters of the heart—the family and the question of marriage. Hunter, despite his seeming goodness, seeks to defend the perimeters of his family's colonial whiteness, hence their power and privilege vis-à-vis the natives and in relation to their fellow white Americans in the United States. He is ashamed of his own hypocrisy in preaching universal love and yet setting a limitation to it on the basis of race.[134]

At the point when Hunter begins to question his fidelity to his own ideals, a Spaniard, Don Vicente, steps into the picture. Described as one with the visage of a priest, hearkening back to the archetypal prelate of Spanish times, Don Vicente is noble in his idealistic desire to help the people but debased by his adulterous affairs. The Spaniard does not criticize Hunter for exploiting the natives, whose labor and sexuality he himself exploits as well, but the difference between them is that he acknowledges that he owes the natives.[135] The Spaniard calls upon the minister to be honest with himself, to acknowledge that what he is doing by giving to the natives is in fact not out of love for them but to enable himself to play God. Indeed, his argument implies that each act of giving is a display of power, because the gift makes the American appear large and the native small and humbled. Moreover, the American has created material and cultural wants and needs in the native that he never had any intention of honoring. He has made "parrots" out of them, miming the American anthem, saluting the American flag, and making them desire everything American. For Don Vicente, part of this honesty is acknowledging one's passions, one's feelings, that one will die among a sea of brown faces. This acknowledges the dependence of the colonizer upon the colonized. Hunter pejoratively labels it sentimentality, however, not acknowledging his own sentimental imperialism.[136]

Finally, there are the Filipinos, represented by two allegorical figures of loyalty and betrayal, Badong and Tito. While physically weak, Badong is studious, articulate, and devoted to the Americans. To them, he is both a hard-working domestic servant and a student. He dreams of going to America to study and to become an American.[137] In wartime, this America-oriented colonized Filipino risks his life to find his master's son, Junior, and suffers torture at the hands of the enemy, never revealing any secrets that could jeopardize his masters. He and the minister's daughter, Florence, subsequently fall in love and make love in the caves.[138] Dr. Hunter's opposition to the marriage creates tensions for the first time between the Hunters and their native converts, especially Badong's parents. But given the suspension of power and social norms created by the war, symbolized by their hiding in the mountains, Hunter is in a sense forced to acquiesce to the young couple's wish to marry, especially with Junior, now a guerrilla, approving the union.[139] Badong's older brother, Tito, represents the other Filipino type; he is a physically vigorous man who criticizes his brother for being a "slave" of the Americans. He claims he never would be a slave. While Junior is his best friend, he will serve neither his family nor the colonial mission. He is proud of his country. During the war, he becomes a leader of the guerrillas and fights the enemy from the mountains, jungles, and caves. He returns a hero and assumes a government position.[140]

Santos represents the postwar, postcolonial moment as a confused tangle of emotions that leads to renegotiations of power. There were moments during the war when it appeared that a true nonracial solidarity would emerge among Americans and Filipinos. When the members of the Red Cross first arrive, they are unable to distinguish the Hunters from the natives. The Hunters have quite literally turned brown while working and living among the natives. They have become naturalized as a result of their common plight in the jungle with the Filipino poor. But alas, as soon as the U.S. Army and the Red Cross reestablish American colonial hegemony, the Hunters revert back to being colonialists and shed their acquired brownness. The sign of their renewed power is in their ability once again to dole out "gifts." Meanwhile, the natives reassert their dignity and their *supog*.[141] Again, the specter of racism rears its ugly head when Hunter engages in a series of lies to his daughter, to Badong, to his family, and to the native community in order to separate his daughter from her husband. Angry members of the community are not fooled, however, and resort to throwing stones on his roof every night. In the end, the family is humiliatingly driven out by the growing nationalist atmosphere, away from the new nation and a country where they had thought they would spend the rest of their lives.[142] Meanwhile, disease afflicts Don Vicente, who requires the amputation of a limb, perhaps the price of his personal and moral corruption.[143] The Filipinos face a series of betrayals. Badong knows that his erstwhile patrons are leaving without him not out of necessity but because they are ashamed of him. Tito is disillusioned by the realization that the wartime collaborators with the Japanese have assumed power. The pro-Americans in office in turn hurl the epithet of "anti-American" at anyone who is critical of the elite and America's neocolonial policies. There is little room for anything in between. In the aftermath of war and the colonialists' vacating of the territory, the Filipino nation is left with divisive questions of authenticity: who represents it? Who are the authentic leadership of the country? Mocking Badong, Tito says he can go to the United States if he wishes, but that he has strong feelings against those who go and come back (thus commenting indirectly on Santos's own plight as a repatriated Filipino). "Our place is here," he tells the Doctor. "For many of the young people who go to America, the experience does them no good. They become impatient and highly critical of the way things are in our country, and instead of helping correct them, they speak with nostalgia, longing for the conveniences they enjoyed in your country." Santos invests Tito with a particular insight into the Filipino's postcolonial identity. At a dinner at the Hunters' residence, Tito talks comically and dramatically about the plight of the Filipino, in words reminiscent of Teodoro Agoncillo's analysis of Manila intellectuals at the beginning of World War II, discussed in the previous chapter. "Be yourself. What is being ourselves? Partly this and partly that and being something else which we are not?"[144] The novel ends with no set resolution. The Americans leave, but Santos's other stories indicate that the problems of the postcolonial and neocolonial Filipino American "special relations" exposed by the novel will continue.[145]

〜

The unresolved problems at the conclusion of *The Volcano* are perhaps a fitting reminder of the troubled postcolonial relationship between Americans and Filipinos. Like Rizal's *El Filibusterismo*, Santos shows the ability to transcend his own ethnic and national boundaries to empathize with the various segments of Filipino society. Perhaps the very dislocations in his own life and his problematic relationship with authentic nationalism and Philippine citizenship allowed him to represent these problems, to dramatize the ambivalence at the heart of colonialism, postcolonialism, and nationalism. Indeed, as I have shown in this chapter, expatriation produced a social mobility, freedom, and material well-being that, in response to family, community, and national expectations, led Santos to profound feelings of guilt and shame (*hiya, supog*) and of betrayal of the nation-state. For Santos, unlike for Romulo and Bulosan, expatriation was neither affirming nor provided a stable position from which to construct the Filipino nation. Yet it was also something whose real effects on him and upon other expatriates he could not deny, as Gonzalez attempted to do. Expatriation had its rewards, but it was equally an indeterminable position of stress, pain, and frustration that evoked dreams of home and an end to what became a routine transpacific commute. Over time and with the physical hardships of advancing age, neither homecoming nor leave-taking provided moments of joy and celebration, but rather of guilt, worry, and doubt. As Santos writes, "Returning to either country . . . is always full of anticipation, and leaving one for the other, full of regret, sometimes fear. In the back of my mind, I wonder, is this the last time I'll say good-bye to my children? The last time I'll see the country?"[146]

Santos's ambivalent relationship with nationalism and national cultures can be seen in various ways throughout this chapter. On the one hand, the strong maternal and feminized spiritual element in his life reconnects Santos with the tradition of the pasyon and animism. Likewise, his relationship to friends and patrons indicates his implication in forms of patronage that have historically shaped the relationship between colonizers and colonized, Americans and Filipinos. These relationships and problems in his life found metonymic expression in much of his writing, and indeed it becomes difficult at times to draw the lines between biography and fiction. On the other hand, Santos also tended to frame his relationship to history and tradition in reductive, essentialist ways, embodied in his insecure nationalism. He valorized tradition over modernity, the country over the city, the plain, submissive, or maternal rural woman over the assertive, "painted," self-confident urban woman, and the Philippines over the United States. The ironies, of course, are that his life as a literary expatriate subverted his attempts to put down roots, and that most of the women with whom he cultivated relationships were modern and assertive, not passive and traditional. His life in America, supported by white American friends and patrons, reflected "home" as much as the Philippines he nostalgically longed for. In some sense, Santos came to recognize, much more than Gonzalez did, how important his American life was to him. A good indicator of this is his acceptance of designations such as "Filipino American" and "Asian American" writer to describe himself, which Gonzalez rejected. Santos's life in exile, with its painful ambivalence and its shame and guilt stemming from the inability to find a home, recalls the Filipino saying that the "crime" of "leaving one's own country carries with it its own penalty." That "crime" now burdens Filipino expatriates the world over, from overseas contract workers to nurses to mail-order brides.[147]

Conclusion: Toward a Transnational Asian American Intellectual History

The Complexities of Filipino American Intellectual Culture

We may now be able to draw conclusions from the experiences of the five Filipino American intellectual travelers and expatriates that have been the subject of this book. Each of the different chapters has attempted to underscore some aspect of the combination of cultural hybridity and ambivalence rooted in actual experiences of travel and expatriation. In Chapter 1, I explored Carlos Romulo's shifting self-definitions during the period of American colonial rule—as "Oriental," westernized Filipino, and American—and as a Third World politician and First World cultural broker during the postcolonial period. In Chapter 2, I showed how the plagiarism case involving Carlos Bulosan was only the tip of the iceberg for this socialist intellectual's deeper involvement in premodern Philippine oral culture. In Chapter 3, I traced the traditional influences on José García Villa of social class and ethnic nationalism coexisting with his ongoing modernist manifestoes and his performances as a diva and master teacher. Finally, in Chapters 4 and 5, I explored the tensions arising from N. V. M. Gonzalez's and Bienvenido Santos's attempts to manage the difficult pressures exerted by the nation-state during the post–World War II era and their commitment to literary art for Asian and Asian American audiences.

Yet, while all five men embodied and recognized the "heterogeneity, hybridity, and multiplicity" of Asian and Asian American cultures,[1] each took a different view of his sojourns away from the Philippines and his "foreign" experiences. The five men deploy their narratives of expatriation with distinctive agendas. Romulo saw his experiences away from the homeland as formative of his national identity and regarded "expatriate affirmation" as crucial to the construction of Philippine nationalism. This position both facilitated his adoption of a transnational, Philippine-American cultural identity and justified his "pro-American" politics (rooted in the synthesis of nationalism and liberal free market ideology). Bulosan's expatriation was more circumscribed than Romulo's. As we have seen, the very nation-state that supported Romulo in the 1950s engaged in a witch-hunt that sought to ensnare Bulosan and his Communist friends. Bulosan in effect regarded himself as belonging to a diaspora of Filipino migrant laborers in Hawaii, Alaska, and the western United States, although he did not use the word "diaspora." For the expatriates, who were constructing a more progressive political culture and fraternal community in exile, the Philippines constituted a common point of origin and reference but it was not the sole focus of their culture in America, which also drew upon common experiences of hardship, racism, and union organizing. Bulosan experienced something of the economic exploitation and racial discrimination faced by his compatriots and shared their sense of deracination and homelessness, for they were accepted neither in the United States nor in the Philippines. In his writing, Bulosan sought to depict the hardships of his social class—pointedly excluding the pensionados, the middle class, and the upper-class diplomats in the eastern United States—and to unify them through the pasyon idiom and his own example of self-sacrifice.

Villa initially saw himself as an exile fleeing the cultural provincialism and sexual restraints of the homeland, symbolized in his writings by a peremptory, brooding, backward-looking—indeed Oedipal—Father, who closely resembled his real father. For Villa, expatriation was inextricably bound up with living in Greenwich Village, which stood for the experimental, avant-garde, and cosmopolitan artistic life. Just as important, perhaps, Greenwich Village represented sexual freedom for Villa, the space upon which to discover and explore his homosexuality, alongside numerous "queer" American writers and artists who had likewise found refuge there. This view of expatriation was consistent with Villa's poetics, his transcendent conception of "Man" (although not woman) and his disdain for nationalist and proletarian outlooks, which for him were pedestrian propaganda (unmindful of the propaganda of his own art for art's sake approach). Similarly, Villa's return trips to the Philippines and his public appearances there, calculated for shock value and to maximize his reputation as a diva, sought to reassure Filipinos that he remained Filipino despite a long expatriation. Quite simply, he described himself neither as an American nor as a Filipino American nor an Asian American poet, but as a "Filipino poet in New York." The description had the curious effect of downplaying whatever "foreign" influences and lived experiences might have shaped his life. Although it is a subdued theme in Villa, this obscuring of expatriate experiences would find greater articulation in the younger Gonzalez, whose artistic career paralleled Villa's.

Gonzalez and Santos differed from Romulo, Bulosan, and Villa in their obsession with the problem of authenticity as Filipinos. During World War II and in the postwar period, Filipino intellectuals increasingly embraced a Filipino cultural nationalism that was simultaneously pan-Asian in perspective and at times anti-American in rhetoric. It was ironically during this time of national assertion that Gonzalez and Santos traveled extensively outside of the Philippines and constructed their binational lives. Gonzalez, a classic sojourner, sought to better his economic life and his literary opportunities in America before returning to the Philippines. Martial law foiled his dreams of an early return. Despite his encounters with social movements on college campuses, often involving Asian American students, and his inclusion in Filipino American or Asian American anthologies, conferences, and events, Gonzalez never wavered in his self-designation as a "Philippine writer." In fact, he sought to downplay or erase the influence of expatriation in his public pronouncements and to advance the creation of a truly national Philippine culture. That culture would be unified by new myths and metaphors that valorized the dignity, ingenuity, and diversity of Filipinos and their vast, pre-Hispanic cultural resources. In line with this expanded nativist project, Gonzalez constructed his own myth about expatriation, claiming that he had never actually left the Philippines, despite his long sojourn in America and his transpacific life. Moreover, he felt that those who left their Philippine homeland *could* return, indeed *had to* return, in order to draw upon their ethnic culture and vernacular languages and to regain their equanimity and balance, destroyed by colonialism and migration. The irony, of course, is that those essential ethnic and vernacular cultures were in large part shaped by colonialism and migration.

Unlike Gonzalez, Santos recognized his identities as a Filipino, a Filipino American, and an Asian American writer, although this was dependent on his location and his audiences. In speeches in the Philippines, where he received several honorary doctorates, he highlighted his nostalgia for the Philippines and downplayed his American experiences and U.S. citizenship. Conversely, in his letters and speeches to American audiences, Santos emphasized his affinities with Filipino American, Asian American, and ethnic American writers, downplaying his desire to return to the Philippines. Indeed, given his widespread acceptance across the Pacific and the bifurcation of his family that resulted from martial law, Santos regarded expatriation with immense feelings of guilt and insecurity. His attempt to fulfill family, literary, and personal expectations by traveling across the Pacific involved him in a physically demanding schedule that nonetheless left him uncertain and ambivalent about satisfying anyone. This combination of mobility, homelessness, and the conflict of Filipino nationalist ideals with American experiences found poignant expression in Santos's writings.

The experiences of these Filipino American intellectuals across the Pacific during the colonial and postcolonial periods had important consequences for the construction of both Philippine and Filipino American identities and solidarities. First, it must be noted that by the fact of travel, Filipino intellectual migrants to the United States occupied a liminal position, which created the opportunity to reenvision Philippine cultures and to see the American cultural landscape anew. Second, intellectual expatriate experiences challenge the perception that the Filipino national and Filipino American ethnic cultures are monolithic, undifferentiated, and unchanging (a view that reflects the influence of elite nationalist ideologies or aspirations). Rather, side by side in the Philippines and in Filipino America, there are myriad regional, class, ethnic, linguistic, and religious cultures, with both colonial and postcolonial histories, as well as internal hierarchies. These cultures have changed over time and continue to change, vis-à-vis both expatriates and American-born Filipinos. Third, Filipino cultural heterogeneity provides a rich resource for the construction of new cultural forms and national imaginings in the diaspora, which persist even when such elements are repressed by an attempt to embrace modernity or social mobility.

Just as important, the American culture that Filipino American writers encountered in the United States involved a variety of cultural experiences. Filipino intellectual migrants to the United States sought to incorporate not only Filipino immigrant and working-class experiences on the West Coast but also white American popular and elite cultures (political, academic, and avant-garde) throughout the country. Filipino migrant intellectual experiences in the United States led to a wide range of responses, from the rejection or blocking of American influences characteristic of Filipino nativism to an incorporation of the multicultural, multiracial, and intergenerational experiences that typify acculturation in American society. Indeed, these cultural positions should not be seen as definitive or mutually exclusive. Intellectual expatriates' ambivalent bicultural, transpacific cultures exposed these stances as points on a continuum of cultural positions. Moreover, both the neocolonial hegemony of the United States in the Philippines and the race, class, and cultural exclusions faced by Filipinos and Filipino Americans continue to provide the material basis for such bicultural perspectives.[2]

In light of these complex historic and contemporary factors, the difficulties faced by contemporary Filipino Americans with regard to naming themselves and defining their collective identities appear less problematic. Rather than seeing these designations—Filipino, Pilipino, Filipino American, Pilipino American, Asian American, Pacific Islander, Latino, and so on—as mutually exclusive, it is perhaps more fruitful to regard them as reflections of complex cultural negotiations that have historically faced Filipinos on both sides of the Pacific. Indeed, the dynamism of Philippine and Filipino American life in the United States makes the attempt to limit Filipino self-naming an impossible task, if not something undesirable.

The Denial of "Empire" and Asian American Intellectuals

This critical study of Filipino American intellectual expatriate experiences also has important implications for the writing of American intellectual history and the interdisciplinary field of Asian American Studies, which are increasingly taking place in the context of the American assertion of global hegemony in the twenty-first century. For instance, since the terrorist attack upon the symbols of American power on September 11, 2001, and the American invasion of Iraq, public and academic concern has meshed over the question of America's identity as an "empire." In an editorial for the *New York Times*, Harvard's Michael Ignatieff argued that empire "in a place like Iraq" has become "the *last hope* for democracy and stability alike" (emphasis added), although he cautioned that "empires survive only by understanding their limits."[3] Some time after this article, Niall Ferguson, a New York University professor, wrote that America is "an empire in denial."[4] Examining the British Empire's contributions to free trade and liberal political institutions around the world, he urged America to "export its capital, its people, and its culture to those *backward* regions that need them most urgently" (emphasis added). He warned that if these regions "are neglected," they "will breed the greatest threats to its security."[5]

Both the romanticism and the developmentalism of these reflections upon empire, presented as sober assessment and realpolitik, recall the exclusions in the imperialist discourse of American foreign policy at the beginning of the twentieth century. It is disconcerting that neither Ignatieff nor Ferguson attends to the perspectives of the "Other," the varied discourses of the colonized or racialized peoples of these empires and the consequences of imperialist and anti-imperialist arguments *for them*. With this ominous erasure, they build their arguments for American intervention in the world.

These kinds of exclusions are reproduced in a recent appraisal of global and transnational discourses in U.S. history, *Rethinking American History in a Global Age*.[6] The book represents a pioneering attempt at assessing the impact of global processes and trends, especially as they impinge on the writing of cultural and intellectual history. The collection charts possible directions for transnational research. In particular, Prasenjit Duara (a historian of China), Akira Iriye, and Charles Bright and Michael Geyer, respectively, challenge the limitations of historical narratives centered upon the development of the nation, examine international bodies whose activities transcend nation-state boundaries, and problematize the meaning of American "sovereignty" in an era of globalization.[7] At the same time, it is the premier intellectual historians Thomas Bender and David Hollinger who provide the cautious, if not skeptical, remarks against the erasure of the American "nation." In their attempts to recenter American national history, they seem to leave their national narratives vulnerable to being appropriated by the triumphalism about empire that infuses the analyses of Ignatieff and Ferguson.[8]

Bender's and Hollinger's essays, for instance, might be taken as rejoinders to Duara's questioning of the nation, which is often quoted by different authors throughout the book. In *Rescuing History from the Nation* (1995), Duara argues for the importance of subnational (intrastate) and supranational (international) approaches to the history of China and calls for a "rescue" of historiography from nationalist or nation-state narratives.[9] In contrast, Bender writes in his introduction to the anthology that it is not "the purpose of this work to subvert the nation," without defining what that means. Indeed, the somewhat conservative tenor of this statement is reflected in his tendentious view of transnationalism and his unproblematized assumption of community and history with anonymous readers, which reinforces precisely the nationalism that critical studies of nationalism have questioned. "It seems important at this moment in *our* own history," says Bender, "when there is a heightened awareness of both transnational connections and particularistic solidarities, to explore those stories of *our* past, those experiences at scales other than the nation, that have been . . . obscured by the emphasis upon the centrality of the nation" (emphases added).[10] Despite Bender's work in editing this pioneering work, he is not an enthusiastic proponent of transnational or global developments. In part, his goal is to rehabilitate American national historiography. For instance, Bender highlights the importance for transnationalism of an essay by Frederick Jackson Turner, whose work on the frontier has provided such a provocative and at the same time problematic basis for Western history. He argues that Turner's less famous essay "The Significance of History," written after his famous essay outlining the frontier thesis, is an early transnational piece that argues for the impossibility of a truly *national* history divorced from international developments. Instead of a critical view of the contradictory aspects of Turner, Bender seems to imply that Turner was a transnationalist all along.[11]

Meanwhile, David Hollinger's more substantive essay, which concludes the book, responds to Duara by claiming that "nations are not the only formations that threaten to turn historians into tools" and that "[n]onnational and antinational movements and solidarities can do the same."[12] Hollinger sees the telling of U.S. history as imperative, given his nationalistic claim that the United States "displays the most successful nationalist project in all of modern history."[13] Responding to the American cultural historian David Thelen's attack on nation-centered narratives, Hollinger provides excellent readings of works that reflect "a nation-centered scholarship that speaks both to a global community of professional historians and to citizens of the United States."[14] Hollinger, however, goes beyond these examples. He claims that future national narratives should have a programmatic focus. For him, this involves "the notion of *a national solidarity committed—but often failing—to incorporate individuals from a great variety of communities of descent, on equal but not homogeneous terms, into a society with democratic aspirations inherited largely from England*" (emphasis in original).[15]

One can only be cautious of the apparent Eurocentrism of these two approaches. Like those of Ignatieff and Ferguson, neither Bender's nor Hollinger's essay includes perspectives from America's racialized or colonized others or writings by contemporary scholars of color. Bender's recapitulation of Turner and his attempt to transnationalize him fails to engage, much less to credit, contemporary "borderlands" studies, for instance, José David Saldivar's *Border Matters: Remapping American Cultural Studies* (1997), which have problematized Turner's teleological story of westward movement and Americanization by imagining "new cultural affiliations and negotiations . . . in terms of multifaceted migrations across borders."[16] Hollinger's examples of "*American* intellectual history" tellingly exclude seminal works on African American intellectuals and the African diaspora.[17] Given these omissions, one becomes skeptical of following Hollinger's path to national narratives. Indeed, his statement seems to reflect a static notion of political indebtedness and tradition. It highlights America's *inheritance* of democratic principles *from* England (and Europe by extension) rather than emphasizing the rich *inheritance* of American democratic struggles to actualize, indeed transform, the flawed imaginings of democracy at the nation's founding.

Rethinking American History has little to say about Asian Americans, Pacific Islanders, and their transpacific movements and cultures, even as it highlights transatlantic connections. This might leave the mistaken impression that nothing has been done in this direction. On the contrary, there has been an increasing engagement with transnational issues in Asian American Studies that has yet to be explored by American historians. In a field such as Asian American Studies, which has been so identified with immigration studies and with "Asia," it might seem that few would disagree with the importance of transnationalism. Yet developments in Asian American studies have tended to mirror the concerns of *Rethinking American History*. In the past ten years, there has been a growing debate in the cultural studies field between those enthusiastic about transnationalism and those who caution against its too ready adoption.[18] On the one hand, the literary critic Sau-ling Wong's landmark essay "Denationalization Reconsidered" (1995) raised the specter of diaspora studies potentially undermining the domestic subject-position of Asian *American* studies and its critique of race and class *in* America. On the other hand, several scholars, including Susan Koshy, take issue with Wong's usage of the word "denationalization" and its potentially treasonous implication, as with the simplistic dualism between diaspora and domestic that seems to pervade Wong's argument.[19]

Perhaps more important than these debates in the literary and cultural realm is the growing historiography on transnational, transpacific concerns. Much of this involves work on Chinese and Chinese American transnational relations, the most recent being the social histories of Cantonese migrants by Madeline Hsu and Yong Chen, which trace the lives of workers, married men and women, and entrepreneurs between Guangdong and California.[20] These two recent works join a host of writings on Chinese in Latin America and the Caribbean, a series of explorations of Chinese national political figures like Sun Yat-sen, Liang Qichao, and Kang You-wei, and a recent comparative study of Chinese migrant networks in Peru, Chicago, and Hawaii.[21] Transpacific studies have also emerged in the study of other Asian groups. Indeed, the spate of writings on transnationalism, taken together, is redefining and radically expanding the meaning of Asian American and Asian American studies.[22] Contrary to Sau-ling Wong's fears, transnational and diaspora studies have broadened the scope of the field and at the same time kept attuned to political and social developments and racial conditions in the United States.

This rise in transnational concerns in Asian American studies also parallels the rise of the emergent field of Asian American intellectual history. Hitherto, the study of Asian American intellectuals has not been an important contributor to transnational studies, especially since Asian American scholars, suspicious of the elitist or conservative assumptions of the word "intellectual," have long ignored intellectual history. There are signs, however, of a reconsideration of intellectual studies. For instance, Henry Yu's *Thinking Orientals* is the first book of its kind to explore Asian American intellectuals, specifically, the dynamics of race involving Asian American sociologists and the Chicago School. Viet Thanh Nguyen's *Race and Resistance* also examines contemporary Asian American intellectuals, including Asian American writers, artists, and academics, in the context of the representational conflicts within the contested field of Asian American studies. Concerned with race relations and ethnic formation in response to specific institutional and political developments in the United States, these works have understandably focused on national institutional developments and counterpublics.[23]

My own work on Filipino American intellectual expatriates addresses the exclusion of racial others, especially transpacific Asian American intellectuals, in the field of American intellectual history. At the same time, it seeks to recenter intellectual history, albeit nontraditional intellectual history, in transnational studies of Asian Americans. Of crucial importance to my approach to intellectual history and transnationalism are the colonial context and postcolonial relations, which shape the terrain of intellectual activities and relationships. Hence, one might term the new discursive space that I am attempting to clear "transnational Asian American intellectual studies."

Toward a Transnational Asian American Intellectual History

Contemporary discussions of intellectual history and transnationalism have thus far been mired in binary thinking. Social history, as I explored in the Introduction, has been set against intellectual history and vice versa. Nationalism has been set in opposition to transnationalism. Historians have raised the question of transnationalism by taking sides on Prasenjit Duara's provocative dictum of "rescuing history from the nation," resting upon the false choice between abolishing or defending the nation. This dichotomy obscures the complex relationship between the nation-state and the transnational or subnational processes that seem to defy it. The transnational Asian American intellectual history I am concerned with attempts to overcome these binaries. As I explain in the Introduction, I have attempted to build upon the insights of Ruby Paredes and others who argue that the national or colonial state is itself transnational. As we have seen, relationships of power, patronage, and reciprocity were crucial to the construction, reception, and reproduction of Filipino American intellectual lives and discourses. Perhaps more important, my work on expatriate Filipino intellectuals calls into question this nation-transnationalism dichotomy by examining the lived social experiences of the intellectuals themselves through their own discursive lenses. Such an examination, in particular, reveals that the sense of deracination, displacement, and doubleness that characterizes transnational intellectual discourse derives not from an experimental, postmodernist conception of ethnicity or a choice to be "postnationalist" or "postethnic." Rather, transnationality arises precisely from the ironic failure of expatriate intellectuals to come home or feel at home, whether as a result of their rejection by the nation-state, or by their compatriots, or of their inability to meet the demands of ethnic community, kin, or nation.

Despite their overseas contexts, transnational Filipino intellectuals and writers of the colonial era saw themselves as good Filipino nationalists in the service of the Philippine-American state (before Philippine independence in 1946) and the emergent postcolonial Philippine nation-state. They felt a tremendous sense of loyalty to the Philippines, evidenced by their service to the Commonwealth government, the state-sponsored University of the Philippines and other state-run schools, their common goal of building a national literature, and their relations of obligation with Philippine political leaders. Their nationalism was also evident in the stubbornness with which they clung to Filipino citizenship and refused the urgings of friends that they become U.S. citizens. Romulo and Gonzalez are today buried in the Libingan ng mga Bayani, the Cemetery of Heroes, exclusively reserved for Philippine citizens. Although they died in America, Bulosan and Villa remained Philippine "nationals" to the end of their days. Santos was the only one to opt for naturalization, at the ripe age of sixty-five, but his reasons for doing so included self-protection and nationalism. He was convinced that this was the only way to protect himself and his family from the Marcos dictatorship and to facilitate his journeys back to his homeland. He is buried today in his home province of Albay.

Exile and expatriation were a constituent experience of Filipino nationalism, and at least during the formal colonial era, there was no conflict between leaving one's country and being Filipino. Indeed, as a famous scholar of nationalism writes, "Exile is the cradle of nationalism." And as migration scholars have argued, separation from home, encounters with racial differ- ence, and regional loyalties in diasporas sharpened (rather than diminished) both ethnic American and Old World national identities. Romulo's first years at Columbia during the Jazz Age, Bulosan's sojourn in the West, Villa's seclusion in the New Mexico desert during the Depression, Santos's wartime exile at the University of Illinois, and Gonzalez's journey across the United States four years after the war's end—all of these first pilgrimages to the metropole evoked deep feelings of nostalgia, nationalist pride, and home- coming. At the same time, intellectual expatriates had distinctive American racial experiences. Romulo found himself caught in the racial divide be- tween blacks and whites in America and forced to assert a third, nonaligned path. Racism opened Bulosan's eyes to widespread discrimination against Filipinos, and Villa's to a greater sense of the importance of his career for the Filipino nation. Expatriation alerted Gonzalez to stereotypes of Filipinos in America and the malaise of the Filipino middle class on both sides of the ocean. Finally, Santos became increasingly aware of racial difference through his fleeting encounters with Filipino farm laborers and urban service work- ers. Expatriation tended to blur Philippine regional differences for all the in- tellectuals, although homeland class distinctions held firm in the diaspora, separating Bulosan's experiences from the elite, middle-class, or upper-class experiences of the others.

Expatriation, however, often frustrated transnational intellectual aspira- tions for national service and authenticity in unpredictable ways. For in- stance, national publics, whether envious of migrant intellectuals or wary of their ties to the foreign, questioned their authenticity. Romulo failed to win a Philippine presidential nomination in part because of the populace's sus- picion of his transnational, Philippine-American diplomatic experience and the assumption of disloyalty. Bulosan became the target of anticommunist witch-hunts and the snobbery of the educated elite. Villa escaped the con- fining sexual morality of the Philippine colony. Gonzalez fled an economi- cally unrewarding public school system, while Santos, after obtaining U.S. citizenship, bemoaned his exclusion from consideration as a National Artist, an honor reserved for Philippine citizens. The Marcos dictatorship had con- tradictory effects on these expatriates, enlisting the loyalty or tacit cooperation of Romulo and Villa and discouraging the Philippine return of Gonzalez and Santos.

Simultaneously, various aspects of American life, including the pulls exerted by Filipino American communities, undermined their resolve to return home. Their fictional characters might return to the Philippines, but their own homecoming was a "dream deferred." America represented or embodied many things for these men. For most of the five, America was a space of sexual freedom, if not, transgression, as can be seen in the interracial relationships of Romulo, Bulosan, Villa, and Santos. For these, World War II offered opportunities for economic advancement, social interaction with the white majority, and openings for Filipino literature. Meanwhile for all five, America's universities and libraries became intellectual havens, in contrast to the provincialism of their Philippine counterparts. Filipino American communities exerted their greatest pulls upon Bulosan, Santos, and Gonzalez, although they were also crucial in Villa's later life. Romulo was a fleeting presence at respectable Filipino American community events during the war. Bulosan was attracted to the Filipino laborers' transient life, the progressive ideals of radical Filipinos, and their efforts at union organizing. Santos identified with Filipino old-timers' feeling of rootlessness and their inability to return home. Their poverty reminded him of his own class origins, even as the expatriate Filipino professionals after 1965 welcomed him into their luxurious homes. Both he and Gonzalez found support and admiration among Filipino American and Asian American intellectuals, even if their Filipinoness did not always mesh with their America-centered perspectives. Villa always maintained contact with Philippine intellectuals at the United Nations, hosted visiting Filipino writers, and toward the end of his life, socialized with a younger generation of Filipino expatriate intellectuals who identified with his early literary triumphs. It should be stated here that Filipino expatriate intellectuals themselves formed an important part of Filipino American communities in various parts of the United States. Villa married a white American woman and lived with her and their two children in New York until the couple's divorce. Bulosan had in effect a common law marriage with Josephine Patrick in Seattle. Santos, his wife Beatriz, and their son Tomas were among the pioneers of Filipino communities in Iowa City, Iowa, Wichita, Kansas, and later Greeley, Colorado. Gonzalez, his wife Narita, and their children lived in Hayward, California, for several decades, near the large, long-established San Francisco Filipino community. As these examples show, even as Filipino intellectual expatriates identified with the Philippines and Filipino nationalism, they were rooted in American realities through their racial and multiracial encounters and their experiences of education, labor, marriage, family, and community life in America. In various ways, these inevitably found expression in their writing.

These examples show that there are rich possibilities for transnational intellectual exploration between the nation and transnationalism. The nation need not be eradicated—indeed, the nation as ideal and reality was central to the experience and imagining of Filipino American intellectual life. But expatriation created its own pathos, stemming from the volatility of neocolonial Philippine life, which tended to exclude Filipino intellectual expatriates even as they sought inclusion and recognition from the Philippine state and Philippine national communities. Expatriation also produced simultaneous experiences in the United States of inclusion and exclusion, irreducible to a Philippine nationalist paradigm. Indeed, it is in the ironic and continuing failure of Filipino American expatriate writers to find lasting acceptance in either the Philippine nation-state or their second home in the United States that one can define the space of transnational culture. Transnationalism is inconceivable without the national or colonial state or the desire for national belonging. Simultaneously, the nation paradoxically finds confirmation through the limits that it sets upon those who can belong to its imagined community and the failed or incomplete integration experienced by those in-between figures whose lives hover at its margins.

REFERENCE MATTER

Notes

1. Matei Calinescu, *Five Faces of Modernity: Modernism, Avant-Garde, Decadence, Kitsch, Postmodernism* (Durham, N.C.: Duke University Press, 1987).

2. That these key intellectuals all happen to have been men stems from the nature of the historiographic intervention, as will become clear in the text. Arguably, it also stems from the relative absence of Filipina expatriate writers during the first half of the twentieth century. I was struck by the interest of Asian American literary critics, especially in the early 1970s, when the Asian American movement was just emerging, in these Filipino intellectuals as *Asian American* writers and participants in various *Asian American* projects. At the same time, I found it curious that these Filipinos were marginalized from Asian American literary discourse.

3. This global diaspora, I argue, exerts pressures to expand the label "Filipino American," which I use to describe these border-crossing intellectuals. This designation, which emerged in the late 1960s as a result of the influence of American ethnic political movements, came to refer to those born or raised in the United States. But I doubt if it can be limited to that population alone. Filipino immigrants, from the very beginnings of labor migration in this century to the present wave of professionals and military personnel, have always been an integral part of America's Filipino communities. Likewise, Filipino immigrants today are transforming America and are in turn being transformed by their experience in this country. Throughout most of their lives, Filipino expatriate intellectuals embraced the term "Filipino" rather than "Filipino American." Nonetheless, their long peri-

ods of residence and travel in the United States embody a range of ethnic American experiences, of racism, class, and multicultural relations, that go beyond Filipino experience. Indeed, Filipino expatriate intellectual lives would not be legible if seen exclusively from the standpoint of the Philippines and a territorially defined Filipino perspective. And, vice versa, their American contributions would appear warped without examination of the strands connecting them across the Pacific to their "homeland." Thus, I use the ethnic label "Filipino American" in an expansive sense to include the heterogeneous experiences of the Filipino population in America, especially the exiles and migrants at its margins.

4. While there are numerous definitions of the concept of nation, I understand it in terms of Benedict Anderson's classic formulation of it as an "imagined political community," which brings together people unknown to each other in bonds of fictive kinship, forged especially through participation in mass democratic social movements. See his *Imagined Communities: Reflections on the Origin and Spread of Nationalism* (1983; reprint, New York: Verso, 1991).

5. Yuji Ichioka, "*Kengakudan*: The Origin of Nisei Study Tours of Japan," *California History* 73, no. 1 (Spring 1994): 31.

6. I use the term "cosmopolitanism" here in the conventional sense of the attributes of a "cosmopolitan" or "cosmopolite," i.e., a sophisticate with a worldwide rather than a provincial scope. The term "cosmopolitanism" is not to be confused with David Hollinger's identification, in debates among liberal intellectuals in the 1920s, of a distinct cultural position against ethnic pluralism, in his "Ethnic Diversity, Cosmopolitanism, and the Emergence of the American Liberal Intelligentsia," in *In the American Province: Studies in the History and Historiography of Ideas* (Bloomington: Indiana University Press, 1985), 56–73. The term "archipelagic," which nicely conveys the simultaneous diversity, multiplicity, and isolation of the Philippines' 7,107 islands, comes from Oscar Campomanes, "N. V. M. Gonzalez and the Archipelagic Poetics of Filipino Postcoloniality," in N. V. M. Gonzalez, *Work on the Mountain* (Quezon City: University of the Philippines Press, 1995), vii–xx.

7. Citing Veblen, Sollors argues that modernity and ethnicity need not contradict each other. In his discussion of Jewish intellectuals, Veblen argued, for instance, that it was their "escape" from their cultural environment and exposure to culture contact and doubleness that encouraged "pioneering" in artistic endeavors—this he termed "divided allegiance." Thorstein Veblen, "The Intellectual Preeminence of Jews in Modern Europe," in *The Portable Veblen* (New York: Viking, 1948), 467–79, quoted in Werner Sollors, *Beyond Ethnicity: Consent and Descent in American Culture* (New York: Oxford University Press, 1986), 243; and see also Edward Said, *Culture and Imperialism* (New York: Knopf, 1993), 51. Said writes else-

where that the exile sees things from a "double perspective" that always compares "every scene or situation in the old country" with the "new country." This exilic mental activity provides the basis for an intellectual approach that "counter-pose[s]" ideas and experiences, "making them both appear in a sometimes new and unpredictable light." Edward Said, *Representations of the Intellectual* (New York: Vintage Books, 1994), 60.

8. Anthony Giddens, *Central Problems in Social Theory: Action, Structure and Contradiction in Social Analysis* (Berkeley: University of California Press, 1979), 1–8, 57. Giddens defines "practical consciousness" as "tacit stocks of knowledge" that are "skillfully applied in the enactment of courses of conduct . . . which the actor is not able to formulate discursively." For the notion of "rearticulation" and "resignification," see Judith Butler, *Excitable Speech: A Politics of the Performative* (New York: Routledge, 1997), 28, 40–41. In discussing "agency" and structure, Butler argues that "agency" is "a reiterative or rearticulatory practice, immanent in power and not a relation of external opposition to power." Using the example of the word "queer," Butler shows how the resignification of this word from a mark of opprobrium to a symbol of ownership and empowerment in the gay movement has opened new contexts and produced legitimation in new forms. Performativity, says Butler, is not only "defined by social context [but] by its capacity to break with social context." The analytic power of these dimensions of performativity theory will become apparent when applied to the formation of national identities in diaspora or exile. As we shall see, Filipino expatriate intellectuals in Spain and then in the United States became aware of themselves and continually reimagined themselves as "Filipinos" and "Filipino Americans" *retrospectively*. This national consciousness was often articulated in the wake of performative responses (oratory, acts of defiance, and masculine gestures) to colonial racist acts and epithets, which served to unify Filipino intellectuals who had hitherto regarded themselves as part of distinct regional identities.

9. Sollors also uses the term "double audience" to describe the ethnic writer's problem of addressing two distinct groups at different points in time—natives and noninitiates, insiders and outsiders—whether real or imagined. This becomes a source of playfulness for ethnic writers. See Sollors, *Beyond Ethnicity*, 249ff.

10. Reynaldo Ileto, *Pasyon and Revolution: Popular Movements in the Philippines, 1840–1910* (Quezon City: Ateneo de Manila University Press, 1979, 1989).

Introduction

1. My account draws principally on three works: for the ilustrados, John N. Schumacher's classic *The Propaganda Movement, 1880–1895: The Creators of a Fil-*

ipino Consciousness, the Makers of the Revolution (Quezon City: Ateneo de Manila University, 1973); for popular nationalism, Reynaldo Ileto, *Pasyon and Revolution: Popular Movements in the Philippines, 1840–1910* (Quezon City: Ateneo de Manila University Press, 1979, 1989); and for patronage, the collected essays in Ruby R. Paredes, ed., *Philippine Colonial Democracy* (New Haven, Conn.: Yale University Southeast Asia Studies, 1988).

2. Schumacher, *Propaganda Movement*, 70. Creoles were full-blooded Spaniards born in the Philippines. *Indio* was the Spanish term for all nonwhite Filipinos. Spanish mestizos were children of Spanish and indio parentage, and Chinese mestizos were children of Chinese and indio parentage. The term "Filipino" was only used to describe full-blooded Spaniards born in the Philippines, the "Españoles-Filipinos."

3. Ibid., 5–8, 50–51. See also Ambeth Ocampo, *Rizal Without the Overcoat* (Metro Manila: Anvil, 1990), for accounts of ilustrados' travels throughout Europe, and Cesar Majul, "Anticlericalism During the Reform Movement and the Philippine Revolution," in *Studies in Philippine Church History*, ed. Gerald H. Anderson (Ithaca, N.Y.: Cornell University Press, 1969), 152–71.

4. Schumacher, *Propaganda Movement*, passim, and Nick Joaquin, "What Signified the Expatriates?" in *A Question of Heroes* (Manila: National Book Store, 1981), 39–53.

5. For examples of these masculine displays, see Schumacher, *Propaganda Movement*, 174–75; Ocampo, *Rizal Without the Overcoat*, 121ff.; and Vicente Rafael, "Nationalism, Imagery, and the Filipino Intelligentsia in the Nineteenth Century," *Critical Inquiry* 16 (Spring 1990): 591–611.

6. Schumacher, *Propaganda Movement*, 57–67, 185–90.

7. Renato Constantino, *The Philippines: A Past Revisited* (Manila: Renato Constantino, 1975), 152.

8. José Rizal, *Noli Me Tangere*, trans. Soledad Lacson-Locsin (Honolulu: University of Hawai'i Press, 1996); id., *The Subversive (El Filibusterismo)*, trans. León Ma. Guerrero (Bloomington: Indiana University Press, 1962).

9. John Schumacher, *The Making of a Nation: Essays on Nineteenth-Century Filipino Nationalism* (Quezon City: Ateneo de Manila University Press, 1991), 93–101; Teodoro Agoncillo, *History of the Filipino People*, 8th ed. (Quezon City: Garotech, 1990), 149, 175.

10. Ileto, *Pasyon and Revolution*, 22–25.

11. Ibid., 22.

12. Ibid., 119ff.

13. Ibid., 50, 108; 99ff.; 139–41. In folk belief, a mythical figure named Bernardo Carpio, trapped in the San Mateo caves southeast of Manila, would one

day return to free his people. Lower-class revolutionaries reasoned that although Filipinos had once owed a "debt of education" to Mother Spain, her children had now adequately repaid her through their labor and by shedding their blood to defend her against the Moros (Muslims from the southern Philippines) and other colonial powers. Moreover, Spain herself, in the guise of her cruel, greedy friars, had violated the mutual trust between the two peoples, abrogating any prior union between them.

14. Vicente Rafael, *Contracting Colonialism: Translation and Christian Conversion in Tagalog Society under Early Spanish Rule* (Quezon City: Ateneo de Manila University Press; Ithaca, N.Y.: Cornell University Press, 1988), 121–35. See, e.g., "Tomas Pinpin and the Shock of Castilian," ibid., 55–83.

15. Rafael refers to Tagalog strategies of decontextualization of colonial speech as "fishing," which refuses to internalize religious principles as demanded by Catholic conversion and instead grafts them onto native worldviews. See Rafael, *Contracting Colonialism*, 1–22.

16. Glenn May, "Civic Ritual and Political Reality: Municipal Elections in the Late Nineteenth Century," in *Philippine Colonial Democracy*, ed. Paredes et al., 13–40.

17. Ruby R. Paredes, "Ilustrado Legacy: The Pardo de Taveras of Manila," in *An Anarchy of Families: State and Family in the Philippines*, ed. Alfred W. McCoy (Quezon City: Ateneo de Manila University Press, 1994), 373, 397; Estebana A. de Ocampo, *First Filipino Diplomat: Felipe Agoncillo, 1859–1941* (Manila: National Historical Institute, 1994), 3; and Michael Cullinane, "Playing the Game: The Rise of Sergio Osmeña, 1898–1907," *Philippine Colonial Democracy*, ed. Paredes et al., 77–78.

18. See Ruby R. Paredes, "The Origins of National Politics: Taft and the Partido Federal," in *Philippine Colonial Democracy*, ed. id. et al. Taft and other American politicians were, after all, drawing on a long history of American political patronage, including Republican Party (and, generally, white) patronage of blacks, New York's Tammany Hall politics, and Democratic Party patronage of the Irish. See Eric Foner, *A Short History of Reconstruction, 1863–77* (San Francisco: Perennial Library, 1990); Edward L. Ayers, *The Promise of the New South: Life after Reconstruction* (New York: Oxford University Press, 1992), 35, 38ff.; Richard L. McCormick, *The Party Period and Public Policy: American Politics from the Age of Jackson to the Progressive Era* (New York: Oxford University Press, 1986), 234–35, 291–310; Richard Hofstadter, *American Political Tradition* (New York: Vintage Books, 1978), 220–22; Alan Trachtenberg, *The Incorporation of America: Culture and Society in the Gilded Age* (New York: Hill & Wang, 1982), 161–73; and David Roediger, *The Wages of Whiteness: Race and the Making of the American Working Class* (New York: Verso, 1991), 140–44.

19. Established in 1902, the Resident Commissioner's Office allowed Filipino colonials the opportunity to send a nonvoting representative to Congress to argue on behalf of Filipino rights. In 1903, the *pensionado* system was established to send promising high school youth, with Philippine colonial government scholarships, to American universities. It was the brainchild of T. H. Pardo de Tavera, then a member of the Philippine Commission. After the establishment of the University of the Philippines in 1908, the pensionado system shifted toward sending students abroad for professional or graduate education. See Constantino, *The Philippines: A Past Revisited*, 300; "The First One Hundred Filipinos," *Graphic*, Oct. 22, 1927; Romeo V. Cruz, *America's Colonial Desk and the Philippines, 1898–1934* (Quezon City: University of the Philippines Press, 1974), 119ff. See also William Alexander Sutherland, *Not By Might: The Epic of the Philippines* (Las Cruces, N.M.: Southwest Publishing Co., 1953).

20. Paredes, "Origins of National Politics," 58ff.; Alfred W. McCoy, "Quezon's Commonwealth: The Emergence of Philippine Authoritarianism," in *Philippine Colonial Democracy*, ed. Paredes et al., 114–60.

21. See Manuel Arguilla, Esteban Nedruda, and Teodoro Agoncillo, eds., *Literature under the Commonwealth* (Manila: Philippine Writers' League, 1940); Grant K. Goodman, "Japan and Philippine Radicalism: The Case of Benigno Ramos," in *Four Aspects of Philippine-Japanese Relations, 1930–1940*, Monograph Series, no. 9 (New Haven, Conn.: Yale University Southeast Asia Studies 1967), 135–36.

22. On the historical development of state patronage of the arts in the United States, see Michael Kammen, "Culture and the State in America," *Journal of American History,* December 1996, 791–814.

23. Nathan Irvin Huggins, *Harlem Renaissance* (New York: Oxford University Press, 1971), 85, 117–18, 127–28.

24. Maximo C. Manzon, *The Strange Case of the Filipinos in the United States* (New York: American Committee for Protection of Foreign Born, 1938); *Letters in Exile: An Introductory Reader on the History of Pilipinos in America* (Los Angeles: Asian American Studies Center, 1976).

25. See Harvey Klehr and John Earl Haynes, *The American Communist Movement: Storming Heaven Itself* (New York: Twayne, 1992), esp. ch. 3; Richard H. Pells, *Radical Visions & American Dreams: Culture and Social Thought in the Depression Years* (1973; repr., Urbana: University of Illinois Press, 1998), 151–93. For the debate in the Philippines between a socially responsible literature and "art for art's sake," see Salvador P. Lopez's essays on Philippine literature in the 1930s in id., *Literature and Society: Essays on Life and Letters* (Manila: University Publishing Co., 1940).

26. Sucheng Chan, *Asian Americans: An Interpretive History* (Boston: Twayne, 1991), 121–22, 141–42.

27. On the impact of the Cold War on various American intellectuals, see John Patrick Diggins, *The Proud Decades: America in War and in Peace, 1941–1960* (New York: Norton, 1989), 220–72. On the anticommunist campaign of terror in the Philippines during the 1950s, see Benedict J. Kerkvliet, *The Huk Rebellion: A Study of Peasant Revolt in the Philippines* (Honolulu: University of Hawai'i Press, 1977).

28. Mike Murase, "Ethnic Studies and Higher Education for Asian Americans," in *Counterpoint: Perspectives on Asian America,* ed. Emma Gee et al. (Los Angeles: Asian American Studies Center, 1976), 205–23; Madge Bello and Vince Reyes, "Filipino Americans and the Marcos Overthrow," *Amerasia Journal* 13, no. 1 (1986–87): 73–84; and Mark R. Thompson, *The Anti-Marcos Struggle: Personalistic Rule and Democratic Transition in the Philippines* (New Haven, Conn.: Yale University Press, 1995).

29. See Edward Said, "Introduction," in id., *Orientalism* (New York: Vintage Books, 1978).

30. Edward Said, *Culture and Imperialism* (New York: Knopf, 1993). The arrangement of the book shows this bipolar thinking. While chapter 1 shows the complexities of "Overlapping Territories, Intertwined Histories," the next two chapters divide hegemony and resistance—chapter 2 presents the "Consolidated Vision" of empire of European modernists, while chapter 3 presents "Resistance and Oppression." Antoinette Burton's excellent study of postcolonial Indian intellectuals, *At the Heart of the Empire: Indians and the Colonial Encounter in Late-Victorian Britain* (Berkeley: University of California Press, 1998), presents a more nuanced example of this overlap between resistance and hegemony.

31. See Homi Bhabha, "Introduction: Narrating the Nation," in *Nation and Narration,* ed. id. (New York: Routledge, 1990), 91–97.

32. See Paul Gilroy, *The Black Atlantic: Modernity and Double Consciousness* (Cambridge, Mass.: Harvard University Press, 1993), ch. 1, "The Black Atlantic as a Counterculture of Modernity," 1–40; and Gilroy's specific readings of black intellectuals, such as Martin Delaney and W. E. B. Du Bois, 19–30, 111–45.

33. James Clifford, "Traveling Cultures," in *Cultural Studies,* ed. Lawrence Grossberg et al. (New York: Routledge, 1992), 97, 100. See also James Clifford, *Routes: Travel and Translation in the Late Twentieth Century* (Cambridge, Mass.: Harvard University Press, 1997).

34. For a review of this literature, see Patrick Wolfe, "History and Imperialism: A Century of Theory, from Marx to Postcolonialism," *American Historical Review* 102, no.2 (April 1997): 410–13.

35. Ed Cohen, "Posing the Question: Wilde, Wit, and the Ways of Man," in *Performance and Cultural Politics,* ed. Elin Diamond (New York: Routledge, 1996), 35–47. See also Mary Louise Pratt, "Reinventing America/Reinventing Europe:

Creole Self-Fashioning," in id., *Imperial Eyes: Travel Writing and Transculturation* (New York: Routledge, 1992), 172–97; and Vicente Rafael, "Nationalism, Imagery, and the Filipino Intelligentsia in the Nineteenth Century," *Critical Inquiry* 16 (Spring 1990): 591–611. See also Doreen G. Fernández, "From Ritual to Realism," in *Palabas: Essays on Philippine Theater History* (Quezon City: Ateneo de Manila University Press, 1996), 2–26.

36. Benedict Anderson, *Imagined Communities: Reflections on the Origin and Spread of Nationalism* (New York: Verso, 1991), 47–65.

37. Victor Turner, *Dramas, Fields, and Metaphors: Symbolic Action in Human Society* (Ithaca, N.Y.: Cornell University Press, 1974), chs. 5 and 6; Joseph Campbell, *The Hero of a Thousand Faces* (Princeton, N.J.: Princeton University Press, 1949, 1973), 3–25, 315–64. For Arnold van Gennep, rites of passage or transition rites involved three phases: separation, margin (or *limen,* Latin for threshold), and reaggregation. It is the second, liminal stage, when the ritual subject's identity is ambiguous, neither here nor there, that has interested social theorists, for, in Turner's words, this is where "communitas"—or a deep feeling of community, equality, and comradeship—emerges. See Turner, *Dramas, Fields, and Metaphors,* 232.

38. This involves a large literature. Important texts include *Counterpoint: Perspectives on Asian America,* ed. Emma Gee et al. (Los Angeles: Asian American Studies Center, 1976); *Letters in Exile: An Introductory Reader on the History of Pilipinos in America* (Los Angeles: Asian American Studies Center, 1976); Fred Cordova, *Filipinos: Forgotten Asian Americans* (Dubuque, Iowa: Kendall/Hunt, 1983); Yuji Ichioka, *The Issei: The World of the First Generation Japanese Immigrants, 1885–1924* (New York: Free Press, 1988); Ronald Takaki, *Strangers from a Different Shore* (New York: Penguin Books, 1989); Karen Leonard, *Making Ethnic Choices: California's Punjabi Mexican Americans* (Philadelphia: Temple University Press, 1992); Evelyn Nakano Glenn, *Issei, Nisei, War Bride: Three Generations of Japanese American Women in Domestic Service* (Philadelphia: Temple University Press, 1986); Barbara Posadas and Roland Guyotte, "Unintentional Immigrants: Chicago's Filipino Foreign Students Become Settlers, 1900–1941," *Journal of American Ethnic History* 9, no. 2 (Spring 1990): 26–48; Valerie Matsumoto, *Farming the Home Place: A Japanese American Community in California, 1919–1982* (Ithaca, N.Y.: Cornell University Press, 1993); and Judy Yung, *Unbound Feet: A Social History of Chinese Women in San Francisco* (Berkeley: University of California Press, 1995).

39. Don Nakanishi, "Asian American Politics: An Agenda for Research," *Amerasia Journal* 12, no. 2 (1985–86): 1–27; Sucheta Mazumdar, "Asian American

Studies and Asian Studies: Rethinking Roots," in *Asian Americans: Comparative and Global Perspectives*, ed. Shirley Hune et al. (Pullman: Washington State University Press, 1991), 29–44; Oscar Campomanes, "Filipinos in the United States and Their Literature of Exile," in *Reading the Literatures of Asian America*, ed. Shirley Lim and Amy Ling (Philadelphia: Temple University Press, 1992), 49–78; R. Radhakrishnan, "Postcoloniality and the Boundaries of Identity," *Callaloo* 16, no. 4 (1993): 750–71; Sau-ling C. Wong, "Denationalization Reconsidered: Asian American Cultural Criticism at a Theoretical Crossroads," *Amerasia Journal* 21, nos. 1–2 (1995): 1–27; King-Kok Cheung, ed., *An Interethnic Companion to Asian American Literature* (New York: Cambridge University Press, 1997); Elaine H. Kim and Lisa Lowe, "Introduction," in "New Formations, New Questions: Asian American Studies," special issue, *Positions: East Asia Cultural Critique* 5, no. 2 (Fall 1997): v–xiii; and David L. Eng, "Out Here and Over There: Queerness and Diaspora in Asian American Studies," *Social Text* (Fall–Winter 1997): 31–52.

40. Wong, "Denationalization Reconsidered," 5–12. See also Arif Dirlik, "Asians on the Rim: Transnational Capital and Local Community in the Making of Contemporary Asian America," *Amerasia Journal* 22, no. 3 (1996): 1–24.

41. Louis A. Perez Jr., "Incurring a Debt of Gratitude: 1898 and the Moral Sources of United States Hegemony in Cuba," *American Historical Review* 104, no. 2 (April 1999): 356–98; Ramón Grosfoguel et al., "Beyond Nationalist and Colonialist Discourses: The *Jaiba* Politics of the Puerto Rican Ethno-Nation," in *Puerto Rican Jam: Rethinking Colonialism and Nationalism: Essays on Culture and Politics*," ed. Francis Negrón-Muntaner and Ramón Grosfoguel (Minneapolis: University of Minnesota Press, 1997), 1–38; Enrique de la Cruz, ed., "Essays into American Empire in the Philippines, Part I: Legacies, Heroes, and Identity," special issue, *Amerasia Journal* 24, no. 2 (1998); id., ed., "Essays into American Empire in the Philippines, Part II: Culture, Community, and Capital," special issue, ibid., no. 3 (1998); Sharon Delmendo, "The Star Entangled Banner: Commemorating 100 Years of Philippine (In)dependence and Philippine-American Relations," *Journal of Asian American Studies* 1, no. 3 (October 1998); and "Islands in History," special issue, *Radical History Review* 73 (Winter 1999).

42. Exceptions include Campomanes, "Filipinos and Their Literature of Exile"; Vicente Rafael, "Anticipating Nationhood: Collaboration and Rumor in the Japanese Occupation of Manila," *Diaspora* (Spring 1991): 67–82; and id., "White Love: Surveillance and Nationalist Resistance in the U.S. Colonization of the Philippines," in *Cultures of United States Imperialism*, ed. Amy Kaplan and Donald E. Pease (Durham, N.C.: Duke University Press, 1993), 185–218.

43. For a genealogy of race discourse and the colonial state, see David Theo

Goldberg, "Racial Rule," in *Relocating Postcolonialism*, ed. David Theo Goldberg and Ato Quayson (Malden, Mass.: Blackwell, 2002), 82–102; and Vicente Rafael, "White Love: Census and Melodrama in the U.S. Colonization of the Philippines," in id., *White Love and Other Events in Filipino History* (Durham, N.C.: Duke University Press, 2000), 32–38. For the seminal studies of whiteness and the desire to become white among subaltern groups, see David R. Roediger, *The Wages of Whiteness: Race and the Making of the American Working Class* (New York: Verso, 1991); and David R. Roediger and James Barrett, "Inbetween Peoples: Race, Nationality, and the 'New-Immigrant' Working Class," in David R. Roediger, *Colored White: Transcending the Racial Past* (Berkeley: University of California Press, 2002), 138–68. Finally, on the importance of race and everyday experience, see Philomena Essed, "Everyday Racism: A New Approach to the Study of Racism," in *Race Critical Theories*, ed. Philomena Essed and David Theo Goldberg (Malden, Mass.: Blackwell, 2002), 176–94.

44. Stuart Hall, "Gramsci's Relevance for the Study of Race and Ethnicity," *Journal of Communication Inquiry* 10, no. 2 (1986): 23–25, and id., "New Ethnicities," in Kobena Mercer et al., *Black Film, British Cinema* (London: Institute of Contemporary Arts, 1988), 135ff.; and Renato Rosaldo, "Cultural Citizenship: Attempting to Enfranchise Latinos," *Nueva Visión* (Stanford Center for Chicano Research) 1–2 (Summer 1992): 7, cited in José David Saldivar, *Border Matters: Remapping American Cultural Studies* (Berkeley: University of California Press, 1997), 206 n. 4.

45. On masculinism and its relation to American empire, see Ronald Takaki, "The Masculine Thrust Toward Asia," in id., *Iron Cages: Race and Culture in Nineteenth-Century America* (1979; repr., New York: Oxford University Press, 1990), 253–79; Amy Kaplan, "Romancing the Empire: The Embodiment of American Masculinity in the Popular Historical Novel of the 1890s," *American Literary History* 2, no. 4 (Winter 1990): 659–90; and Kristin Hoganson, *Fighting for American Manhood: How Gender Politics Provoked the Spanish-American and Philippine-American Wars* (New Haven, Conn.: Yale University Press, 1998). For a critique of gender and its representations in the colonial and nationalist context, see Ashis Nandy, "The Psychology of Colonialism: Sex, Age and Ideology in British India," in id., *The Intimate Enemy: Loss and Recovery of Self under Colonialism* (Delhi: Oxford University Press, 1983, 1994), 9–18; Gayatri Chakravorty Spivak, "Can the Subaltern Speak?" in *Marxism and the Interpretation of Culture*, ed. Cary Nelson and Lawrence Grossberg (Urbana: University of Illinois Press, 1988), 271–313; and Jenny Sharpe, "Introduction," in id., *Allegories of Empire: The Figure of Woman in the Colonial Text* (Minneapolis: University of Minnesota Press, 1993), 16–19.

Chapter 1. "Expatriate Affirmation": Carlos Romulo

1. Carlos P. Romulo, *I Walked with Heroes* (New York: Holt, Rinehart & Winston, 1961), 125, 128, 135, 151.
2. Ibid., 136–37.
3. Ibid., 144–45.
4. *Current Biography, 1943* (New York: H. W. Wilson, 1943), 626–28. Also, *U.P. Biographical Directory* (Quezon City: Library of the University of the Philippines, 1964), 141.
5. *Current Biography, 1957* (New York: H. W. Wilson, 1957), 474.
6. *Current Biography, 1943*, 626–28.
7. Ibid., 623.
8. Carlos P. Romulo, *I Saw the Fall of the Philippines* (Garden City, N.Y.: Doubleday, Doran, 1942); *Mother America: A Living Story of Democracy* (Garden City, N.Y.: Doubleday, Doran, 1943); *My Brother Americans* (Garden City, N.Y.: Doubleday, Doran, 1945); and *I See the Philippines Rise* (Garden City, N.Y.: Doubleday, 1946).
9. The Russian foreign minister Andrei Vishinsky described Romulo as "this little man with the big, big voice . . . [with a] gift of ready wit and fluent words." *Current Biography, 1957*, 475.
10. An essay in *Aiiieeeee!!!: An Anthology of Asian American Writers*, ed. Frank Chin et al. (Washington, D.C.: Howard University Press, 1974), lvi, mentions Romulo's novel *The United* (New York: Crown, 1951) as a work similar to Carlos Bulosan's *America Is in the Heart* (1946; reprint, Seattle: University of Washington Press, 1973) and Celso Al. Carunungan's *Like a Big Brave Man* (New York: Farrar, Straus & Cudahy, 1960) in extolling the virtues of America.
11. Renato Constantino, *The Making of a Filipino: A Story of Philippine Colonial Politics* (Quezon City: Malaya Books, 1969), inside cover. See also Constantino's general historical survey, *The Philippines: The Continuing Past* (Quezon City: Foundation for Nationalist Studies, 1978).
12. Constantino, *Making of a Filipino*, 161.
13. These were the captions to his discussion of Romulo. See Constantino, *Making of a Filipino*, 165, 167.
14. Raymond Bonner, *Waltzing with a Dictator: The Marcoses and the Making of American Policy* (New York: Vintage Books, 1987), 231; Pio Andrade, *The Fooling of America: The Untold Story of Carlos P. Romulo* (1985), rev. ed. (Manila: Ouch, 1990). While right to question the basis of Romulo's claims, Andrade's account is marred by a tendency to demonize Romulo. See ibid., 10–36, 98–127.
15. For the notions "residual," "dominant," and "emergent," see Raymond

Williams, *Marxism and Literature* (Oxford: Oxford University Press, 1977). However, whereas Williams uses these terms to refer to the passage of modes of production, I am using them here to describe the cultural relations accompanying the end of one colonial order, the establishment of a new one, and the anticipation of a postcolonial nation.

16. Colonial racism sorted Americans and Filipinos out as civilized and savage, respectively; it further separated Filipinos into those who are urban, Christian, and cultured on the one hand (although misguided by centuries of Spanish rule) and "wild," "tribal" Filipinos who are non-Christian peoples who live in mountains and remote forests. American race relations creates a binary in allowing non-white peoples to participate in all facets of society, although as second-class citizens, who up until recently were socially segregated and discriminated against in higher-paying and higher-status occupations.

17. Romulo's autobiographical *I Walked With Heroes* is the starting point for the following biographical details of his life, especially for the pre–World War II era.

18. The Romulos of Camiling, Tarlac, were similar in means to the prominent families of the Philippine Republic who fought the Americans—the Aquinos of Murcia, Tarlac, and the Aguinaldos of Kawit, Cavite. See Nick Joaquin, *The Aquinos of Tarlac: An Essay on History as Three Generations* (Metro Manila: Cacho Hermanos, 1983), 35. The Romulos were part of the middle class of rural gentry that Joaquin argues was the fundamental class that led the revolution. Romulo grew up speaking the vernacular, Pangasinense, and some Tagalog. His grandmother taught him Spanish. See Nick Joaquin, *The Seven Ages of Romulo* (Manila: Filipinas Foundation, 1977); *Aquinos of Tarlac*, 27 n. 7; and Jesús Z. Valenzuela, *History of Journalism in the Philippine Islands* (Manila, privately printed, 1933), 151.

19. Romulo also befriended Mauro Mendez, who would become one of his lifelong friends. Sylvia Mendez Ventura, *Mauro Mendez: From Journalist to Diplomat* (Quezon City: University of the Philippines Press, 1978), 1–3; and *Carlos P. Romulo* (Manila: Tahanan Books for Young Readers, 1995), 7–8.

20. Romulo especially "gloated" over O. Henry's short stories. See Carlos P. Romulo, "O. Henry" (M.A. thesis, Columbia University, 1921).

21. The report that earned this invitation was Romulo's coverage of Quezon fulminating against the newspaper *La Vanguardia*, which had been attacking him. The paper was owned by the powerful Roces family, which was a great supporter of Quezon's rival for political supremacy, Sergio Osmeña, the Speaker of the House. See Romulo, *I Walked with Heroes*, 89.

22. Ibid., 91.

23. Ibid., 92.

24. Ibid., 86–87. Quezon wore the first two-tone shoes Romulo had ever seen, black and white, and his tie and pocket handkerchief matched. Romulo's second wife, Beth Day, described Romulo at a much later age in words similar to his own description of Quezon: "A dapper, fastidious man, the General, despite his small stature (he was five feet four), managed to dominate a room when he entered it through a combination of self-assurance and great charm. . . . [He] considered good grooming and being a good host important adjuncts to diplomatic life and gave them serious attention. 'A person who is well dressed is at ease and sure of himself,' he maintained. His clothes—even pajamas and robes—were well tailored." She also found Romulo the speaker "a great performer," although unlike Quezon, he was more like a "Jack Benny," who spiced up serious matter with anecdotes and jokes. See Beth Day Romulo, *Inside the Palace: The Rise and Fall of Ferdinand and Imelda Marcos* (New York: G. P. Putnam's Sons, 1987), 29–30.

25. See Anthony Reid, *Southeast Asia in the Age of Commerce, 1450–1680* (New Haven, Conn.: Yale University Press, 1988), 120; Reynaldo Ileto, *Pasyon and Revolution: Popular Movements in the Philippines, 1840–1910* (Quezon City: Ateneo de Manila University Press, 1989), 22–27.

26. Romulo, *I Walked with Heroes*, 116–19.

27. Ibid., 135–45.

28. Carlos P. Romulo, "The Tragedy of Our Anglo-Saxon Education" (1923), reprinted in *Encyclopedia of the Philippines: The Library of Philippine Literature, Art, and Science,* vol. 1: *Literature,* ed. Zoilo Galang (Manila: P. Vera & Sons, 1935), 255, 256–58.

29. Ibid., 258–59.

30. Ibid., 261.

31. Despite being an able administrator, Wood had opposed Francis Burton Harrison's liberal policies and seemed to close the door on the possibilities for Philippine independence and self-rule. Bernardita Reyes Churchill, *The Philippine Independence Missions to the U.S., 1919–1934* (Manila: National Historical Institute, 1983), 53–55.

32. Ibid., 429, 431. Romulo again accompanied Quezon as a representative of the press in the "Mixed Mission" of March 1933. He was by then editor-in-chief of the Manila *Tribune.*

33. Joaquin, *Seven Ages of Romulo,* 29. Even those who disdained the influence of American culture recognized Romulo's popularity among the youth. See, e.g., Manuel C. Briones, "Our Path to Follow," in *Discursos y ensayos temarios y vida filipina* (Manila, 1931), reprinted in *Philippine Literature: From Ancient Times to the Present,* ed. Teofilo del Castillo and Buenaventura S. Medina Jr. (Quezon City: Del Castillo & Sons, 1964), 244.

34. Carlos P. Romulo, *The Real Leader: A Play in One Act,* in id., *Daughters for Sale and Other Plays* (Manila: Manila Book Co., 1924). Romulo says in the preface that these plays were "not originally intended for publication," "hurriedly written," and meant to satisfy the demand for "plays in English by Filipinos on Filipino themes."

35. Valenzuela, *History of Journalism in the Philippine Islands,* 146, 147.

36. Romulo, *I Walked with Heroes,* 185.

37. Churchill, *Philippine Independence Missions,* 148–49.

38. Theodore Friend, *Between Two Empires: The Ordeal of the Philippines, 1929–1946* (New Haven, Conn.: Yale University Press, 1965), 115–16. In 1937, the chain was reorganized to include the Spanish-language paper *El Debate,* and became the D-M-H-M chain, with Romulo as its publisher.

39. *Philippines Herald Year Book,* Sept. 29, 1934, 7.

40. Romulo, *I Walked with Heroes,* 199.

41. Carlos P. Romulo, "The Mind of a New Commonwealth" (speech accepting honorary doctorate of laws, Notre Dame University, 1935), 231.

42. Ibid., 229.

43. Ibid., 231.

44. Romulo, *I Walked with Heroes,* 201–10. On various occasions, Quezon promised to support Romulo as senator and to make him secretary of public instruction.

45. William Manchester, *American Caesar: Douglas MacArthur, 1880–1964* (Boston: Little, Brown, 1978), 177. In the mid 1930s, President Quezon had appointed MacArthur field marshal of the Philippines and tasked him with developing a national defense plan to meet the threat of Japanese aggression. Douglas MacArthur, *Reminiscences* (New York: Crest Books, 1964), 113–25; Alfred W. McCoy, "Quezon's Commonwealth: The Emergence of Philippine Authoritarianism," in *Philippine Colonial Democracy,* ed. Ruby R. Paredes et al. (New Haven, Conn.: Yale University Southeast Asia Studies, 1988), 144–145; Manchester, *American Caesar,* 160–204.

46. Manuel E. Arguilla, Esteban Nedruda, and Teodoro Agoncillo, eds., *Literature under the Commonwealth* (Manila: Philippine Writers' League, 1940), 5, 7, 101–3; Teodoro Agoncillo, *The Fateful Years: Japan's Adventure in the Philippines, 1891–1945,* vol. 2 (Quezon City: R. P. Garcia, 1965), 594.

47. *Newsweek,* May 1942, 28.

48. Carlos P. Romulo, "Billion Orientals Look to America for Aid in Crisis," *Philippines Herald,* Sept. 15, 1941.

49. Carlos P. Romulo, "'Closed Waters': Indomitable Will of New China Shown in Chungking," *Philippines Herald,* Sept. 16, 1941; id., "Appeasement of Japan Fatal, Say Chinese Leaders," *Philippines Herald,* Sept. 17, 1941.

50. Carlos P. Romulo, "Chiang Confident . . . 'Our Fight Is Your Fight,' Romulo Told," *Philippines Herald*, Sept. 18, 1941.

51. Carlos P. Romulo, "Romulo Sees Flow of American Aid on Famed Burma Road," *Philippines Herald*, Sept. 24, 1941; id., "Burma's Agitation for Freedom Affects Asia," ibid., Sept. 27, 1941; id., "Thailand Neutrality Principle Is Clarified," ibid., Sept. 30, 1941; id., "Singapore's Urgent Role Is to Keep Burma Road Safe," ibid., Oct. 11, 1941; id., "NEI [Netherlands East Indies] More Prepared for War Than Any Far Eastern State," ibid., Oct. 17, 1941.

52. Carlos P. Romulo, "Indonesians' Struggle for Liberty Accelerated by War Against Fascism," *Philippines Herald*, Oct. 17, 1941.

53. Carlos P. Romulo, "U.S. Arming . . . Romulo Sees Flow of American Aid on Famed Burma Road," *Philippines Herald*, Sept. 24, 1941. Fernando Amorsolo (1892–1972) was one of the best-loved and influential painters in the Philippines. According to one Ateneo University curator, Amorsolo and his paintings were enormously popular. He was posthumously granted official recognition as "National Artist" for depicting peasants in colorful rustic scenes, including the planting or harvesting of rice or "dancing at fiestas," as though scarcity and "injustice did not stalk the countryside." See Emmanuel Torres, "Introduction," in *One Hundred Years of Philippine Painting* (Pasadena, Calif.: Pacific Asia Museum, 1984), 9. Tondo, a crowded district of Manila that has subsequently come to be known for its poverty, was the destination of many migrants from the provinces in the 1920s and 1930s. It was also where Bienvenido Santos grew up. See Petronilo Bn. Daroy, "Tondo: The Triumph of Reality," *Panorama* 11, no. 8 (Aug. 1959): 43–45.

54. Carlos P. Romulo, "Nippon Massing 8 More Divisions in French Indo-China," *Philippines Herald*, Oct. 8, 1941.

55. Carlos P. Romulo, "Nippon Exploiting Indo-China along Manchukuo Lines," *Philippines Herald*, Oct. 10, 1941.

56. Carlos P. Romulo, "NEI [Netherlands East Indies] Believes War Outbreak Not Imminent," *Philippines Herald*, Oct. 22, 1941.

57. Carlos P. Romulo, *Philippines Herald*, Nov. 1, 1941, repr. in John Hohenberg, ed., *The Pulitzer Prize Story: News Stories, Editorials, Cartoons, & Pictures* (New York: Columbia University Press, 1959), 147.

58. Hohenberg, ed., *Pulitzer Prize Story,* 147. Altogether Romulo traveled over 20,000 miles in 1941. King Features distributed his reports for the *Herald* to 112 newspapers, and in 1942 he won the Pulitzer Prize in Journalism for distinguished correspondence. The award was to come, however, during a period of violent transition in Romulo's life. Heinz-Dietrich Fischer de Gruyter, *Outstanding International Press Reporting: Pulitzer Prize Winning Articles in Foreign Correspondence,* vol. 1: *1928–1945* (New York: Walter de Gruyter, 1984), xxxviii–xl.

59. H. W. Brands, *Bound to Empire: The U.S. and the Philippines* (New York: Oxford University Press, 1992), 192–94. This decision sealed the fate of U.S. troops in the Philippines, who would suffer serious food and supply shortages.

60. *Current Biography 1943*, 623; Vicente Albano Pacis, *President Sergio Osmena: A Fully Documented Biography* (Quezon City: Phoenix Press, 1971), 141.

61. Ibid., 623.

62. Page numbers in the text refer to Romulo, *I Saw the Fall of the Philippines*.

63. Ibid., 1. Apparently, this claim was made earlier in an article Romulo published in *Cosmopolitan*. See the inside back cover.

64. Ibid., back jacket to hardcover edition.

65. Harrison's entry of July 3, 1942, in *Origins of the Philippine Republic: Extracts from the Diaries and Records of Francis Burton Harrison*, ed. Michael P. Onorato, Data Papers, no. 95 (Ithaca, N.Y.: Cornell University Department of Asian Studies, Southeast Asia Program, 1974), 173.

66. Romulo, *I Saw the Fall of the Philippines*, 169–177, 206–19.

67. Manchester, *American Caesar*, 236, 237–38.

68. Romulo, *I Saw the Fall of the Philippines*, 2–4. See mention of Madrigal in Romulo, "NEI Believes War Outbreak Not Imminent." Romulo credited MacArthur with having suggested his tour of Asia, but Romulo himself had publicly thanked Vicente Madrigal for the idea and for having provided the funds for the trip.

69. *Origins of the Philippine Republic*, ed. Onorato, 177–78 (July 1942).

70. Ibid., 205 (January 1942). Elizalde said of the publication of *I Saw the Fall of the Philippines* that Romulo was forced "to have the book recast and to pay $1,800 to the publishers for resetting and renumbering the pages. . . . This came out of his first payment of $2,500. That the blackouts in the book were really at the instance of the War Department; they were left in the book to add importance to it. Romulo has sold already 25,000 copies—will probably get $20,000 out of the book" (ibid.).

71. The Atlantic Conference between Roosevelt and Churchill occurred in August 1941. The two leaders proclaimed common war aims that they called the "Atlantic Charter." This had eight aspects, including opposition to Anglo-American imperialist ventures and fascism, defense of self-government for all peoples, free trade, economic collaboration, postwar peace, and disarmament of aggressor nations. See Robert Dallek, *Franklin D. Roosevelt and American Foreign Policy, 1932–1945* (New York: Oxford University Press, 1979), 283.

72. Romulo, *Mother America*, xiii.

73. Ibid., xiv.

74. Nowhere in the book does Romulo explain the meaning of the term

"Mother America." In nineteenth-century Tagalog culture, however, the bonds between mother and son were so important that they shaped native perceptions of
the meaning of the revolution against Spanish colonial rule. This was often figured
as a sentimental separation between Mother Spain and her Filipino children, who
had grown up and had to leave home. Tagalog revolutionary literature depicts Filipinos as having already repaid their debts to Spain (see Introduction, n. 13,
above). Quite unconsciously perhaps, Romulo was drawing on precolonial Southeast Asian conceptions of indebtedness. See Reynaldo Ileto, *Pasyon and Revolution:
Popular Movements in the Philippines, 1840–1910* (Quezon City: Ateneo de Manila
University Press, 1989), 104–5, 139.

75. Romulo, *Mother America*, 6–9, 13.

76. See, e.g., *Letters in Exile: An Introductory Reader on Pilipino Americans* (Los
Angeles: Asian American Studies Center, 1976).

77. His appointment as resident commissioner was in part Romulo's reward for
his splendid job of publicizing the Philippines during the war. See Pacis, *President
Sergio Osmeña*, 210.

78. As H. W. Brands writes, the Filipinos had very little leverage upon Americans, given the wartime devastation of the country. Americans had economic leverage: the Philippines needed reconstruction aid, and the United States could potentially drag its feet on Philippine independence. See Brands, *Bound to Empire*,
219–21.

79. Romulo, *I Walked with Heroes*, 245–48.

80. See P. C. Morantte, *Remembering Carlos Bulosan: His Heart Affair with
America* (Quezon City: New Day, 1984), 134–38; Bienvenido N. Santos, "José Gar-
cía Villa in Exile," in *Philippine Harvest: an Anthology of Filipino Writing in
English*, ed. Maximo D. Ramos (Manila: E. F. David, 1953), 22–26.

81. Romulo, *I Walked with Heroes*, 322; *Bataan*, November 1943, 11.

82. Mendez Ventura, *Mauro Mendez*, 113–14; Romulo, *I Walked with Heroes*,
322.

83. Roger Bresnahan, "Salvador P. Lopez," in id., *Angles of Vision: Conversations on Philippine Literature* (Quezon City: New Day, 1992), 112.

84. "[W]hen I travel, the young men I helped train and encourage[d] welcome
me all over the world," he boasted. "They are still my boys." Romulo, *I Walked
with Heroes*, 323.

85. Jorge R. Coquia, *The Philippine Presidential Election of 1953* (Manila: University Publishing Co., 1955), 81–99; see appendix and Romulo's letter to Quirino.
The Communist insurgency and Quirino's corrupt government were causing
alarm in Washington, D.C. See "A Report to the President by the National Security Council on the Position of the U.S. with Respect to the Philippines," Nov. 9,

1950, 6, 9, in Enrique de la Cruz, "The Philippine Progressive Movement and the Philippine Support Movement in the U.S., 1972–1992, Reader for Asian American Studies 197, Spring 1993" (an unpublished collection of documents from the anti–Marcos dictatorship movement in the United States during the 1970s and 1980s).

86. Coquia, *Philippine Presidential Election of 1953*, 119–20. According to the *Manila Times*, Nov. 8, 1953, the feud between Romulo and Elizalde started during World War II; José V. Abueva, *Ramon Magsaysay: A Political Biography* (Manila: Solidaridad, 1971), 124–25.

87. Coquia, *Philippine Presidential Election of 1953*, 92–93.

88. Ibid., 264–65. Based on a *Weekly Women's Magazine* article on Cabili, July 7, 1953.

89. Ibid., 263–64.

90. Romulo spent 200,000 pesos of his own money, while the Lopez family was reputed to have spent over 300,000. See ibid., 262–63, 272–73.

91. Ibid., 268.

92. Ibid., 272–73.

93. Teodoro M. Locsin, "Backward Is Forward," *Philippines Free Press*, Sept. 12, 1953, repr. in *The NP-DP Coalition: A Milestone in Philippine Political Development* (n.p, n.d.), 16, Carlos P. Romulo Papers, Ayala Museum Library, Metro Manila.

94. Coquia, *Philippine Presidential Election of 1953*, 271. Locsin wrote glowingly of Romulo's skills as a politician. "[Romulo] performed so brilliantly that he seemed to be transcending the law about water not being able to rise above its level." For Locsin, Romulo worked "diplomatic magic," as though conjuring "international rabbits . . . out of hats" or making "women vanish into thin air." See Locsin, "Backward Is Forward," 16.

95. Abueva, *Ramon Magsaysay*, 157. I discuss this charge below.

96. Ibid., 252; Constantino, *Making of a Filipino*, 190.

97. Romulo argued that the Igorots, whom he described as "primitive black people" and Philippines' "aborigines," had a claim to the country similar to that of American Indians to the United States, but he rejected the view that they were "representative" of all Filipinos, as the American press inferred. More controversially, he asserted that "the Igorot is *not* Filipino and we are *not* related" (Romulo, *Mother America*, 59; emphases added).

98. From photographs in the Carlos P. Romulo Papers, Ayala Museum, Metro Manila.

99. Gabriel S. Castro, letter to the editor, *Philippines Free Press*, July 6, 1953, Carlos P. Romulo Papers, Ayala Museum, Metro Manila.

100. Carlos P. Romulo, letter to Gabriel S. Castro, July 20, 1953, Carlos P.

Romulo Papers, Ayala Museum, Metro Manila. For instance, Romulo wrote, "I am a Filipino—inheritor of a glorious past, hostage to an uncertain future." He boasted of having "sprung from a hardy race." He claimed that "the immortal seed of heroes" ran through his "blood." He was quoting from his August 1941 editorial for the *Philippines Herald.*

101. Ibid.

102. Carlos P. Romulo, *Crusade in Asia: Philippine Victory* (New York: John Day, 1955); id., *The Magsaysay Story,* with Marvin M. Gray (1956; repr., New York: Pocket Books, 1957). According to the title page, Marvin M. Gray was "an American journalist who for several years published the *Manila Evening News* and became a close friend and frequent adviser of the later President Magsaysay."

103. Page nos. cited in the text here refer to Romulo, *Magsaysay Story.*

104. In *Crusade in Asia,* 213–14, Romulo also heroized himself, telling of how he had shouted down pro-Quirino goon squads in Bacolod who were trying to intimidate him from speaking on one of his forays into the rural Philippines as Magsaysay's campaign manager. In his review of *Crusade,* the critic Petronilo Bn. Daroy accused Romulo of creating "unrecognizable caricatures of Philippine life" and of exaggerating Philippine poverty and concocting scenes of goon squads and political violence "to make Asia the 'display window' (the phrase is Romulo's) of America's psychological warfare." See Petronilo Bn. Daroy, "Romulo's Crusade," *This Week* 12, no. 26 (June 30, 1957): 9, 35.

105. Page numbers cited in the text are from *America in Vietnam: A Documentary History,* ed. William Appleman Williams et al. (Garden City, N.Y.: Anchor Press, 1985). The United States had sought to discredit the Vietminh, the Vietnamese national resistance against the French, by claiming that it was Communist, and had installed the monarch Bao Dai, who was perceived as a puppet of U.S. interests (ibid., 56).

106. In 1959, Romulo told Felixberto Serrano, Philippine foreign secretary under President Carlos P. Garcia, that the United States did not know what it was getting into in Laos and Vietnam. The United States failed to realize that neither Moscow nor its rival Beijing had any control of these Communist insurgencies, although they were jockeying for position. See Brands, *Bound to Empire,* 269.

107. Citations in the text here refer to Romulo, *Crusade in Asia.*

108. Milton J. Meyer, *A Diplomatic History of the Philippine Republic* (Honolulu: University of Hawai'i Press, 1965), 221. Citations in the text here refer to Romulo, *The Meaning of Bandung* (Chapel Hill: University of North Carolina Press, 1956).

109. First, Romulo said, Asian delegates felt that although the United States preached freedom and human rights, it in practice supported the colonial powers

against decolonizing countries. Its record in the United Nations was also decidedly against resolutions that supported anticolonial struggles. Second, the American hysteria over Communism made its leadership of Asian countries questionable. Third, Asians criticized America's reliability, its boasting about its superior way of life, and its attitude of condescension toward smaller nations because of its nuclear advantage.

110. Carlos P. Romulo and Pearl S. Buck, *Friend to Friend: A Candid Exchange Between Pearl S. Buck and Carlos P. Romulo* (New York: John Day, 1958). Pearl Sydenstricker Buck (1892–1973) was an American novelist who lived most of her life in China. Her novel *The Good Earth* (1931), a story of Chinese peasant life, received the Pulitzer Prize, and in 1938, she was awarded the Nobel Prize for literature. See Peter J. Conn, *Pearl S. Buck: A Cultural Biography* (New York: Cambridge University Press, 1996). This was a particularly nationalistic period, which saw attempts to increase Filipino ownership of businesses in the country vis-à-vis the Americans and the enlargement of the Filipinos' share of large corporations. See Carlos P. Romulo, keynote address to the Nacionalista Party Convention, June 3, 1961, Manila Philippines, 10–11, Carlos P. Romulo Papers, Ayala Museum, Metro Manila.

111. Citations in the text here refer to Romulo and Buck, *Friend to Friend*.

112. Buck describes her affinity with Romulo as that of two people who understand their "two sides of the world," Asia and America, "because we live on two sides" (ibid., 71).

113. Joaquin, *Seven Ages of Romulo*, 51.

114. Silvino V. Epistola, "Romulo's Design for the Filipino University: The Vision That Brought on Student Activism and Faculty Dissent," in *University of the Philippines: The First 75 Years, 1908–1983*, ed. Oscar M. Alfonso (Quezon City: University of the Philippines Press, 1985), 391–95.

115. Ibid., 392, 394, 395. Indeed, Romulo set precedent by abolishing the position of faculty adviser to the campus student newspaper, the *Philippine Collegian*, which ended faculty supervision of student political views, thus enabling unhampered student expression in the 1960s. See also ibid., p. 430.

116. Ibid., 399–401.

117. Ibid., 401, 404.

118. Ibid., 402, 403.

119. Ibid., 418.

120. For instance, on his 20-day tour of Thailand, India, and Indonesia to foster cultural and educational exchanges between those countries and the Philippines, Romulo was treated not as the visiting president of a university but as a head of state. He was welcomed by no less than President Sukarno of Indonesia

and Prime Minister Kittikachorn of Thailand. In India, he was granted a doctorate of laws at Delhi University and was invited to return several months later to give the Azad Memorial Lectures. Carlos P. Romulo, *Mission to Asia: The Dialogue Begins* (Quezon City: University of the Philippines, 1964), 7–9. See also photos and newspaper clippings section of *Mission to Asia*.

121. Citations in the text here refer to Romulo, *Mission to Asia*. Under Romulo's direction, Asian studies courses were integrated into the educational program and the MA program was developed.

122. Carlos P. Romulo, *Contemporary Nationalism and the World Order* (New York: Asia Publishing House, 1964), 11–12. Page numbers cited in the text here refer to this source.

123. Carlos P. Romulo, *Identity and Change* (Manila: Solidaridad, 1965), introduction.

124. Citations in the text here refer to Romulo, *Identity and Change*.

125. Epistola, "Romulo's Design for the Filipino University," 426–28, 430–33. Romulo was not content with his administrative duties, however, but hungered for the opportunity of teaching and lecturing. His lectures on American literature were published as *Evasions and Response: Lectures on the American Novel, 1890–1930* (Quezon City: Phoenix, 1966), and those he gave at SUNY as *Clarifying the Asian Mystique* (Manila: Solidaridad, 1970).

126. Epistola, "Romulo's Design for the Filipino University," 440–41.

127. Ibid., 441.

128. Senator Lorenzo Tañada, letter to President Carlos P. Romulo, Aug. 2, 1968, *Philippine Collegian*, Aug. 7, 1968, 4–5, cited in Epistola, "Romulo's Design for the Filipino University," 677.

129. Epistola, "Romulo's Design for the Filipino University," 441.

130. Carlos P. Romulo to Lorenzo M. Tañada, Senate of the Philippines, Aug. 8, 1968, 1–23, Carlos P. Romulo Papers, Ayala Museum, Metro Manila. For instance, Romulo defended his goal of upgrading the university's backward facilities, which of necessity required extensive funding from American philanthropic organizations. He also claimed that the university was not under the dictates of any foreign agencies; indeed, that the great diversity of donors made the possibility of a conspiracy very remote. Finally, Romulo rejected Tañada's charge that free speech was being suppressed.

131. Epistola, "Romulo's Design for the Filipino University," 440. Probably no other Filipino intellectual was closer to Romulo than Lopez, who loyally served Romulo for three decades. Romulo selected Lopez from the University of the Philippines to work as a columnist for the *Philippines Herald*. He presided over the Commonwealth Literary Awards of 1940 that awarded Lopez the first prize for his

classic *Literature and Society: Essays on Life and Letters* (Manila: University Publishing Co., 1940). It was Romulo who brought Lopez to New York and the United Nations and launched him on a career in the foreign service. In turn, Lopez remained loyal to Romulo and helped to build his reputation. Lopez was Romulo's principal speechwriter, especially in the conflict with Recto in the 1950s. In the 1960s, Lopez became undersecretary and for a brief time secretary of foreign affairs under the Macapagal administration, before becoming permanent delegate to the UN in the Marcos administration. See Mendez Ventura, *Mauro Mendez*, 114, 128–30; Arguilla et al., eds., *Literature under the Commonwealth*, 117–18; Edilberto N. Alegre and Doreen G. Fernandez, "Salvador P. Lopez," in *Writers and Their Milieu: An Oral History of First Generation Writers in English, Part I* (Manila: De La Salle University Press, 1984, 1993), 154–78.

132. *Writers and Their Milieu, Part I*, ed. Alegre and Fernandez, 168–69.

133. Ibid., 169. Over a decade later, Marcos was to sum up this shuffling of positions in a humorous vein. He contrasted the skills of his two men. Romulo he labeled a good "guerrillero" (guerrilla) "who knew how to run away from danger," while Lopez ran in the opposite direction "to serve the University" although he knew an "ambuscade" was waiting for him. Indeed, upon assuming office, U.P. President Lopez faced the practical rebellion of students and faculty and the threat of a military takeover of the university. Yet, despite Romulo's attempts to get rid of his competitor, Lopez succeeded in preserving the university's integrity, with some help from Marcos, who was not unaware of the propaganda value of preserving "academic freedom." See Oscar L. Evangelista, "Lopez' Beleaguered Tenure," in *University of the Philippines: The First 75 Years*, 445.

134. Carlos P. Romulo with Beth Day Romulo, *The Philippine Presidents: Memoirs of Carlos P. Romulo* (Quezon City: New Day, 1988), 137ff., quoted in José D. Ingles, *Philippine Foreign Policy* (Manila: Lyceum Press, 1980), 37; Romulo, *Philippine Presidents*, 138.

135. Ingles, *Philippine Foreign Policy*, 34.

136. Ibid., 34–35; Romulo, *Philippine Presidents*, 137ff.

137. *Philippine Colonial Democracy*, ed. Paredes et al., 1. As Romulo was to write of the early 1970s, "At that time, Marcos' overweening ambition had not yet become apparent." Romulo believed that Marcos had passed laws beneficial to the country and, as his foreign minister, felt compelled "to defend his martial law." See Romulo, *Philippine Presidents*, 138.

138. See Lewis E. Gleeck Jr., *The Third Philippine Republic, 1946–1972* (Quezon City: New Day, 1993), 400; and *Philippine Colonial Democracy*, ed. Paredes et al., 1. "Clearly the collapse of Philippine democracy," Paredes says, "was the product of a deep malaise and not just the work of one man."

139. See *An Anarchy of Families: State and Family in the Philippines*, ed. Alfred W. McCoy (Quezon City: Ateneo de Manila University Press, 1994), introduction.

140. Beth Day Romulo, *Inside the Palace*, 129.

141. Romulo, *Philippine Presidents*, 137–38; also in Gleeck, *Third Philippine Republic*, 394.

142. Romulo, *Philippine Presidents*, 138; Gleeck, *Third Philippine Republic*, 395.

143. Beth Day Romulo, *Inside the Palace*, 129; Gleeck, *Third Philippine Republic*, 395–96. Amnesty International reported that in May 1975, the regime still held 4,553 political prisoners and that torture was "part of the general approach to the treatment of suspects." See Amnesty International, *Report of an Amnesty International Mission to the Republic of the Philippines, 22 November–5 December 1975* (London: n.p., 1977), 6, cited in Mark R. Thompson, *The Anti-Marcos Struggle: Personalistic Rule and Democratic Transition in the Philippines* (New Haven, Conn.: Yale University Press, 1995), 72. Thompson's text also details the complex anti–martial law organizations that sprang up in both the Philippines and the United States to contest Marcos's rule.

144. Bonner, *Waltzing with a Dictator*, 99. Romulo claimed that Marcos had consulted with Nixon and had received his approval before he made his declaration.

145. Andrade, *Fooling of America*, 123.

146. Bonner, *Waltzing with a Dictator*, 230–31. Assistant Secretary of State Derian paid a visit to Manila in 1978 especially to meet with the jailed opposition leader Benigno Aquino. Marcos and many Asian leaders detested Derian's forthrightness about human rights, and Romulo, consonant with the wishes of his bosses, treated her with disdain. Asked by reporters about his meeting with her, he likened her to the "durian," a "Southeast Asian tree fruit that is edible—if one can get past the foul odor." Back in Washington, Secretary Romulo boycotted a meeting of Asian allies of the United States because of Derian's planned attendance, thus helping to delegitimize U.S. attempts to curb international human rights abuses.

147. Beth Day Romulo, *Inside the Palace*, 130–132.

148. Bonner, *Waltzing with a Dictator*, 235–38. Had the polls not been tampered with, Romulo might have garnered the most votes. In the elections, Romulo was gratified by his continued popularity, which testifies to his ability to disassociate himself from the regime's corruption and brutality. Given his duties, Romulo was away from the country much of the time.

149. From the front page of the *Bulletin Today*, Apr. 15, 1978, cited in Andrade, *Fooling of America*, 177.

150. Carlos P. Romulo, "The Media and the State" (address to the Philippine

Association of Broadcast Journalists, n.d.; ca. 1970s), Carlos P. Romulo Papers, Ayala Museum, Metro Manila.

151. Carlos P. Romulo, *The Diplomacy of Consent* (Manila: Department of Foreign Affairs, 1976), 17, 29, 49, 55, 83. Romulo argued that although the U.S. Constitution was "one of the best in the world" and served "the special needs of the American people," the Philippines, as an emerging nation attempting to fashion "new values" for its people, had adopted a democracy "different [in form] from that of the U.S" (97).

152. Carlos P. Romulo, "A Grandfather's Advice to His Granddaughter" (commencement address at the Assumption Convent, Mar. 19, 1975), Carlos P. Romulo Papers, Ayala Museum, Metro Manila. In this beautiful piece of advice for his granddaughter, Carissa Romulo, Romulo spoke of how different the world that women now faced was from that of their grandmothers. He advised his granddaughter to seek equality, to plan, and to cope with disappointments with a sense of humor. He subtly appropriated the women's movement for the dictatorship, claiming that the new dispensation had begun to make women "the full partner of man in promoting our national growth" and urging his granddaughter to "participate" in that "program."

153. William Safire, "Romulo, Drowning," *New York Times*, Apr. 7, 1977, A25.

154. Lopez retired from the U.P. presidency in 1975 and returned to editorial writing. In his October 1976 speech to the Literature and Society Conference in Manila, Lopez fondly recalled Romulo's praise for his book *Literature and Society*. See Salvador P. Lopez, "Literature and Society—A Literary Past Revisited," in *Literature and Society: Cross-Cultural Perspectives*, ed. Roger J. Bresnahan (Manila: Philippine American Educational Foundation and the American Studies Association of the Philippines, 1976), 7. In turn, Romulo wrote to Lopez that although he might not have agreed with him over all these years, he had always respected his views. See Carlos P. Romulo to Salvador P. Lopez, Apr. 20, 1977, Carlos P. Romulo Papers, Ayala Museum, Metro Manila.

155. Bresnahan, "Salvador P. Lopez," in id., *Angles of Vision*, 113. Note that this essay was not published until eleven years later, after the Marcos era had ended and when Romulo himself was dead.

156. Lopez was with Romulo "at the height of his powers" when he was Philippine ambassador to the United Nations. Lopez regarded that period as "the best years of [Romulo's] life" and Lopez's work for him had the effect of sharpening his "political awareness." See *Writers and Their Milieu, Part I*, ed. Alegre and Fernández, 172. Although it was only published after his death in 1985, Romulo had been working on *The Philippine Presidents* in that year and was obviously proud of having served all the presidents of the Philippines. See his introduction.

157. Bonner, *Waltzing with a Dictator*, 359. Prior to the Aquino assassination,

Marcos and the Reagan administration had renewed the military bases agreement, after tortuous negotiations between Philippine and American diplomats. Marcos received close to $1 billion. U.S.-Philippine relations were described as "excellent." Ibid., 339–41; quotation from 341. Reagan was a good friend of Romulo and the Marcoses. See Beth Day Romulo, *Inside the Palace*, 175.

158. Ricardo J. Romulo, address to "Professionals for Justice, Freedom and Sovereignty," Ugarte Field, Makati, Nov. 11, 1983, Carlos P. Romulo Papers, Ayala Museum, Metro Manila.

159. Carlos P. Romulo to Jerome Dunlevy, Sept. 1, 1983, Carlos P. Romulo Papers, Ayala Museum, Metro Manila.

160. Carlos P. Romulo to Roger Enloe, president, UN We Believe, Sept. 12, 1983, Carlos P. Romulo Papers, Ayala Museum, Metro Manila.

161. Carlos P. Romulo to Minister of Labor Blas F. Ople, Oct. 21, 1983, 2, 3, Carlos P. Romulo Papers, Ayala Museum, Metro Manila.

162. Ibid., 3, Carlos P. Romulo Papers, Ayala Museum, Metro Manila. Romulo wrote here that he was eighty-five years old, although most credible sources say he was born in 1899, which would have made him only eighty-four.

163. Roberto Romulo, interviews by the author, Metro Manila, Jan. 22 and 31, 1996.

164. This has been challenged for some time, e.g., in Sucheta Mazumdar, "Asian American Studies and Asian Studies: Rethinking Roots," in *Asian Americans: Comparative and Global Perspectives*, ed. Shirley Hune et al. (Pullman: Washington State University Press, 1991), 29–44; *Reading the Literatures of Asian America*, ed. Shirley Lim and Amy Ling (Philadelphia: Temple University Press, 1992); and *Claiming America: Constructing Chinese American Identities During the Exclusion Era*, ed. K. Scott Wong and Sucheng Chan (Philadelphia: Temple University Press, 1998).

165. Romulo, *Philippine Presidents*, 137, 138ff.

166. See Andrade, *Fooling of America*, 126–27. After receiving the National Artist Award, Romulo sent thank-you letters to Lucrecia Kasilag, Cultural Center of the Philippines (Jan. 15, 1982); Imelda Marcos, described as "Minister of Human Settlements/Governor, Metro Manila/and Patroness of art" (Jan. 16, 1982); and Edgardo J. Angara, president of the University of the Philippines (Feb. 4, 1982), Carlos P. Romulo Papers, Ayala Museum, Metro Manila.

Chapter 2. Suffering and Passion: Carlos Bulosan

1. Reynaldo Ileto, *Pasyon and Revolution: Popular Movements in the Philippines, 1840–1910* (Quezon City: Ateneo de Manila University Press, 1989), 256.

2. For the following biographical account, I have relied on these three reliable

sources: Susan Evangelista, *Carlos Bulosan and His Poetry: A Biography and Anthology* (Quezon City: Ateneo de Manila University Press, 1985), P. C. Morantte, *Remembering Carlos Bulosan: His Heart Affair with America* (Quezon City: New Day, 1984), and Licerio Lagda, "Women in the Life and Poetry of Carlos Bulosan" (M.A. thesis, University of the Philippines, 1988). All three show meticulous attention to the details of Bulosan's life and rely on their own interviews of people who knew Bulosan, primary sources, and readings of his works. In particular, I make frequent use of the work of Pantaleon Cambio (P. C.) Morantte (1909–2001) in this chapter and in Chapter 3 on Villa. Morantte was a journalist for the Manila-based *Graphic* in the late 1930s and the 1940s who had personal acquaintance with Villa and Bulosan, as well as with Romulo. He also knew N. V. M. Gonzalez and Bienvenido Santos. Morantte and Bulosan became close friends, sharing similar interests in literature, Filipino nationalism, and common friends or patrons, like Carey McWilliams. Morantte lived in Los Angeles near Bulosan until 1946, when he returned to the Philippines to pursue a career in the Philippine government. His sensitive biography of Bulosan covers this period of his acquaintance with Bulosan, whom he read as one who had become a successful writer despite numerous obstacles. Influenced by his own brand of Christian mysticism, Morantte nevertheless diverged from Bulosan's Marxist views. P. C. Morantte, interview by the author, Lompoc, Calif., Jan. 31, 1997.

3. Carey McWilliams, "Introduction," in Carlos Bulosan, *America Is in the Heart* (Seattle: University of Washington Press, 1973), xiv. See the similar case of Indian Americans during World War II in Leonard A. Gordon's "Bridging India and America: The Art and Politics of Kumar Goshal," *Amerasia Journal* 15, no. 2 (1989): 72. Gordon observes that "before World War II, visitors or expatriates from foreign parts were assumed to be experts on their places of origin and to know more than almost anyone in their new country about those areas."

4. See, e.g., John Monaghan, *Commonweal*, May 24, 1946, 149.

5. The critical literature on Bulosan is vast. My concern is to tease out two important themes in Bulosan's work that critics have little explored—the question of authenticity (plagiarism) in Bulosan's writing and the prevalence of suffering in his works. These then provide the cornerstones for my construction of the central insights of this chapter.

During the postwar era, Philippine critics took stock of Bulosan's writings after their country emerged from the Japanese occupation into the exhilaration of "liberation" and the trials of "independence" from the United States. Bienvenido Lumbera and Cynthia Lumbera, *Philippine Literature: A History and Anthology* (Metro Manila: National Book Store, 1982), 117. Bulosan's reputation rose and waned with the changing currents of postcolonial politics. Critical attention largely focused on *The Laughter of My Father*. From the late 1940s to the 1950s, Filipino critics questioned Bulosan's authenticity as a Filipino writer, blaming him for the negative responses of American critics to his satires of Philippine rural life. See A. G. Roseburg, *Pathways to Philippine Literature in English*, rev. ed. (Quezon City: Alemar-Phoenix, 1966), 98. Some took issue with Bulosan's support of radical groups on both sides of the Pacific—the Communist-led Huks in Central Luzon and the International Longshoreman's and Warehouseman's Union in the state of Washington, which was then a target of McCarthyism. Bulosan was alleged to have ties to Communist parties, which resulted in the blacklisting of his works in the Philippines. Epifanio San Juan Jr., "Introduction," in *On Becoming Filipino: Selected Writings of Carlos Bulosan* (Philadelphia: Temple University Press, 1995), 28–29. In 1956, Bulosan's death in poverty at the age of forty-four attracted hardly any attention in the Philippine media. One hostile newspaper called him a "plagiarist and a literary bum." Dolores S. Feria, "Carlos Bulosan: Gentle Genius," *Comment* 1 (1957): 57.

In the two decades after Bulosan's death, a wave of anti-American nationalism and the rise of a new left movement swept the Philippines and led to a rediscovery of Bulosan, especially as a proletarian, internationalist writer and political figure. This renewed interest led to the publication of his hitherto unpublished letters, essays, and fiction, which brought a deeper understanding of his personal life. See Dolores S. Feria, ed., *Sound of Falling Light: Letters in Exile* (Quezon City: Dolores S. Feria, 1960); Petronilo Bn. Daroy, "Carlos Bulosan: The Politics of Literature," *Saint Louis Quarterly* 6, no. 2 (June 1968): 195; Epifanio San Juan Jr., *Carlos Bulosan and the Imagination of the Class Struggle* (Quezon City: University of the Philippines Press, 1972); and Evangelista, *Carlos Bulosan and His Poetry*. See also Bulosan's *The Power of the People* (Metro Manila: National Book Store, 1986) and *The Philippines Is in the Heart*, ed. Epifanio San Juan Jr. (Quezon City: New Day, 1978). In the 1980s and 1990s, Bulosan criticism moved in two directions—toward an interest in the traditional, native elements in his writings and an increasing engagement with postcolonial theories. Morantte, *Remembering Carlos Bulosan*; Luis V. Teodoro, "Notes on the Power of the People," *Mithi* 1 (1985): 3–14; Delfin Tolentino. "Satire in Carlos Bulosan's *The Laughter of My Father*," *Philippine Studies* 34 (1986): 452–61.

Perhaps reflective of the emergent character of postwar Philippine studies, critics have been concerned with questions of authenticity. Discussions of Bulosan's literary art and political perspectives have been interwoven with debates about his honesty and originality as a Filipino writer, a concern linked to Philippine literature's quest to establish its legitimacy vis-à-vis American letters. The issue of his alleged plagiarism has thus understandably plagued Philippine scholars. Yet, while scholars have charged Bulosan with ignorance of literary protocols and cited his lack of education, they have been content to leave the matter of the supposed plagiarism unexplored. They have especially failed to compare Bulosan's story with the story he was alleged to have plagiarized. Those who hated Bulosan took the plagiarism charge as a confirmation of his lack of originality, while those who admired him have failed openly to grapple with the two stories for fear of sullying the reputation of their hero.

Unlike Philippine scholars, Asian American studies critics in the United States have shown less concern with charges of plagiarism and more interest in the political authenticity of *America Is in the Heart*. They have grappled with the question of whether or not Bulosan's book deserves to be included in the Asian American literary canon. Identity and empowerment movements for people of color in the 1970s led to the founding of Asian American studies and a search for a different kind of authenticity, the establishment of a legitimate body of literary works and exemplary heroes vis-à-vis these social movements. In this context, Asian American activists rediscovered Bulosan's *America Is in the Heart*. During the 1970s and 1980s, the struggle for a relevant, multicultural curriculum in opposition to white racism helped shape readings of Bulosan, leading to his inclusion in the Asian American canon. "Selected Writings of Carlos Bulosan," special issue, *Amerasia Journal* 6, no. 1 (1979): 135–38; Mark States, "Third World American Dream: Unionist and Socialist Politics in the Art of Hughes and Bulosan," *Critical Perspectives of Third World America* 1, no. 1 (Fall 1983): 91–115; Epifanio San Juan Jr., "Carlos Bulosan," in *American Radical*, ed. Mari Jo Buhle et al. (New York: Routledge, 1994), 253–60, and "Bulosan, Carlos," in *The Asian American Encyclopedia*, vol. 1, ed. Franklin Ng (New York: Marshall Cavendish, 1995), 149–52; Oscar Campomanes, "Carlos Bulosan," in *Encyclopedia of the American Left* (Chicago: University of Illinois Press, 1992), 115–16; Robert Lee, "Carlos Bulosan," in *Encyclopedia of Folklore and Literature*, ed. Mary Ellen Brown and Bruce A. Rosenberg (Santa Barbara, Calif.: ABC-CLIO, 1998), 70–72.

Crucial to the resurgence of interest in Bulosan was the republication of *America Is in the Heart* in 1973 by the University of Washington Press. The event introduced the book to the left intellectuals and the activist-scholars of the Asian American movement and clearly established Bulosan as a progressive, Asian *American* writer. Selections from the autobiography were quickly reprinted in basic texts of Asian American studies, including *Asian American Heritage: An Anthology of Prose and Poetry*, ed. David Hsin-Fu Wand (New York: Washington Square Press, 1974); *Aiiieeeee!!! An Anthology of Asian American Writers*, ed. Frank Chin et al. (1974; reprint, New York: Penguin Books, 1983); *Letters in Exile: An Introductory Reader on the History of Pilipinos in America* (Los Angeles: Asian American Studies Center, 1976); and *Counterpoint: Perspectives on Asian America*, ed. Emma Gee et al. (Los Angeles: Asian American Studies Center, 1976), 485–88. *Amerasia Journal*, published by UCLA's Asian American Studies Center, contributed to the renewed interest in Bulosan by printing many of his unpublished stories, essays, and letters. Numerous journal and encyclopedia articles addressing a more general audience have since been written.

Bulosan increasingly became a principal subject of critical discussion in Asian American studies. In 1972, the Filipino diasporic scholar Epifanio San Juan Jr. emphasized Bulosan's role as a Filipino worker-intellectual and critic of American capitalism. Ten years later, Elaine Kim, in her seminal work, *Asian American Literature*, included Bulosan among the "goodwill ambassadors" of the 1930s and 1940s who laid the foundation for Asian American literature. And, in the following year, Sam Solberg found in *America Is in the Heart* a convincing epical synthesis of the early Filipino American experience. San Juan, *Carlos Bulosan and the Imagination of the Class Struggle*; Elaine Kim, *Asian American Literature: The Writings and Their Social Contexts* (Philadelphia: Temple University Press, 1982); Sam Solberg, "An Introduction to Filipino American Literature," in *Aiiieeeee!* ed. Chin et al., 39–58. By the 1980s, Bulosan's place in the canon of Asian American studies was firmly established. In 1991, the critic Amy Ling recognized *America Is in the Heart* as one of the "unquestioned classics in Asian American literature courses all over the country." Amy Ling, "Emerging Canons of Asian American Literature and Art," in *Asian Americans: Comparative and Global Perspectives*, ed. Shirley Hune et al. (Pullman: Washington State University Press, 1991), 192.

In the 1990s, the influence of postcolonial theory became apparent in the responses of various critics to Bulosan. In 1992, Oscar Campomanes questioned the "immigration narrative" underlying Asian American criticism, which assumed that all Asian migrants to the United States sought eventual assimilation into American culture. His alternative view, what he called "reverse telos," identified a longing for identification with or return to a Philippine homeland fractured by U.S. colonialism. Campomanes's reading of Bulosan and allied interpretations by critics such as Shirley Lim and Lisa Lowe have thus centered on the paradoxical moments in *America Is in the Heart* and Bulosan's life. Campomanes, "Filipinos in the United States and Their Literature of Exile," in *Reading the Literatures of Asian America*, ed. Shirley Lim and Amy Ling (Philadelphia: Temple University Press, 1992), 49–78, and Shirley Lim, "The Ambivalent American," ibid., 13–32. Lisa Lowe, *Immigrant Acts: On Asian American Cultural Politics* (Durham, N.C.: Duke University Press, 1996), 47. For instance, Lim cites Bulosan's resistance to being categorized either as Filipino or as American, while Lowe has focused on the ways Bulosan's "America" instances "a stratified, contradictory figure divided between the named promise of democracy and the unnamed refugees, immigrants, and victims of violence who live beneath that promise." Bulosan, Lowe says, does not identify with the "national fiction of inclusion" but contests it with a heterogeneous definition of the American polity.

In response to postcolonial theory's emphasis on doubleness and ambivalence, recent criticisms of *America Is in the Heart* have taken a similar tack. The critic Sau-ling Wong sees a "mobility narrative" in the book, an obsession with naming places that seems to undercut the book's dominant narrative of the transformation of political consciousness. Wong believes that these conflicting stories in *America Is in the Heart* are a "formal manifestation of Bulosan's impossible self-assignment, which is a legacy of his colonial upbringing. . . . 'Taught to regard Americans as [his] equals' while 'Western people are brought up to regard Orientals or colored peoples are inferior,' Bulosan appears reluctant or unable to let go of his old conviction, feeling compelled instead to reconcile the discrepancy by alternating between the two rival stories." Wong, *Reading Asian American Literature: From Necessity to Extravagance* (Princeton, N.J: Princeton University Press, 1993), 135–36. Wong quotes from Feria, ed., *Sound of Falling Light*, 191–92. In her gloss on Bulosan, however, Wong ignores the author's account of his upbringing in the Philippines, which occurs in part 1. In this section of the book, numerous accidents and sufferings befall the narrator, and a pattern of tragedy develops that continues in other parts of the book. Thus, a narrative of suffering seems to override the one of mobility proposed by Wong.

Indeed, suffering recurs in the passages in Bulosan most often cited by Asian American critics, as does the related idea of sacrifice. Yet no one has even considered this theme as worthy of critical examination. For instance, Marilyn Alquizola's articles responding to allegations that the book was not "subversive" cite the final paragraph of the book, which appears as a "naïve" conclusion to the sufferings encountered by the narrator. Alquizola, "The Fictive Narrator of *America Is in the Heart*," in *Frontiers of Asian American Studies: Writing, Research, and Commentary*, ed. Gail Nomura et al. (Pullman: Washington State University Press, 1989), 211–17, and id., "Subversion or Affirmation: The Text and Subtext of *America Is in the Heart*," in *Asian Americans: Comparative and Global Perspectives*, ed. Hune, 199–210. Kenneth Mostern too sees anti-Marxist implications in the book's "immigrant" narrative. Citing its similarity to European American immigrant narratives, he calls vehemently for rejection of this "rhetoric." Mostern, "Why Is America in the Heart?" *Critical Mass: A Journal of Asian American Cultural Criticism* 2, no. 2 (Spring 1995): 35–65.

Alquizola and Mostern fail to take note of the religious themes, imagery, and language of these passages. In fact, the concluding passage of *America Is in the*

Heart is an extremely dense one, which requires careful reading. As Alquizola has rightly pointed out, its placement at the end must be seen in conjunction with the rest of the text. But is it, as Alquizola claims, "ironic"? Is Bulosan using a "naïve narrator" as a backdrop for highlighting the racial, class, and gender exploitation exposed by the book? In making such a claim, Alquizola would probably concede that the passage is not subversive but affirmative of a faith in an exceptionalist notion of America. However, Bulosan's description of "faith" does not show that he was interested in a teleological notion of the American dream, the proverbial rags-to-riches scheme. Note that the emphasis of the passage is on the *way* in which that faith arose and developed. Several times, Bulosan repeats that his vision grew "out of" several sources of suffering, including the labors of his family members, whose lives transcend the immediate geography of America to include the Philippines. Indeed, the juxtaposition of church bells in the Philippines and in America marks the boundaries of a kind of spiritual geography. One might argue that it is the act of suffering itself that is redemptive, and along with it, the continuous act of believing and having faith, which the word "America" has come to signify for Bulosan. In the second passage, despite the stated meaning of America as "land," the emphasis remains on other significations of suffering—toil, sacrifice, laying down one's life—for an America that remains "unfinished." Bulosan is calling attention to something quite different here than the Americanism that Alquizola and Mostern fear. What Bulosan lays out exceeds the purely political view of a bounded American nation-state or of a benevolent, unblemished nation blessing its immigrants. There is a religious quality at work, a certain spiritualism whose possibilities are indicated by Bulosan's use of eschatological language. The narrator's desire "to contribute something to [America's] *final fulfillment*" calls to mind several discourses, including a Marxist revolutionary utopianism and a Christian millenialism. At the very least, both of these passages hint at possibilities of overlapping cultural outlooks that demand a more involved investigation.

Thus, combined with the plagiarism charge against Bulosan, the tantalizing suggestion of religious themes informing Bulosan's politics provides the basis for a new look at this Filipino American author.

New perspectives from Filipino postcolonial criticism help to address the seemingly aberrant phenomena of plagiarism and suffering in Bulosan within the contexts of nationalism, social change, and migration. For instance, historical forgeries, similar to plagiarisms, have been a consistent presence in Philippine historiography, as the studies of Fr. Schumacher and Glenn May have shown. Vicente Rafael proposes that we look at the forgers "not as *failed historians . . .* but as *aspiring storytellers*" transmitting various historic "possibilities" and as a "starting point," rather than a final authority, for inquiring into Filipino nationalist narratives under American colonial rule. See his review of Glenn Anthony May's *Inventing a Hero: The Posthumous Re-creation of Andres Bonifacio* (Madison: University of Wisconsin Center for Southeast Asian Studies, 1996), *American Historical Review* 103, no. 4 (Oct. 1998): 1304–6.

Reynaldo Ileto's studies of religio-political movements help to reinforce Rafael's call and provide a cultural basis for understanding Bulosan's emphasis on religious language and symbolism. Ileto calls attention to an "*underside* of Philippine history" consisting of the worldview of social groups excluded from the mestizo-elite narrative of national independence. See Reynaldo Ileto, "Rizal and the Underside of Philippine History," in *Moral Order and the Question of Change: Essays on Southeast Asian Thought*, ed. David K. Wyatt and Alexander Woodside (New Haven, Conn.: Yale University Southeast Asia Studies, 1982). Ileto discovers an idiom called the *pasyon*, based upon the Holy Week celebrations of the suffering, death, and resurrection of Christ, overlaid with pre-Christian animist conceptions of talismanic power, light or radiance, and charisma. See Reynaldo Ileto, *Pasyon and Revolution: Popular Movements in the Philippines, 1840–1910* (Quezon City: Ateneo de Manila University Press, 1979, 1989).

6. Carlos Bulosan to Dorothy Babb, Dec. 10, 1937, in San Juan, *On Becoming Filipino*, 194. See also Herminia Q. Meñez, "The Performance of Folk Narrative in California's Filipino Communities," in *Explorations in Philippine Folklore* (Quezon City: Ateneo de Manila University Press, 1996), 49–60. Meñez's article shows the continuity and change in the folklore of Filipino migrants to the United States. She divides these narratives into personal histories, ethnic jokes, and belief stories. Her discussion of the first provides an epic cast to the oft-repeated truth of the representativeness of Bulosan's *America Is in the Heart*. In a telling passage on p. 54, Meñez writes of the recurring themes of immigrant personal histories, the common voyage across the Pacific on steamships, their itinerant lives of farm laborers or urban service workers, the encounters with prejudice, the "attempts to return to the homeland," and the aging of a population "in an alien country." It is, as Meñez writes, through the "periodic retellings" of these stories that they acquire "common themes and episodes," such that "[o]nce you've heard one, you've heard them all."

7. Morantte, interview by the author. A year before he died, Bulosan was to write of the principles that captured his career—his "grand dream of equality" for all, his particular goal of representing his "voiceless" fellow Filipinos in the United States, and his desire to "translate" the "aspirations" of all Filipinos—in the Philippines and America—for "contemporary history." See *Twentieth Century Authors* (New York: H. W. Wilson, 1957), quoted in Evangelista, *Carlos Bulosan and His Poetry*, 29–30.

8. Carlos Bulosan, "Freedom from Want," in *On Becoming Filipino*, 131–34. See also "Message to Congress, January 6, 1941," in *My Friends: Twenty-eight History Making Speeches by Franklin Delano Roosevelt*, ed. Edward H. Kavinoky and Julian Park (Buffalo, N.Y.: Foster & Stewart, 1945), 76–83.

9. Benét wrote "Freedom from Fear," Tarkington "Freedom of Speech," and Durant "Freedom of Worship." See Morantte, *Remembering Carlos Bulosan*, 132.

10. Ibid., 124–25.

11. Thomas Sugrue, *New York Times Book Review*, Apr. 23, 1944, 7, and Clara Savage Littledale, *Saturday Review of Literature*, June 3, 1944, 22.

12. Susan Evangelista, "Carlos Bulosan: A Sociohistorical Biography," *Philippine Social Sciences and Humanities Review* 44, nos. 1–4 (Jan.-Dec. 1980), 262.

13. Florentino Rodao, "Spanish Falange in the Philippines, 1936–1945," *Philippine Studies* 43 (1st quarter 1995): 3–26. At that time, Hartendorp was battling the antidemocratic and anti-American propaganda of the Falange, a fascist group in the Philippines affiliated with the Franco regime in Spain. See *Philippine Magazine*, Aug. 1941, 341. In the same letter, Bulosan also solicited stories and poems for his planned anthology of Philippine writing. With regard to fascism in the Philippines, see Bulosan, *America Is in the Heart*, 291, where an American leftist who had just returned from the Philippines during the 1930s is quoted as saying, "I didn't know that Philippine capitalists were closely tied up with the Falangist movement in Spain." To which Bulosan replies, "I think the Falange gets its orders direct from Berlin."

14. Carlos Bulosan to José de los Reyes, in Feria, ed., *Sound of Falling Light*, 21–22.

15. Alfred McCoy notes that Quezon had a penchant for wine, women, and song that helped to contribute to the consolidation of his political friends. It probably worsened his tuberculosis. See *Philippine Colonial Democracy*, ed. Ruby R. Paredes et al. (New Haven, Conn.: Yale University Southeast Asia Studies, 1988), 132–36.

16. Feria, ed., *Sound of Falling Light*, 22, 23.

17. Ibid., 24.

18. Aurelio Bulosan, "When Carlos Went to Washington, D.C."(MMS 1–5, University of Washington Libraries, Manuscripts and University Archives Division, 2329–2, box 1, folder 5); Feria, ed., *Sound of Falling Light*, 23.

19. Carlos P. Romulo, "Foreword," in Carlos Bulosan, *Voice of Bataan*, pp. xi–xii. Romulo wrote a favorable review of *America Is in the Heart* for the *New York Times Book Review*, which appeared on the book's back cover.

20. Carlos Bulosan to Carlos P. Romulo, cablegram, Dec. 10, 1943, Carlos P. Romulo Papers, University of the Philippines. Romulo discusses his visit to Cali-

fornia in *My Brother Americans* (Garden City, N.Y.: Doubleday, Doran, 1945), 169. Romulo's concern for the Filipinos appears genuine, but his language is that of their superior, a patron who surveys the situation and speaks for his people to the white community of businessmen and respectable citizens. Romulo excludes the voices of Filipinos, both laborers and intellectuals—neither Morantte, Bulosan, nor any intellectuals (e.g., newspapermen or union organizers) are mentioned.

21. Carlos Bulosan to Grace Cunningham, May 18, 1946, in Feria, ed., *Sound of Falling Light*, 33.

22. Aurelio Bulosan, "When Carlos Went to Washington, D.C.," 4.

23. Morantte, *Remembering Carlos Bulosan*, 25–26. Morantte's account is backed up by Bienvenido Santos's own recollections of the cabinet members during this time. Santos worked for Philippine Resident Commissioner Joaquin Elizalde, one of those whom Santos describes as "really Spaniards or mestizos." See Santos, *Memory's Fictions* (Quezon City: New Day, 1993), 90–92.

24. Morantte claims that the original title of the story was "The Soldier." See his *Remembering Carlos Bulosan*, 155. The account of plagiarism is on 155–56.

25. Morantte does not give the reasons why Romulo had rejected the story and thus leaves us to speculate as to whether he had political reasons for doing so. See the *New Yorker*, Sept. 2, 1944, 21–24; San Juan, *On Becoming Filipino*, ix.

26. Guido D'Agostino, "The Dream of Angelo Zara," in *The Best American Short Stories, 1943, and the Yearbook of the American Short Story*, ed. Martha Foley (Boston: Houghton Mifflin, 1943), 47–55.

27. We have no knowledge of the substance of the negotiations, or of whether the *New Yorker*'s editors at that time did or did not acknowledge plagiarism. All we have is the testimony of Epifanio San Juan. In 1970, San Juan wrote to the *New Yorker* editor, who dismissed the charge and asserted Bulosan's "originality." San Juan claimed that a "comparison" between the two pieces would prove the "falsity of the charge," but he eschewed any such comparison in his book. See San Juan, *Carlos Bulosan and the Imagination of the Class Struggle*, 56. Subsequent critics have cited San Juan and relied on his conclusion about the matter. These include Morantte, *Remembering Carlos Bulosan*, 156 and Kim, *Asian American Literature*, 46.

28. The phrase "articulate silence," which profoundly captures the deep silences, evasions, and rationalizations in Bulosan's letters, is from King-Kok Cheung, *Articulate Silences: Hisaye Yamamoto, Maxine Hong Kingston, Joy Kogawa* (Ithaca, N.Y.: Cornell University Press, 1993).

29. See *Asian American Literature: An Annotated Bibliography*, ed. King-Kok Cheung and Stan Yogi (New York: Modern Language Press, 1988).

30. Carlos Bulosan to Ray [no last name], Mar. 23, 1955, 2, University of Washington Libraries, Manuscripts and University Archives Division, box 6, folder 23.

31. Bulosan's bitterness toward the elites is so pronounced in this work that it probably contributed to the exaggerations and hyperbolic claims he made about his life in the book.

32. *America Is in the Heart*, 5.

33. Ibid., 23.

34. Ibid., 24.

35. Ibid., 243.

36. Feria, "Carlos Bulosan: Gentle Genius," 61.

37. Carlos Bulosan to Leopoldo Yabes, Jan. 6, 1947, in Feria, ed., *Sound of Falling Light*, 40.

38. Carlos Bulosan to José de los Reyes, July 27, 1948, in ibid., 68.

39. Carlos Bulosan to Leopoldo Yabes, Apr. 13, 1948, in ibid., 64. It is strange that Bulosan would accuse Romulo of this when *America Is in the Heart* itself exhibits universalist pretensions. Romulo, of course, had become a standby during the war whenever there was mention of Bataan and Corregidor (see, e.g., Bulosan's cablegram to Romulo cited in n. 21 above). He wrote several books that received wide acclaim, including *I Saw the Fall of the Philippines* (Garden City, N.Y.: Doubleday, Doran, 1942) and *I See the Philippines Rise* (Garden City, N.Y.: Doubleday, 1946).

40. Much later, Bulosan was to accuse Manuel Roxas of being America's "nominee for president," "protector of the landlords," and a Japanese collaborator who had become president only as a result of the presence of U.S. troops in the Philippines and an elitist electoral system. See *ILWU Yearbook, Cannery Workers, ILWU Local 37*, 1952, 27.

41. Carlos Bulosan to Leopoldo Yabes, Jan. 6, 1947, in Feria, ed., *Sound of Falling Light*, 42. The Philippine Trade Act, also called the Bell Trade Act, was a postwar treaty that maintained the Philippine economy's dependence upon U.S. markets. It established a graduated schedule for the introduction of tariffs on Philippine goods and set quotas for popular Philippine exports to the United States. The infamous parity provision was an amendment introduced by Rep. Charles Jasper Bell (D-Mo.) himself that gave Americans the unfair privilege of exploiting Philippine natural resources and purchasing property in the Philippines equal to any Filipino citizen, without however granting a reciprocal right to Philippine citizens to do the same in the United States. See Stephen Shalom, *The United States and the Philippines: A Study of Neocolonialism* (Quezon City: New Day, 1986), 43–50.

42. Carlos Bulosan to José de los Reyes, Nov. 2, 1949, in Feria, ed., *Sound of Falling Light*, 70.

43. Carlos Bulosan to José de los Reyes, July 27, 1948, in ibid., 68.

44. Carlos Bulosan to José de los Reyes, June 7, 1946, in ibid., 33.

45. The Huks—the name is short for Hukbalahap (Hukbo ng Bayan Laban sa Hapon), or "People's Army Against the Japanese"—originated in the Filipino guerrilla resistance during World War II, when they succeeded in creating "liberated zones" in Central Luzon prior to the arrival of MacArthur's invasion force. The liberation of the Philippines brought the return of elites like Osmeña who had been exiled to the United States and likewise the restoration of elite landlords to power. While the Huks acknowledged their rule and participated in electoral politics to advance peasant interests, they were soon barred from taking over positions they had legally won. This and a host of other repressive measures by landlords and Philippine government officials led to an armed Huk rebellion that lasted three years, which was ultimately suppressed by a combination of government-sponsored reforms, the appeal of the populist president Ramon Magsaysay, and a CIA-sponsored counterinsurgency campaign in the 1950s. See Renato Constantino, *The Philippines: The Continuing Past* (Quezon City: Foundation for Nationalist Studies, 1978) and Benedict J. Kerkvliet, *The Huk Rebellion: A Study of Peasant Revolt in the Philippines* (Honolulu: University of Hawai'i Press, 1977).

46. "Defense Chief Orders Arrest" (fragment of a longer article), n.d., n.p., Carlos Bulosan Papers, 2329, 2329–2, box 1, folder 11, University of Washington Libraries, Manuscript and University Archives Division.

47. "Excerpt from the Minutes of the Municipal Council of Binalonan, Pangasinan, in Its Special Session Held at the Municipal Hall, on the 29th Day of September, 1956."

48. *New Yorker*, Sept. 2, 1944, 21–24. This is reprinted in Bulosan, *On Becoming Filipino*, 100–108, whence I cite it.

49. Bulosan, *On Becoming Filipino*, 103.

50. Ibid., 104, 105.

51. See Gerald T. Burns, "American Folklore," in *Presenting America, Encountering the Philippines* (Quezon City: University of the Philippines Press, 1992), 76–97; Walter Ong, *Orality and Literacy: The Technologizing of the Word* (New York: Methuen, 1988); and Christine Goldberg, "Folktale," in *Encyclopedia of Folklore and Literature*, ed. Mary Ellen Brown and Bruce A. Rosenberg (Santa Barbara, Calif.: ABC-CLIO, 1998), 219–20.

52. See, e.g., Dean Fansler, *Filipino Popular Tales* (Lancaster, Pa.: American Folk-lore Society, 1921); "E. Arsenio Manuel," in *Contemporary Authors Autobiography Series* 9 (Detroit: Gale Research, 1989), 157. Through the narrator of *America Is in the Heart*, Bulosan speaks of the vital role played by folklore in the establishment of every modern national literature. After reading the world's famous fairy tales, the narrator decides on a new vocation: "Now I must live and

integrate Philippine folklore in our struggle for liberty." See Bulosan, *America Is in the Heart*, 260.

53. Vicente Rafael, "White Love: Census and Melodrama in the U.S. Colonization of the Philippines," in id., *White Love and Other Events in Filipino History* (Durham, N.C.: Duke University Press, 2000), 34. Cf. Romulo's attack on Tom Inglis Moore for his unsubstantiated claim that 90 percent of the students at the University of the Philippines cheated. See Bernardita Reyes Churchill, "Palma's Momentous Decade (1923–1933)," in *University of the Philippines: The First 75 Years (1908–1983)*, ed. Oscar M. Alfonso (Quezon City: Univ. of the Philippines, 1985), 176.

54. Walter Benjamin, "The Storyteller," in *Illuminations*, ed. Hannah Arendt (New York: Schocken Books, 1968), 103. Ong claims that such cultures appear strange because we have become so habituated to our own literate world. For instance, the mind-set of oral narratives, such as those that influenced Bulosan, differs considerably from "chirographic" (writing) psyches. Oral narratives tend to be "aggregative" (rather than analytic) and repetitive in structure. They also eschew abstractions and instead make close reference to the human life world. See Ong, *Orality and Literacy*, 38, and his discussion of writing cultures, 78–116. Walter Benjamin's reflections in "The Storyteller" add to Ong's insights. Benjamin argues that there is a profound kinship between storytelling and fairy tales, which "[contain] figuratively mythical elements . . . whose effect is certainly captivating and static, and yet not outside man."

55. Meñez, "Performance of Folk Narratives," in *Explorations in Philippine Folklore*, 56. For instance, the anthropologist Stephen Griffiths shows the transnational dimensions of folk belief systems. He follows the travels of Ilokano migrants in Hawaii back to the Philippines and notes the importance of "touching" in their interactions with persons possessing unusual healing powers and *anting-anting* (amulets). Meñez also refers to "belief stories" that show the influence of the supernatural among Bulosan's fellow Filipino migrants in California. "Belief stories," Meñez says, "[have] retained the status of legend in the repertory of Filipino immigrants. Narratives about witches, ghosts, *kapre* (giants), and *ingkanto* (environmental spirits) are exchanged, often during discussions involving the validity of supernatural beliefs." See Griffiths, *Emigrants, Entrepreneurs, and Evil Spirits: Life in a Philippine Village* (Honolulu: University of Hawai'i Press, 1988, 71–81.

56. Benjamin, "The Storyteller," 108.

57. Carlos Bulosan, *Voice of Bataan* (New York: Coward-McCann, 1943), published under the auspices of the American-Philippine Foundation.

58. Carlos Bulosan, *The Laughter of My Father* (New York: Harcourt, Brace, 1944).

59. Carlos Bulosan, preface to "The Death of a Rich Man: Story," *Philippine*

Free Press 38 (Dec. 13, 1947): 20, cited in Grace F. Bulaong, "Filipino Satire in English" (M.A. thesis, University of the Philippines, 1967), 97.

60. Carlos Bulosan to José de los Reyes, Feb. 11, 1948, in Feria, ed., *Sound of Falling Light*, 60.

61. Morantte writes that Bulosan's "poetic insight" was honed by life with his father in the province and the daily encounter with the land, the plants, and the animals, all of which would continue to "haunt" him well after his arrival in the United States. See Morantte, *Remembering Carlos Bulosan*, 36.

62. Ibid., 37–38.

63. Carlos Bulosan, "How My Stories Were Written," in id., *On Becoming Filipino*, 111ff.

64. Carlos Bulosan to Dorothy Babb, June 2, 1953, in Feria, ed., *Sound of Falling Light*, 81.

65. Bulosan, *America Is in the Heart*, 235. See Bienvenido Lumbera, *Tagalog Poetry, 1570–1898: Tradition and Influences in Its Development* (Quezon City: Ateneo de Manila University Press, 1986). At the same time, one can see a pattern developing: Bulosan was *living dangerously*—pushing the limits of borrowing and retelling to an extreme that flirted with disaster.

66. Carlos Bulosan to Leopoldo Yabes, Jan. 6, 1947, in Feria, ed., *Sound of Falling Light*, 40.

67. Carlos Bulosan to José de los Reyes (1950?), in ibid., 73.

68. Morantte, *Remembering Carlos Bulosan*, 131.

69. Bulosan, *America Is in the Heart*, 3, 280–83, 286–87.

70. Rocky Chin, "Interview with Aurelio Bulosan," in "Selected Writings of Carlos Bulosan," special issue, *Amerasia Journal* 6, no. 1 (1979): 159.

71. Morantte, *Remembering Carlos Bulosan*, 22.

72. Griffiths, *Emigrants, Entrepreneurs, and Evil Spirits*, 71–81; Meñez, *Explorations in Philippine Folklore*, 55.

73. Carlos Bulosan to Marjorie Barrows, May 27, 1956, University of Washington Libraries, Manuscripts and University Archives Division, Aurelio Bulosan Papers, 2329, 2329–2, box 1, folder 7.

74. Carlos Bulosan, *The Philippines Is in the Heart*, ed. Epifanio San Juan Jr. (Quezon City: New Day, 1978). The title was San Juan's, not Bulosan's.

75. Ibid., 185, 181–82.

76. Ibid., 185.

77. Bulosan, *America Is in the Heart*, 44–45.

78. Ibid., 250.

79. According to Bienvenido Lumbera, Aquino de Belen, a native of Rosario, Batangas, was the author of the first written narrative poem in Tagalog, *Ang Mahal na Pasion*, the *Sacred Passion*. Lumbera believes that the pasyon was not derived

from a Spanish original but was a native adaptation of the New Testament. In the nineteenth century, it was to become popularized in the Pasion Pilapil. The pasyon combined the story of Christ with *aral,* or lessons, thus serving a didactic purpose. See Lumbera, *Tagalog Poetry, 1570–1898,* 57.

80. Ileto, *Pasyon and Revolution,* 22.

81. The *lakaran* was also "[t]raditionally referrred to [as] a pilgrimage with biblical connotations." Also prominent in the pasyon tradition was *liwanag,* the image and symbolism of light, with all of its biblical connotations. See Ileto, *Pasyon and Revolution,* 269.

82. See Evangelista, *Carlos Bulosan and His Poetry,* 121–35.

83. Bulosan, *Voice of Bataan,* 121, 135.

84. See Evangelista, *Carlos Bulosan and His Poetry,* 146–47.

85. See discussion of Alquizola and Mostern in the Introduction to the chapter and Bulosan, *America Is in the Heart,* 311–12.

86. Page numbers cited in the text refer to Bulosan, *America Is in the Heart.*

87. Ileto, *Pasyon and Revolution,* 91–93.

88. See Evangelista, *Carlos Bulosan and His Poetry,* 146–47.

89. Bulosan, *America Is in the Heart,* 227–28.

90. Carlos Bulosan to Harriet Monroe, Feb. 3, 1936. See Licerio Lagda, "Women in the Life and Poetry of Carlos Bulosan," appendix, Carlos Bulosan to Florentino Valeros, Apr. 8, 1955, Carlos Bulosan Papers.

91. Dorothy Babb to P. C. Morantte, in Morantte, *Remembering Carlos Bulosan,* 92, 93.

92. Ibid., 11.

93. John Fante, quoted by McWilliams, "Introduction," in Bulosan, *America Is in the Heart,* xviii.

94. Matias J. Lagunilla to Mrs. Jean Antles, King County Department of Public Assistance, Seattle, Mar. 25, 1954, 2.

95. Alfonso P. Santos, *Literary Apprentice,* 1957, 96.

96. Feria, "Carlos Bulosan: Gentle Genius," 61.

97. Carlos Bulosan to Aurelio Bulosan, n.d. (Sept. 16, 1950s?), University of Washington Libraries, Manuscripts and University Archives Division, Aurelio Bulosan Papers, 2329–2, box 1, folder 1.

98. Luis Taruc, *Born of the People* (New York: International Publishers, 1953). And see flyer for "Born of the People: Autobiography of Luis Taruc," by the Committee to Sponsor Luis Taruc's Autobiography, University of Washington Libraries, Manuscript and University Archives Division, Carlos Bulosan Papers, 589–12, box 3, folder 14.

99. See Dolores S. Feria, "Bulosan's Power, Bulosan's People," in id., *Red Pencil, Blue Pencil: Essays & Encounters* (Manila: Kalikasan Press, 1991), 190–95.

100. See Carlos Bulosan to Aurelio Bulosan, n.d., University of Washington Libraries, Manuscripts and University Archives Division, Aurelio Bulosan Papers, 2329–2, box 1, folder 1.

101. Epifanio San Juan Jr., "Introduction," in Carlos Bulosan, *The Power of the People* (Metro Manila: National Book Store, 1986). Reprinted as *The Cry and the Dedication,* ed. Epifanio San Juan Jr. (Philadelphia: Temple University Press, 1995).

102. Gerald Burns, "The Repatriate Theme in Philippine Second-Language Fiction," in id., *Presenting America, Encountering the Philippines* (Quezon City: University of the Philippines Press, 1992), 209–15.

103. San Juan, "Introduction," in Bulosan, *Power of the People,* 8–10.

Chapter 3. The Artistic Vanguard: José García Villa

1. Carlos Bulosan to José de los Reyes, ca. 1950, in Dolores S. Feria, ed., *Sound of Falling Light: Letters in Exile* (Quezon City: Dolores S. Feria, 1961), 73.

2. The critic Sam Solberg described the two poets as separated by a "three thousand mile wide landmass" (Bulosan lived in Los Angeles, Villa in New York City), but their distance was more than physical, it was spiritual—"a state of mind, a feeling, a dream and a promise." See Solberg, "Bulosan-Theseus-Villa: A Cryptography of Coincidence," *MELUS* 15, no. 2 (Summer 1988): 3–25.

3. I take as a point of departure Werner Sollors's perspective on ethnic modernists in *Beyond Ethnicity: Consent and Descent in American Culture* (New York: Oxford University Press, 1986), 235ff.

4. Juan Luna entered an artistic competition in Madrid in which he garnered one of three gold medals for his painting *Spoliarium,* which had no Philippine theme, although the reference to "spoliation" was read as a criticism of Spanish colonialism in the Philippines. See John N. Schumacher, *The Propaganda Movement: 1880–1895: The Creators of a Filipino Consciousness, the Makers of the Revolution* (Quezon City: Ateneo de Manila University, 1973), 44, and Ambeth R. Ocampo, "Deflating the Historical Ego," in id., *Rizal Without the Overcoat* (Metro Manila: Anvil, 1990), 13–14.

5. See, e.g., Susan Kalcik, "Ethnic Foodways in America: Symbol and the Performance of Identity," in *Ethnic and Regional Foodways in the United States: The Performance of Group Identity,* ed. Linda Keller Brown and Kay Mussell (Knoxville: University of Tennessee Press, 1984), 37–65.

6. José García Villa, *Footnote to Youth: Tales of the Philippines and Others* (New York: Scribner's, 1933); id., *Many Voices: Selected Poems* (Manila: Philippine Book Guild, 1939); id., *Poems by Doveglion* (Manila: Philippine Writers' League, 1941);

id., *Have Come, Am Here* (New York: Viking, 1942); id., *Volume Two* (New York: New Directions, 1949); id., *Selected Poems and New* (New York: McDowell, Oblensky, 1958).

7. Carmen Guerrero Nakpil, "A Personal Reminiscence," *Malaya*, Feb. 12, 1997.

8. Ibid; Nick Joaquin, "Viva Villa," in id., *Doveglion and Other Cameos* (Manila: Nick Joaquin, 1977), 187; Gemino Abad and Edna Manlapaz, *Man of Earth: An Anthology of Filipino Poetry and Verse from English, 1905 to the Mid-50s* (Quezon City: Ateneo de Manila University Press, 1989), 411–14. Accounts of Villa's father's plight include Simeon Villa, *The Flight and Wanderings of General Emilio Aguinaldo from Bayambang to Palanan, 1899–1901: A Diary*, in *Aguinaldo's Odyssey, as Told in the Diaries of Col. Simeon Villa and Dr. Santiago Barcelona* (Manila: Bureau of Public Libraries, 1963); Stanley Karnow, *In Our Image: America's Empire in the Philippines* (London: Century, 1990), 158; Roger Bresnahan, ed., *In Time of Hesitation: American Anti-Imperialists and the Philippine-American War* (Quezon City: New Day, 1981), 62. Bresnahan details his humiliating capture by General Frederick Funston's men.

9. Letty Jimenez-Magsanoc, "Viva Villa: Poet Celebrates 60th Birthday Today," *Philippine Panorama*, Aug. 7, 1973, 15.

10. Joaquin, "Viva Villa," 192; Abad and Manlapaz, eds., *Man of Earth*, 412.

11. *Clay: A Literary Notebook* 1 (1931). Sanora Babb was, of course, the sister of Dorothy Babb, and both were close friends and supporters of Carlos Bulosan.

12. Edward J. O'Brien, ed., *The Best Short Stories of 1932 and the Yearbook of the American Short Story* (New York: Dodd, Mead, 1932). Another collection that showcased Villa's stories was Blanche Colton Williams, ed., *O. Henry Memorial Award: Prize Stories of 1932* (Garden City, N.Y.: Doubleday, Doran, 1932).

13. Villa, *Footnote to Youth*, 3–5. O'Brien speaks of a "lyrical quality," an "innocence of eye," and an "energy" in Villa's stories, qualities he locates in the "two widely different cultures" Villa fuses. However, O'Brien lapses into cultural stereotypes: Villa's "Filipino sense of race," he asserts, blends with "a strong Spanish sense of form and color"; his "native sensuousness of perception and expression" draws on "the ascetic pattern of the American desert" and the "asceticism of the Spanish short story."

14. Salvador P. Lopez, "The Poetry of José García Villa," in id., *Literature and Society: Essays on Life and Letters* (Manila: University Publishing Co. 1940), 152, 161ff. Lopez quotes the term "white hope" from Federico Mangahas. Cf. Elmer Ordoñez, "Send in the Clowns," *Literary Apprentice*, 1957, 59. The American publisher A. V. H. Hartendorp concurred with Lopez's assessment, adding, "[Villa's] out-put has been . . . alive and interesting, provocative, stimulating, not as to

thought but as to form and manner . . . he has always had an ear for the music of his lines in poetry; in fact, it is mostly sound rather than sense." *Philippine Magazine*, January 1939, 37.

15. Among the prominent members of the Philippine Writers League advocating a socially conscious literature were Lopez, Arturo B. Rotor (one of Villa's close friends), the essayist Fred Mangahas, and, later, the short story writer Manuel Arguilla. Villa lined up with those who valued a formal approach to art, including A. E. Litiatco, literary editor of the *Graphic*. See Ordoñez, "Send in the Clowns," 63–64.

16. José García Villa, interview by the author, with the assistance of Luis Cabalquinto, Greenwich Village, New York, August 15, 1996.

17. Villa divided the 127 poems of the book into four sections of lyric poetry (reflecting his predilection for lyricism and musicality) and an extended section on artistic self-fashioning called "Divine Poems."

18. Among the fellowships Villa won were an American Academy of Arts and Letters grant (1942) and a Guggenheim fellowship (1943). See *Contemporary Authors*, vol. 12 (Detroit: Gale Research, 1984), 492. Villa and Lamb were divorced in the late 1940s and the children went to live with their mother. Villa often visited them, however, and helped to pay for their schooling all through college. See further Abad and Manlapaz, eds., *Man of Earth*, 413.

19. There is an extensive body of Villa criticism, which falls into two main periods. The first was from World War II to the 1960s in the United States, where Villa published his landmark poetry collections *Have Come, Am Here* (1942) and *Volume Two* (1949). Villa was hailed as an "American" poet, praised and patronized by established white American critics and poets like Alfred Kreymborg, Marianne Moore, and Babette Deutsch, and especially by the British poet Edith Sitwell, who was astounded by his "perfectly original gift." See Alfred Kreymborg, "From Masters to Master Villa," *Saturday Review of Literature*, Oct. 10, 1942, 18; Marianne Moore, "Who Seeks Shall Find," *Nation* 155 (Oct. 17, 1942): 394; Babette Deutsch, "The Poet's Signature," *Literary Apprentice* 12, no. 15 (1948–49): 68–71; Dame Edith Sitwell, "Preface," in *Selected Poems and New* by José García Villa (1958; reprint, Metro Manila: Bookmark, 1993), x, xv.

In the Philippines during the same period, Villa was hailed as a national hero by leading newspapers and appropriated for a politically conservative cause as a champion of art against proletarian literature. For favorable, if not laudatory, accounts of Villa, see Teodoro Locsin, "The Dove, the Eagle, and the Lion," *Philippines Free Press* 38, no. 3 (Jan. 18, 1941): 4, 5; Ricaredo Demetillo, "Villa: An Estimate," *Sands and Coral: Literary Magazine of Silliman University,* 1950, 45–48; id., "José García Villa vs. Salvador P. Lopez," *Silliman Journal* 1, no. 3 (July 1954):

14–33; and David Quemada, "Major Influences on Seven Leading Philippine Poets in English: José García Villa et al.," ibid., 43–55. Frankly hagiographic is Leonidas V. Benesa's "José, García, Villa: Poet, Par, Excellence: A Review of Villa's *Selected Poems and New*," *Commen*t 14 (1962): 89–91. Poet-critics like Manuel Viray, Epifanio San Juan Jr., Gémino Abad, Rolando Tinio, and Amador Daguio debated the question of spirituality in Villa's poetry and his connection to religiously inspired poets like Donne, Blake, Hopkins, and Whitman. See Manuel Viray, "Transformations," *Literary Apprentice*, 1948–49: 80–91; Epifanio San Juan Jr., "The Vision of the Contemporary," *Panorama*, September 1960; Gémino Abad, "The Self as Genius and God as Peacock: A Study of 'Mysticism' in José García Villa's Poetry," *University College Journal* 8 (n.d. [ca. 1960s]): 172–85; Rolando Tinio, "Villa's Values; or, The Poet You Cannot Always Make Out, or Succeed In Liking Once You Are Able To," in *Brown Heritage: Essays on Philippine Cultural Tradition and Literature*, ed. Antonio P. Manuud (Quezon City: Ateneo de Manila University Press, 1967), 722–38; and Amador Daguio, "The Doveglion Book of Philippine Poetry," *Comment* 14 (1962): 138–47.

The second period of Villa criticism was from the 1970s to the 1990s. In the emerging field of Asian American literary studies, Villa received some recognition as an Asian American poet from the critics and anthologists Bruce Iwasaki, Kai-yu Hsu and Helen Palubinskas, and Hsin-fu Wand for his eccentricity and bold experimentation, which they sensed as a challenge to the project of an Asian American literature. See Bruce Iwasaki, "Response and Change for the Asian in America: A Survey of Asian American Literature," in *Roots: An Asian American Reader*, ed. Amy Tachiki et al. (Los Angeles: Continental Graphics, 1971), 90–91; Kai-yu Hsu and Helen Palubinskas, eds., *Asian American Authors* (Boston: Houghton Mifflin, 1972), 132–34; and Hsin-fu Wand, ed., *Asian-American Heritage: An Anthology of Prose and Poetry* (New York: Washington Square Press, 1974), 125. Villa then disappeared from Asian American literature. It was only in the late 1980s and early 1990s that liberal white critics like Sam Solberg and Werner Sollors saw Villa's usefulness for myth criticism and ethnic modernism. See Solberg, "Bulosan-Theseus-Villa"; Sollors, *Beyond Ethnicity*, 235ff., 237–58.

In Philippine literary criticism, no new critical work was done on Villa during the 1970s and 1980s, reflecting the shifting political winds of Philippine politics. In the 1990s, the expatriate white woman author Dolores Stephens Feria, a close friend and critic of Bulosan's, saw significance in Villa as an expatriate author who spoke to the theme of "exile" in Philippine literature. Epifanio San Juan Jr. carried this insight further, identifying in Villa's art an example of a "Third World sublime," an allegorical challenge to a conservative white literary world that sought to assimilate (and blunt the impact of) his "strange" Philippine poetic discourse. See

Feria, "Filipino Writers in Exile," in id., *Red Pencil, Blue Pencil: Essays & Encounters* (Manila: Kalikasan Press, 1991), 179–89, and Epifanio San Juan Jr., "José García Villa: Toward a Poetics of Disappearance and Resistance," in *Reading the West/Writing the East: Studies in Comparative Literature and Culture* (San Francisco: Peter Lang, 1992), 126, 95–132.

20. See, e.g., the discussion of the avant-garde in Matei Calinescu's *Five Faces of Modernity: Modernism, Avant-Garde, Decadence, Kitsch, Postmodernism* (Durham, N.C.: Duke University Press, 1987), 116ff., and Jochen Schulte-Sasse, "Foreword: Theory of Modernism Versus Theory of the Avant-Garde," in Peter Burger, *Theory of the Avant-Garde* (Minneapolis: University of Minnesota Press, 1984), viii and passim.

21. Francisco Arcellana, interview in *Writers and Their Milieu, Part II: An Oral History of Second Generation Writers in English*, ed. Edilberto N. Alegre and Doreen G. Fernández (Manila: De La Salle University Press, 1987), 46.

22. Edward Said, *Representations of the Intellectual* (New York: Vintage Books, 1994), 56.

23. Other literary figures who faced the wrath of the censors on "obscenity" charges include James Joyce for *Ulysses* and D. H. Lawrence for *Lady Chatterley's Lover* and other writings. See M. H. Abrams et al., eds., *The Norton Anthology of English Literature: Major Authors Edition* (New York: Norton, 1975), 2390; D. H. Lawrence, *Sex, Literature, and Censorship*, ed. Harry Moore (New York: Viking, 1959).

24. Elmer A. Ordoñez, "Remembered by the Clowns," *Literary Apprentice* 20, no. 2 (1957): 58, 60.

25. See "José García Villa: A Bio-Bibliography" (Quezon City: Library of the University of the Philippines, 1973), exhibits A and C (n.p.).

26. Villa was a prelaw student, hence Bocobo's involvement. He had once enrolled in medicine to please his father. However, he disliked medicine, and against his father's wishes, he changed career paths. See Villa's best friend, Arturo B. Rotor, interview in *Writers and Their Milieu, Part I: An Oral History of First Generation Writers in English*, ed. Edilberto Alegre and Doreen Fernandez (Manila: De La Salle University Press, 1984), 192–94.

27. Maximo M. Kalaw, *An Introduction to Philippine Social Science* (Manila: Philippine Education Co., 1939), 187–89, repr. Manila: Solar, 1986.

28. Manuel Buaken, *I Have Lived with the American People* (Caldwell, Idaho: Caxton, 1946), 244.

29. "José García Villa: A Bio-Bibliography," exhibit D, 1. Villa's conception of the grotesque and ugliness as beautiful echoes Sherwood Anderson's exploration of the grotesque and physical deformity in *Winesburg, Ohio* (1919; repr., New York:

Penguin Books, 1993). See Irving Howe's introduction to these 1919 stories, ibid., xii–xiv.

30. "José García Villa: A Bio-Bibliography," exhibit D, 2.

31. Ibid.

32. Ibid., 2–5. Villa idolized Sherwood Anderson, whose *Winesburg, Ohio* chronicles a young reporter's rebellion against the stilted lives of an American small town and his flight from these confines.

33. Ibid., exhibit D, 2.

34. The quotations from Anderson liberally mention the word "body," e.g., "My body does not belong to me" but "to tired women who have found no lovers" or to "those who lust and those who shrink from lusting." Ibid., exhibit D, 4.

35. "Excerpts from the Minutes of the 251st meeting of the Executive Committee of the University Council of the University of the Philippines," ibid.

36. José García Villa, interview by the author, Greenwich Village, New York, August 1996.

37. See Alegre and Fernandez, *Writers and Their Milieu, Part I,* 289. Every writer who was interviewed, the editors observe, mentioned José García Villa and his varied influences upon his contemporaries.

38. O'Brien, ed., *Best Short Stories of 1932,* 293.

39. The trilogy includes "Untitled Story," "White Interlude," and "Walk at Midnight: A Farewell." The recurrent symbols here are the "purple flower" and the color white, which express the values of tenderness, sensuality, and vision that help the artist make the decisive break away from family and from tradition.

40. See esp. "White Interlude."

41. See, e.g., "Footnote to Youth," "The Fence," "The Woman Who Looked Like Christ," "The Man Who Looked Like Rizal," "The Daughter of Rizal," "The Son of Rizal," and, finally, the moving "Yet Do They Strife."

42. José García Villa, "Letter from New York: The Man Who Led Me to Poetry," *Archipelago* A-7, 1, no. 7 (July 1974): 6; P. C. Morantte, "Two Filipinos in America," *Books Abroad* 18 (1944): 326; José García Villa, interview by the author, Greenwich Village, New York, August 1996. Villa claimed to have been the victim of numerous racial incidents, but underscored only one. In 1941, as a graduate student at Columbia, he telephoned the managers of a vacant apartment. When he arrived at the apartment to inspect the place, the manager told him that the apartment was no longer vacant. Many decades later, Luis Francia tells the story of Villa's row with a bartender at one of his favorite bars, in which he was called a "Chinese cocksucker." See Luis Francia, "Villanelles," in *The Anchored Angel: Selected Writings by José García Villa,* ed. Eileen Tabios (New York: Kaya Press, 1999), 172.

43. Belinda Olivares, "Angry Young Men of the Thirties," *Panorama* 12, no. 5 (May 1960): 68–69; Teresita E. Erestain, "A Veronican Revisited: Delfin Fresnosa and His Works," *Likha* 13, no. 1 (1991–92): 6ff. Olivares claims that these angry young men (except for Alfon) "declared a local war on morality in Literature," and that their "Grand Ally" was Villa, who had been "expelled" from the University of the Philippines. They were called "Veronicans" because they sought "to make their writing bear the imprint of the Face of the Philippines" in the same way that Veronica's cloth "bore the imprint of the face of Christ." See Francisco Arcellana, *The Francisco Arcellana Sampler* (Quezon City: University of the Philippines Creative Writing Center, 1990), inside front cover.

44. Lopez, "Poetry of José García Villa," 162.

45. Quoted by Hilario S. Francia, "Remembering José García Villa," *Manila Chronicle*, Feb. 13, 1997, 18.

46. See Villa, *Poems by Doveglion*. His first collection was *Many Voices* (1939). In later poems, Villa was to attribute a generative power to this mystical name. In one poem, for instance, the narrator claims to be "Doveglion" and says that his "business" is "ascension." At times, Villa seems to subsume his "biography" into his artistic persona: "Doveglion," he writes, "is the *author* of José García Villa" (emphasis added). See "A Composition," *Literary Apprentice*, 1953, 59–61.

47. In the last three decades of his life, Villa used the pen name "Xoce García Villa." His use of "Xoce" would again signal a movement back to prose, this time philosophical prose, and to what he considered a maturing of the poet into philosopher. The constant renaming was Villa's way, not only of marking his development, but also of keeping the interest of his audience in the artist. For every new self-designation destabilized old conceptions and demanded that Villa be read anew. His explanation for switching to Xoce appears in part 2 of "On the Human Condition," a compilation of Villa sayings from 1970 to 1988 by Larry Francia (courtesy of Hilario Francia). Villa met the prize-winning Russian poet Yevgeny Yevtushenko in 1973 when he returned to the Philippines to receive the National Artist Award, and he subsequently visited Yevtushenko in Russia. He and another famous Philippine author, Carmen Guerrero Nakpil, were invited to attend an international Writers' Symposium at Alma Ata. Villa enjoyed his nonstop "Russian Sojourn," and the Russians were "so sweet and warm and outgoing" that he called them "the Filipinos of Europe." It was at this point that he decided to change his name from José to the russified spelling Xoce, which he regarded as "an improvement." See also Carmen Guerrero Nakpil, "A Personal Reminiscence," *Malaya*, Feb. 12, 1997.

48. Villa, *Volume Two*, reprinted in *Selected Poems and New*, 81–82. As regards the false analogy with pointillism, Tinio, "Villa's Values," points out that the basic

element of the painting is the brush stroke, but for poetry, it is the word, not the comma. An example of Villa's comma poems is "The, bright, Centipede," which begins: "The,bright,Centipede,/Begins,his,stampede!/His,spiritual,might,/Golding,the,night," etc. One wonders here whether the beauty of the poem is achieved by the commas or by Villa's adept use of internal and external rhymes. Villa's "Adaptations," in his collection *Selected Poems and New,* were his last poetic innovation.

49. See Villa's "Index of Short Stories Published in Philippine Magazines, 1926 to 1934," in *The Best Filipino Short Stories,* ed. O. O. Sta. Romana (Manila: Wightman, 1935), 141–51. See also, "José García Villa's Roll of Honor of Short Stories (1926 to 1940)," in *Midcentury Guide to Philippine Literature in English,* ed. Alberto S. Florentino (Manila: Filipiniana Publishers, 1963), 83–95. Among the authors to consistently earn Villa's three stars were Estrella Alfon, Francisco Arcellana, Manuel Arguilla, Consorcio Borje, Casiano T. Calalang, Delfin Fresnosa, N. V. M. Gonzalez, Paz Latorena, Loreto Paras-Sulit, Ligaya Victorio Reyes, Arturo Rotor, and Bienvenido N. Santos.

50. Josephine B. Serrano and Trinidad M. Ames, eds., *A Survey of Filipino Literature in English* (Quezon City: Phoenix, 1988), 2.

51. Olivares, "Angry Young Men of the Thirties," 69.

52. A. V. H. Hartendorp, "Four O'Clock in the Editor's Office," *Philippine Magazine,* September 1933.

53. Edna Z. Manlapaz, *Our Literary Matriarchs, 1925–1953: Angela Manalang Gloria, Paz M. Latorena, Loreto Paras Sulit, and Paz Marquez Benitez* (Quezon City: Ateneo de Manila University Press, 1996), 28.

54. José García Villa, "The Status of Philippine Poetry," *Graphic,* June 6, 1935, cited in Manlapaz, *Our Literary Matriarchs,* 63.

55. Edilberto K. Tiempo, *Literary Criticism in the Philippines and Other Essays* (Manila: De La Salle University Press, 1995), 13.

56. *Harvard Wake* 5 (1945), E. E. Cummings issue; *Quarterly Review of Literature,* Winter 1946–47, Marianne Moore issue. Villa's selection of Marianne Moore's poetry helped contribute to Moore's reputation, as it included notable writers like Elizabeth Bishop, William Crowe Ransom, William Carlos Williams, and Wallace Stevens. See Charles Molesworth, *Marianne Moore: A Literary Life* (New York: Atheneum, 1990), 333; José García Villa, ed., *A Celebration for Edith Sitwell* (1948; repr., Freeport, N.Y.: Books for Libraries Press, 1972). Several decades later, Villa published *Bravo: The Poet's Magazine,* which won the coveted Pushcart Prize for small presses in 1981. See back cover of vol. 2 (1982).

57. Edith Sitwell, *The American Genius: An Anthology of Poems with Some Prose* (London: John Lehmann, 1951). Villa, *Selected Poems and New,* "Introduction," ix.

58. Villa was at this party and hobnobbed with famous literary personalities like Tennessee Williams, Stephen Spender, W. H. Auden, Elizabeth Bishop, Marianne Moore, Gore Vidal, and Randall Jarrell. A photograph of the occasion was taken for *Life*. See Victoria Glendinning, *Edith Sitwell: A Unicorn Among Lions* (London: Weidenfeld & Nicolson, 1981), 277.

59. Of Villa's poems, Sitwell wrote to Stephen Spender that some "are really *lovely*" and others "so awful that my blood turns to blocks of ice in my veins." See Edith Sitwell to Stephen Spender, Sept. 8, 1944, cited in Glendinning, *Edith Sitwell*, 245.

60. Villa's poems did eventually appear in Cyril Connolly's *Horizon* in May 1949, a few months before the magazine ceased publication. See Glendinning, *Edith Sitwell*, 246.

61. Edith Sitwell to John Lehmann, Dec. 19, 1949, in Edith Sitwell, *Selected Letters, 1919–1964* (New York: Vanguard Press, 1970), 169.

62. Friedrich Nietzsche, *Human, All Too Human*, trans. Marion Faber (Lincoln: University of Nebraska Press, 1986), 113.

63. Morantte, "Two Filipinos in America," 326–27.

64. P. C. Morantte, "Filipino Writers in America III: José García Villa," *This Week*, Sept. 4, 1949, 26.

65. Bienvenido N. Santos, "José García Villa in Exile," in *Philippine Harvest: An Anthology of Filipino Writing in English*, ed. Maximo D. Ramos (Manila: E. F. David, 1953), reprint of earlier article published in *Philippine American*, May 1946, 22–26. See also Santos's *Memory's Fictions: A Personal History* (Quezon City: New Day, 1993), 91.

66. Morantte, "Filipino Writers in America III," 26. According to Morantte, Villa was called up for the draft but was rejected by the army. See his "Villa in Retrospect," *This Week*, May 9, 1948, 14.

67. Morantte, "Filipino Writers in America III," 28. Thus began Villa's lifelong antipathy to Romulo. As Morantte wrote, Ambassador Romulo promised to get Villa a job but it never materialized. Romulo also had a habit of slighting Villa by calling him "Joe," which Villa hated.

68. Locsin, "The Dove, the Eagle, and the Lion," 5ff.

69. Amador T. Daguio, letter to the *Philippines Free Press*, Feb. 22, 1947, 12. Daguio's concern was shared by two other readers responding to Locsin's article on Villa.

70. Nick Joaquin, "Viva Villa" and "What Signified the Expatriates?" in id., *A Question of Heroes* (Manila: National Book Store, 1981), 39–53. Joaquin clearly sympathizes with Villa, at times excusing his irresponsible behavior, although he manages to present less flattering views of the poet by his detractors. By the time

these articles were written, Joaquin had established himself as a poet, fiction writer, and playwright. His novel *Woman with Two Navels* had been highly acclaimed, as was his play *The Portrait of the Artist as Filipino*. Joaquin's perspective on Villa was shaped by a similarity of social class background. Joaquin's father, like Villa's, had been a colonel in the Philippine revolutionary forces and was humiliated by the American victory. Joaquin's own artistic project during this period of intense postwar nationalism was to have Filipinos acknowledge the importance of Spain and Hispanic-Filipino culture (economy, language, religion, etc.) in the constitution of modern-day Filipino culture. See, e.g., his *Culture and History: Occasional Notes on the Process of Philippine Becoming* (Metro Manila: Solar, 1988). In this project, Romulo and Villa, given their families' high birth and social participation in the Spanish colonial period, provided Joaquin with signal studies (e.g., *The Seven Ages of Romulo*), although the two authors' high degree of Americanization left him ambivalent about them. See, e.g., Joaquin's assessment of Villa in *The Aquinos of Tarlac: An Essay on History as Three Generations* (Metro Manila: Cacho Hermanos, 1983), 132–33, which seems to take Villa out of the Philippine intellectual tradition of Rizal and the ilustrados. Unless otherwise indicated, the following account draws on "Viva Villa."

71. Fred and Gloria McDarrah, *Beat Generation: Glory Days in Greenwich Village* (New York: Schirmer Books, 1996), 10, 12, 143, has several snapshots of Villa at the February 15, 1959, reading of the Beats, with the poets Gregory Corso and Amiri Baraka. Villa loved to tell stories about Allen Ginsberg's visits to his apartment and the bugs he left in his wake. See Luis Cabalquinto, "José García Villa: What's He Been Up To?" *Filipinas: A Magazine for All Filipinos* 3, no. 30 (October 1994): 18; and José García Villa, interview by the author, Greenwich Village, New York, August 1996.

72. Villa was supposed to have said that the Guerreros were "a terrible family," because they all had "personality," unlike his family, where he was "the only one with personality." Nakpil, "Personal Reminiscence."

73. Page numbers cited in the text refer to Joaquin, "Viva Villa."

74. Literary critics like Dolores Feria frowned on this attention paid to Villa and the indifference to Bulosan, who, unlike Villa, had identified and advanced a Filipino agenda. See Feria, "Carlos Bulosan: Gentle Genius," 58.

75. Villa's dislike for public displays or performances seems to have originated in an elitist disdain for the commodification of the artist. Cirilo Bautista hazards a similar observation in his "Conversations with José García Villa," *Archipelago* A60 (August 1979): 29–30. Villa, says Bautista, dreaded being in the "spotlight" and refused to be "a performing artist." Despite numerous offers, he never gave poetry readings in either New York or the Philippines. Cirilo hypothesizes that Villa "dis-

dained poets who recited their poems in public" as "no better than circus barkers or market vendors."

76. Joaquin's reportage on Villa ends here.

77. Imelda Marcos was the chair of the Cultural Center of the Philippines' board of trustees, which nominated Villa and the others for the award. See Federico Pascual Jr., "The National Artists," *Fookien Times Yearbook*, 1973, 248. The National Artists Award was only one of the projects of the Cultural Center patronized by the Marcoses. It went hand in hand with the construction of the Cultural Center of the Philippines, the Theater for the Performing Arts, the National Museum, the Design Center of the Philippines, and the Folk Arts Theater, as well as numerous projects and performances on a national and international scale. See Mercy S. Tolentino, "The CCP Record: A Fruitful Decade for the Arts," *Archipelago* A53 (January 1979): 4–5.

78. See "José García Villa: A Bio-Bibliography." Its subtitle was "on the occasion of the conferment of the Degree of Doctor of Humane Letters Honoris Causa upon José García Villa."

79. Pascual, "National Artists," 248; Andres Cristobal Cruz, "Contemporary Philippine Literature: Themes and Trends," *Fookien Times Yearbook*, 1973, 264. Cristobal Cruz quotes Marcos on his so-called "Democratic Revolution," then being waged on two fronts: "the first is in the heart of the individual Filipino. The second is in the being of Philippine society." This was putatively the foundation of the "cultural development objectives of the New Society."

80. Pascual, "National Artists," 248ff. The artists included Francisca Reyes Aquino (dance), Carlos V. Francisco (painting), Amado V. Hernandez (novel), Antonio J. Molina (music), Juan F. Nakpil (architecture), Guillermo E. Tolentino (sculpture), and Villa for poetry.

81. Pascual, "National Artists," 248.

82. Jimenez-Magsanoc, "Viva Villa: Poet Celebrates 60th Birthday Today," 14.

83. Ibid., 16. Many of Villa's aphorisms on sex are collected in "Reflections on Poetry and Sex by José García Villa, 1970–1990," compiled by Larry Francia and John Cowen, *Philippine Graphic*, May 6, 1990, 23–25. These reflect the continuing centrality of sex and the body for Villa's conception of life and poetry, as well as his constant search for the crisp, shocking turn of phrase. For instance, he claimed that he taught poetry that was "between consenting adults." He enjoined others to cultivate their "passions of the spirit" to "create works that endure." At another time, he reveled in his "animality," his "animalship," and his "animalhood."

84. Jimenez-Magsanoc, "Viva Villa: Poet Celebrates 60th Birthday Today," 14, 16.

85. Carlos Angeles, interview in *Writers and Their Milieu, Part II*, ed. Alegre and Fernández, 26.

86. Nakpil, "Personal Reminiscence"; Pio Andrade, *The Fooling of America: The Untold Story of Carlos P. Romulo* (Manila: Ouch, 1985, 1990), 127.

87. Andrade, *Fooling of America*, 127.

88. *Writers and Their Milieu*, ed. Alegre and Fernandez, 291. Romulo, of course, was born in 1899, Villa in 1908.

89. For an enthusiastic account of Villa's methods of teaching poetry during his return to the Philippines in 1960, see Beatrice and Jorma Kaukonen, "The Philippines and Jose Garcia-Villa *[sic]* Remembered," *Bulletin of the American Historical Collection* 20, no. 1, 78 (January-March 1992): 24–34.

90. Joaquin, "Viva Villa," 216.

91. John Cowen, a professor in education at Farleigh Dickinson University, first met Villa in 1964 and was "enamored of his brilliant, imaginative and lyrical poems." Despite a shaky first meeting, Villa came to respect him. Cowen studied with Villa through 1967 and all the way through Villa's death in 1997. In later years, the teacher-student relationship between the two was transformed into a collaborative effort on literary projects and finally into a father-son relationship. John King, a New York lawyer, took two courses with Villa at the New School in 1969. He was told that for the serious poetry student, "there was no one better." Robert L. King to the author, in response to interview questions, May 8, 1999, 1; Arthur Vanderborg, letter to the author, in response to interview questions, May 6, 1999. Besides Cowen, King, and Vanderborg, other students included Gloria Potter, who studied with Villa for over a decade, and Mort Malkin who had studied with Villa in the late 1960s and returned in 1980 to study with him again until 1997. John Cowen, interview by the author, June 17, 1997, 4. Cowen became a lifelong friend of Villa's. The poet and short story writer Arthur Vanderborg thought Villa "a poetic genius" and found his lectures and workshops "excellent." Vanderborg stayed with Villa for ten years.

92. Bautista, "Conversations with José García Villa," 30.

93. "Calvin Forbes," in *Contemporary Authors Autobiography Series* 16 (Detroit: Gale Research, 1984), 112. At the same time, however, students were attracted to Villa's easygoing style outside the classroom. For several years, Villa met after class with students at the Smith Bar on Sixth Avenue, and much later at the Cedar Bar on Twelfth Street and University Place near New York University. Forbes describes the informal settings where Villa continued to interact with students and to perform. Villa, he wrote, gathered students to eat and drink at Smith's and spoke of poetry "while he sipped martinis," discoursing most often on E. E. Cummings and Dylan Thomas, two he had personally known. John Cowen, interview by the author, 1, and "Calvin Forbes," in *Contemporary Authors Autobiography Series*, 112.

94. John Cowen, interview by the author, June 17, 1997, 1.

95. Bautista, "Conversations with José García Villa," 30.

96. Robert L. King to author, 1.

97. Leonidas V. Benesa, "Viva Villa?" *Focus Philippines*, Dec. 2, 1972.

98. Ibid., 16–18.

99. Robert L. King to author, 1; John Cowen, interview by the author, June 17, 1997, 4.

100. "A Note on the Adaptations," in José García Villa, *Selected Poems and New*, 160–61. Villa borrowed the collage concept from painting.

101. "Guideline Notes for Adaptations," José García Villa, Poetry Workshop 3, 1977, 4A (courtesy of John Cowen).

102. Luis Francia, "Villanelles," in *Anchored Angel*, ed. Tabios, 169.

103. Ibid., 169. Villa traced his discovery of the "spirit of lyricism" to E. E. Cummings, from whom he also learned the "sense of language and great experimentation in technique." "Letter from New York" (cited n. 42 above), 6.

104. Luis Francia, "Villanelles," 170. To "form," King added Villa's belief in "musicality" and "the importance of tension" in a poem's verses and stanzas. Villa himself attempted to diagram his own poetic scheme for the class: in it, he broke down the essentials of poetry into a pie chart expressive of the balance between language (diction, rhythm, tone, economy, and meaning) and craft (line, stanza, internal structure). From Xoce García Villa, A theoretical model of poetry [not the title], May 16, 1978 (courtesy of John Cowen). Note that meaning occupies a small, subordinate place under language.

105. Luis Francia, from an early draft of "Villanelles," 11 (courtesy of author). Luis Cabalquinto, telephone interview, November 1996.

106. Luis Cabalquinto, telephone interview, 2.

107. John Cowen, interview by the author, June 17, 1997, 6.

108. José García Villa, interview by the author, Greenwich Village, New York, August 1996, and *Writers and Their Milieu, Part I*, ed. Alegre and Fernández, 308.

109. F. Sionil José, interview by the author, Manila, Feb. 1, 1996.

110. Arnold Azurin, *Reinventing the Filipino Sense of Being and Becoming* (Quezon City: University of the Philippines Press, 1995), 179–80.

111. The poem was written in 1934. See Abad and Manlapaz, eds., *Man of Earth*, 153.

112. Villa, ,,A Composition,,, 59.

113. José García Villa, interview by the author, Greenwich Village, New York, August 1996.

114. Jonathan Chua, "A Visit with José García Villa," *Evening Paper*, Thursday, Jan. 16, 1996, 11.

115. Hilario S. Francia, letter to the author, in response to interview questions, June 2, 1999, 3.

116. Joaquin, "Viva Villa," 197.

117. John Cowen, interview by the author, June 17, 1997, 1.

118. Cabalquinto, "José García Villa: What's He Been Up To?" 18. *Adobo* is chicken, pork, or beef marinated in vinegar and soy sauce. *Kare-kare* is a stew of oxtail, beef, and mixed vegetables in peanut sauce. *Pansit* is the generic name for Chinese Filipino noodles of various kinds. "Crispy *pata*" are deep-fried pig's trotters. Finally, *lumpia* is the generic designation for a variety of Filipino-style egg rolls.

119. Hilario S. Francia, "Remembering José García Villa, Part 2," *Manila Chronicle*, Feb. 20, 1997.

120. A. Z. Jolicco Cuadra, "Viva Villa: Have Come Am Here (again)," *Manila Chronicle*, Jan. 29, 1995.

121. Adrian Cristobal, "The Exiled Nightingale," *Philippine Daily Inquirer*, Feb. 6, 1997.

122. Marites Paez, "'A poem must be magical, as musical as a seagull': Doveglion Buried," *Malaya*, Feb. 12, 1997, 1, 6.

Chapter 4. Nativism and Negation: N. V. M. Gonzalez

1. The term *balikbayan* refers to overseas Filipinos "returning home," including Filipino immigrants from North America and overseas contract workers (OCW's). See Vicente L. Rafael, *White Love and Other Events in Filipino History* (Durham, N.C.: Duke University Press, 2000), 206.

2. James McEnteer, "You Can't Go Home Again If You Never Left," *Filipinas: A Magazine for All Filipinos* 6, no. 57 (Jan. 1997): 43. McEnteer was a visiting Fulbright professor at the University of the Philippines, 1994–95, who lived in Mindanao at the time, according to the article.

3. Oscar Campomanes calls homecoming a "classic scene in exilic writing"— "the actual and transient return and the first glimpse of home after an absence of many years." See his "Filipinos in the United States and Their Literature of Exile," in *Reading the Literatures of Asian America*, ed. Shirley Lim and Amy Ling (Philadelphia: Temple University Press, 1992), 67.

4. See A. V. H. Hartendorp, "Four O'Clock in the Editor's Office," *Philippine Magazine*, September 1933 and July 1938. "Local color" writing came to prominence in late nineteenth-century America, capturing "the unique customs, manners, speech, folklore, and other qualities of a particular regional community, usually in humorous short stories." See Chris Baldick, *The Concise Oxford Dictionary of Literary Terms* (New York: Oxford University Press, 2001), 142–43.

5. N. V. M. Gonzalez, *Seven Hills Away* (Denver: Swallow Press, 1947); and see id., *Kalutang: A Filipino in the World* (Manila: Kalikasan Press, 1990).

6. In the 1950s and early 1960s, Gonzalez produced a spate of books: *Children of the Ash-Covered Loam and Other Stories* (1954), the novels *Season of Grace* (1956) and *The Bamboo Dancers* (1959), and the story collection *Look, Stranger, on This Island Now* (Manila: Benipayo Press, 1963). This was followed by a retrospective collection, *Selected Stories* (1965). Some complained that Gonzalez's writings were "dull" and that nothing ever happened in them, rejecting their "slice of life" approach. See review of Gonzalez, *Seven Hills Away*, by F. Sionil José, *Manila Chronicle*, n.d. (ca. 1949); Arturo Roseburg, "N. V. M. Gonzalez," *Pathways to Philippine Literature in English* (Quezon City: Alemar-Phoenix, 1966), 112–36; Teodoro Locsin, cited in "Francisco Arcellana," in *Writers and Their Milieu: An Oral History of Second Generation Writers in English, Part II*, ed. Edilberto N. Alegre and Doreen G. Fernndez (Manila: De La Salle University Press, 1987), 63. Others scrutinized his style and diction. And still others looked down on his "peasant" subjects. Edilberto K. Tiempo, "The Fiction of N. V. M. Gonzalez," in *Literary Criticism in the Philippines and Other Essays* (Manila: De La Salle University Press, 1995), 281–320, repr. of original essay, "The Stories of N. V. M. Gonzalez: Destination Unknown," in *Sands and Coral*, October 1955; Gracianus Reyes, "N. V. M. Gonzalez Revisited," *Mithi* 9 (1985): 76–78; review of *Seven Hills Away*, by Jolico Cuadra, *Chronicle Magazine*, June 6, 1964, 3. He did, however, have admirers who claimed that he had been misread. Through their careful readings of Gonzalez's works, they brought to light the author's artistry and the lasting cultural values in his works. Valdemar Olaguer, "The Criticism of E. K. Tiempo: Destination Missed," *Literary Apprentice* 20, no. 2 (1957): 84–95; Edilberto de Jesús Jr., "On This Soil, in This Climate: Growth in the Novels of N. V. M. Gonzalez," in N. V. M. Gonzalez, *The Bamboo Dancers* (Manila: Bookmark, 1993), 331–58. The latter essay first appeared in *Brown Heritage: Essays on Philippine Cultural Tradition and Literature*, ed. Antonio G. Manuud (Quezon City: Ateneo de Manila University Press, 1967), 739–64.

7. Miguel A. Bernad, S.J., *Bamboo and the Greenwood Tree: Essays on Filipino Literature in English* (Manila: Bookmark, 1961), 115–21. Father Miguel Bernad generously included an essay by Gonzalez in response to his own essay on Gonzalez's novels *A Season of Grace* and *The Bamboo Dancers*. Bernad's own critical method, as Gonzalez's response makes clear, is based upon Catholic moral assumptions and a laudable cosmopolitanism, although one limited to Western Christian civilization. Leonard Casper, "Folk Culture and City Commerce," in *New Writing from the Philippines* (Syracuse, N.Y.: Syracuse University Press, 1965), 42–55. Casper identifies the use of formal techniques in Gonzalez's fiction such as the use of "limited narrators," "objective correlative," and "understatement" that highlight the importance of "technique" in the construction of a literary work. Limited narrators are an expression of point of view in fiction in which a first-person or third-

person narrator has a confined knowledge of the events being described. Objective correlative, defined as "an external equivalent for an internal state of mind" or a "situation" that evokes a particular "mood" or "emotion," comes from T. S. Eliot's essay "Hamlet and His Problems" (1919), in which Eliot criticizes the play for its failure to match Hamlet's emotion with the action. And finally, "understatement" is a subset of irony, which gives the impression of "unemotional detachment" or "restraint." See Baldick, *Concise Oxford Dictionary of Literary Terms*, 166, 176, 198; and William Harmon, *A Handbook to Literature*, 9th ed. (Upper Saddle River, N.J.: Prentice-Hall, 2003). Casper's essay is for the most part a sensitive reading of Gonzalez's stories and novels. It does on occasion suffer from Orientalism, a superficial understanding of Philippine cultures that one can detect in his repetition of the word "primitive" to describe Gonzalez's rural subjects.

8. See Jesús, "On This Soil, in This Climate." Richard R. Guzman, "'As in Myth, the Signs Were All Over': The Fiction of N. V. M. Gonzalez," *Virginia Quarterly Review* 60, no. 1 (Winter 1984): 102–18, repr. in Gonzalez, *Work on the Mountain* (Quezon City: University of the Philippines Press, 1995), echoes this approach. Guzman was one of Gonzalez's students at California State University, Hayward. Petronilo Bn. Daroy, "Aspects of Philippine Writing in English," *Philippine Studies* 17, no. 2 (April 1969): 249–65.

9. For a review of this Asian American criticism, see my essay, "The 'Pre-History' of an 'Asian-American' Writer: N. V. M. Gonzalez' Allegory of Decolonization," *Amerasia Journal* 24, no. 3 (Winter 1998): 126–42. During this long period of time, Gonzalez produced only a few original short stories. He concentrated on producing synoptic essays, including his literary autobiography, "Moving On: A Filipino in the World," in *Foreign Values and Southeast Asian Scholarship*, ed. Joseph Fischer (Berkeley: Center for South and Southeast Asia Studies, University of California, 1973), 123–57, later reprinted as *Kalutang*. This was followed by examinations of Philippine writing and the literatures of "emerging nations," which presaged the interest in postcolonial criticism. For instance, "Holding the Rainbow: Notes on the English Literatures of the Third World," *Manila Review* 1, no. 3 (April 1975): 59–69. Gonzalez also published a retrospective story collection, which was reissued in 1989 and received positive reviews. See *Mindoro and Beyond* (1979; repr., Quezon City: University of the Philippines Press, 1989). In the last decade of his life, Gonzalez concentrated on reissuing his works for a new generation that had not read him. These included *Bread of Salt and Other Stories* (Seattle: University of Washington Press, 1993), his first book published in the United States since 1947; *The Winds of April* (1998); and *Work on the Mountain* (1995). The last included *The Father and the Maid: Essays on Filipino Life and Letters* (Quezon City: University of the Philippines Press, 1990). He also collected another set of essay

reprints, *The Novel of Justice* (Manila: National Commission for Culture and the Arts, 1996). Finally, he published a collection of new and hitherto uncollected stories, *A Grammar of Dreams* (Quezon City: University of the Philippines Press, 1997).

10. See Oscar Campomanes's essays, including "Filipinos in the United States and Their Literature of Exile," in *Reading the Literatures of Asian America,* ed. Shirley Lim and Amy Ling (Philadelphia: Temple University Press, 1992); "Introduction," in Gonzalez, *Work on the Mountain*; and "Looking Homeward," in *An Interethnic Companion to Asian American Literature,* ed. King-Kok Cheung (New York: Cambridge University Press, 1997).

11. For the connection between travel and identity suggested by "routes," as opposed to the traditional notion of identity represented in terms of the metaphor of planting "roots," see Paul Gilroy, *Black Atlantic: Modernity and Double Consciousness* (Cambridge, Mass: Harvard University Press, 1993), 1–40.

12. Narita Gonzalez states that Gonzalez provided workshops at their U.P. home for practically anyone interested in writing, including students in the sciences. According to Gémino Abad, one of his former students, Gonzalez was chair of the second U.P. Writers' Summer Workshop in Los Baños in 1967. Narita Gonzalez, "Our Life on File," *The Writer's Wives,* ed. Narita M. Gonzalez (Pasig City, Philippines: Anvil, 2000), 106; Gémino Abad and Edna Zapanta Manlapaz, eds., *Man of Earth: An Anthology of Filipino Poetry and Verse from English, 1905 to the Mid-50s* (Quezon City: Ateneo de Manila University Press, 1989), 378.

13. Ann Evory, ed., *Contemporary Authors New Revision Series* 2 (1981): 259; Philip J. Belarmino, "Bananas and Blades: A Stylistic Analysis of N. V. M. Gonzalez's Mindoro and Beyond" (M.A. thesis, University of the Philippines, 1997), 202–4.

14. Danton Remoto, with Ma. Elena Paterno, "N. V. M. Gonzalez: Writing as a Celebration of Life," *Chimera: Voices, Tales, and Visions* 1, no. 1 (1996): 9–10. According to Michael Gonzalez, Nestor Ibarra was born in 1943, Anselma ("Selma") in 1945, Michael himself in 1948, and Lakshmi in 1953. Selma, "believed to be a Mangyan princess," was born during their exile in Mindoro. Michael Gonzalez, E-mail to the author, Friday, May 16, 2003.

15. N. V. M. Gonzalez, interview by the author, Los Angeles, Oct. 24, 1998.

16. Ibid.

17. Teodoro A. Agoncillo, *The Fateful Years: Japan's Adventure in the Philippines, 1941–45* (1965; repr. Quezon City: University of the Philippines Press, 2001), 602–3. Agoncillo (1912–1985) was Gonzalez's contemporary and fellow faculty member at the University of the Philippines. He might also be regarded as a language nationalist, for whom Tagalog, especially formal Tagalog as opposed to

Taglish and other lingua francas, was extremely important to Filipino national identity. He was a professor in the History Department starting in 1958 and later served as its chair until his retirement. He wrote for local periodicals in both Pilipino and English and worked for the Institute of National Language. Agoncillo wrote pathbreaking histories from a nationalist viewpoint, including *Revolt of the Masses: The Story of Bonifacio and the Katipunan* (Quezon City: University of Philippines, 1956); and *Malolos: The Crisis of the Republic* (Quezon City: College of Liberal Arts, University of the Philippines, 1960). See Florentino B. Valeros and Estrellita V. Gruenberg, *Filipino Writers in English* (Quezon City: New Day, 1987), 3–4.

18. See Andrew Gonzalez, FSC, *Language and Nationalism: The Philippine Experience Thus Far* (Quezon City: Ateneo de Manila University Press, 1980), 60–96.

19. Agoncillo, *Fateful Years*, 638.

20. Gonzalez, *Kalutang*, 66–71.

21. Agoncillo, *Fateful Years*, 634–35.

22. Ibid., 604. Filipino writers were well aware of the Japanese colonial government's attempts to use Tagalog to get rid of English and replace it with "Nippongo," Agoncillo writes (ibid. 641–42), but this did not negate the cultural impact of the language change upon Filipino intellectuals' identity and culture.

23. I am thinking here, for instance, of *négritude* poets of the 1950s like Léopold Sédar Senghor and Aimé Césaire, as well as of the more recent Afrocentric theorists. In response to the West's racial disparagement of blacks all over the world, the latter celebrated what they believed united them, namely, their emotional, instinctive, and artistic culture. Ironically, these notions reflected the influence of French anthropologists, who also passed on their "negrophilia" and their notions of black exoticism. See Tyler Stovall, *Paris Noir: African Americans in the City of Light* (Boston: Houghton Mifflin, 1996), ch. 3. For criticisms of nativist currents among contemporary African and African American intellectuals, see Kwame Anthony Appiah's, "Topologies of Nativism," in *The Bounds of Race: Perspectives on Hegemony and Resistance*, ed. Dominick LaCapra (Ithaca, N.Y.: Cornell University Press, 1991); and Paul Gilroy, *The Black Atlantic: Modernity and Double Consciousness* (Cambridge, Mass.: Harvard University Press, 1993).

24. This is a tradition that Gonzalez conveniently ignores in his desire to construct a subservient intellectual class of the colonial period. See William Henry Scott, "A Minority Reaction to American Imperialism: Isabelo de los Reyes," in *Cracks in the Parchment Curtain and Other Essays in Philippine History* (Quezon City: New Day, 1982, 1985), 285–99. De los Reyes's broadsides against the Americans in his newspaper *El Grito del Pueblo* spanned the entire period of formal U.S. colonial rule (ibid., 286, 297). Scott seems to have been influenced by this reduc-

tive nationalism, which consigned an entire generation of Filipinos socialized under the U.S. dispensation to the charge of having sold out the country. See also
Fidel Reyes, "Aves de Rapiña," *El Renacimiento*, Oct. 30, 1908, an editorial criticiz-
ing Secretary of the Interior Dean Worcester as a man with "the characteristics of
the vulture, the owl, and the vampire." This was in reference to his allegedly having used public money to prospect for gold in the mountains of Benguet for his
own profit. Worcester sued the publisher and the editor, Teodoro M. Kalaw, for
libel and won his case. Having lost the suit, Kalaw was forced to sell the newspaper at auction and served jail time before being pardoned by Governor-General
Francis Burton Harrison. See Teodoro Agoncillo, *Filipino Nationalism, 1872–1970*
(Quezon City: R. P. Garcia, 1974), 25–26, 251–54.

25. Nick Joaquin, *La Naval de Manila and Other Essays* (Manila: Alberto S.
Florentino, 1964), 28–29. The essay first appeared in October 1943 in a Philippine
journal. Moreover, as both Benedict Anderson and Vicente Rafael have subsequently pointed out, Joaquin argued that the American conquest made 400 years
of Filipino culture under the Spaniards distant, if not inaccessible, to a generation
trained exclusively in English. See Vicente Rafael, "Introduction," in id., *White
Love and Other Events in Filipino History* (Durham, N.C.: Duke University Press,
2000), 1, 17.

26. Agoncillo, *Fateful Years*, 641–42.

27. Ibid., 642.

28. For works surveying various aspects of Tagalog literature, see Bienvenido
Lumbera and Cynthia Lumbera, *Philippine Literature: A History and Anthology*
(Metro Manila: National Book Store, 1982); Bienvenido Lumbera, *Tagalog Poetry,
1570–1898: Tradition and Influences in Its Development* (Quezon City: Ateneo de
Manila University Press, 1986); Doreen G. Fernandez, *Palabas: Essays on Philippine
Theater History* (Quezon City: Ateneo de Manila University Press, 1996); and
Soledad Reyes, *Nobelang Tagalog, 1905–1975: Tradisyon at Modernismo* (Quezon
City: Ateneo de Manila University Press, 1982).

29. *Writers and Their Milieu, Part II*, ed. Alegre and Fernández, 172.

30. Ibid. See also Arnold Molina Azurin, "Letter from Mindoro: Lures of San
José," *Archipelago* A60 (August 1979): 6.

31. The realities of life under the new colonial and technological dispensation
for the Hanunoo and their more numerous relatives among the Mangyans were
more daunting than their idyllic stereotype might suggest. One observer has commented that while the Mangyans could assume a "romantic aura" as "noble savage[s]," they have had to pay a steep price in terms of "progress" and "assimilation"
for their "isolation" during the last four centuries. Leonidas V. Benesa, "The Van-
ishing Mangyans," *Archipelago* 5: 8, A50 (1978): 41. Gonzalez was obviously not

engaged in this kind of stereotyping, but he would rarely comment on the changes that were transforming, if not destroying, the lifeways of the Hanunoo-Mangyan.

32. See Kwame Anthony Appiah, "Race," in *Critical Terms for Literary Study*, ed. Frank Lentricchia and Thomas McLaughlin (Chicago: University of Chicago Press, 1995), 274–87.

33. Herbert Schneider, S.J., "The Period of Emergence of Philippine Letters (1930–1944)," in *Brown Heritage: Essays on Philippine Cultural Tradition and Literature*, ed. Antonio G. Manuud (Quezon City: Ateneo de Manila University Press, 1967), 588.

34. This group included H. Otley Beyer of the Anthropology Department at the University of the Philippines, Dean Fansler of the English Department, and A. V. H. Hartendorp of the *Philippine Magazine*. See Joy Marsella, "Some Contributions of the *Philippine Magazine*," *Philippine Studies* 17, no. 2 (April 1969): 316; Dean Fansler, ed., *Filipino Popular Tales* (Lancaster, Pa.: American Folk-lore Society, 1921). For the emergence of cultural anthropology in the early twentieth century, see George W. Stocking Jr., *Race, Culture, and Evolution: Essays in the History of Anthropology* (New York: Free Press, 1968).

35. See Vincent B. Leitch's excellent survey, *American Literary Criticism from the 30s to the 80s* (New York: Columbia University Press, 1988), 528–29.

36. Ibid., 26–30. See also Mark Schorer, "Technique as Discovery," in *The World We Imagine: Selected Essays* (New York: Farrar, Straus & Giroux, 1968), 5.

37. Wallace Stegner likewise became a celebrated chronicler of the "West" and of American realist writing, as Robert Penn Warren did of the South. See *Dictionary of Literary Biography Yearbook, 1993* (Farmington Hills, Mich.: Thomson Gale, 1994), 309. For the following biographical information on Ransom, Tate, and Gordon, I have relied on Daniel Young, "John Crowe Ransom," *Dictionary of Literary Biography* 45 (1986), 344–58; Everett C. Wilkie Jr., "Allen Tate," ibid., 4 (1980), 378–82; and Robert H. Brinkmeyer Jr., "Caroline Gordon," ibid., 102 (1991), 118–27.

38. N. V. M. Gonzalez, "Letter from Breadloaf," *This Week,* Oct. 16, 1949, 12.

39. Leitch, *American Literary Criticism,* 119.

40. Charles Eric Reeves, "Myth Theory and Criticism," in *The Johns Hopkins Guide to Literary Theory and Criticism*, ed. Michael Groden and Martin Kreiswirth (Baltimore: Johns Hopkins University Press, 1994), 521. Langer translated Cassirer's *Language and Myth* (New York: Dover, 1946), published in 1925 in German.

41. Helene Dwyer Poland, updated by Nick Assendelft, *American Women Writers,* vol. 7, ed. Laurie Champion (Westport, Conn.: Greenwood Press, 2000).

42. Reeves, "Myth Theory and Criticism," 521.

43. Leitch, *American Literary Criticism,* 133.

44. Ibid.

45. Ibid., 140.

46. See, e.g., these indicative *Graphic* pieces by Gonzalez: "Encore for Barong Tagalog" (the national dress for men), May 19, 1938, 20ff.; "We Have Rare Books in the National Library," Jan. 21, 1937, 60; "About Vocational Schools," June 10, 1937, 26; and "Bacteria Farm," Aug. 25, 1938, 6ff. I thank the University of the Philippines Main Library for providing me with copies of these articles.

47. N. V. M. Gonzalez, "Time as Sovereign: A Reading of Joseph Conrad's *Youth*," *Literary Apprentice*, 1954, 106–22; id., "Notes on a Culture and a Method," *University College Journal* 4 (n.d. [ca. late 1950s]): 87–94, reprinted in *Manila Review* 4, no. 2 (June 1978): 36–39; id., "Language and the Filipino Writer," *Philippines Quarterly* 1, no. 3 (December 1951): 9, 12, 13; id., "The Rich Man's House," *Diliman Review* 13, no. 1 (January 1965): 72–78.

48. Gonzalez, "Language and the Filipino Writer"; id., "The Writers Talk Back: N. V. M. Gonzalez," in Bernad, *Bamboo and the Greenwood Tree*, 115–21; id., "Rizal and the Monomyth: Hero's Life and Work Reflect Constant Filipino Theme," *Sunday Times Magazine* 16 (June 11, 1961): 25–27, rev., repr. as "The Poetic Myth in Philippine Literature," *Diliman Review* 8, no. 2 (April 1965): 157–76.

49. N. V. M. Gonzalez, "The Sound of Waves," *Panorama* 8, no. 10 (October 1956): 52–53 (on a Yukio Mishima novel); id., "The Artist in Southeast Asia," *Literary Apprentice* 20, no. 2 (1957): 77–83; id., "Korean Writing," *Collegian Monthly*, September 1957, 13–14; id., "The Filipino Writer in Asia," *Panorama* 12, no. 4 (April 1960): 24–26; and id., "Asian Literature: Some Figures in the Landscape," *Asian Studies* 2, no. 1 (April 1964): 76–81.

50. Guzman, "As in Myth, the Signs Were All Over," repr. in Gonzalez, *Work on the Mountain*, 187–88.

51. For Gonzalez, this is a mark of opprobrium, for progress, especially the evils of technological progress, is what negates the values of the folk, and, as we see in *The Bamboo Dancers*, even threatens humanity itself.

52. Gonzalez, *Season of Grace*, 14–15.

53. "The Writers Talk Back: N. V. M. Gonzalez," in Bernad, *Bamboo and the Greenwood Tree*, 117.

54. Gonzalez, *Bamboo Dancers*, 109. Ernie reads an "item" on Paul Gauguin and Paul Serusier. See also Herbert Read, *Art Now: An Introduction to the Theory of Modern Painting and Sculpture* (New York: Pitman, 1960), 49.

55. When he goes spin fishing off the shore of Sipolog, Ernie thinks that perhaps in some distant corner of the earth "another mushroom cloud had already burst open in the sky" (Gonzalez, *Bamboo Dancers*, 324).

56. See ibid., 330.

57. Claro M. Recto, "Our Lingering Colonial Complex" (1951), in *Recto Reader: Excerpts from the Speeches of Claro M. Recto*, ed. Renato Constantino (Manila: Recto Memorial Foundation, 1965), 8–10.

58. The poem concerns the Mesopotamian mythic figure Tammuz, a symbol of fertility, whose death or disappearance leads to the impotence of the natural (animal, plant, human, and water) world. See the reference provided by Gonzalez, Jessie L. Weston, *From Ritual to Romance* (Garden City, N.Y.: Doubleday Anchor Books, 1957), 39–40.

59. I am indebted for the thematic synthesis of the novel offered here to Jesús, "On This Soil, in This Climate."

60. "Where's My Baby Now" is in *Children of the Ash Covered Loam* (1954; Manila: Bookmark, 1992), 121–34.

61. "On the Ferry" and "The Popcorn Man" are in Gonzalez's *Look, Stranger, on This Island Now*, 139–56, 175–200.

62. For Gonzalez's account of his travels, see *Writers and Their Milieu, Part II*, ed. Alegre and Fernandez, 151–202. Information on his 1962 trip to Taiwan comes from Belarmino, "Bananas and Blades," 213–17, and N. V. M. Gonzalez, "In the World," *Weekly Nation* 1, no. 19 (Dec. 31, 1965): 80.

63. Gonzalez met Usmar Ismail and S. H. Vatsyayan, both of whom were distinguished writers in their native languages, Bahasa Indonesian in the case of the former and Hindi in that of the latter. This perhaps helped to imbue Gonzalez with the self-confidence to write in his own native language. Biographical information in English is difficult to obtain for Usmar Ismail (1921–1971), who is described in the Internet Movie Database as an Indonesian director and writer. See http://us.imdb. com/name/nm0411344 (last accessed August 24, 2004). According to critics, Sachchidanand Hirnand Vatsyayan, or "Agyeya" (1911–1987), "ranks among the most prominent Hindi writers of the twentieth century." His career lasted five decades, during which he wrote poetry, fiction, and criticism, and "distinguished himself as one of Hindi culture's especially sophisticated writers." See *Contemporary Authors* 158, ed. Scott Peacock (Detroit: Gale Research, 1998), 411–12.

64. In 1963, Santha Rama Rau writing for the *New York Times Book Review* (April 14, 1963) said of Rao that he was "perhaps the most brilliant—and certainly the most interesting—writer of modern India." See *Contemporary Authors New Revision Series* 51, ed. Jeff Chapman and Pamela S. Dear (Detroit: Gale Research, 1996), 347, 348. According to the editors of *Chinese America: History and Perspectives: Journal of the Chinese Historical Society of America* 14 (2000), Wang Gungwu had a distinguished career as a historian in Singapore and Australia before he became vice-chancellor of the University of Hong Kong.

65. Wang Gungwu, E-mail to the author, Oct. 6, 2002.

66. *Writers and Their Milieu, Part II*, ed. Alegre and Fernández, 177, 178; James King, *The Last Modern: A Life of Herbert Read* (London: Weidenfeld & Nicolson, 1990), 306–9.

67. See Gonzalez, *Kalutang*, 26–27; and *Writers and Their Milieu, Part II*, ed. Alegre and Fernandez, 177.

68. N. V. M. Gonzalez, "Introduction," in *You Lovely People* by Bienvenido N. Santos (Manila: Benipayo Press, 1955).

69. *Writers and Their Milieu, Part II*, ed. Alegre and Fernandez, 173–74.

70. Ibid., 173–74, 199.

71. See Gémino Abad and Edna Zapanta Manlapaz, eds., *Man of Earth: An Anthology of Filipino Poetry and Verse from English: 1905 to the Mid-50s* (Quezon City: Ateneo de Manila, 1989), 412.

72. *Writers and Their Milieu, Part II*, ed. Alegre and Fernandez, 196; Narita Gonzalez, "Our Life on File" (MS), 109; id., telephone interview with Edward Loomis, July 2002; N. V. M. Gonzalez to Wallace Stegner, Dec. 6, 1967, Department of Special Collections, Stanford University Libraries.

73. See, e.g., Gonzalez's discussion of the importance of university patronage of letters in his "Where All the Rays Meet . . ." *Solidarity* 2, no. 10 (November-October 1967): 35.

74. *Writers and Their Milieu, Part II*, ed. Alegre and Fernández, 180–81.

75. N. V. M. Gonzalez, "Language and the Filipino Writer," *Philippines Quarterly* 1, no. 3 (December 1951), 13; id., *Kalutang*, 67–68; and id., "Writing from the Outside: Two Notes on Bienvenido N. Santos (1911–96)," *Philippines Free Press* (Apr. 13, 1996), 37–38.

76. Gonzalez, *Kalutang*, 67–68.

77. Ibid., 70.

78. N. V. M. Gonzalez, "In the World," *Weekly Nation* 1, no. 19 (Dec. 31, 1965): 80, reviewed the so-called "Bagay" ("thing") group, which included poets, essayists, activists, and academics who wrote successfully in Tagalog (or Pilipino) during much of their careers, among them Rolando S. Tinio, José F. Lacaba, and Bienvenido Lumbera. On Lualhati Bautista, the most successful writer in Taglish and Tagalog of the 1970s, see Jacqueline Siapno's "Alternative Filipina Heroines: Contested Tropes in Leftist Feminisms," in *Bewitching Women, Pious Men: Gender and Body Politics in Southeast Asia*, ed. Aihwa Ong and Michael G. Peletz (Berkeley: University of California Press, 1995), 216–43.

79. Gonzalez's annual salary increased from 6,540 pesos as assistant professor, step IV, to 9,108 pesos. At UC Santa Barbara alone, Gonzalez noted, he was already making U.S.$14,000, which at the current exchange rate would have been

at least five times what he had been making at the University of the Philippines. In 1962, one dollar was worth 3.9 pesos. In December 1970, after devaluation, it was worth 6.4 pesos. See "Exchange Rate Policy in Philippine Development," by Romeo M. Bautista, PIDS-PES Distinguished Speakers Lecture, Carlos P. Romulo Hall, NEDS sa Makati Building, Aug. 29, 2002, 2, http://dirp3.pids.gov.ph/silver/documents/ Bautista%20paper.pdf (last accessed August 21, 2004). And see the entry on "N. V. M. Gonzalez," *UP Faculty Directory*, ca. 1960, 3, and "Certification of Approval of Permanent Appointment," signed by Iluminada Panlilio, secretary of the university, and Francisco Nemenzo, dean, College of Arts and Sciences, Apr. 24, 1966, in Belarmino, "Bananas and Blades," 202–3, 221; *Writers and Their Milieu, Part II*, ed. Alegre and Fernandez, 196.

80. N. V. M. Gonzalez to Wallace Stegner, Dec. 6, 1967, Department of Special Collections, Stanford University Libraries.

81. One of Gonzalez's children, Lakshmi, could not afford the high price of nonresident tuition fees in 1974 and had to return to the Philippines. N. V. M. Gonzalez to Bienvenido N. Santos, Mar. 20, 1975, MS 86–6, box 1, FF 17, Bienvenido Santos Papers, Special Collections, Wichita State University; Bienvenido N. Santos to Leonard Casper, Nov. 2, 1972, in id., *Letters: Book 2* (Pasig City: Anvil, 1995) [henceforth cited as Santos, *Letters 2*], 136. Santos and Gonzalez spoke on the phone every day during the first few weeks of martial law.

82. Bienvenido N. Santos to David and Noree Briscoe, Sept. 25, 1972, in *Letters 2*, 221; id. to Noree, David, and Jeleen Briscoe, Nov. 1, 1972, ibid., 222.

83. Bienvenido N. Santos to N. V. M. Gonzalez, Mar. 31, 1974, MS 86–6, box 1, FF 17, Bienvenido Santos Papers, Special Collections, Wichita State University.

84. Gonzalez, *Kalutang*, 38.

85. N. V. M. Gonzalez, "Drumming for the Captain," in *World Literature Written in English* 15, no. 2 (November 1976): 415–27. The central image of this essay is that of Africans captured by English sailors and forced to beat drums that signaled the arrival of the colonialists. See also id., "Writing from the Outside," 37–38.

86. This was a U.S. congressional act that promised independence to the Philippines in 1916 once Filipinos had established a stable government.

87. Gonzalez, "Writing from the Outside," 37–38.

88. Gonzalez, "Drumming for the Captain," 419.

89. Gonzalez, "Writing from the Outside," 37–38.

90. Gonzalez, "Drumming for the Captain," 422.

91. Gonzalez, "Writing from the Outside," 38.

92. Ruby R. Paredes, ed., *Philippine Colonial Democracy* (New Haven, Conn.: Yale University Southeast Asia Studies, 1988); Michael Salman, *The Embarrassment*

of Slavery: Controversies over Bondage and Nationalism in the American Colonial Philippines (Berkeley: University of California Press, 2001); Alfredo T. Morales, "Contributions of American Thought to Filipino Ideas of Independence," *Philippine Social Science and Humanities Review* 14, no. 3 (September 1949): 249–94.

93. Maximo Kalaw, *An Introduction to Philippine Social Science* (Manila: Philippine Education Co., 1938).

94. Claro Recto, for instance, regarded any Filipino with pro-American politics as guilty of having a "colonial complex" and a "colonial consciousness," reducing complex strategic and cultural calculations to essentialist notions. Constantino likewise spoke about his mentor Recto's roots of "ambivalence," and of losing and rediscovering his own identity as a Filipino, clearly with a clear nationalist agenda as the criterion for such evaluations. See the table of contents in Renato Constantino, *The Making of a Filipino: A Story of Philippine Colonial Politics* (Quezon City: Malaya Books, 1969), and the speech titles in *Recto Reader,* ed. id.

95. See William Henry Scott, "Isabelo de los Reyes: *Provinciano* and Nationalist," *Cracks in the Parchment Curtain* (Quezon City: New Day, 1982), 274.

96. See Alfred W. McCoy, "Baylan: Animist Religion and the Philippine Peasant Ideology," *Philippine Quarterly of Culture and Society* 10 (1982): 141–84; Reynaldo Ileto, "Outlines of a Nonlinear Emplotment of Philippine History," in *The Politics of Culture in the Shadow of Capital,* ed. David Lloyd and Lisa Lowe (Durham, N.C.: Duke University Press, 1997), 98–130; and Vicente Rafael, "Patronage, Pornography, and Youth: Ideology and Spectatorship During the Early Marcos Years," in id., *White Love,* 137.

97. Gonzalez, *Kalutang,* 64–68.

98. *Writers and Their Milieu, Part II,* ed. Alegre and Fernandez, 180. See Gonzalez's comment: "[R]etrievals are only documentary. What's retrieved still needs to be interpreted, understood."

99. N. V. M. Gonzalez, "The Edenic Myth: The Ideology of Filipino Fiction," *Mithi* 8 (1985): 65. In an interview, "Working in the Shade," Gonzalez described these motifs somewhat differently—his list included the search for home, the search for mobility, the search for healing powers, and the Lost Eden. See "Working in the Shade with N.V.M.," *Kultura* 3, no. 4 (1990): 39–43.

100. N. V. M. Gonzalez, "The Difficulties with Filipiniana," in Antonio P. Manuud, *Brown Heritage* (Quezon City: Ateneo de Manila University Press, 1967), 542, 544.

101. While Gonzalez discusses this in several pieces, his most explicit statement about it is in his response in Bernad, *Bamboo and the Greenwood Tree,* 117–19.

102. See Manuel Arguilla, "How My Brother Leon Brought Home a Wife," in *How My Brother Leon Brought Home a Wife and Other Stories* (1940; repr. Manila:

De La Salle University Press, 1998); and N. V. M. Gonzalez, "The Father and the Maid," in id., *The Father and the Maid*, 2–8.

103. N. V. M. Gonzalez, "Whistling Up the Wind: Myth and Creativity," *Philippine Studies* 31 (2d quarter 1983): 216–26.

104. In the Philippine literature class he taught in the winter quarter of 1992 at UCLA, Gonzalez was almost rhapsodic in his discussion of Arguilla's accomplishment.

105. N. V. M. Gonzalez, "Even as the Mountain Speaks," *Amerasia Journal* 18, no. 2 (1992): 55–66.

106. N. V. M. Gonzalez, interview by Roger J. Bresnahan, Hayward, Calif., Sept. 8, 1980, in *Conversations with Filipino Writers* (Quezon City: New Day, 1990), 38.

107. N. V. M. Gonzalez, "The Novel and Its Reader," in id., *The Father and the Maid,* 44ff.

108. Gonzalez, *Father and the Maid,* 50. For a sense of the complexities of historical narrative and its relation to fiction, periodization, and literary tropes, see Ileto, "Outlines of a Nonlinear Emplotment of Philippine History"; Dominick LaCapra, *History, Politics, and the Novel* (Ithaca, N.Y.: Cornell University Press, 1987); and Hayden White, *Metahistory: The Historical Imagination in Nineteenth-Century Europe* (Baltimore: Johns Hopkins University Press, 1973).

109. At UCLA, Gonzalez taught Asian American literature in the fall quarter of 1987, Philippine American Literature in the winter quarter of 1991, and a seminar on Filipino literature in the mid 1990s.

110. N. V. M. Gonzalez, interview by the author, Mindoro, Philippines, Feb. 23, 1996. For another perspective of the same course and of his ideas as a teacher, see Anna Alves, "Remembering N. V. M. Gonzalez," *Disorient Journalzine* 9 (2001): 27–30.

111. From 1968 to 1983, Gonzalez taught expository writing, an introduction to the study of literature, critical writing, introduction to creative writing / beginning workshop in fiction, discursive writing, advanced expository writing, intermediate workshop in fiction, and the writing of fiction. Gonzalez's course offerings courtesy of Lucille Klovdahl, Archives and Special Collections, California State University, Hayward, Library. See *University Catalog, 1977–1978* (California State University, Hayward), *Class Schedule (Including Non-Catalog Listed Courses), Winter 1976* (California State University, Hayward), and *Schedule of Classes Fall 1974* (California State University, Hayward).

112. E. James Murphy (chair of the English Department at Cal State Hayward from 1977 to 1985), letter to the author, June 5, 2002. In addition, other courses, such as Reading Ethnic Literatures, Asian Literature, and the Literature of Emerg-

ing Nations, reflected Gonzalez's interest in Asian American writing, postcolonial literature, and contemporary world English literature. This course emphasized "forms in English literary tradition that appear to have been supportive of the multi-cultural life of various new nations that have achieved political independence since WWII." See *Class Schedule (Including Non-Catalog Listed Courses) Winter 1976* (California State University, Hayward).

113.   Gonzalez developed hypertension at this time, perhaps owing to the stress of the job, Narita Gonzalez surmised. See her "Our Life on File,"109; Gonzalez to Santos, Sept. 22 and Nov. 23, 1971, MS 86–6, box 1, FF 17, Bienvenido N. Santos Papers, Special Collections, Wichita State University.

114.   Carlos Quirino, "Three Expatriate Filipino Writers Prefer to Live Amidst the Scent of Apples," *Philippine Panorama* 10 (Oct. 11, 1981): 9–11; Efren Padilla, telephone interview by the author, July 2, 2002.

115.   Edward Loomis, telephone interview by the author, July 2002.

116.   Hatch Williams, telephone interview by the author, July 3, 2002.

117.   Douglas Peterson, professor of English (and colleague of N. V. M. Gonzalez's until 1976), telephone interview by the author, July 2, 2002.

118.   Ibid.; Alan Smith, dean of the School of Arts and Letters, California State University, Hayward (1977–1992), interview by the author, San Francisco, June 18, 2002.

119.   Jack Conner, CSU Hayward professor of English, telephone interview by the author, July 2002.

120.   N. V. M. Gonzalez to Bienvenido Santos, Aug. 26, 1974, Dec. 8, 1974, Mar. 30, 1975, and Narita Gonzalez to Beatriz Nidea, n.d. (ca. 1974), MS 86–6, box 1, FF 17, Bienvenido Santos Papers, Special Collections, Wichita State University.

121.   Narita M. Gonzalez, "Our Life on File," in *Writers' Wives*, ed. id., 115.

122.   Ibid.

123.   *Writers and Their Milieu, Part II*, ed. Alegre and Fernandez, 176.

124.   Quirino, "Three Expatriate Filipino Writers Prefer to Live Amidst the Scent of Apples," 9.

125.   N. V. M. Gonzalez to Bienvenido N. Santos, Oct. 28, 1981, MS 86–6, box 1, FF 17, Bienvenido Santos Papers, Special Collections, Wichita State University.

126.   See Mark R. Thompson, *The Anti-Marcos Struggle: Personalistic Rule and Democratic Transition in the Philippines* (New Haven, Conn.: Yale University Press, 1995), esp. chs. 8 and 9. Aquino came to power in 1986 as a result of a popular revolt that toppled the Marcos dictatorship. She ruled a provisional government for the next six years, abolishing the old Constitution and establishing a new one, which became the basis for legislative elections and a democratic transition. While

challenged by a number of coup attempts against her, Aquino held firm. During her term, popular sentiment and volcanic explosions led to the dismantling of the U.S. military bases. After six years, Aquino facilitated a smooth transition to power of a member of her cabinet, Fidel V. Ramos, a former Marcos constabulary chief who had rebelled against his old boss in 1986, who then became the first president elected since 1969. In 1998, a year before Gonzalez's death, another smooth transition to power took place with the election of the former actor Joseph "Erap" Estrada. In the thirteen years after Marcos, freedom of the press was reinstated and the Philippine newspapers became as freewheeling as they had been before the dictatorship. It was an atmosphere conducive to the return of dissident elites and intellectuals, who assumed positions in the new government.

127. Alan Smith, interview by the author, San Francisco, June 18, 2002.

128. René Cruz, *Katipunan*'s editor, a longtime activist at the University of the Philippines from the anti–Vietnam War period to the anti–martial law protests in the United States, believed that Gonzalez was a liberal with anti-imperialist sentiments. While Gonzalez may have privately held these views, he never articulated them as *Katipunan*'s literary editor. René Cruz, E-mail to the author, Aug. 2, 2002.

129. S. Lily Mendoza, *Between the Homeland and the Diaspora: The Politics of Theorizing Filipino and Filipino American Identities: A Second Look at the Poststructuralism-Indigenization Debates* (New York: Routledge, 2002), 133.

130. David Clive Price, "Tales of Home," *Far Eastern Economic Review* 30 (September 1993): 56–57.

131. Caroline Hau, "N. V. M. Gonzalez the Teacher" (II), LegManila.com, 12/14/1999, http://www.legmanila.com/us/article/448.asp (ceased publication). Hau, the associate editor of LegManila, is the author of *Necessary Fictions: Philippine Literature and the Nation, 1946–1980* (Quezon City: Ateneo de Manila University Press, 2000) and the editor of *Intsik: An Anthology of Chinese Filipino Writing* (Pasig: Anvil, 2000). Literary awards always preoccupied Gonzalez, as they did his contemporaries, especially the National Artist Award, which obsessed Romulo and flattered Villa. See, e.g., Arcellana's ruminations about the great book that he felt Gonzalez was tending toward in Francisco Arcellana, "Towards the Great Filipino Novel," *Philippines Quarterly* 1, no. 4 (March 1952): 36–39. See also Gonzalez, "Among the Wounded," in *Novel of Justice*, 141–44, on Gonzalez's ruminations about the Nobel Prize and its snubbing of Asian writers.

132. N. V. M. Gonzalez, interview by the author, Oct. 24, 1998, Los Angeles.

133. The stories include "Crossing Over," "The Tomato Game," "In the Twilight," "The Gecko and the Mermaid," "A Shelter of Bamboo and Sand," and "The Long Harvest." See Gonzalez, *The Bread of Salt and Other Stories*.

134. Inspired by Gonzalez, Efren Padilla, one of his colleagues at Hayward,

started writing poetry in Hiligaynon, a language he had not spoken in years. Efren Padilla, telephone interview by the author, July 2, 2002. A European American student noted the important effect of Gonzalez's rigorous classes in fiction writing on his own career as a writer. A Filipino American activist couple in Los Angeles have been inspired to write essays and to learn classical Philippine songs on the violin and guitar, both of which Gonzalez played. Prosy Abarquez-Delacruz, Sept. 15, 2000, "N. V. M. Guestbook," <http://www.stanford.edu/~sierrag/NVM/bio. htm> ©Sierra Gonzalez. Critics like De Jesús, Guzman, and Campomanes—all of whom have written beautiful pieces on Gonzalez—benefited from their association with him. Meanwhile, the Chinese American author and journal editor Russell Leong, one of Gonzalez's close friends, considers him as one of his principal influences. See *Asian American Authors,* ed. Kai-yu Hsu and Helen Palubinskas (Boston: Houghton Mifflin, 1972), 88; *Contemporary Authors,* vol. 142 (Detroit: Gale Research, 1994), 245–46; and William Wei, *The Asian American Movement* (Philadelphia: Temple University Press, 1993), 125. Filipino American authors like Jessica Hagedorn, Cecilia Manguerra-Brainard, Peter Bacho, and Linda Ty-Casper have all professed their love for Gonzalez's stories or acknowledged his importance to their development as writers, their understanding of fiction, and their awareness of being Filipino. No doubt the list could be extended.

Chapter 5. Fidelity and Shame: Bienvenido Santos

1. Diary entry, Dec. 8, 1941, Bienvenido N. Santos Papers, Special Collections, Wichita State University, MS 86–6, box 2, FF 10.

2. Bienvenido N. Santos, *Memory's Fictions: A Personal History* (Quezon City: New Day, 1993), 168.

3. Bienvenido N. Santos, diary, in id., *Letters: Book 1* (Pasig City: Anvil, 1995) [henceforth cited as Santos, *Letters 1*], 56; id., *Memory's Fictions*, 73, 77; Bienvenido N. Santos to P. C. Morantte, in *Letters 2* (Pasig City: Anvil, 1995), 7.

4. *Writers and Their Milieu, Part I: An Oral History of First Generation Writers in English*, ed. Edilberto N. Alegre and Doreen G. Fernandez (Manila: De La Salle University Press, 1984), 242. See also William Alan Sutherland, *Not by Might: The Epic of the Philippines* (Las Cruces, N.M.: Southwest Publishing Co., 1953).

5. Santos, *Letters 1*, 48; id., *Memory's Fictions*, 119–20.

6. Florentino B. Valeros and Estrellita V. Gruenberg, *Filipino Writers in English* (Quezon City: New Day, 1987), 201. Other postwar Philippine critics observed the same human qualities in Santos's writings—the serious tone and the guilt—and praised the literary sensibility that, at least with his stories, successfully contained his sentimentality. Among them were N. V. M. Gonzalez, who in his "Introduc-

tion" to Santos's *You Lovely People* (Manila: Benipayo Press, 1955), identifies the ideal of the Filipino woman as a symbol of the Filipino nation among expatriate nationalists. In commenting on Santos's poetry, Manuel A. Viray, in his introduction to *The Wounded Stag: 54 Poems* (Manila: Capitol, 1956), highlights the themes of love, tragedy, and religion, and the artist remaining intact, although "wounded." Epifanio San Juan Jr., in "The Vision of the Contemporary," *Panorama*, September 1960, 28–29, hails the lyricism, mournfulness, and rhythm of Santos's poetry, although critical of the "minor thoughts" behind them. Leonard Casper, in his "Introduction" to *Brother My Brother* (1960; repr., Manila: Bookmark, 1991) notes the dialectic of rejection and embrace, departure and return, among Santos's "pilgrims," who fear betraying their origins and abandoning their country. And Miguel Bernad, S.J., "Filipino Exile," in *Bamboo and the Greenwood Tree: Essays on Filipino Literature in English* (Manila: Bookmark, 1961), 33–41, highlights the moral dislocations of Santos's characters and the lyricism of his writing, reminiscent for him of Bulosan.

Meanwhile, among Marxist critics, Petronilo Bn. Daroy's "Aspects of Philippine Writing in English," *Philippine Studies* 17, no. 2 (April 1969): 249–65, and Milagros C. Guerrero's "Proletarian Consciousness in Philippine Literature, 1930–1970," in *Society and the Writer: Essays on Literature in Modern Asia*, ed. Wang Gungwu et al. (Canberra: Research School of Pacific Studies, 1981) chide Santos for the class outlook underlying his serious tone. The former accuses him of a moralistic view of the wealthy, while the latter argues that Santos's writing reveals the way characters of peasant origin who move up to the middle class are "smothered by the superstructure."

More recent Philippine critics like Leonor Aureus-Briscoe, "Foreword," in Bienvenido Santos, *Dwell in the Wilderness: Selected Short Stories 1931–1941* (Quezon City: New Day, 1985), recall themes of death and pain in Santos's stories. Tomas N. Santos, in his introduction to *The Volcano* (Quezon City: New Day, 1986) points to cosmic forces of destruction and regeneration that overlaid the human conflicts of the postcolonial Filipino nation. And Isagani R. Cruz, "Bienvenido, Our Brother: The Man Behind the Author (1992)," in *The Alfredo E. Litiatco Lectures*, ed. David Jonathan Y. Bayot (Manila: De La Salle University Press, 1996), 202–15, points to Santos's blurring of the distinction between fact and fiction.

For an exhaustive survey that focuses attention on the various schools of criticism, see David Jonathan Y. Bayot, "Bienvenido N. Santos: A Review of Studies and Criticism," in *Reading Bienvenido N. Santos*, ed. Isagani R. Cruz and David Jonathan Y. Bayot (Manila: De La Salle University Press, 1994), 1–11.

Asian American critics have especially remarked at length upon Santos's identification with outsiders, especially in his short stories. Like Bernad, Bruce Iwasaki,

"Literature: Introduction," in *Counterpoint: Perspectives on Asian America*, ed. Emma Gee et al. (Los Angeles: Asian American Studies Center, 1976), 461, notes Santos's similarity to Bulosan as a chronicler of the *manong* experience of racial exclusion. Elaine H. Kim, *Asian American Literature: An Introduction to the Writings and Their Social Context* (Philadelphia: Temple University Press, 1982), 265–72; Paul B. Phelps, "The Philippines: An Exile's Dreams," *Washington Post*, Apr. 20, 1980, 6; and Maxine Hong Kingston, "Precarious Lives," *New York Times Book Review*, May 4, 1980, 15, 28–29, all identify exile as a central theme in Santos's works. Kim observes Santos's juxtaposition of the longings of Filipinos across the oceans, especially the opposite trajectories of middle-class Filipinos seeking escape from their homelands and those Filipinos seeking to return to the Philippines. Kingston's influential review called attention to the urban geography traversed by the exiles and delighted in Santos's rendition of Philippine vernacular speech in English. Reviewing Santos's collection of stories *Scent of Apples* (Seattle: University of Washington Press, 1979), Hisaye Yamamoto, *MELUS* 7, no. 2 (1980): 92–93, admires Santos's self-deprecating humor, and Wakako Yamauchi, *Amerasia Journal* 6, no. 2 (1979): 196–98, notes his evocations of memories through food.

Recalling Gonzalez's comments, King-Kok Cheung, "Bienvenido N. Santos: Filipino Old-Timers in Literature," *Markham Review* 15 (1986): 49–53, points to the idealization of the homeland as woman and youth among Filipino old-timers, seeing their attempts at escape as responses to social discrimination. Meanwhile, Oscar Campomanes, "Filipinos in the United States and Their Literature of Exile," in *Reading the Literatures of Asian America* (Philadelphia: Temple University Press, 1992) blames U.S. colonialism for creating a wedge of language, education, and social class among Filipino old-timers. Sau-ling Wong, *Reading Asian American Literature: From Necessity to Extravagance* (Princeton, N.J.: Princeton University Press, 1993), 162–63, notes the importance of mobility in Santos's novel *What the Hell for You Left Your Heart in San Francisco*. Rachel Lee, "Short Fiction: An Introduction," in *Asian American Literature*, ed. Sau-ling Wong and Stephen Sumida (New York: Modern Language Association of America, 2001), 264–265, identifies gender and race oppression and the resilience of the old-timers.

Most critics, however, have been less concerned with integrating Santos's fiction with his transnational life. With few exceptions, Asian American criticism of Santos has been limited to those stories reflecting an American geography, but especially "Scent of Apples" and "The Day the Dancers Came." One consequence is that Santos's culturally hybrid and transnational qualities have been appropriated for exclusively national literatures, serving the purposes of geographically bounded Philippine nationalism or Asian American pan-ethnicity. It is with a view of addressing this yawning gap in studies of Santos, exploring the complexities of his life on *both* sides of the ocean as well as his precolonial, national, and postcolonial periods that this chapter is concerned.

7. For the Tagalog affect of *hiya*, see Vicente Rafael, *Contracting Colonialism: Translation and Christian Conversion in Tagalog Society under Early Spanish Rule* (Quezon City: Ateneo de Manila University Press; Ithaca, N.Y.: Cornell University Press, 1988), 121–35; Reynaldo Ileto, *Pasyon and Revolution: Popular Movements in the Philippines, 1840–1910* (Quezon City: Ateneo de Manila University Press, 1979, 1989), 9, 10; and for *supog*, its Bicolano equivalent, see Fennela Cannell's *Power and Intimacy in the Christian Philippines* (New York: Cambridge University Press, 1999), xxiv, 15–22.

8. See Ileto, *Pasyon and Revolution*, 22–25, for discussion of animism and folk Christianity; and see also Benedict R. O'G. Anderson, "The Idea of Power in Javanese Culture," in *Culture and Politics in Indonesia*, ed. Claire Holt, Benedict R. O'G. Anderson, and James Siegel (Ithaca, N.Y.: Cornell University Press, 1972), 1–70.

9. Edna Zapanta Manlapaz and Ruth B. Cudala, "Wrestling with Maria Clara: Filipino Women Poets in English, 1905–50," *Philippine Studies* 38 (1990): 317. Citing Carmen Guerrero Nakpil's classic study, "Maria Clara," in *Woman Enough and Other Essays* (Manila: Vibal, 1963), Manlapaz and Cudala trace the cult to the character in José Rizal's novel *Noli Me Tangere*. The readers who came afterwards "wilfully misread" her character, which was supposed to be noble and strong, fetishizing instead her external attributes, her blushing and fainting. "In Filipino idiom," write the authors, "to be called Maria Clara is to be viewed as a virgin who, to protect that supreme virtue of her womanhood, must observe the most minute rituals of maidenly modesty. As though to protect herself from any male tactile advances . . . Maria Clara hides her body beneath the multilayered, voluminous gown that has since borne her name."

10. Bienvenido Santos, *Memory's Fictions* (266 pp.); id., *Postscript to a Saintly Life* (Metro Manila: Anvil, 1994) (171 pp.); *Letters 1* (360 pp.); and *Letters 2* (336 pp.).

11. For an introduction to Jacques Derrida's critique of the logocentrism of Western philosophy and its privileging of binary oppositions, see Madan Sarup, *An Introductory Guide to Post-Structuralism and Postmodernism,* 2d ed. (Athens: University of Georgia Press, 1993), 36–38.

12. Santos, *Letters 1*, 143–44.

13. Bienvenido Santos, *The Day the Dancers Came: Selected Prose Works* (1967; repr., Manila: Bookmark, 1991), 7.

14. Santos quoted in Leonard Casper, "Truth in Fiction and History" (sum-

mary of conference panel on "The Place of History in Fiction," held at Ann Arbor, Mich.) *Pilipinas* 6 (Spring 1986): 53–54. Santos was agreeing with a comment by N. V. M. Gonzalez.

15. The epigraph to the book claims that the author's most vivid "memories" were "those that never really happened." The prologue states that "memory fictionizes" and that the author will play with his readers "a game like truth without consequence." Finally, Santos says that compared to the imagination, memory "is honest but weak." *Memory's Fictions*, 4, 6, 102.

16. *Contemporary Authors New Revision Series* 46 (Detroit: Gale Research, 1995), 346–48; Gémino Abad and Edna Z. Manlapaz, eds., *Man of Earth: An Anthology of Filipino Poetry and Verse from English, 1905 to the Mid-50s* (Quezon City: Ateneo de Manila University Press, 1989), see esp. "Biographical Notes: Bienvenido N. Santos," 400–405. On countercolonial remapping, see, e.g., Thongchai Winichakul, *Siam Mapped: A History of the Geo-Body of a Nation* (Honolulu: University of Hawai'i Press, 1994).

17. For discussion of these racial stereotypes of Filipinos under American colonial rule, see Vicente Rafael, "White Love: Census and Melodrama in the U.S. Colonization of the Philippines," in id., *White Love and Other Events in Filipino History* (Durham, N.C.: Duke University Press, 2000), 32–38; Robert W. Rydell, "The Louisiana Purchase Exposition, Saint Louis, 1904: The Coronation of Empire," in *All the World's a Fair: Visions of Empire at American International Expositions, 1876–1916* (Chicago: University of Chicago Press, 1984); and Bruno Lasker, *Filipino Immigration to the Continental United States and to Hawaii* (1931; repr. New York: Arno Press, 1969), 92ff.

18. Abad and Manlapaz, eds., *Man of Earth*, 400–405.

19. These are based on my own count. Twenty-one stories are set in the United States and forty-nine in the Philippines. One is set in Japan.

20. Santos, *Postscript to a Saintly Life*, 4.

21. The Pensionado Act of 1903 had established the program as a means of selecting the brightest and most pliable Filipino students and sending them for training in the imperial education system for the benefit of the emergent Philippine nation. William Sutherland's hagiographic book on pensionados shows how reflective the program was of the imperial civilizing mission to teach the Filipino natives the arts of self-government. See Bonifacio Salamanca, *The Filipino Reaction to American Rule, 1901–1913* (Hamden, Conn.: Shoe String Press, 1968), 90–92, 243–44; William Sutherland, *Not by Might*, passim; Santos, *Memory's Fictions*, chs. 11 and 12; Santos, *Postscript to a Saintly Life*, ch. 12.

22. *Writers and Their Milieu*, ed. Alegre and Fernandez, 242.

23. Santos, *Memory's Fictions*, 180.

24. *University of the Philippines: The First 75 Years, 1908–1983*, ed. Oscar M. Alfonso (Quezon City: University of the Philippines Press, 1985), 275, 276. "Antinationalism" in this context implies wanting either to remain under American supervision or to flee the Philippines' multiple problems.

25. Nidea was of Chinese mestizo background from Bicol province. She was an excellent student at the University of the Philippines, eventually obtained her PhD in education at the University of Iowa, and wrote textbooks and examinations for the state of Iowa. For a long time, she earned more as a teacher than Santos. Apart from the emotional bonds of marriage, she played an important role in stabilizing Santos's occupational and family life, thus providing him extensive support to write. See Santos, *Memory's Fictions*, 52, 88, 181, 233, 244. Their first separation occurred during their courtship from 1931 to 1933, when Nidea graduated from the University of the Philippines and returned to Bicol, while Santos remained to finish his education. The second time was from 1933 to 1934, when Santos, on his first teaching assignment, taught at an elementary school in Bacon, Sorsogon, until he passed the senior teacher's examination. The third time they were separated, during which their three daughters also remained in the war-torn Philippines, was the longest, from October 11, 1941, until early February 1946. After Nidea's death in 1981, Santos spent half of each year with his son Tomas and his family in Colorado and the other half with his daughters in the Bicol region. *Contemporary Authors New Revision Series* 46, 346–48; *Letters 1*, 2; *Letters 2*, 110.

26. They were married for nearly half a century, forty-eight years, the marriage ending only upon Nidea's mysterious death on November 1, 1981. *Contemporary Authors New Revision Series* 46, 346–48; Santos, *Postscript to a Saintly Life*, 65; id., *Letters 1*, 2; id., *Memory's Fictions*, 229–30.

27. Santos to P. C. Morantte, in *Letters 2*, 20.

28. Santos, *Memory's Fictions*, 42. What I have in mind here is the colonialists' paternalist desire for their colonized "children's" well-being and the disjuncture between those relationships and the real relations of power and violence between colonialists and natives. See, e.g., Frank Gibney, *The Pacific Century: Asia and America in a Changing World* (New York: Maxwell Macmillan International, 1993), and the critique of sentimental imperialism in Rafael, "White Love: Census and Melodrama," 19–51.

29. Santos's "The Filipino Writer in English as Storyteller and Translator," was first published in *The Quill* 3, no. 1 (1991): 4–12, and then reprinted in *Reading Bienvenido N. Santos*, ed. Cruz and Bayot, 38–39.

30. *Writers and Their Milieu, Part I*, ed. Alegre and Fernandez, 219.

31. The encounter with the sentimental teacher would find fictional representation in Santos's story "Surprise Ending" (see his collection *Dwell in the Wilder-*

ness) and reappear in *Villa Magdalena, The Volcano, The Man Who (Thought He) Looked Like Robert Taylor,* and *What the Hell for You Left Your Heart in San Francisco.*

32. See Judith Butler, "Burning Acts, Injurious Speech," in *Excitable Speech: A Politics of the Performative* (New York: Routledge, 1997), 43–70.

33. Santos, *Memory's Fictions,* 42–43.

34. Ibid., 43.

35. Rafael, "White Love: Census and Melodrama," 34. We saw this in Romulo's protest against T. Inglis Moore, the lawsuit against Bulosan for plagiarism, and the charge of Magsaysay's men that Romulo had plagiarized Adlai Stevenson's speech.

36. Santos, *Memory's Fictions,* 44; *Writers and Their Milieu, Part I,* ed. Alegre and Fernandez, 224.

37. Santos, *Memory's Fictions,* 242–43, 55–56; id., *Letters 1,* 40–41.

38. Doreen G. Fernandez, *Palabas: Essays on Philippine Theater History* (Quezon City: Ateneo de Manila University Press, 1996), 67–68.

39. For a survey of Philippine theater and performativity from the pre-Spanish period to the present, see Doreen G. Fernandez, "From Ritual to Realism," ibid., 2–26; Vicente Rafael, "Tomas Pinpin and the Shock of Castilian," in id., *Contracting Colonialism,* 55–83.

40. Santos, *Letters 1,* 142.

41. *Writers and Their Milieu, Part I,* ed. Alegre and Fernandez, 243.

42. Santos, *Memory's Fictions,* 200–201; *The Writers and Their Milieu, Part I,* ed. Alegre and Fernandez, 230. Both stories appeared in Santos's *You Lovely People.*

43. See the epigraph to this chapter; Santos to Leonard Casper, Sept. 8, 1966, in id., *Letters 2,* 47–48; and id., *Memory's Fictions,* 214.

44. See, e.g., his letters to various women friends, Marlis Broadhead, Noree Briscoe, and Doreen Fernandez, in Santos, *Letters 1,* 280ff., and id., *Letters 2,* 79ff. and 178ff. Santos's principal written language was English, but he often switched to Tagalog, Bicolano, Pampango, or even Spanish or Hawaiian, for effect. For instance, in one example that combines sexual banter (and sexism) with language switching, Santos writes that the school semester was concluding and he could not remember the names of his students. He failed to recall "even the loveliest of them, the sexiest, those who come to class in their hot pants and spread their legs like the spread-eagled symbol of America. Disgusting (intentionally vague) *Talaga* ["Really" in Tagalog]." Santos to Doreen Fernandez, May 13, 1983, in *Letters 2,* 87.

45. His father's first cousin, Inda Duni, made the enigmatic statement that he was not even a Santos, making him think that he was a "bastard child." Indeed,

Santos says that even as a child he had heard words "said in jest" that caused him lifelong "insecurity." Santos, *Memory's Fictions*, 16.

46. Ibid., 55.

47. *The Writers and Their Milieu, Part I*, ed. Alegre and Fernandez, 236, 239.

48. N. V. M. Gonzalez, "Writing from the Outside: Two Notes on Bienvenido N. Santos (1911–96)," *Philippines Free Press*, Apr. 13, 1996, 37–38, and Santos, *Memory's Fictions*, 190, 252.

49. Abad and Manlapaz, eds., *Man of Earth*, 403.

50. Santos, *Memory's Fictions*, 178–79, 184–85, 241.

51. Santos to Leonard Casper, Aug. 14, 1963, in *Letters 2*, 112.

52. Ibid., 67, 68.

53. Ibid., 233, 231.

54. Bienvenido Santos to Lee Tzu Pheng [Anne], Sept. 12, 1991, in *Letters 2*, 311.

55. Doreen G. Fernandez, "Teaching Creative Writing: An Interview with Bienvenido N. Santos," in *Postscript to a Saintly Life*, 105.

56. Santos to Nidea, Aug. 18, 1945, in id., *Letters 1*, 76.

57. Santos to Estela Detera Diolata, Mar. 7, 1985, in id., *Letters 1*, 165.

58. *The Writers and Their Milieu*, ed. Alegre and Fernandez, 234.

59. Bienvenido Santos, "The Personal Saga of a Straggler" (1976), in *Reading Bienvenido N. Santos*, 32.

60. Bienvenido Santos, "Pilipino Old Timers: Fact and Fiction" (1982), in *Reading Bienvenido N. Santos*, 24.

61. Santos, *Memory's Fictions*, 58, 88, 198, 214.

62. See, e.g., the dramatic footage of popular resistance to the eviction of Filipino and Chinese residents of the International Hotel, San Francisco, in the 1993 Chonk Moonhunter film *Fall of the I-Hotel*, written, produced, and ed. Curtis Choy, distributed by NAATA.

63. Santos, *Memory's Fictions*, 21; Santos to Estela Detera Diolata, June 20, 1941, in id., *Letters 1*, 144; Santos to Beatriz Nidea, December 1931 and Oct. 14, 1932, ibid., 3, 23.

64. For background on the Virgin of Antipolo, see "Antipolo: Mecca and Playground," *Panorama* 8, no. 5 (May 1956): 82–84. For the widespread practice of Virgin worship, see Nicanor G. Tiongson, "The Virgin in a Feudal Time: The Blessed Virgin's Role in the Economics of Salvation," in *Filipino Heritage: The Making of a Nation*, vol. 7, *The Spanish Colonial Period (Late 19th Century): The Awakening* (Metro Manila: Lahing Pilipino, 1978), 1733–36.

65. Santos, *Memory's Fictions*, 49–52.

66. Ibid., 225.

67. Ibid., 53–54.

68. Santos to Beatriz Nidea, July 28 and Nov. 22, 1932, and Apr. 1, 1933, in id., *Letters 1*, 11; 28–29; 46.

69. Santos, *Memory's Fictions*, 67; 173–75.

70. Like many Filipino housewives, Nidea managed their finances and invested in land, a jeepney business, and houses in the Philippines and America. She took care of Santos when he became ill, cared for their grandchildren, and at the same time continued to earn money for the family. She was a great dresser, sewed her own clothes, and also made stylish new clothes for her husband. See *Letters 1*, 255, 264, 267.

71. Santos, *Memory's Fictions*, 208; Santos to Dolores Hernandez Sison, July 7, 1968, Apr. 5, 1972, and Nov. 30, 1975, in id., *Letters 1*, 251; 255–56; 267.

72. Santos to Susie L. Tan, July 20, 1987, in id., *Letters 2, 321*.

73. Santos diary, Oct. 16, 1941, in id., *Letters 1*, 58; Roger Bresnahan, *Angles of Vision: Conversations on Philippine Literature* (Quezon City: New Day, 1992), 106–7.

74. As a teacher in Manila in the 1930s, Santos wrote that there were "many lost women nowadays" and mentioned a young woman who had boarded a bus in Pulilan, Bulacan, and been abducted (he says seduced and presumably raped) and taken to Manila. "[T]here is no such blood on my hands," he exclaimed. Santos to Beatriz Nidea, Mar. 15, 1933, in id., *Letters 1*, 42.

75. Santos to Ambeth Ocampo, May 8, 1989, in id., *Letters 1*, 325.

76. Santos to Beatriz Nidea, Nov. 20, 1932, in id., *Letters 1*, 27.

77. *Writers and Their Milieu, Part I*, ed. Alegre and Fernandez, 243; Santos, *Memory's Fictions*, 82, 84, 86.

78. Santos, *Memory's Fictions*, 241.

79. Ibid., 86–87.

80. Lewis Putnam Turco, "Engle, Paul [Hamilton]" *Encyclopedia of American Literature* (New York: Continuum, 1999), 332–33.

81. Santos, *Memory's Fictions*, 80–81; Santos to Gonzalez, June 7, 1967, in id., *Letters 2*, 46; Santos to F. Sionil José, Oct. 8, 1971, ibid., 64.

82. Santos, *Letters 2*, 243; "Remembering Ben Santos" (MS) 3, Bienvenido N. Santos Papers, courtesy of the Santos family, Naga, Camarines Sur; Santos, *Memory's Fictions*, 170.

83. Santos to Leonard Casper, Sept. 8, 1966, in id., *Letters 2*, 121; Santos to N. V. M. Gonzalez, May 31, 1968, ibid., 48.

84. Santos hinted that readers of his letters to her should read between the lines. Santos to Dolores Hernandez Sison, June 14, 1968, in id., *Letters 1*, 248.

85. Santos to Dolores Hernandez Sison, June 10, 1970, in id., *Letters 1*, 254; *Letters 1*, 252.

86. Santos, *Memory's Fictions*, 204.

87. Santos, *Letters 1*, 222; id., *Memory's Fictions*, 201, 204–5, 212–13; Santos to Magelli, July 26, 1983, and Apr. 9, 1984, in id., *Letters 1*, 223–24.

88. This was the successful and important Filipino American writer Linda Ty-Casper.

89. For biographical information on Leonard Ralph Casper, see *Contemporary Authors*, vol. 1–4, first revision (Detroit: Gale Research, 1967), 162–63.

90. Santos also asked Casper to take autographed copies of his *The Wounded Stag* to his summer session teacher at Harvard, I. A. Richards. Santos to Leonard Casper, July 15, 1957, in id., *Letters 2*, 105.

91. Bienvenido N. Santos to Leonard Casper, Oct. 1, 1959, in id., *Letters 2*, 110.

92. The University of the Philippines' Alfredo Morales and the critic Manuel Viray wrote the other two letters. Santos to Leonard Casper, Nov. 17, 1964, in id., *Letters 2*, 113.

93. See Leonard Casper to Santos, July 16, 1960, and Santos to Casper, July 19, 1960, box 5, FF 12, Bienvenido N. Santos Papers, Special Collections, Wichita State University.

94. *Midcentury Guide to Philippine Literature in English*, ed. Alberto S. Florentino (Manila: Filipiniana Publishers, 1963). Santos to Leonard Casper, Aug. 14, 1963, in id., *Letters 2*, 112.

95. Santos to Leonard Casper, Apr. 10, 1966, in id., *Letters 2*, 118.

96. Santos, *Memory's Fictions*, 156.

97. Ibid., 156; Santos, *Postscript to a Saintly Life*, 60.

98. See, e.g., Rafael, *Contracting Colonialism*.

99. Santos to Nidea, July 23 and Aug. 2, 1945, in id., *Letters 1*, 73, 74; id., *Memory's Fictions*, 178–79.

100. Santos, *Memory's Fictions*, 179.

101. Ibid.

102. While Santos made little public fuss about it at the time, his private correspondence and his redoubled efforts to publish the novel over the next decade show the extent of his disappointment with the censorship decision. See his correspondence with F. Sionil José, in id., *Letters 2*, 52–69.

103. Santos, *Memory's Fictions*, 198; Santos to Gonzalez, Nov. 2, 1972, in id., *Letters 2*, 136–37; Santos to Leonard Casper, ibid., 136, 139; id., *Memory's Fictions*, 200; Bresnahan, *Angles of Vision*, 109–10.

104. From Santos, "Thoughts of a Famous Writer on His Becoming a U.S. Citizen," *Philippine Times*, Jan. 1–15, 1976, repr. in id., *Postscript to a Saintly Life*, 76–77.

105. Santos to Ambeth Ocampo, July 26, 1990, in id., *Letters 1*, 329, and Santos to F. Sionil José, Apr. 20, 1973, and Mar. 24, 1980, in id., *Letters 2*, 67, 68; id., *Memory's Fictions*, 225, 226; Santos to Estela Detera Diolata, July 26, 1984, in id., *Letters 1*, 156; "Why I Became a Writer," in Cruz and Bayot, eds., *Reading Bienvenido Santos*, 47; and Santos to Estela Detera Diolata, Jan. 9, 1985, in id., *Letters 1*, 163.

106. "Child" was originally published in *Literary Apprentice*, 1933, and was reprinted in *Dwell in the Wilderness* (1985), 11–15.

107. "Far From the City" was first published in *Philippine Magazine* (August 1933) and reprinted in *Brother My Brother* (1960), 45–57. "Early Harvest" was first published in *Story Magazine* (1944) and also reprinted in *Brother My Brother*, 187–211.

108. Santos, *Villa Magdalena* (Quezon City: New Day, 1986); orig. Manila: Erewhon, 1965.

109. Santos, *The Praying Man* (Quezon City: New Day, 1982); orig. *Solidarity*, May 1971–February 1972.

110. Santos, *The Man Who (Thought He) Looked Like Robert Taylor* (Quezon City: New Day, 1983).

111. Bresnahan, *Angles of Vision*, 96.

112. Santos, correspondence with Beatriz Nidea, in id., *Letters I*, 12, 14, 19, 28, 29.

113. Santos, *Letters*, 30.

114. In *Villa Magdalena*, illicit affairs dramatize the corruption and decadence of money and high social class. Don Magno has built the opulent villa for his wife, Doña Magdalena, and named it after her. He has a long-lasting extramarital affair with a younger woman named Pat, however, to whom Fred acts as go-between. Don Magno's infidelity and ruthlessness devastate Doña Magdalena, but she has become too dependent on him to change her life, and her sister, the strong-willed Doña Asuncion, who stands up to Don Magno, becomes her will and conscience, until her death. Ultimately, Doña Magdalena becomes insane, assuming the personality of her sister. Don Magno's mother is represented by Balatong, a withered woman, who suffers from echolalia, repeating and reflecting back to Don Magno all of his words. Meanwhile, after a torrid affair with Manang, a beautiful social climber from Sulucan, Fred marries Nora, one of the daughters of Don Magno and Doña Magdalena. (The other daughter is Isabel.) Their marriage suffers, however, because Nora has only married Fred to punish her lover, Nick Calderon, for his indiscretion. Soon, Fred himself becomes involved in an adulterous affair with Doña Magdalena's niece, Elisa, the daughter of Isabel and Dr. Vidal, now a doctor who has studied in the United States. This last relationship is also unhappy be-

cause of Dr. Vidal's bouts of alcoholism, and because at the time of his death, Isabel leaves him and runs away to Japan with Sol King, a lower-class Filipino whose mother had been a servant and seamstress at the villa. Indeed, the action of the novel begins with Fred's visit to this exiled couple in Japan, on orders from Don Magno, to obtain Isabel's permission to transfer power of attorney for all of her properties to Don Magno.

115. Santos's story "The Portrait" was originally published in *Graphic Magazine* (Sept. 7, 1933) and was reprinted in *Dwell in the Wilderness* (1985), 21–26. "School-house in the Foothills" was originally published in *Sunday Tribune Magazine* (Dec. 29, 1935) and reprinted in ibid., 52–57.

116. One sees these tensions in gender relations in Santos's story "Friends of Mine," in the male narrator's disdain for Luz, a local girl who outgrows her male playmates and becomes a beautiful model or actress. The narrator "liked" Luz when she was a child but does not like the woman who "adorns the society pages." While he feels sexually attracted to her, he is discomfited by her "high-heeled shoes" and "proud gait" like "a pampered queen," and worse, by her failure to "recognize us." The story was first published in *Graphic Magazine* (Sept. 23, 1933), and was reprinted in *Dwell in the Wilderness* (1985), 18.

117. See, e.g., Maria Rosa Henson, *Comfort Woman: A Filipina's Story of Prostitution and Slavery under the Japanese Military* (Lanham, Md.: Rowman & Littlefield, 1999).

118. The change was never so great as many Filipino men on both sides of the ocean perhaps imagined, however, because even during the Commonwealth period, traditional notions of women's place as being in the home led many young women workers to stop working when they married or had children. Meanwhile, even modern, high-class intellectual women of the 1930s chose to remain in the Philippines to secure marriages with fellow male intellectuals rather than risk their chances of remaining unmarried by going abroad, despite being highly qualified, respected pensionados. See Daniel F. Doeppers' discussion of women in *Manila, 1900–1941: Social Change in a Late Colonial Metropolis* (New Haven, Conn.: Yale University Southeast Asia Studies, 1984), 91, 94–95, 106, and Edna Zapanta Manlapaz's account of the poet's choice to abandon her Barbour scholarship for marriage, *Angela Manalang Gloria: A Literary Biography* (Quezon City: Ateneo de Manila University Press, 1993), 40–42.

119. "Scent of Apples" was originally published two years after Santos's return to the Philippines from the United States, *This Week*, 14 Nov. 1948, 20–21, reprinted in *You Lovely People* (1956) and in *Scent of Apples: A Collection of Stories* (1979).

120. Santos's "Footnote to a Laundry List" was first published in *Philippines*

Free Press (Oct. 13, 1962), 20–22, 67–69, and reprinted in *The Day the Dancers Came* (1967), 23–38. The same trope is presented negatively in the later story "Brother My Brother" (cited n. 122 below).

121. Santos's "The House on the Hill" was originally published in *This Week,* Aug. 22, 1948, 8–9, 24, 35, and was reprinted in *Brother My Brother* (1960), 91–102.

122. Santos's "Brother, My Brother" originally appeared in *Philippines Free Press,* Oct. 5, 1957, 12–13, 44, and was reprinted in *Brother My Brother* (1960), 267–81.

123. Santos's *The Volcano* was originally serialized in *Weekly Women's Magazine,* Apr. 2–June 18, 1965, and subsequently published in book form by Alemar-Phoenix (Quezon City, 1965); the latest version, on which the discussion here is based, was published by New Day Publishers (Quezon City, 1986).

124. Santos, *Memory's Fictions,* 87.

125. Writing about his experience rereading the novel for his memoir in 1993, Santos expressed his fondness for the book he had written a quarter of a century ago. He felt he had accomplished what he had set out to do—to make alive the people living near Mount Mayon whom he had known, their "goings on," their "tragedies," and their "secrets" during "30 years [1928 to 1958] in the history of the Philippines." Santos, *Memory's Fictions,* 89.

126. Ibid.

127. The novel itself uses the phrase "sentimental imperialism," with reference to a newspaper article written by an American writer who nostalgically remembers Americans of the colonial period, of which an American teacher says, "This guy's an imperialist, the worst kind, a sentimental one" (51).

128. Santos, *The Volcano,* 27ff.

129. Ibid., 28.

130. Ibid., 37. This is analogous to Rafael's account in *Contracting Colonialism* (e.g., 1–22) of native resistance to the imposition of the Spanish religious worldview through various forms of displacement.

131. Ben Whitaker, *The Foundations: An Anatomy of Philanthropy and Society* (London: Eyre Methuen, 1974), 18.

132. Santos, *The Volcano,* 67–68.

133. Ibid., 112.

134. Ibid., 129–34.

135. The Spaniard does business in copra and hemp and exploits the labor of the native poor, although indirectly. The common folk harvest the abundant hemp and coconuts and sell them to Chinese wholesalers, who then transport and sell them to Don Vicente's warehouses in Legazpi. Don Vicente is also an inveterate womanizer and adulterer. Santos, *The Volcano,* 161; 29, 30, 36.

136. Ibid., 161–67.

137. Ibid., 42–77.

138. Junior, the minister's son also falls in love with a Filipino woman, Tina, although it is interesting that it is Florence's interracial relationship that poses the dilemma for Hunter.

139. Ibid., 144; 132–33, 139–40.

140. Ibid., 7, 45, 204.

141. Ibid., 187ff.

142. Ibid., 223, 232ff.

143. Ibid., 224–28.

144. Ibid., 234; 235–36.

145. Indeed, *Villa Magdalena* shows the lingering resentments of Japan and the United States created by the war. In Chapter 11, Fred visits Sol and Isabel in Tokyo, seeking to fulfill Don Magno's wish to have certain properties transferred from Isabel to Don Magno. In scenes reminiscent of Ernie Rama's experiences in Tokyo in *The Bamboo Dancers*, the couple take Fred out on the town. He wants to see the forbidden places, the geishas, and the steamy side. Instead, he is stuck in a tense and uncomfortable situation with two Japanese men who accost them at a restaurant, including one whose father died in Tabaco, Albay, near Mayon Volcano. For an unknown reason, he is annoyed at their interminable bowing, until he recalls the bowing of Japanese soldiers in the Philippines he had feared and hated. Fred is haunted by memories of the war, and his own bitterness surfaces over the injustice of Tokyo rebuilt, with America giving Japan millions, while the ruins remain all over Manila. Fred is overwhelmed *(hiya)* by the "courtesy" with which the Japanese, "former enemies," greet him. Later, he realizes, if only in the form of a fleeting "grudge," that the source of his discomfort lies in the discrepancy ("something was not right") between a Philippines still in ruins and the fact that there are no ruins to be seen in Japan, the former enemy (*Villa Magdalena*, 222–23).

146. *Memory's Fictions*, 215–16.

147. N. V. M. Gonzalez, "Drumming for the Captain," *World Literature Written in English* 15, no. 2 (November 1976): 421.

Conclusion: Toward a Transnational Asian American Intellectual History

1. See Lisa Lowe, "Heterogeneity, Hybridity, and Multiplicity: Marking Asian American Differences," in id., *Immigrant Acts: On Asian American Cultural Politics* (Durham, N.C.: Duke University Press, 1996).

2. For instance, Filipinos have continued to rely upon emigration to various parts of the world, and especially to the United States, as a solution to the unem-

ployment and underemployment facing them in the Philippines. At the same time, Filipino Americans in search of cultural validation and economic opportunities have increasingly sought them in the post-Marcos Philippine economy, particularly in the arena of culture—book publication, movies, and the arts.

3. Michael Ignatieff, "The Burden," *New York Times*, Jan. 5, 2003; Andrew Bacevich, *American Empire: The Realities & Consequences of U.S. Diplomacy* (Cambridge, Mass: Harvard University Press, 2002).

4. Niall Ferguson, "America: An Empire in Denial," *Chronicle of Higher Education*, Mar. 28, 2003, B7.

5. Ibid., B10.

6. Thomas Bender, ed., *Rethinking American History in a Global Age* (Berkeley: University of California Press, 2002).

7. See Prasenjit Duara, "Transnationalism and the Challenge to National Histories," 25–46; Akira Iriye, "Internationalizing International History," 47–62; and Charles Bright and Michael Geyer, "Where in the World Is America? The History of the United States in the Global Age," 63–100, all in Bender, ed., *Rethinking American History in a Global Age*.

8. Thomas Bender, "Introduction: Historians, the Nation, and the Plenitude of Narratives," 1–22; and David A. Hollinger, "The Historian's Use of the United States and Vice Versa," 381–96, both in Bender, ed., *Rethinking American History in a Global Age*.

9. Prasenjit Duara, *Rescuing History from the Nation: Questioning Narratives of Modern China* (Chicago: University of Chicago Press, 1995), 4–5.

10. Bender, "Introduction," in id., ed., *Rethinking American History in a Global Age*, 1–2.

11. Ibid., 4.

12. Hollinger, "Historian's Use of the United States," in Bender, ed., *Rethinking American History in a Global Age*, 382.

13. Ibid.

14. Ibid., 391. These works include David M. Kennedy's *Freedom from Fear: The American People in Depression and War* (New York: Oxford University Press, 1999); Daniel T. Rodgers' *Atlantic Crossings: Social Politics in a Progressive Age* (Cambridge, Mass.: Belknap Press of Harvard University Press, 1998); and James T. Kloppenberg's *Uncertain Victory: Social Democracy and Progressivism in European and American Thought, 1870–1920* (New York: Oxford University Press, 1986).

15. Bender, ed., *Rethinking American History in a Global Age*, 392.

16. José David Saldívar, *Border Matters: Remapping American Cultural Studies* (Berkeley: University of California Press, 1997), 1, 172–173. See also *Unequal Sisters: A Multicultural Reader in U.S. Women's History*, ed. Vicki L. Ruiz and Ellen

Carol DuBois (New York: Routledge, 2000); Renato Rosaldo, *Culture and Truth: The Remaking of Social Analysis* (Boston: Beacon Press, 1989), for his concept of "borderlands" studies; Mary Louise Pratt, *Imperial Eyes: Travel Writing and Transculturation* (New York: Routledge, 1992), for her notions of "contact zones"; Juan Gómez-Quiñones, *Sembradores: Ricardo Flores Magón y el Partido Liberal Mexicano: A Eulogy and Critique* (Los Angeles: Aztlán Publications, 1973); Américo Paredes, *Folklore and Culture on the Texas-Mexican Border*, ed. Richard Bauman (Austin, Tex.: Center for Mexican American Studies, 1993); and *Criticism in the Borderlands: Studies in Chicano Literature, Culture, and Ideology*, ed. Hector Calderon and José David Saldivar (Durham, N.C.: Duke University Press, 1991).

17. Robin D. G. Kelley's essay, "How the West Was One: The African Diaspora and the Re-Mapping of U.S. History" does appear in Bender, ed., *Rethinking American History in a Global Age*, 123–47, but Hollinger fails to address it. Among the most incisive writings on this subject, one might include Wilson Jeremiah Moses, *The Golden Age of Black Nationalism, 1850–1925* (Hamden, Conn.: Archon Books, 1978), Robert A. Hill, ed., *Pan-African Biography* (Los Angeles: African Studies Center, University of California, Los Angeles, and Crossroads Press / African Studies Association, 1987); Paul Gilroy, *Black Atlantic* (Cambridge, Mass.: Harvard University Press, 1993); Kevin Gaines, *Uplifting the Race: Black Leadership, Politics, and Culture in the Twentieth Century* (Chapel Hill, N.C., 1996); Tyler Stovall, *Paris Noir: African Americans in the City of Light* (Boston: Houghton Mifflin, 1996); and Penny M. Von Eschen, *Race Against Empire* (Ithaca, N.Y.: Cornell University Press, 1997).

18. For a critical review of this debate, see my "Asian American Global Discourses and the Problem of History," in *After the Imperial Turn: Thinking Through the Nation, Post-Colonialism*, ed. Antoinette Burton (Durham, N.C.: Duke University Press, 2003).

19. Sau-ling Wong, "Denationalization Reconsidered: Asian American Cultural Criticism at a Theoretical Crossroads," *Amerasia Journal* 21, nos. 1 and 2 (1995): 1–27; and Susan Koshy, "The Fiction of Asian American Literature," in *Asian American Studies: A Reader*, ed. Jean Yu-wen Shen Wu and Min Song (New Brunswick, N.J.: Rutgers University Press, 2000), 467–96.

20. Yong Chen, *Chinese San Francisco, 1850–1943: A Trans-Pacific Community* (Stanford: Stanford University Press, 2000); and Madeline Hsu, *Dreaming of Gold, Dreaming of Home: Transnationalism and Migration Between the United States and South China, 1882–1943* (Stanford: Stanford University Press, 2000).

21. Sucheng Chan, "European and Asian Immigration: A Comparative Approach," in *Immigration Reconsidered: History, Sociology, and Politics*, ed. Virginia Yans-McLaughlin (New York: Oxford University Press, 1990), 37–75; L. Eve Ar-

mentrout Ma, *Revolutionaries, Monarchists, and Chinatowns: Chinese Politics in the Americas and the 1911 Revolution* (Honolulu: University of Hawai'i Press, 1990); Him Mark Lai, "The Kuomintang in Chinese American Communities," in *Entry Denied: Exclusion and the Chinese Community in America, 1882–1943,* ed. Sucheng Chan (Philadelphia: Temple University Press, 1991); K. Scott Wong, "Liang Qichao and the Chinese of America: A Re-evaluation of His Selected Memoir of Travels in the New World," *Journal of American Ethnic History* 11, no. 4 (Summer 1992): 3–24; id., "The Transformation of Culture: Three Chinese Views of America," *American Quarterly* 48, no. 2 (1996): 201–32; id., "Cultural Defenders and Brokers: Chinese Responses to the Anti-Chinese Movement," in *Claiming America: Constructing Chinese American Identities During the Exclusion Era,* ed. K. Scott Wong and Sucheng Chan (Philadelphia: Temple University Press, 1998), 3–40; Yansheng Ma Lum and Raymond Mun Kong Lum, *Sun Yat-sen in Hawaii: Activities and Supporters* (Honolulu: Hawaii Chinese History Center, 1999); and Adam McKeown, *Chinese Migrant Networks and Cultural Change: Peru, Chicago, Hawaii, 1900–1936* (Chicago: University of Chicago Press, 2001).

22. The literature on transnational issues involving Japanese, Korean, Asian Indian, and Filipino Americans is extensive. See, e.g., on Japanese Americans, Yuji Ichioka, "Japanese Immigrant Nationalism: The Issei and the Sino-Japanese War, 1937–1941," *California History* 59, no. 3 (Fall 1990): 260–75, id., "*Kengakudan*: The Origin of Nisei Study Tours of Japan," *California History* 73, no. 1 (Spring 1994): 30–43; Brian Hayashi, "*For the Sake of Our Japanese Brethren*": *Assimilation, Nationalism, and Protestantism Among the Japanese of Los Angeles, 1895–1942* (Stanford: Stanford University Press, 1995); Eiichiro Azuma, "Racial Struggle, Immigrant Nationalism, and Ethnic Identity: Japanese and Filipinos in the California Delta, 1930–1941," *Pacific Historical Review* 67, no. 2 (May 1998); and id., "The Politics of Transnational History Making: Japanese Immigrants on the Western 'Frontier,' 1927–1941," *Journal of American History* 89, no. 4 (March 2003): 1401–30. On Korean Americans, see Helen Heran Jun, "Contingent Nationalisms: Renegotiating Borders in Korean and Korean American Women's Oppositional Struggles," in "New Formations, New Questions: Asian American Studies," special issue, *Positions: East Asia Cultures Critique* 5, no. 2 (Fall 1997): 325–56; Laura Hyun Yi Kang, "Si(gh)ting Asian/American Women as Transnational Labor," *Positions* 5, no. 2 (Fall 1997): 403–38; Gordon H. Chang, "Whose 'Barbarism'? Whose 'Treachery'? Race and Civilization in the Unknown United States–Korea War of 1871," *Journal of American History* 89, no. 4 (March 2003): 1331–65. On Asian Indians, see Kumari Jayawardena, "Going for the Jugular of Hindu Patriarchy: American Women Fundraisers for Ramabai," in *Unequal Sisters: A Multicultural Reader in U.S. Women's History,* ed. Vicki L. Ruiz and Ellen Carol DuBois (New York: Routledge,

2000), 197–204; Dhan Gopal Mukerji, *Caste and Outcast* (1923), ed. Gordon H. Chang, Purnima Mankekar, and Akhil Gupta (Stanford: Stanford University Press, 2002). And on Filipino Americans, see Steffi San Buenaventura, "The Master and the Federation: A Filipino-American Social Movement in California and Hawaii," *Social Process in Hawaii* 33 (1991): 169–93; Melinda Tria Kerkvliet, "Pablo Manlapit's Fight for Justice," ibid. (1991): 153–68; and id., "Interpreting Pablo Manlapit," ibid. 37 (1996): 1–25.

23. Henry Yu, *Thinking Orientals: Migration, Contact, and Exoticism in Modern America* (New York: Oxford University Press, 2001); and Viet Thanh Nguyen, *Race & Resistance: Literature and Politics in Asian America* (New York: Oxford University Press, 2002).

Select Bibliography

Archives and Manuscript Collections

PHILIPPINES

American Historical Collection
Aquinas University (formerly Legazpi College) Library
Bienvenido N. Santos Papers, De La Salle University Library
Carlos P. Romulo Papers, Ayala Museum
Carlos P. Romulo Papers, University of the Philippines Library Archives
José Rizal Library, Filipiniana Collection, Ateneo de Manila
National Library
University of Nueva Cáceres Library
University of the Philippines Main Library

UNITED STATES OF AMERICA

Aurelio Bulosan Papers, University of Washington Libraries, Manuscript and University Archives Division
Bienvenido N. Santos Papers, Wichita State University, Manuscript Archives Collection
Carey McWilliams Papers, Special Collections, Young Research Library, University of California, Los Angeles
Carlos Bulosan Papers, University of Washington Libraries, Manuscript and University Archives Division
Wallace Stegner Papers, Department of Special Collections, Stanford University Libraries

Interviews

F. Sionil José, Manila, Philippines, Feb. 1, 1996
N. V. M. Gonzalez, Oct. 24, 1998, Los Angeles, California
N. V. M. Gonzalez and Narita Gonzalez, Feb. 23, 1996, San Aquilino, Roxas, Mindoro
P. C. Morantte, Lompoc, California, Jan. 31, 1997
Beth Day Romulo, Metro Manila, Philippines, Jan. 16, 1996
Ricardo Romulo, Metro Manila, Philippines, Jan. 31, 1996
Roberto Romulo, Metro Manila, Philippines, Jan. 22, 1996
Alan Smith, San Francisco, California, June 18, 2002

CORRESPONDENCE, TELEPHONE CALLS, E-MAIL

Luis Cabalquinto, Nov. 15, 1996
Jack Conner, July 6, 2002
John Cowen, June 17, 1997
Hilario S. Francia, June 2, 1999
Robert L. King, May 8, 1999
Edward Loomis, July 7, 2002
Efren Padilla, July 2, 2002
Douglas Peterson, July 2, 2002
Arthur Vanderborg, May 6, 1999
José García Villa (with Luis Cabalquinto), Aug. 15, 1996
Hatch Williams, July 3, 2002

Philippine Periodicals Cited

Unless otherwise noted, Manila is the place of publication. Periodicals marked with an asterisk are defunct.

*Archipelago**
Asian Studies
Bulletin of the American Historical Collection
Bulletin Today
Chimera: Voices, Tales, and Visions
*Comment**
Diliman Review (University of the Philippines, Diliman, Quezon City)
The Evening Paper
Focus Philippines
Fookien Times Yearbook

*Graphic**
*El Grito del Pueblo**
Likha (De La Salle University, Manila)
Literary Apprentice (University of the Philippines, Diliman, Quezon City)
Malaya
The Manila Chronicle
*Manila Review**
Mithi
Panorama
Philippine Collegian (University of the Philippines, Diliman, Quezon City)
Philippine Daily Inquirer
*Philippine Magazine**
Philippine Quarterly of Culture and Society
Philippine Studies (Ateneo de Manila University)
Philippines Free Press
*Philippines Herald**
The Philippines Quarterly
*El Renacimiento**
Sands and Coral: Literary Magazine of Silliman University (Dumaguete City, Negros Oriental)
The Silliman Journal
*Solidari*ty
Sunday Times Magazine
*Taliba**
This Week
University College Journal (University of the Philippines, Diliman, Quezon City)
*La Vanguardia**
*Weekly Nation**
*Weekly Women's Magazine**

Writings by Bulosan, Gonzalez, Romulo, Santos, and Villa

Bulosan, Carlos. *America Is in the Heart*. New York, 1946. Reprint. Seattle: University of Washington Press, 1973.

———. *The Laughter of My Father*. New York: Harcourt, Brace, 1943.

———. *On Becoming Filipino: Selected Writings of Carlos Bulosan* . Edited by Epifanio San Juan Jr. Philadelphia: Temple University Press, 1995.

———. *The Philippines Is in the Heart*. Edited by Epifanio San Juan Jr. Quezon City: New Day, 1978.

———. *The Power of the People.* Metro Manila: National Book Store, 1986. Reprinted as *The Cry and the Dedication,* ed. Epifanio San Juan Jr. (Philadelphia: Temple University Press, 1995).

———. *Voice of Bataan.* New York: Coward-McCann, 1943.

———, ed. *Chorus for America: Six Philippine Poets.* Los Angeles: Wagon and Star, 1942.

Gonzalez, Nestor Vicente Madali. *The Bamboo Dancers.* Quezon City: Diliman Review, 1959. Reprint. Manila: Bookmark, 1993.

———. *The Bread of Salt and Other Stories.* Seattle: University of Washington Press, 1993.

———. *Children of the Ash-Covered Loam and Other Stories.* Manila: Benipayo Press, 1954.

———. "The Enchantment of Old Manila." *Sunday Times Magazine* 18 (July 7, 1963): 14–15.

———. "Even as the Mountain Speaks." Lecture to the "Columbus Conference Paradox" of the UCLA Center for Medieval and Renaissance Studies. *Amerasia Journal* 18, no. 2 (1992): 55–66.

———. *The Father and the Maid: Essays on Filipino Life and Letters.* Quezon City: University of the Philippines Press, 1991.

———. "First Literary Symposium." *Comment* 8 (1st quarter 1959): 177.

———. *A Grammar of Dreams.* Quezon City: University of the Philippines Press, 1997.

———. "In the World: Bolo Men." *Weekly Nation* 3, no. 8 (Oct. 16, 1967): 85.

———. "Kalatong: Notes on an Other-World." *Sunday Times Magazine* 13 (July 6, 1958): 4–5.

———. *Kalutang: A Filipino in the World.* Manila: Kalikasan Press, 1990.

———. "Letter from Breadloaf." *This Week,* Oct. 16, 1949, 12, 19.

———. *Look, Stranger, on This Island Now.* Manila: Benipayo Press, 1963.

———. "Memo to a Survivor." *Greenfield Review* 6 (Spring 1977): 56–57.

———. *Mindoro and Beyond: Stories.* Quezon City: New Day, 1989.

———. *Mindoro and Beyond: Twenty-One Stories.* Quezon City: University of the Philippines Press, 1979.

———. "Moving On: A Filipino in the World." In *Foreign Values and Southeast Asian Scholarship,* ed. Joseph Fischer. Berkeley: Center for South and Southeast Asia Studies, University of California, 1973. Later published under the title *Kalutang: A Filipino in the World.*

———. "New Windows: Tale of Two Overcoats." *Manila Times* 37 (Mar. 1, 1995).

———. "Notes on a Method and a Culture." *University College Journal* 4 (ca. 1961).

———. *The Novel of Justice.* Manila: National Commission for Culture and the Arts, 1996.

———. "Rizal and the Monomyth: Hero's Life and Work Reflect Constant Filipino Theme." *Sunday Times Magazine* 16 (June 11, 1961): 25–27.

———. *A Season of Grace.* Manila: Benipayo Press, 1956.

———. *Seven Hills Away.* Manila: Halcon House, 1947. [Published by Alan Swallow].

———. "Tradition and Modernity in Literature." *Comment* 17 (1st quarter 1963): 73–74, Asian Writers Conference, Manila, Philippines, Dec. 26–29, 1962.

———. "Where All the Rays Meet . . ." *Solidarity* 2, no. 10 (Nov.-Oct. 1967): 35.

———. "Whistling Up the Wind: Myth and Creativity." *Philippine Studies* 31 (2d quarter 1983): 216–26.

———. *The Winds of April.* Quezon City: University of the Philippines Press, 1998.

———. "Working in the Shade with N.V.M." *Kultura* 3, no. 4 (1990).

———. *Work on the Mountain.* Quezon City, University of the Philippines Press, 1995.

Romulo, Carlos Peña. "Appeasement of Japan Fatal, Say Chinese Leaders." *Philippines Herald*, Sept. 17, 1941.

———. "Billion Orientals Look to America for Aid in Crisis." *Philippines Herald*, Sept. 15, 1941.

———. "Burma's Agitation for Freedom Affects Asia." *Philippines Herald*, Sept. 27, 1941.

———. "Chiang Confident . . . 'Our Fight Is Your Fight,' Romulo Told." *Philippines Herald*, Sept. 18, 1941.

———. "'Closed Waters': Indomitable Will of New China Shown in Chungking." *Philippines Herald*, Sept. 16, 1941.

———. *Contemporary Nationalism and the World Order.* Azad memorial lectures, 1964. New York: Asia Publishing House, 1964.

———. *Crusade in Asia: Philippine Victory.* New York: John Day, 1955.

———. *Daughters for Sale and Other Plays.* Manila: Manila Book Co., 1924.

———. *The Diplomacy of Consent.* Manila: Department of Foreign Affairs, 1976.

———. *Evasions and Response: Lectures on the American Novel, 1890–1930.* Quezon City: Phoenix, 1966.

———. *Identity and Change.* Manila: Solidaridad, 1965.

———. "Indonesians' Struggle for Liberty Accelerated by War Against Fascism." *Philippines Herald*, Oct. 17, 1941.

———. *The Meaning of Bandung.* The Weil lectures on American citizenship. Chapel Hill: University of North Carolina Press, 1956.

———. *I Saw the Fall of the Philippines*. Garden City, New York: Doubleday, Doran, 1942.

———. *I See the Philippines Rise*. Garden City, N.Y.: Doubleday, 1946.

———. *I Walked With Heroes*. New York: Holt, Rinehart & Winston, 1961.

———. *The Magsaysay Story*, with Marvin M. Gray. 1956. Reprint. New York: Pocket Books, 1957.

———. *Mission to Asia: the Dialogue Begins*. Quezon City: University of the Philippines, 1964.

———. *Mother America: A Living Story of Democracy*. Garden City, New York: Doubleday, Doran, 1943.

———. "NEI [Netherlands East Indies] Believes War Outbreak Not Imminent." *Philippines Herald*, Oct. 22, 1941.

———. "NEI [Netherlands East Indies] More Prepared for War Than Any Far Eastern State." *Philippines Herald*, Oct. 17, 1941.

———. "Nippon Massing 8 More Divisions in French Indo-China." *Philippines Herald*, Oct. 8, 1941.

———. "Nippon Exploiting Indo-China Along Manchukuo Lines." *Philippines Herald*, Oct. 10, 1941.

———. "O. Henry." MA thesis, Columbia University, May 9, 1921.

———. "Romulo Sees Flow of American Aid on Famed Burma Road." Sept. 24, 1941.

———. "Singapore's Urgent Role Is to Keep Burma Road Safe." *Philippines Herald*, Oct. 11, 1941.

———. "Thailand Neutrality Principle Is Clarified." *Philippines Herald*, Sept. 30, 1941.

———. "The Tragedy of Our Anglo-Saxon Education." *Encyclopedia of the Philippines*, 1923, 255, 256–58.

———. "U.S. Arming: Romulo Sees Flow of American Aid on Famed Burma Road." *Philippines Herald*, Sept. 24, 1941.

Romulo, Carlos P., and Pearl S. Buck. *Friend to Friend: A Candid Exchange Between Pearl S. Buck and Carlos P. Romulo*. New York: John Day, 1958.

Romulo, Carlos P., with Beth Day Romulo. *The Philippine Presidents: Memoirs of Carlos P. Romulo*. Quezon City: New Day, 1988.

Santos, Bienvenido Nuqui. *Brother My Brother*. Manila: Bookmark, 1991.

———. *The Day the Dancers Came: Selected Prose Works*. 1967. Reprint. Manila: Bookmark, 1991.

———. *Distances: In Time: Selected Poems*. Quezon City: Ateneo de Manila University Press, 1983.

———. *Dwell in the Wilderness: Selected Short Stories 1931–1941*. Quezon City: New Day, 1985.

————. "Filipino American Writing and Its Audience." *Kultura* 4, no. 4 (1991): 2–9.

————. "Filipinos at War." *Philippines* (1943). Reprinted in *Letters in Exile: An Introductory Reader on the History of Pilipinos in America.* Los Angeles: UCLA Asian American Studies Center, 1976.

————. "José García Villa in Exile." *Philippine Harvest: An Anthology of Filipino Writing in English,* ed. Maximo D. Ramos. Manila: E. F. David, 1953.

————. *Letters: Book 1.* Pasig City: Anvil, 1995.

————. *Letters: Book 2.* Pasig City: Anvil, 1995.

————. *The Man Who (Thought He) Looked Like Robert Taylor.* Quezon City: New Day, 1983.

————. *Memory's Fictions: A Personal History.* Quezon City: New Day, 1993.

————. *Postscript to a Saintly Life.* Manila: Anvil, 1994.

————. *The Praying Man.* Quezon City: New Day, 1982.

————. *Scent of Apples: A Collection of Stories.* Seattle: University of Washington Press, 1979.

————. *Villa Magdalena.* Quezon City: New Day, 1986.

————. *The Volcano.* Quezon City: New Day, 1986.

————. *What the Hell for You Left Your Heart in San Francisco.* Quezon City: New Day, 1987.

————. *The Wounded Stag: 54 Poems.* Manila: Capitol, 1956.

————. *You Lovely People.* Manila: Benipayo Press, 1955.

Villa, José García. *Bravo: The Poet's Magazine.* Vol. 2 (1982).

————. *A Celebration for Edith Sitwell.* 1948. Reprint. Freeport, N.Y.: Books for Libraries Press, 1972.

————. "A Composition." *Literary Apprentice,* 1953: 59–61.

————. *Clay: A Literary Notebook* 1 (1931).

————. *Harvard Wake* 5, E. E. Cummings issue (1945).

————. *Have Come, Am Here: Poems.* New York: Viking, 1942.

————. "Index of Short Stories Published in Philippine Magazines, 1926 to 1934." In *The Best Filipino Short Stories,* ed. O. O. Sta. Romana. Manila: Wightman, 1935, 141–51.

————. *Footnote to Youth: Tales of the Philippines and Others.* New York: Scribner's, 1933.

————. "José García Villa's Roll of Honor of Short Stories (1926 to 1940)." In *Midcentury Guide to Philippine Literature in English,* ed. Alberto S. Florentino, 83–95. Manila: Filipiniana, 1963.

————. "Letter from New York: The Man Who Led Me to Poetry." *Archipelago* A–7, 1, no. 7 (July 1974).

————. *Many Voices: Selected Poems.* Manila: Philippine Book Guild, 1939.

———. *Poems by Doveglion*. Manila: Philippine Writers' League, 1941.

———. *Quarterly Review of Literature,* Marianne Moore issue, Winter 1946–47.

———. "Reflections on Poetry and Sex by José García Villa, 1970–1990." Compiled by Larry Francia and John Cowen. *Philippine Graphic,* May 6, 1990, 23–25.

———. *Selected Poems and New*. New York: McDowell, Oblensky, 1958.

———. *Volume Two*. New York: New Directions, 1949.

Secondary Sources

Abad, Gémino, ed. *A Native Clearing: Filipino Poetry and Verse from English since the '50s to the Present: Edith L. Tiempo to Cirilo F. Bautista*. Quezon City: University of the Philippines Press, 1993.

Abad, Gémino, and Edna Manlapaz, eds. *Man of Earth: An Anthology of Filipino Poetry and Verse from English, 1905 to the Mid-50s*. Quezon City: Ateneo de Manila University Press, 1989.

Abueva, Ramon V. *Ramon Magsaysay: A Political Biography*. Manila: Solidaridad, 1971.

Agoncillo, Teodoro. *Filipino Nationalism, 1872–1970*. Quezon City: R. P. Garcia, 1974.

———. *History of the Filipino People*. 8th ed. Quezon City: Garotech, 1990.

———. *The Fateful Years: Japan's Adventure in the Philippines, 1891–1945*. Vol. 2. Quezon City: R. P. Garcia, 1965.

Aiken, Conrad, ed. *A Comprehensive Anthology of American Poetry*. New York: Modern Library, 1929, 1944.

Alegre, Edilberto N., and Doreen G. Fernandez, eds. *Writers and Their Milieu, Part I: An Oral History of First Generation Writers in English*. Manila: De La Salle University Press, 1984.

———. *Writers and Their Milieu, Part II: An Oral History of Second Generation Writers in English*. Manila: De La Salle University Press, 1987.

Alfonso, Oscar M., ed. *University of the Philippines: The First 75 Years, 1908–1983*. A Diamond Jubilee Publication. Quezon City: University of the Philippines Press, 1985.

Alquizola, Marilyn. "Subversion or Affirmation: The Text and Subtext of *America Is in the Heart*." In *Asian Americans: Comparative and Global Perspectives*, ed. Shirley Hune et al., 199–210. Pullman: Washington State University Press, 1991.

———. "The Fictive Narrator of *America Is in the Heart*." In *Frontiers of Asian American Studies: Writing, Research, and Commentary*, ed. Gail Nomura et al., 211–17. Pullman: Washington State University Press, 1989.

Anderson, Benedict R. O'G. *Imagined Communities: Reflections on the Origin and Spread of Nationalism.* 1983. Reprint. New York: Verso, 1991.

———. "The Idea of Power in Javanese Culture." In *Culture and Politics in Indonesia,* ed. Claire Holt, Benedict R. O'G. Anderson, and James Siegel, 1–70. Ithaca, N.Y.: Cornell University Press, 1972.

Anderson, Sherwood. *Winesburg, Ohio.* 1919. Reprint. New York: Penguin Books, 1993.

Andrade, Pio. *The Fooling of America: The Untold Story of Carlos P. Romulo.* 1985. Rev. ed. Manila: Ouch, 1990.

"Antipolo: Mecca and Playground." *Philippine Panorama* 8, no. 5 (May 1956): 82–83.

Appiah, Kwame Anthony. "Race." In *Critical Terms for Literary Study,* ed. Frank Lentricchia and Thomas McLaughlin, 274–87. Chicago: University of Chicago Press, 1995.

———. "Topologies of Nativism." *The Bounds of Race: Perspectives on Hegemony and Resistance,* ed. Dominick LaCapra. Ithaca, N.Y.: Cornell University Press, 1991.

Arcellana, Francisco. *The Francisco Arcellana Sampler.* Quezon City: University of the Philippines Creative Writing Center, 1990.

Arguilla, Manuel E. *How My Brother Leon Brought Home a Wife and Other Stories.* Manila: Philippine Book Guild, 1940. Reprint. Manila: De La Salle University Press, 1998.

Arguilla, Manuel E., Esteban Nedruda and Teodoro Agoncillo, eds. *Literature under the Commonwealth.* Manila: Philippine Writers' League, 1940.

Ayers, Edward L. *The Promise of the New South: Life After Reconstruction.* New York: Oxford University Press, 1992.

Azurin, Arnold. *Reinventing the Filipino Sense of Being and Becoming.* Quezon City: University of the Philippines Press, 1995.

Bacevich, Andrew. *American Empire: The Realities & Consequences of U.S. Diplomacy.* Cambridge, Mass: Harvard University Press, 2002.

Bautista, Cirilo. "Conversations with José García Villa." *Archipelago* A60 (Aug. 1979): 29–30.

Bayot, David Jonathan Y. "Bienvenido N. Santos: A Review of Studies and Criticism." In *Reading Bienvenido N. Santos,* ed. Isagani R. Cruz and David Jonathan Y. Bayot, 1–11. Manila: De La Salle University Press, 1994.

Belarmino, Philip J. "Bananas and Blades: A Stylistic Analysis of N. V. M. Gonzalez's *Mindoro and Beyond.*" MA thesis, University of the Philippines, Diliman, 1994.

Bello, Madge and Vince Reyes. "Filipino Americans and the Marcos Overthrow." *Amerasia Journal* 13, no. 1 (1986–87): 73–84.

Bender, Thomas. *Rethinking American History in a Global Age.* Berkeley: University of California Press, 2002.

Benjamin, Walter. "The Storyteller." In *Illuminations: Essays and Reflections,* ed. Hannah Arendt. New York: Schocken Books, 1968.

Bernad, Miguel A., S.J. *Bamboo and the Greenwood Tree: Essays on Filipino Literature in English.* Manila: Bookmark, 1961.

Bhabha, Homi, ed. *Nation and Narration.* New York: Routledge, 1990.

Boguslav, David. "Recollections of Thirty Years of Philippine Journalism." *Fookien Times Yearbook,* 1956: 51, 52, 82.

Bonner, Raymond. *Waltzing with a Dictator: The Marcoses and the Making of American Policy.* New York: Vintage Books, 1987.

Brands, H. W. *Bound to Empire: The U.S. and the Philippines.* New York: Oxford University Press, 1992.

Bresnahan, Roger. *Angles of Vision: Conversations on Philippine Literature.* Quezon City: New Day, 1992.

———, ed. *In Time of Hesitation: American Anti-Imperialists and the Philippine-American War.* Quezon City: New Day, 1981.

———, ed. *Literature and Society: Cross-Cultural Perspectives.* Manila: Philippine American Educational Foundation and the American Studies Association of the Philippines, 1976.

Brown, Mary Ellen, and Bruce A. Rosenberg, eds. *Encyclopedia of Folklore and Literature.* Santa Barbara, Calif.: ABC-CLIO, 1998.

Brown, Linda Keller, and Kay Mussell. *Ethnic and Regional Foodways in the United States: The Performance of Group Identity.* Knoxville: University of Tennessee Press, 1984.

Buaken, Manuel. *I Have Lived with the American People.* Caldwell, Idaho: Caxton, 1946.

Bulaong, Grace F. "Filipino Satire in English." MA thesis, University of the Philippines, 1967.

Burns, Gerald T. *Presenting America, Encountering the Philippines.* Quezon City: University of the Philippines Press, 1992.

Burton, Antoinette. *At the Heart of the Empire: Indians and the Colonial Encounter in Late-Victorian Britain.* Berkeley: University of California Press, 1998.

Butler, Judith. *Excitable Speech: A Politics of the Performative.* New York: Routledge, 1997.

Cabalquinto, Luis. "José García Villa: What's He Been Up To?" *Filipinas: A Magazine for All Filipinos* 3, no. 30 (Oct. 1994).

Calinescu, Matei. *Five Faces of Modernity: Modernism, Avant-Garde, Decadence, Kitsch, Postmodernism.* Durham, N.C.: Duke University Press, 1987.

Campbell, Joseph. *The Hero of a Thousand Faces*. Princeton, N.J.: Princeton University Press, 1949, 1973.

Campomanes, Oscar. "Carlos Bulosan." In *Encyclopedia of the American Left*, 115–16. Chicago: University of Illinois Press, 1992.

———. "Filipinos in the United States and Their Literature of Exile." In *Reading the Literatures of Asian America*, ed. Shirley Lim and Amy Ling. Philadelphia: Temple University Press, 1992, 49–78.

Casper, Leonard. *Firewalkers: Literary Concelebrations, 1964–1984*. Quezon City: New Day, 1987.

———. *In Burning Ambush: Essays, 1985–90*. Quezon City: New Day, 1991.

———. *New Writing from the Philippines: A Critique and Anthology*. Syracuse, N.Y.: Syracuse University Press, 1966.

Chan, Sucheng. *Asian Americans: An Interpretive History*. Boston: Twayne, 1991.

Chen, Yong. *Chinese San Francisco, 1850–1943: A Trans-Pacific Community*. Stanford: Stanford University Press, 2000.

Cheung, King-Kok. *Articulate Silences: Hisaye Yamamoto, Maxine Hong Kingston, Joy Kogawa*. Ithaca, N.Y.: Cornell University Press, 1993.

———. "Bienvenido N. Santos: Filipino Old-Timers in Literature." *Markham Review* 15 (1986): 49–53.

———, ed. *An Interethnic Companion to Asian American Literature*. New York: Cambridge University Press, 1997.

Cheung, King-Kok, and Stan Yogi. *Asian American Literature: An Annotated Bibliography*. New York: Modern Language Press, 1988.

Chin, Frank, et al., eds. *Aiiieeeee!!!: An Anthology of Asian American Writers*. Washington, D.C.: Howard University Press, 1974. Reprint. New York: Penguin Books, 1983.

Clifford, James. "Traveling Cultures." In *Cultural Studies*, ed. Lawrence Grossberg et al. New York: Routledge, 1992.

———. *Routes: Travel and Translation in the Late Twentieth Century*. Cambridge, Mass.: Harvard University Press, 1997.

Conn, Peter J. *Pearl S. Buck: A Cultural Biography*. New York: Cambridge University Press, 1996.

Coquia, Jorge R. *The Philippine Presidential Election of 1953*. Manila: University Publishing Co., 1955.

Churchill, Bernardita Reyes. *The Philippine Independence Missions to the U.S., 1919–1934*. Manila: National Historical Institute, 1983.

Conklin, Harold C. *Hanunoo Agriculture: A Report on an Integral System of Shifting Cultivation in the Philippines*. Rome: Food and Agriculture Organization of the United Nations, 1957.

Constantino, Renato. *The Making of a Filipino: A Story of Philippine Colonial Politics.* Quezon City: Malaya Books, 1969.

———. *The Philippines: A Past Revisited.* Manila: Renato Constantino, 1975.

———. *The Philippines: The Continuing Past.* Quezon City: Foundation for Nationalist Studies, 1978.

———, ed. *Recto Reader: Excerpts from the Speeches of Claro M. Recto.* Manila: Recto Memorial Foundation, 1965.

Cordova, Fred. *Filipinos: Forgotten Asian Americans.* Dubuque, Iowa: Kendall/Hunt, 1983.

Cruz, Isagani R. "Bienvenido, Our Brother: The Man Behind the Author (1992)." In *The Alfredo E. Litiatco Lectures,* ed. David Jonathan Y. Bayot, 202–15. Manila: De La Salle University Press, 1996.

Cruz, Isagani R., and David Jonathan Y. Bayot, eds. *Reading Bienvenido N. Santos.* Manila: De La Salle University Press, 1994.

Cruz, Romeo V. *America's Colonial Desk and the Philippines, 1898–1934.* Quezon City: University of the Philippines Press, 1974.

Dado, José B. "A Short History of Legazpi Junior Colleges." *Legazpinian* yearbook, 1950. Aquinas University (Legazpi College) Library.

Dallek, Robert. *Franklin D. Roosevelt and American Foreign Policy, 1932–1945.* New York: Oxford University Press, 1979.

Daroy, Petronilo Bn. "Aspects of Philippine Writing in English." *Philippine Studies* 17, no. 2 (Apr. 1969): 249–65.

———. "Area 1, U.P.—Suburb of the Intellect." *Philippine Panorama* 11, no. 7 (July 1959): 50–53.

———. "Carlos Bulosan: The Politics of Literature." *Saint Louis Quarterly* 6, no. 2 (June 1968): 195.

———. "Diliman: University Town." *Philippine Panorama* 8, no. 3 (Mar. 1956), 82.

———. "Legaspi: Margin of Filipino Middleclass." *Philippine Panorama,* Jan. 1960, 51–52.

De la Cruz, Enrique, ed. "Essays into American Empire in the Philippines, Part I: Legacies, Heroes, and Identity." Special issue, *Amerasia Journal* 24, no. 2 (1998).

———, ed. "Essays into American Empire in the Philippines, Part II: Culture, Community, and Capital." Special issue, *Amerasia Journal* 24, no. 3 (1998).

———, ed. "Reader for Asian American Studies 197, Spring 1993, The Philippine Progressive Movement and the Philippine Support Movement in the U.S., 1972–1992." An unpublished collection of documents from the anti–Marcos dictatorship movement in the United States during the 1970s and 1980s. UCLA.

Del Castillo, Teofilo, and Buenaventura S. Medina Jr., eds. *Philippine Literature: From Ancient Times to the Present.* Quezon City: Del Castillo & Sons, 1964.

De Ocampo, Estebana A. *First Filipino Diplomat: Felipe Agoncillo, 1859–1941.* Manila: National Historical Institute, 1994.

Diamond, Elin, ed. *Performance and Cultural Politics.* New York: Routledge, 1996.

Diggins, John Patrick. *The Proud Decades: America in War and in Peace, 1941–1960.* New York: Norton, 1989.

Doeppers, Daniel F. *Manila, 1900–1941: Social Change in a Late Colonial Metropolis.* New Haven, Conn.: Yale University Southeast Asia Studies, 1984.

Duara, Prasenjit. *Rescuing History from the Nation: Questioning Narratives of Modern China.* Chicago: University of Chicago Press, 1995.

Espiritu, Augusto. "The 'Pre-History' of an Asian-American Writer: N. V. M. Gonzalez's Allegory of Decolonization." *Amerasia Journal* 24, no. 3 (1998): 126–42.

Essed, Philomena, and David Theo Goldberg, eds. *Race Critical Theories.* Malden, Mass.: Blackwell, 2002.

Evangelista, Susan. *Carlos Bulosan and His Poetry: A Biography and Anthology.* Quezon City: Ateneo de Manila University Press, 1985.

———. "Carlos Bulosan: A Sociohistorical Biography." *Philippine Social Sciences and Humanities Review* 44: 1–4 (Jan.-Dec. 1980).

Fansler, Dean, ed. *Filipino Popular Tales.* Lancaster, Pa.: American Folk-lore Society, 1921.

Feria, Dolores S. "Carlos Bulosan: Gentle Genius." *Comment* 1 (1957): 57.

———. *Red Pencil, Blue Pencil: Essays & Encounters.* Manila: Kalikasan Press, 1991.

———, ed. *Sound of Falling Light: Letters in Exile.* Quezon City: Dolores S. Feria, 1960.

Fernandez, Doreen G. *Palabas: Essays on Philippine Theater History.* Quezon City: Ateneo de Manila University Press, 1996.

Fischer de Gruyter, Heinz-Dietrich. *Outstanding International Press Reporting: Pulitzer Prize Winning Articles in Foreign Correspondence,* vol. 1: *1928–1945.* New York: Walter de Gruyter, 1984.

Florentino, Alberto S. *Midcentury Guide to Philippine Literature in English.* Manila: Filipiniana Publishers, 1963.

Foley, Martha. *The Best American Short Stories 1943 and the Yearbook of the American Short Story.* Boston: Houghton Mifflin, 1943.

Francia, Hilario S. "Remembering José García Villa, Part 2." *Manila Chronicle,* Feb. 20, 1997.

Friend, Theodore. *Between Two Empires: The Ordeal of the Philippines, 1929–1946.* New Haven, Conn.: Yale University Press, 1965.

Gaerlan, Barbara. "In the Court of the Sultan: Orientalism, Nationalism, and Modernity in Philippine and Filipino American Dance." *Journal of Asian American Studies* 2, no. 3 (Oct. 1999).

Galdon, Joseph A. *Essays on the Philippine Novel in English.* Quezon City: Ateneo de Manila University Press, 1983.

Gee, Emma. *Counterpoint: Perspectives on Asian America.* Los Angeles: UCLA Asian American Studies Center, 1976.

Gibney, Frank. *The Pacific Century: Asia and America in a Changing World.* New York: Maxwell Macmillan International, 1993.

Giddens, Anthony. *Central Problems in Social Theory: Action, Structure and Contradiction in Social Analysis.* Berkeley: University of California Press, 1979.

Gilroy, Paul. *The Black Atlantic: Modernity and Double Consciousness.* Cambridge, Mass.: Harvard University Press, 1993.

Gleeck, Lewis. E., Jr. *The Third Philippine Republic, 1946–1972.* Quezon City: New Day, 1993, 400.

Glendinning, Victoria. *Edith Sitwell: A Unicorn Among Lions.* London: Weidenfeld & Nicolson, 1981.

Goldberg, David Theo, and Ato Quayson, eds. *Relocating Postcolonialism.* Malden, Mass.: Blackwell, 2002.

Gonzalez, Andrew. *Language and Nationalism: The Philippine Experience Thus Far.* Quezon City: Ateneo de Manila University Press, 1980.

Gonzalez, Narita M. "Doing Things the Roman Way." *Weekly Nation* 1, no. 8 (Oct. 15, 1965), 10–11.

———. "'Flying Saucer of a Church.'" Pamphlet on the Chapel of the Holy Sacrifice at the University of the Philippines, Diliman, reprinted from *Philippine Daily Inquirer*, Dec. 11, 1995.

———, ed. *The Writers' Wives.* Pasig City, Philippines: Anvil, 2000.

Gonzalves, Theo. "'The Show Must Go On': Production Notes on the Pilipino Cultural Night." *Critical Mass: A Journal of Asian American Cultural Criticism* 2, no. 2 (Spring 1995): 129–44.

Goodman, Grant K. "Japan and Philippine Radicalism: The Case of Benigno Ramos." In *Four Aspects of Philippine-Japanese Relations, 1930–1940.* Monograph Series, no. 9. New Haven, Conn.: Yale University Southeast Asia Studies, 1967.

Griffiths, Stephen. *Emigrants, Entrepreneurs, and Evil Spirits: Life in a Philippine Village.* Honolulu: University of Hawai'i Press, 1988.

Gungwu, Wang, et al., eds. *Society and the Writer: Essays on Literature in Modern Asia.* Canberra: Research School of Pacific Studies, 1981.

Guzman, Richard R. "'As in Myth, the Signs Were All Over': The Fiction of N. V. M. Gonzalez." *Virginia Quarterly Review* 60, no. 1 (Winter 1984):

102–18. Reprinted in N. V. M. Gonzalez, *Work on the Mountain*, 77–194. Quezon City: University of the Philippines Press, 1995.

Hall, Stuart. "Gramsci's Relevance for the Study of Race and Ethnicity." *Journal of Communication Inquiry* 10, no. 2 (1986): 23–25.

Hayashi, Brian. *"For the Sake of Our Japanese Brethren": Assimilation, Nationalism, and Protestantism Among the Japanese of Los Angeles, 1895–1942.* Stanford: Stanford University Press, 1995.

Henson, Maria Rosa. *Comfort Woman: A Filipina's Story of Prostitution and Slavery under the Japanese Military.* Lanham, Md.: Rowman & Littlefield, 1999.

Hofstadter, Richard. *American Political Tradition.* New York: Vintage Books, 1978.

Hoganson, Kristin. *Fighting for American Manhood: How Gender Politics Provoked the Spanish-American and Philippine-American Wars.* New Haven, Conn.: Yale University Press, 1998.

Hohenberg, John, ed. *The Pulitzer Prize Story: News Stories, Editorials, Cartoons, & Pictures.* New York: Columbia University Press, 1959.

Hollinger, David. *In the American Province: Studies in the History and Historiography of Ideas.* Bloomington: Indiana University Press, 1985.

Hsu, Kai-yu, and Helen Palubinskas, eds. *Asian-American Authors.* Boston: Houghton Mifflin, 1972.

Hsu, Madeline. *Dreaming of Gold, Dreaming of Home: Transnationalism and Migration between the United States and South China, 1882–1943.* Stanford: Stanford University Press, 2000.

Hufana, Alejandrino G. "Transvaluation in N. V. M. Gonzalez's *Mindoro and Beyond: Twenty-one Stories.*" *Likhaan: Multi-Lingual Creative Writing Journal* 1 (Dec. 1979), 145–50.

Huggins, Nathan Irvin. *Harlem Renaissance.* New York: Oxford University Press, 1971.

Hune, Shirley, et al., eds. *Asian Americans: Comparative and Global Perspectives.* Pullman: Washington State University Press, 1991.

Ichioka, Yuji. *The Issei: The World of the First Generation Japanese Immigrants, 1885–1924.* New York: Free Press, 1988.

———. "*Kengakudan*: The Origin of Nisei Study Tours of Japan." *California History* 73 (Spring 1994).

Ileto, Reynaldo. "Outlines of a Nonlinear Emplotment of Philippine History." In *The Politics of Culture in the Shadow of Capital*, ed. David Lloyd and Lisa Lowe, 98–130. Durham, N.C.: Duke University Press, 1997.

———. *Pasyon and Revolution: Popular Movements in the Philippines, 1840–1910.* Quezon City: Ateneo de Manila University Press, 1989.

———. "Rizal and the Underside of Philippine History." *Moral Order and the*

Question of Change: Essays on Southeast Asian Thought, ed. David K. Wyatt and Alexander Woodside. New Haven, Conn.: Yale University Southeast Asia Studies, 1982.

Ingles, José D. *Philippine Foreign Policy*. Manila: Lyceum Press, 1980.

International Longshoreman's and Warehouseman's Union. *ILWU Yearbook, Cannery Workers, ILWU Local 37*, 1952.

"Islands in History." Special issue, *Radical History Review*, ed. Pennee Bender and Yvonne Lassalle, 73 (Winter 1999).

Iwasaki, Bruce. "Response and Change for the Asian in America: A Survey of Asian American Literature." In *Roots: An Asian American Reader*, ed. Amy Tachiki et al., 90–91. Los Angeles: Continental Graphics, 1971.

Jayawardena, Kumari. "Going for the Jugular of Hindu Patriarchy: American Women Fundraisers for Ramabai." In *Unequal Sisters: A Multicultural Reader in U.S. Women's History*, ed. Vicki L. Ruiz and Ellen Carol DuBois, 197–204. New York: Routledge, 2000.

Jesús, Edilberto de, Jr. "On This Soil, in This Climate: Growth in the Novels of N. V. M. Gonzalez." In Gonzalez, *Bamboo Dancers*, 331–58. Manila: Bookmark, 1993. Originally published in *Brown Heritage: Essays on Philippine Cultural Tradition and Literature*, ed. Antonio G. Manuud, 739–64 (Quezon City: Ateneo de Manila University Press, 1967).

Joaquin, Nick. *The Aquinos of Tarlac: An Essay on History as Three Generations*. Metro Manila: Cacho Hermanos, 1983.

———. *Culture and History: Occasional Notes on the Process of Philippine Becoming*. Metro Manila: Solar, 1988.

———. *Doveglion and Other Cameos*. Manila: Nick Joaquin, 1977.

———. *La Naval de Manila and Other Essays*. Manila: Alberto S. Florentino, 1964.

———. *The Seven Ages of Romulo*. Manila: Filipinas Foundation, 1977.

———. "What Signified the Expatriates?" In id., *A Question of Heroes*, 39–53. Manila: National Book Store, 1981.

"José García Villa: A Bio-Bibliography." Quezon City: Library of the University of the Philippines, 1973.

Kalaw, Maximo M. *An Introduction to Philippine Social Science*. Manila: Philippine Education Co., 1939. Reprint. Manila: Solar, 1986.

Kalcik, Susan. "Ethnic Foodways in America: Symbol and the Performance of Identity." In *Ethnic and Regional Foodways in the United States: The Performance of Group Identity*, ed. Linda Keller Brown and Kay Mussell, 37–65. Knoxville: University of Tennessee Press, 1984.

Kammen, Michael. "Culture and the State in America." *Journal of American History*, Dec. 1996, 791–814.

Kaplan, Amy and Donald E. Pease, eds. *Cultures of United States Imperialism.* Durham, N.C.: Duke University Press, 1993.

Karnow, Stanley. *In Our Image: America's Empire in the Philippines.* London: Century, 1990.

Kaukonen, Beatrice, and Jorma Kaukonen. "The Philippines and Jose Garcia-Villa *[sic]* Remembered." *Bulletin of the American Historical Collection* 20: 1, 78 (Jan.-Mar. 1992): 24–34.

Kerkvliet, Benedict J. *The Huk Rebellion: A Study of Peasant Revolt in the Philippines.* Honolulu: University of Hawai'i Press, 1977.

Kerkvliet, Melinda Tria. "Interpreting Pablo Manlapit." *Social Process in Hawaii* 37 (1996): 1–25.

Kim, Elaine H. *Asian American Literature: The Writings and Their Social Contexts.* Philadelphia: Temple University Press, 1982.

Kim, Elaine H., and Lisa Lowe. "Introduction." In "New Formations, New Questions: Asian American Studies." Special issue, *Positions: East Asia Cultural Critique* 5, no. 2 (Fall 1997): v–xiii.

Kingston, Maxine Hong. "Precarious Lives." *New York Times Book Review,* May 4, 1980, 15, 28–29.

Klehr, Harvey, and John Earl Haynes. *The American Communist Movement: Storming Heaven Itself.* New York: Twayne, 1992.

Lagda, Licerio. "Women in the Life and Poetry of Carlos Bulosan." MA thesis, University of the Philippines, 1988.

Lasker, Bruno. *Filipino Immigration to the Continental United States and to Hawaii.* N.p.: Institute of Pacific Relations, 1931. Reprint. New York: Arno Press, 1969.

Leitch, Vincent B. *American Literary Criticism from the 30s to the 80s.* New York: Columbia University Press, 1988.

Letters in Exile: An Introductory Reader on Pilipino Americans. Los Angeles: Asian American Studies Center, 1976.

Lim, Shirley, and Amy Ling. *Reading the Literatures of Asian America.* Philadelphia: Temple University Press, 1992.

Ling, Amy. "Emerging Canons of Asian American Literature and Art." *Asian Americans: Comparative and Global Perspectives,* ed. Shirley Hune et al. Pullman: Washington State University Press, 1991.

Locsin, Teodoro. "The Dove, the Eagle, and the Lion." *Philippines Free Press* 38, no. 3 (Jan. 18, 1941): 5ff.

Lopez, Salvador P. *Literature and Society: Essays on Life and Letters.* Manila: University Publishing Co., 1940.

Lowe, Lisa. *Immigrant Acts: On Asian American Cultural Politics.* Durham, N.C.: Duke University Press, 1996.

Lumbera, Bienvenido. *Tagalog Poetry, 1570–1898: Tradition and Influences in Its Development*. Quezon City: Ateneo de Manila University Press, 1986.

Lumbera, Bienvenido, and Cynthia Lumbera. *Philippine Literature: A History and Anthology*. Metro Manila: National Book Store, 1982.

MacArthur, Douglas. *Reminiscences*. New York: Crest Books, 1964.

Malay, Armando J. "A Short History of the Philippine Press." *Panorama* 13, no. 8 (Aug. 1961).

Manchester, William. *American Caesar: Douglas MacArthur, 1880–1964*. Boston: Little, Brown, 1978.

Manlapaz, Edna Z. *Angela Manalang Gloria: A Literary Biography*. Quezon City: Ateneo de Manila University Press, 1993.

———. *Our Literary Matriarchs, 1925–1953: Angela Manalang Gloria, Paz M. Latorena, Loreto Paras Sulit, and Paz Marquez Benitez*. Quezon City: Ateneo de Manila University Press, 1996.

Manuud, Antonio G., ed. *Brown Heritage: Essays on Philippine Cultural Tradition and Literature*. Quezon City: Ateneo de Manila University Press, 1967.

Manzon, Maximo C. *The Strange Case of the Filipinos in the United States*. New York: American Committee for Protection of Foreign Born, 1938.

Marsella, Joy A. "Some Contributions of the *Philippine Magazine* to the Development of Philippine Culture." *Philippine Studies* 17 (1969): 326.

Mazumdar, Sucheta. "Asian American Studies and Asian Studies: Rethinking Roots." *Asian Americans: Comparative and Global Perspectives*, ed. Shirley Hune et al., 29–44. Pullman: Washington State University Press, 1991.

McCormick, Richard L. *The Party Period and Public Policy: American Politics from the Age of Jackson to the Progressive Era*. New York: Oxford University Press, 1986.

McCoy, Alfred W., ed. *An Anarchy of Families: State and Family in the Philippines*. Quezon City: Ateneo de Manila University Press, 1994.

———. "Baylan: Animist Religion and the Philippine Peasant Ideology." *Philippine Quarterly of Culture and Society* 10 (1982): 141–84.

McDarrah, Fred W., and Gloria S. McDarrah. *Beat Generation: Glory Days in Greenwich Village*. New York: Schirmer Books, 1996.

McEnteer, James. "You Can't Go Home Again If You Never Left." *Filipinas: A Magazine for All Filipinos* 6, no. 57 (Jan. 1997).

Meñez, Herminia Q. *Explorations in Philippine Folklore*. Quezon City: Ateneo de Manila University Press, 1996.

Meyer, Milton J. *A Diplomatic History of the Philippine Republic*. Honolulu: University of Hawai'i Press, 1965.

Molesworth, Charles. *Marianne Moore: A Literary Life*. New York: Atheneum, 1990.

Morantte, P. C. "Filipino Writers in America III: José García Villa." *This Week,* Sept. 4, 1949, 26.

———. *Remembering Carlos Bulosan: His Heart Affair with America.* Quezon City: New Day, 1984.

———. "Two Filipinos in America." *Books Abroad,* 1944.

———. "Villa in Retrospect." *This Week,* May 9, 1948.

Mostern, Kenneth. "Why Is America in the Heart?" *Critical Mass: A Journal of Asian American Cultural Criticism* 2, no. 2 (Spring 1995): 35–65.

Mukerji, Dhan Gopal. *Caste and Outcast.* Edited by Gordon H. Chang. Stanford: Stanford University Press, 2002.

Murase, Mike. "Ethnic Studies and Higher Education for Asian Americans." *Counterpoint: Perspectives on Asian America,* ed. Emma Gee et al., 205–23. Los Angeles: Asian American Studies Center, University of California, 1976.

Nakanishi, Don. "Asian American Politics: An Agenda for Research." *Amerasia Journal* 12, no. 2 (1985–86): 1–27.

Nakpil, Carmen Guerrero. "Maria Clara," *Woman Enough and Other Essays.* Manila: Vibal, 1963.

Nandy, Ashis. *The Intimate Enemy: Loss and Recovery of Self under Colonialism.* 1983. Reprint. Delhi: Oxford University Press, 1994.

Negrón-Muntaner, Francis, and Ramón Grosfoguel, eds. *Puerto Rican Jam: Rethinking Colonialism and Nationalism: Essays on Culture and Politics.* Minneapolis: University of Minnesota Press, 1997.

Nguyen, Viet Thanh. *Race & Resistance: Literature and Politics in Asian America.* New York: Oxford University Press, 2002.

Nietzsche, Friedrich. *Human, All Too Human.* Translated by Marion Faber. Lincoln: University of Nebraska Press, 1986.

O'Brien, Edward J. *The Best Short Stories of 1932 and the Yearbook of the American Short Story.* New York: Dodd, Mead, 1932.

Ocampo, Ambeth R. *Rizal Without the Overcoat.* Metro Manila: Anvil, 1990.

Olivares, Belinda. "Angry Young Men of the Thirties." *Panorama* 12, no. 5 (May 1960).

Ong, Walter. *Orality and Literacy: The Technologizing of the Word.* New York: Methuen, 1988.

Onorato, Michael P., ed. *Origins of the Philippine Republic: Extracts from the Diaries and Records of Francis Burton Harrison.* Data Papers, no. 95. Ithaca, N.Y.: Cornell University Department of Asian Studies, Southeast Asia Program, 1974.

Ordoñez, Elmer. "Remembered by the Clowns." *Literary Apprentice* 20, no. 2 (1957).

———. "Send in the Clowns." *Literary Apprentice,* 1957.

Pacis, Vicente Albano. *President Sergio Osmeña: A Fully Documented Biography.* Quezon City: Phoenix Press, 1971.

Paredes, Ruby R., ed. *Philippine Colonial Democracy.* New Haven, Conn.: Yale University Southeast Asia Studies, 1988.

Pells, Richard H. *Radical Visions & American Dreams: Culture and Social Thought in the Depression Years.* 1973. Reprint. Urbana: University of Illinois Press, 1998.

Perez, Gilbert. "Thomasites: The First American Teachers in the Philippines: They Were Part-time Teachers, Full-time Diplomats." *Archipelago* 1, no. 8 (Aug. 1974): 40–44.

Perez, Louis A., Jr. "Incurring a Debt of Gratitude: 1898 and the Moral Sources of United States Hegemony in Cuba." *American Historical Review* 104, no. 2 (Apr. 1999): 356–98.

Pertierra, Raul. *Religion, Politics, and Rationality in a Philippine Community.* Honolulu: University of Hawai'i Press, 1988.

Phelps, Paul B. "The Philippines: An Exile's Dreams." *Washington Post,* Apr. 20, 1980, 6.

Posadas, Barbara, and Roland Guyotte. "Unintentional Immigrants: Chicago's Filipino Foreign Students Become Settlers, 1900–1941." *Journal of American Ethnic History* 9, no. 2 (Spring 1990).

Pratt, Mary Louise. *Imperial Eyes: Travel Writing and Transculturation.* New York: Routledge, 1992.

Rafael, Vicente. *Contracting Colonialism: Translation and Christian Conversion in Tagalog Society under Early Spanish Rule.* Quezon City: Ateneo de Manila University Press, 1988.

———. "Nationalism, Imagery, and the Filipino Intelligentsia in the Nineteenth Century." *Critical Inquiry* 16 (Spring 1990): 591–611.

———. *White Love and Other Events in Filipino History.* Durham, N.C.: Duke University Press, 2000.

Reid, Anthony. *Southeast Asia in the Age of Commerce, 1450–1680.* New Haven, Conn.: Yale University Press, 1988.

Remoto, Danton R. "N. V. M. Gonzalez: Writing as a Celebration of Life." *Chimera: Voices, Tales & Visions* [Quezon City] 1, no. 1 (1996): 4–11.

Rizal, José. *The Subversive (El Filibusterismo).* Translated by León Ma. Guerrero. Bloomington: Indiana University Press, 1962.

———. *Noli Me Tangere.* Translated by Soledad Lacson-Locsin. Honolulu: University of Hawai'i Press, 1996.

Rodao, Florentino. "Spanish Falange in the Philippines, 1936–1945." *Philippine Studies* 43 (1st quarter 1995): 3–26.

Roediger, David. *The Wages of Whiteness: Race and the Making of the American Working Class*. New York: Verso, 1991.

Roediger, David R., and James Barrett. "Inbetween Peoples: Race, Nationality, and the 'New-Immigrant' Working Class." In David R. Roediger, *Colored White: Transcending the Racial Past*, 138–68. Berkeley: University of California Press, 2002.

Romulo, Beth Day. *Inside the Palace: The Rise and Fall of Ferdinand and Imelda Marcos*. New York: G. P. Putnam's Sons, 1987.

Rosaldo, Renato. *Culture and Truth: The Remaking of Social Analysis*. Boston: Beacon Press, 1989.

Roseburg, A. G. *Pathways to Philippine Literature in English*. Rev. ed. Quezon City: Alemar-Phoenix, 1966.

Rydell, Robert W. *All the World's a Fair: Visions of Empire at American International Expositions, 1876–1916*. Chicago: University of Chicago Press, 1984.

Said, Edward. *Culture and Imperialism*. New York: Knopf, 1993.

———. *Representations of the Intellectual*. The 1993 Reith Lectures. New York: Vintage Books, 1994.

Salamanca, Bonifacio. *The Filipino Reaction to American Rule, 1901–1913*. Hamden, Conn.: Shoe String Press, 1968.

Saldivar, José David. *Border Matters: Remapping American Cultural Studies*. Berkeley: University of California Press, 1997.

Salman, Michael. *The Embarrassment of Slavery: Controversies over Bondage and Nationalism in the American Colonial Philippines*. Berkeley: University of California Press, 2001.

San Buenaventura, Steffi. "The Master and the Federation: A Filipino-American Social Movement in California and Hawaii." *Social Process in Hawaii* 33 (1991): 169–93.

San Juan, Epifanio, Jr. *Carlos Bulosan and the Imagination of the Class Struggle*. Quezon City: University of the Philippines Press, 1972. Reprint. New York: Oriole Editions, 1976

———. "Carlos Bulosan." In *The American Radical*, ed. Mari Jo Buhle et al., 253–60. New York: Routledge, 1994.

———. "José García Villa: Toward a Poetics of Disappearance and Resistance." In *Reading the West/Writing the East: Studies in Comparative Literature and Culture*. San Francisco: Peter Lang, 1992.

Schorer, Mark. *The World We Imagine: Selected Essays*. New York: Farrar, Straus & Giroux, 1968.

Schumacher, John N. *The Propaganda Movement, 1880–1895: The Creators of a Filipino Consciousness, the Makers of the Revolution*. Quezon City: Ateneo de Manila University, 1973.

————. *The Making of a Nation: Essays on Nineteenth-Century Filipino National-ism*. Quezon City: Ateneo de Manila University Press, 1991.

Scott, William Henry. *Cracks in the Parchment Curtain and Other Essays in Philippine History*. Quezon City: New Day, 1982, 1985.

"Selected Writings of Carlos Bulosan." Special issue, *Amerasia Journal* 6, no. 1 (1979).

Serrano, Josephine B., and Trinidad M. Ames, eds. *A Survey of Filipino Literature in English*. Quezon City: Phoenix, 1988.

Shalom, Stephen. *The United States and the Philippines: A Study of Neocolonialism*. Quezon City: New Day, 1986.

Sharpe, Jenny. *Allegories of Empire: The Figure of Woman in the Colonial Text*. Minneapolis: University of Minnesota Press, 1993.

Sitwell, Edith. *The American Genius: An Anthology of Poems with Some Prose*. London: John Lehmann, 1951.

Solberg, Sam. "An Introduction to Filipino American Literature." In *Aiiieeeee! An Anthology of Asian American Writers*, ed. Frank Chin et al., 39–58. New York: Penguin Books, 1983.

————. "Bulosan-Theseus-Villa: A Cryptography of Coincidence." *MELUS* 15, no. 2 (Summer 1988): 3–25.

Sollors, Werner. *Beyond Ethnicity: Consent and Descent in American Culture*. New York: Oxford University Press, 1986.

Spivak, Gayatri Chakravorty. "Can the Subaltern Speak?" In *Marxism and the Interpretation of Culture*, 271–313. Basingstoke: Macmillan Education, 1988.

States, Mark. "Third World American Dream: Unionist and Socialist Politics in the Art of Hughes and Bulosan." *Critical Perspectives of Third World America* 1, no. 1 (Fall 1983): 91–115.

Stocking, George W., Jr. *Race, Culture, and Evolution: Essays in the History of Anthropology*. New York: Free Press, 1968.

Stovall, Tyler. *Paris Noir: African Americans in the City of Light*. Boston: Houghton Mifflin, 1996.

Sutherland, William Alexander. *Not by Might: The Epic of the Philippines*. Las Cruces, N.M.: Southwest Publishing Co., 1953.

Tabios, Eileen, ed. *The Anchored Angel: Selected Writings by José García Villa*. New York: Kaya Press, 1999.

Takaki, Ronald. *Strangers from a Different Shore*. New York: Penguin Books, 1989.

Taruc, Luis. *Born of the People*. With a foreword by Paul Robeson. New York: International Publishers, 1953.

Teodoro, Luis V. "Notes on the Power of the People." *Mithi* 1 (1985): 3–14.

Thompson, Mark R. *The Anti-Marcos Struggle: Personalistic Rule and Democratic Transition in the Philippines*. New Haven, Conn.: Yale University Press, 1995.

Tiempo, Edilberto K. *Literary Criticism in the Philippines and Other Essays.* Manila: De La Salle University Press, 1995.

Tinio, Rolando. "Trying to Read Villa." *Philippine Studies* 7, no. 4 (Oct. 1959): 494–99.

———. "Villa's Values; or, The Poet You Cannot Always Make Out, or Succeed In Liking Once You Are Able To." In *Brown Heritage: Essays on Philippine Cultural Tradition and Literature,* ed. Antonio P. Manuud, 722–38. Quezon City: Ateneo de Manila University Press, 1967.

Tolentino, Delfin. "Satire in Carlos Bulosan's *The Laughter of My Father,*" *Philippine Studies* 34 (1986): 452–61.

Trachtenberg, Alan. *The Incorporation of America: Culture and Society in the Gilded Age.* New York: Hill & Wang, 1982.

Turner, Victor. *Dramas, Fields, and Metaphors: Symbolic Action in Human Society.* Ithaca, N.Y.: Cornell University Press, 1974.

Valeros, Florentino B., and Estrellita V. Gruenberg. *Filipino Writers in English.* Quezon City: New Day, 1987.

Ventura, Sylvia Mendez. *Carlos P. Romulo.* Manila: Tahanan Books for Young Readers, 1995.

———. *Mauro Mendez: From Journalist to Diplomat.* Quezon City: University of the Philippines Press, 1978.

Villa, Simeon. *The Flight and Wanderings of General Emilio Aguinaldo from Bayambang to Palanan, 1899–1901: A Diary,* in *Aguinaldo's Odyssey,* as told in the diaries of Col. Simeon Villa and Dr. Santiago Barcelona. Manila: Bureau of Public Libraries, 1963.

Viray, Manuel A. "Art and Audience: The Poetry of Bienvenido N. Santos." *Diliman Review* 1, no. 3 (July 1953).

Wand, David Hsin-Fu. *Asian American Heritage: An Anthology of Prose and Poetry.* New York: Washington Square Press, 1974.

Williams, Blanche Colton, ed. *O. Henry Memorial Award: Prize Stories of 1932.* Garden City, New York: Doubleday, Doran, 1932.

Williams, Raymond. *Marxism and Literature.* Oxford: Oxford University Press, 1977.

Williams, William Appleman, ed. *America in Vietnam: A Documentary History.* Garden City, N.Y.: Anchor Press, 1985.

Winichakul, Thongchai. *Siam Mapped: A History of the Geo-Body of a Nation.* Honolulu: University of Hawai'i Press, 1994.

Wong, K. Scott, and Sucheng Chan. *Claiming America: Constructing Chinese American Identities During the Exclusion Era.* Philadelphia: Temple University Press, 1998.

Wong, Sau-ling. "Denationalization Reconsidered: Asian American Cultural Criticism at a Theoretical Crossroads." *Amerasia Journal* 21, nos. 1 and 2 (1995).

———. *Reading Asian American Literature: From Necessity to Extravagance.* Princeton, N.J.: Princeton University Press, 1993.

Yu, Henry. *Thinking Orientals: Migration, Contact, and Exoticism in Modern America.* New York: Oxford University Press, 2001.

Yung, Judy. *Unbound Feet: A Social History of Chinese Women in San Francisco.* Berkeley: University of California Press, 1995.

Zuraek, Maria Elnora C. "N. V. M. Gonzalez's *A Season of Grace.*" In *Essays on The Philippine Novel in English,* ed. Joseph A. Galdon, 109–24. Quezon City: Ateneo de Manila University Press, 1983.

Index

In this index an "f" after a number indicates a separate reference on the next page, and an "ff" indicates separate references on the next two pages. A continuous discussion over two or more pages is indicated by a span of page numbers, e.g., "57–59." *Passim* is used for a cluster of references in close but not consecutive sequence.

ASIAN AMERICA

Sexual Naturalization: Asian Americans and Miscegenation

SUSAN KOSHY, FORTHCOMING.

*Better Americans in a Greater America: Japanese American Internment,
Redress, and Historical Memory*

ALICE YANG-MURRAY, FORTHCOMING.

Dhan Gopal Mukerji, *Caste and Outcast*

EDITED AND PRESENTED BY GORDON H. CHANG, PURNIMA MANKEKAR,
AND AKHIL GUPTA, 2002.

*New Worlds, New Lives: Globalization and People of Japanese Descent in the
Americas and from Latin America in Japan*

EDITED BY LANE RYO HIRABAYASHI, AKEMI KIKUMURA-YANO, AND JAMES
A. HIRABAYASHI, 2002.

*Japanese Pride, American Prejudice: Modifying the Exclusion Clause of the
1924 Immigration Act*

IZUMI HIROBE, 2001.

Chinese San Francisco, 1850–1943: A Trans-Pacific Community

YONG CHEN, 2000.

Dreaming of Gold, Dreaming of Home: Transnationalism and Migration Between the United States and South China, 1882–1943

MADELINE Y. HSU, 2000.

Imagining the Nation: Asian American Literature and Cultural Consent

DAVID LEIWEI LI, 1998.

Morning Glory, Evening Shadow: Yamato Ichihashi and His Internment Writings, 1942–1945

EDITED, ANNOTATED, AND WITH A BIOGRAPHICAL ESSAY BY GORDON H. CHANG, 1997.

Mary Kimoto Tomita, *Dear Miye: Letters Home from Japan, 1939–1946*

EDITED, WITH AN INTRODUCTION AND NOTES, BY ROBERT G. LEE, 1995.

Beyond the Killing Fields: Voices of Nine Cambodian Survivors in America

USHA WELARATNA, 1993.

Making and Remaking Asian America

BILL ONG HING, 1993.

Righting a Wrong: Japanese Americans and the Passage of the Civil Liberties Act of 1988

LESLIE T. HATAMIYA, 1993.